# MILITARIA
• FROM THE PACIFIC WAR •
DISCOVERING THEIR STORIES

# MILITARIA

## FROM THE PACIFIC WAR

### DISCOVERING THEIR STORIES

J. Forrest Pollard

Library of Congress Cataloging-in-Publication Data
Pollard, J. Forrest
Militaria From The Pacific War, Discovering Their Stories
ISBN 978-0-692-76921-8
1. World War, 1939-1945 — Campaigns — Pacific Area.
2. World War, 1939-1945 — Naval operations, American.
3. World War, 1939-1945 — Aerial Operations, American.
4. World War, 1939-1945 — Intercept radar — History.
5. World War, 1939-1945 — Prisoners and prisons, Japanese.
6. Nomonhan Incident, Mongolia, 1939 — Personal narratives, Japanese.
7. Tarawa, Battle of, Kiribati, 1943 — Personal narratives, American.
8. Tinian, Battle of, Northern Mariana Islands, 1944 — Personal narratives, American.
9. Iwo Jima, Battle of, Japan, 1945 — Personal narratives, American.
10. Iwo Jima, Battle of, Japan, 1945 — Personal narratives, Japanese.
11. United States. Army Air Force — 4th Photographic Squadron — Biography.
12. United States. Marine Corps — Night Fighter Squadron 531 — Biography.
13. United States. Marine Corps — 2nd Marine Division — Biography.
14. United States. Marine Corps — 5th Marine Division — Biography.
15. Sailors — United States — Biography.
16. Soldiers — Imperial Army — Japan — Biography.
17. Prisoners of war — Singapore — Changi — Personal narratives, American.
18. Yorktown (Aircraft carrier: CV-10).
19. McFarland (Seaplane tender: AVD-14).
20. Night fighter planes — History — 20th century.
21. Night flying — History — 20th century.
22. Air warfare — History — 20th century.
23. Nagasaki-shi (Japan) — History, 1945 — Occupation.   I. Title.

*For my son Dean, serving in Afghanistan.*

# CONTENTS

# INTRODUCTION

I was named after my father's best friend, Forrest Prince, who died in his arms at the Battle of Tarawa. My dad never talked much about the war, and I know nothing about Forrest except that he was from California and looked like Buster Crabbe. Not exactly a fully-fleshed story for a ten-year-old to tell his friends while watching old *Flash Gordon* re-runs.

"The child is father of the man," so the poem goes, and when I grew into adulthood and came across an old war relic, I thought of things I wished I knew about Forrest and wondered, "Who did this belong to? What was his story? Is there any way to find out?" This is how I started collecting relics and researching their stories.

There is no word to describe what I do. Military history archaeologist? Military history detective? Neither of these seems right.

The only way to explain the process is by example. To demonstrate, I will use something that I picked up several months before publishing this book. It is an unusual mess kit that belonged to Howard Schermerhorn, who spent the war as a prisoner of the Japanese. Every story in this book began with the discovery of relics like this. I find them at estate sales, auctions or by word of mouth. Sometimes, a friend will put me on to something.

Although the relics I am drawn to are always connected to a named vet, they almost never come with a story. Deciding if a relic might lead to a story is where luck and a hunch enter into the equation. What drew me to Schermerhorn's mess kit were his engravings. They suggested to me a man with personality, and one who was a good storyteller, so I made an offer to purchase.

Discovering the story behind a relic is a difficult and unpredictable process. The first step is to obtain a copy of vet's military records at the National Archives, but Schermerhorn was in the Army and nearly all U.S. Army files, housed at the National Personnel Records Center in St. Louis, were destroyed by a catastrophic fire there in 1973.

Instead, I searched for his obituary. If I am lucky and can locate his survivors, they may be willing to share stories he told them about the war and perhaps provide me with a few photographs. If I am unusually lucky, there will be a tape recording or manuscript of war stories and recollections.

In the case of Howard Schermerhorn I was

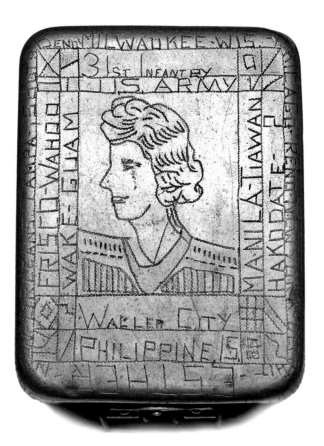

The engraved bottom of Schermerhorn's mess kit. *Author's collection.*

End view of Schermerhorn's mess kit, which was purchased at an auction in 2016. *Author's collection.*

not lucky at all. He died in 1950 from a heart condition, was not married and had no children. He had two sisters, but after more checking I discovered that they, too, were dead and childless, so this path of discovery that is normally very productive quickly came to an end.

Next, I searched for newspaper and magazine articles. Vets with interesting stories were sometimes interviewed after the war and, sure enough, I found a story on Schermerhorn. "Tokyo Trials Too Fair, Says GI" ran the headline in the 20 July 1947 issue of the *Milwaukee Sentinel*.

> "The trials were too fair," said Howard Schermerhorn, 34, former Japanese prisoner of war, of the atrocity trials in Tokyo at which he was a witness against the Jap camp commandant and his hard-boiled subordinates.
>
> The Milwaukeean, who returned from Tokyo 10 days ago to his home told yesterday of his experiences as a Jap prisoner in which his weight fell from 227 to 116 pounds. "It would have saved the government a lot of money if they gave me 20 minutes alone with each of those fellows," said the now husky Schermerhorn, grimacing.
>
> Captured on Bataan as a Pfc in the 31st Infantry, Schermerhorn made the notorious death march to the prison camp at which Americans first tasted Japanese cruelty.

He was transferred many times from one disease ridden camp to another, going from the Philippines to Formosa and then to Japan. It was in Japan that . . . the Americans . . . were submitted to the merciless regime of 1st Lt. Jiro Tendo, camp commandant, and the brutal, one armed Matsuzo Miumi, who was in charge of the work detail.

Gold! And if he testified at the Tokyo War Crimes Tribunal, there must be a record of his participation.

I wrote to the National Archives to see if they could locate the transcript of the trial. A month later I got a response that included a file number. Other clues and avenues of investigation were sure to surface once I visited the Archives and pulled his file.

So that is how my process works: it is unavoidably inefficient, reliant upon intuition and luck, and dependent upon one clue leading to the next.

Approximately half of the artifacts that I acquire never lead to a story. Sometimes the story died with the vet. Other times a good story never existed at all, which is not surprising because most war relics are little more than souvenirs acquired by rear echelon troops to bring home for show.

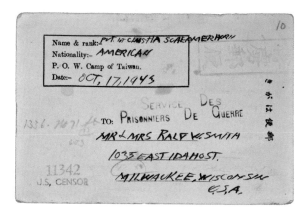

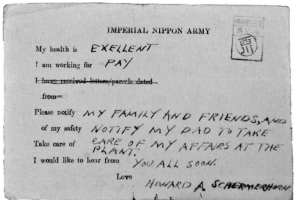

Schermerhorn was occasionally allowed to send cards to family and friends. *My health is* "excellent." *I am working for* "pay" — phrases demanded by his captors which mocked his real circumstances. Ralf W. Smith's connection to Schermerhorn remains a mystery. *Author's collection.*

Another forty percent of the relics produce incomplete stories; they lack a beginning, middle or an end.

The remaining ten percent are exceptional. They are the ones that I share in this book.

As for Japanese diaries, I never know what I will find until I hear back from my translator, so there is a high failure rate there as well. But that's just it — not knowing where I am being taken by a relic is what makes the process so compelling.

Engraved inside the bottom, "Fill To Top." *Author's collection.*

*"All the business of war, and indeed all the business of life,
is to endeavour to find out what you don't know by what you do."*
*— Duke of Wellington*

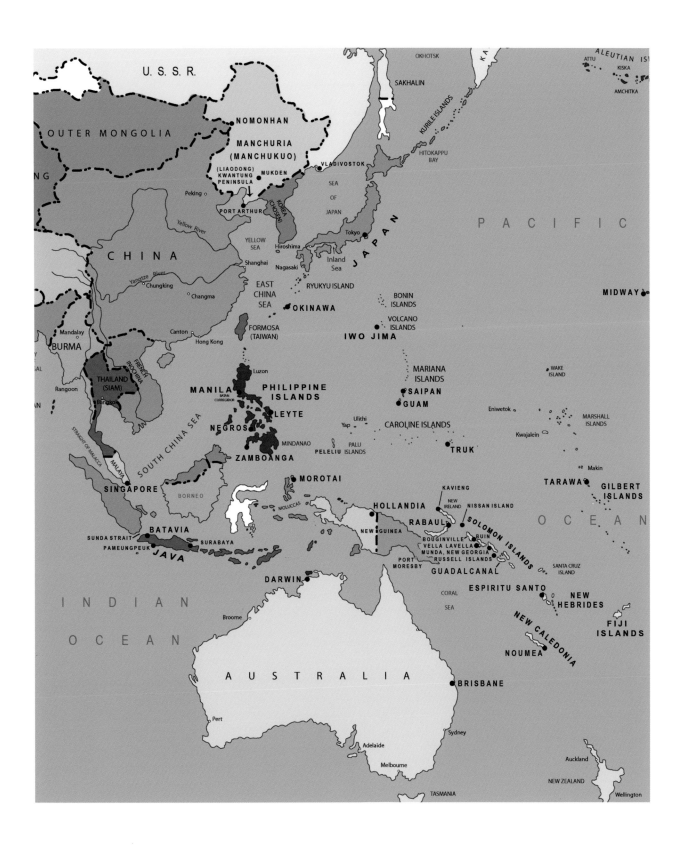

Atsushi Takizawa

# LONG SHADOW AT NOMONHAN

Japanese leaders of the late 19th century believed that colonial expansion was necessary for economic growth and national security. To fulfill these goals two opposing political doctrines were devised: *Hokushin-ron* and *Nanshin-ron*.[1]

Hokushin-ron, the northern road, envisioned Korea, Manchuria and Siberia as areas with the greatest potential to supply raw materials and markets for Japanese-manufactured goods. Nanshin-ron, the southern road, was an alternative plan that expanded the Empire into Southeast Asia, including Singapore, the oil-rich Dutch East Indies and the Pacific Islands. Of the two plans, Hokushin-ron was favored until a little-known border dispute with the Soviet Union forced Tokyo to embrace Nanshin-ron, a doctrine that eventually led Japan into the Pacific War.

In the spirit of Hokushin-ron, Japan moved into Northeast Asia in 1894 and successfully fought the crumbling Chinese Empire for control of Korea and south Manchuria. In the Treaty of Shimonoseki, which ended the First Sino-Japanese War, China recognized the independence of Korea and agreed to cede the Liaodong Peninsula in south Manchuria. China also agreed to pay Japan a large indemnity, and granted Japan trading privileges on Chinese territory.

Russia, which had its own designs on China, intervened over the terms of the treaty. It convinced Germany and France that Japanese control of the Liaodong Peninsula, which was renamed Kwantung by Japan, would have negative effects on the stability of China. This triple intervention by Russia, Germany and France put diplomatic pressure on Japan to return Kwantung to China in exchange for a larger indemnity.

Meanwhile, Russia was completing the Trans-Siberian Railroad which ran from Moscow to Vladivostok, a cold-water eastern seaport that was operational only during the summer months. In search of a warm-water port for her navy and maritime trade, Russia pressured China in 1898 into a lease for Port Arthur, located at the tip of the Liaodong Peninsula. Russia also won rights from the Chinese to extend the Trans-Siberian Railroad south across Manchuria to Port Arthur; this became the southern branch of the Chinese Eastern Railway, known in the West as the South Manchuria Railway. Russia then established it's occupation of the peninsula, even though it had just forced Japan to relinquish such a right.

After securing a military alliance with Great Britain in 1902, Japan sought an agreement with Russia that offered recognition of Czarist railway interests in Manchuria in exchange for Russia's acknowledgement of Japan's political, military

---

1  *Hokushin* literally translates as, "proceeding north," and *Nanshin* translates as "proceeding south." *Ron* means "doctrine."

and economic interests in Korea. Russia refused because it wanted control over the Korean border to Manchuria and other zones in China. In the spirit of compromise, Russia offered Japan a free hand in Korea provided Japan would not use the peninsula as a staging area for military operations. Russia even proposed that Korean territory north of the 39th parallel be declared a neutral zone where neither country would be permitted to station troops. Tokyo rejected Russia's proposal, the two countries went to war, and Russia was defeated.

The 1905 Treaty of Portsmouth formally ended the Russo-Japanese War. The treaty forced Russia to recognize Japan's interests in Korea, surrender its leasehold of the Liaodong Peninsula, and turn over the South Manchuria Railway. Both powers agreed to evacuate resource-rich Manchuria, which had been the principal battleground, and return that province to Chinese administration.

Fearing a Russian war of revenge, Japan came to an understanding with her enemy. In 1907 the two countries signed a secret treaty recognizing Korea as part of Japan's sphere of interest, and Outer Mongolia as a Russian sphere of interest. The treaty also divided meddling rights in Manchuria: Russia would take the northern half of the territory and Japan would take the southern half. By 1910 Japan had annexed Korea. In 1912 Outer Mongolia became a Russian protectorate.

On 18 September 1931 a clique of rogue officers eager to advance Japan's Hokushin-ron doctrine staged an explosion on the South Manchuria Railway at Mukden as a pretext to unleash an invasion north. Troops from Japan's army in the Kwantung Peninsula soon occupied all of Manchuria, separated the region from Chinese control, and created the puppet state of Manchukuo.

The Soviets did not immediately respond. They were in the middle of a massive five-year program of industrial modernization that emphasized basic industries over military production, but by the mid-1930s had strengthened their position in the Far East. Border disputes with Japan followed.

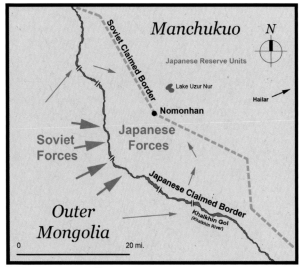

See larger map on page 13.

One of these disputes occurred in an area along the border between Outer Mongolia and Manchukuo, near the village of Nomonhan. The Mongolian Peoples Republic and their Soviet ally maintained that the disputed border was ten miles east of the river Khalkhin Gol, near the village of Nomonhan. The Japanese disagreed, insisting that the border was the river Khalkhin Gol.

Troubles began on 11 May 1939 when seventy to ninety men from a Mongolian cavalry unit entered the disputed area in search of grazing for their horses. They were attacked by the Japanese and driven back across the Khalkhin Gol. Days later the Mongolians returned in greater numbers and were forced again to withdraw. A larger battle was fought in late May, followed by another in July, both ending in stalemate. The Japanese continued to build up their forces through the spring; the Soviets did likewise under a new Corps commander, Georgy Zhukov,[2] who arrived on 5 June.

---

2   It was at Nomonhan that Zhukov tested his pioneering use of tanks. After the battle, which is referred to by Soviet historians as the Battle of Khalkhin Gol, Zhukov transferred his men to units that had not seen action to spread the benefits of their combat experience. The battle also provided practical knowledge that led to the development of the famous T-34 tank, and the phasing out of fire-prone gasoline engines in favor of diesel engines. Zhukov would later claim that the experience he gained at Nomonhan played an important role in his defeat of the Nazis on the Eastern Front.

The climactic battle began on 20 August 1939. Zhukov attacked, directing 500 Soviet tanks, two motorized infantry divisions, 550 fighter and bomber aircraft, and two Mongolian cavalry divisions in a coordinated assault. They were met by elements of Japan's 6th Army, including Lieutenant General Komatsubara's 23rd Infantry Division.

The Soviet air force was first to strike, followed by Zhukov's central ground forces. Initially Zhukov made only modest gains in the face of fierce resistance, but he then engaged the center of the Japanese line so heavily that they could not reinforce their flanks. Soviet armored units swept around the Japanese flanks and attacked from behind — a classic double envelopment. When the Soviet wings linked up at Nomonhan on 25 August, Komatsubara's 23rd Division was trapped. On 26 August a Japanese counterattack to relieve the 23rd Division failed. The 23rd Division then attempted to break out on its own, but that effort also failed. The surrounded troops refused to surrender and were bombarded from the air and by artillery. On 29 August Lieutenant General Komatsubara realized that all was lost. As he prepared to die with his troops by committing suicide, a radio message was received from 6th Army Headquarters instructing Komatsubara to save himself and lead as many men as possible out of the Soviet encirclement. Komatsubara escaped, and by 31 August most of the 23rd Division west of Nomonhan was wiped out, with some remnants left on the Manchukuo side of the border.

As Japan was being handed the worst defeat in its modern history, Joseph Stalin signed the German-Soviet Non-aggression Pact on 23 August 1939, which secured a sphere of influence for the USSR in eastern Europe, bought time to build up the Red Army, and reduced the prospect of a two-front war with Germany and Japan.

Hitler's army invaded Poland, unopposed by the Soviets, on 1 September. Two days later Britain and France declared war on Germany.

Sporadic ground and air combat between Soviet and Japanese forces continued into September. Komatsubara refused to accept the outcome of the battle and was preparing a counter-offensive when a cease-fire agreement was signed in Moscow on 15 September 1939.

Lieutenant General Komatsubara, his black hair turned white from the shock of defeat, returned to Tokyo with his account of the battle. The disaster at Nomonhan cast a long shadow over discussions at a series of Imperial War Conferences where the decision was made to abandon Hokushin-ron in favor of Nanshin-ron. The only thing that might stand in their way was the United States Pacific Fleet.

In April 1941 Japan signed the Soviet–Japanese Neutrality Pact to free up men and materiel for their coming war in the Pacific. Two months later Germany attacked the Soviet Union and enjoyed a string of victories. The Soviets seemed to be on the verge of collapse when Germany urged Japan to avenge her defeat at Nomonhan by opening a second front against the USSR. Had Japan not been defeated at Nomonhan, it would likely have continued to embrace the Hokushin-ron doctrine, and might have joined Hitler in the fight against their mutual communist enemy. The Soviet margin of victory at Moscow, and later at Stalingrad, was thin; Japan could easily have tipped the outcome in favor of Germany.

Colonel Inada Masazumi, the former head of Japan's Army General Staff Operations Section, was forced out in the aftermath of the Nomonhan Incident. In a retrospective article written ten years after the end of the Pacific War, Inada Masazumi had this to say about Nomonhan:

Although very heavy casualties and the dishonor of defeat were among the high prices that we paid, what was more difficult for me to accept was that the Nomonhan Incident destroyed our guiding principle of preparing for global conflict by consolidating our position in the North, which would have been achieved by settling the China War and building up our strength against the Soviet Union. Instead, after the Nomonhan Incident Japan unexpectedly drifted toward the decision to move south, the invasion of French Indo-China, and

The Soviets advancing at Nomonhan, 1939.

Japanese soldiers dug in near Nomonhan, 1939.

Stuck in the mud on the way to the front, Nomonhan, 1939.

The Nomonhan battlefield with a Soviet tank in the foreground.

Destroyed Soviet plane near the Khalkhin Gol, 1939. Photo credits for this page are unknown.

finally the Pacific War. It was this change of policy which I regretted most after being expelled from the Army General Staff. The Nomonhan Incident was a turning point which had great influence on the history of Japan. Even now, when I look back, I think so from the bottom of my heart.[3]

The battle at Nomonhan is reflected in the illustrated diary of Atsushi Takizawa. The diary begins as Takizawa deploys to Nomonhan with a group of reinforcements sent from Kwantung Army headquarters at Hailar, located 93 miles northeast of the fighting. From his reserve position on the battlefield, Takizawa writes and sketches during one of the most pivotal events of the 20th century.

## *Nomonhan Diary*[4]
### *Atsushi Takizaswa*

**August 22nd, *Shōwa* 14 (1939)**[5]
23:22 Left Qiqihar by train.

**August 25th**
Left Hailar by car.

**August 26th**
Rode a cargo truck and arrived before dawn. I heard the sound of artillery fire in the distance. The sound was gradually moving closer when a Soviet aircraft came. It dropped its bombs and the explosions shook the earth. Then our airplanes went to bomb the enemy. I dug in and ate hardtack. The sounds of artillery fire sounded like a thousand thunders.

**The 27th**
The thunder rumbled in the distance. It grew near and is now overhead as I witness a bombing for the first time in my life. One bomb exploded and killed the regimental commander. A sergeant who could not have been more than five steps away from me was wounded. Although there have been endless numbers of aircraft flying overhead, they never dropped bombs on our location until now. Another air attack has been carried out on one of our positions 7,000 meters from here.

**The 28th**
Predawn; everyone in the Regiment gathered together. I met up with Maruyama. We were pleased to see each other alive and well. I did not sleep well because of the cold. Later in the morning I took a break and dozed off in a my dug-out. I had a dream that I was fishing in the countryside. Why did I have such a dream? Airplanes came again. What are they up to? I feel like a fish in a pond being observed from above. We all got into our dug-outs as the enemy approached. Several planes were in a dogfight shooting at one another. It was the first aerial combat I have seen. It seemed the enemy bombed our positions again. We hear the usual sounds of artillery. I'm sure it will be raining by evening. Day by day my dug-out grows larger. In the night a man from brigade headquarters came by and said the bombing they received was severe.

**The 29th**
There were more bombardments. The front line troops came back this morning. The Umibe squad also came back. We prepared a feast and treated them like heroes. Most of the men who returned had been injured; it was a miserable sight. I offered them words of appreciation. Why didn't Captain Umibe come back? What is Ito doing?

---

3   Stuart D. Goldman. *Nomonhan, 1939: The Red Army's Victory That Shaped World War II* (U.S. Naval Institute Press, 2012),172-173.
4   Two illustrated diaries and a *senninbari* piqued my interest when I learned that they were for sale. The seller, who was living in Japan, told me that she found them at a Tokyo antique shop, and that all three had the name Atsushi Takizawa written on them. When asked about the contents of the diaries she said, "The writing is difficult — it is old style." I purchased the lot and sent a few random pages to Kazunori Tanoue, my translator in Japan. Several days later I received the first pages transcribed into English. As I read from the first diary, I wondered if I had made a mistake. The text was typical of a Second Sino-Japanese War diary (1937-1945). It was interesting but off-topic for my concerns. I skipped over to the second diary, and when I read the word "Nomonhan" I knew that I had struck gold.
5   The reign of each Emperor begins a new cycle in the Japanese calendar. The Shōwa era (1926-1989) began with the accession of Emperor Hirohito on 25 December 1926, making it year one in the numbering system. Shōwa 14, the 14th year of the Shōwa era, coincides with1939 on the Gregorian calendar.

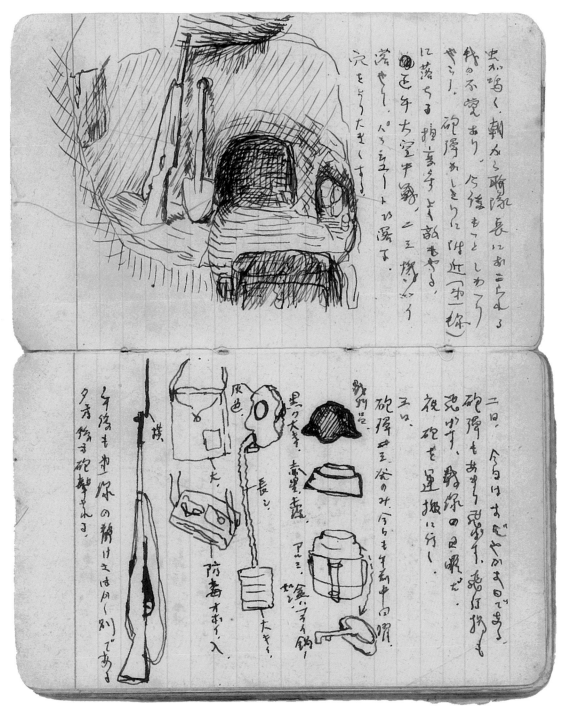

"My residence," Takizawa's grim-looking battlefield dug-out sports an overhead tarp, storage nooks, rifle and shovel. The drawing below depicts all his worldly possessions — the tools of war — neatly illustrated. *Author's collection*.

Takizawa sketched the wounded from the battle at Nomonhan. *Author's collection.*

The night is cold now.
Tonight there is a full moon.
Bright moon over the front-lines.
What are you trying to tell me?

## The 30th

Our pilots made a bombing run in the morning. Ka-boom! And then I felt the ground rumble. Then there was another dogfight high up in the sky. Watching the battlefield in the sky is amazing. I must have been thinking too much about airplanes because the flies also came to attack me. The night was cold and the day was hot. Today is a fine autumn-like day. Insects are chirping and butterflies flutter about. Everyone seems to be overwhelmed by the heat. Even the enemy didn't bother to fire their artillery very often. They probably felt the heat too. After finishing aerial surveillance, I went into my dug-out, dozed off and had a dream that I was born in Tokyo, then moved to Tsuruoka, Tokyo, Hokkaido, Manchuria and then to the border of Central China, and I am in a hole in the ground. Is this true? Yes, it is true, and I am alive! None of us know our destiny. Does my will in any way affect it? In the evening, the ground collapsed in my dug-out because of the intensive bombardment. Black smoke is rising from one of our military positions 5,000 meters from here. What a pity.

## The 31st

The mornings are still cold and the situation has not changed. Air battles at midnight. It was a night attack against the first brigade. There were many air attacks and I am becoming nervous.

## September 1st

September has come at last. This land is filled with autumn-like scenery and the grass seems to have suddenly withered. Grasshoppers were jumping and insects were chirping. The regimental commander scolded me in the morning because I screwed up. He may be on my case from now on. My position on the front line is constantly being bombarded. The enemy is doing well as usual. There were dogfights at noon. Two or three airplanes were shot down and their pilots bailed out with their parachutes. I made my dug-out bigger.

## September 2nd

Today was very calm. There was little incoming artillery and there were no aircraft in the sky. It seemed like Sunday on the battle line. I went outside to help move artillery in the night.

## The 3rd

There were only two or three bombs. Today's morning was like Sunday, too, and the front line was exceptionally tranquil this afternoon as well. We were bombarded in the evening. Three graves were dug for those killed in last night's attack. The

Kwantung Army records reported 16,800 casualties. *Author's collection.*

The Soviets claimed to have inflicted 29,000 Japanese casualties. *Author's collection.*

lonely graves were lined up in a row. There is no way to know whether they were happy or unhappy. Brothers, rest in peace. You will find excellent land in the new world beyond. The sun set behind the meadow again and a beautiful moon appeared. A few men were crushed to death last night by cave-ins because of the rain.

### The 4th
The enemy's bombardment started at around 9 o'clock. Today we got lots of booty. At around 1:20, during air surveillance, artillery shells dropped within twenty to thirty meters from me and continued doing so for about twenty minutes. I felt the heat from each blast as it hit my face. The ground heaved up and a piece of shrapnel glanced off my helmet at a high speed. All day God has given me life.

### The 5th
No bullets came in my direction this morning, except for the occasional long-distance shot. Today was Sunday for the bullet.

### The 6th
Artillery fire came in from three directions this morning. I escaped death by a hair's breadth. One fell silently to the earth and then exploded only 500 meters from me. I have been ordered to dig the dug-out for the squad leader. Three enemy planes were flying overhead.

### The 7th
I finished digging the squad leader's dug-out in the

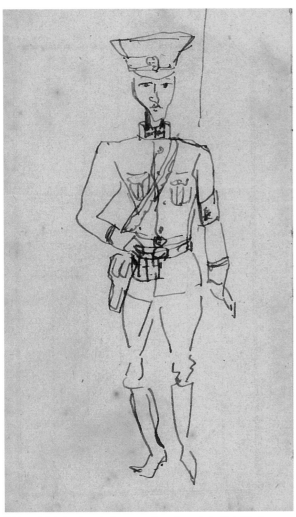

Takizawa's ink drawing of a Japanese officer. It was tucked into his diary on a separate sheet of paper. *Author's collection.*

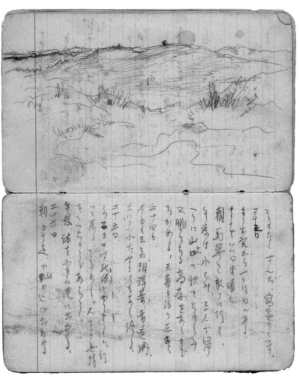

Takizawa's drawing, dirty and smudged from the battlefield, depicts the land-scape of Nomonhan. *Author's collection.*

afternoon. It was big enough for two people. We moved out at night. There was no artillery bombardment.

**The 8th**

Turns out the squad leader's dug-out was a little narrow for two people. I thought I could try enlarging it, but I had a difficult time digging out even another 30 centimeters. Airplanes came from time to time and bombarded us again today. I slept, dozed often, but the night was still cold.

**The 9th**

It was comfortable weather this morning. I worked as air surveillance. There is heavy bombing in the distance. It is autumn and the breeze blows quietly in between the roar of explosions. Insects are chirping. They sound somehow similar to pine crickets we have back home. My beard has grown longer. I have heard rumors from Sergeant Murai that First-Class Private Minamoto is dead. I pray for the repose of his soul. At night I worked hard cooking while the group leader was away, but I was soon overwhelmed by the rain. It leaked through the tent and the wind blew, and so we all spent the day in our dug-outs. The flies came and I moved to the back of the dug-out because of the rain leaking in. At least it dripped in a brash, cheeky manner.

*Takizawa makes no entries until September 16.*

**The 16th**

There was a message that the cease-fire agreement was signed at 8 o'clock in the morning. It was an anticlimactic feeling and I felt disappointed, but it was a good day for the cease-fire. A messenger from the Soviet Army came in the afternoon. Many people went to the signing of the surrender which took place 1,000 meters from here. I cooked *nishime*[6] at night, and it was very delicious and I ate my fill. I was able to relax a little on this, the first night of the cease-fire. I thought nostalgically of Rembrandt as I sit by the fire of a candle. I will sleep well tonight! Good night Father and Mother. Good night! Aman-kun, Yoshikazu and Kiyora!

**The 17th**

The weather was beautiful today. Everyone was re-laxing. A cool wind blanketed my body. This was a lush land when I first arrived, but now it is lonely. The regimental commander laughed out-loud and seemed relaxed. What a beautiful day! After the regular water drawing, I tried to lay down on the grass in spite of the heat. The cool wind felt good under the heat of the sun. When I listened carefully, I could hear insects chirping.

**The 18th**

I did calisthenics in the morning. The anti-aircraft squad executed military exercises at 9:30 a.m. and again for an hour in the afternoon. Private First Class Matsumoto was in charge. I went to bed after eating an early dinner.

**The 19th**

It was raining and I had to spend the day inside my dug-out, which I am not happy about. Tomorrow I am expecting to leave this place. The squad leader went to Hailar to take care of things at midnight. I couldn't sleep at all. I will send letters to the land-owner and to my teacher. Maybe I will send one to an elementary school student as well. I thought to myself: tonight is the last night I will spend in this hole, and then dozed off.

"I went into my dug-out, dozed off and had a dream . . . ." *Author's collection.*

**The 20th**

Departure day has finally come. The squad leader and I checked the signaling device and then put it back in place. I took a nap around noon. I forgot to observe a moment of silence for our heroic war dead, but I always observe a moment of silence for them in my mind. New troops poured into this posi-tion where we had lost more than half of our men in the fighting. The date for departure has been moved to tomorrow but three personnel from headquarters will remain. It was a cold night.

**The 21st**

It was time to prepare breakfast and I looked here and there for something to eat. I found *kiriboshi*[7]

"Carrying water."

and *miso*.[8] I left my dug-out and our battlefield at 10 o'clock in the morning and have now arrived at this hill. I set up a tent in the morning and went to draw water. One of the maidservants won a comfort bag.[9]

---

6  *Nishime* is simmered Japanese vegetables.

7  *Kiriboshi*: dried shreaded daikon radish.
8  *Miso*: a traditional Japanese seasoning. It also means soup.
9  Comfort bag: Is called a *imon-bukuro* (sympathy bag). It was a cotton bag with a drawstring filled with non military issued items, such as toiletries, dried fruits, canned foods and letters of encouragement. They were prepared by school-girls or local patriotic women's societies.

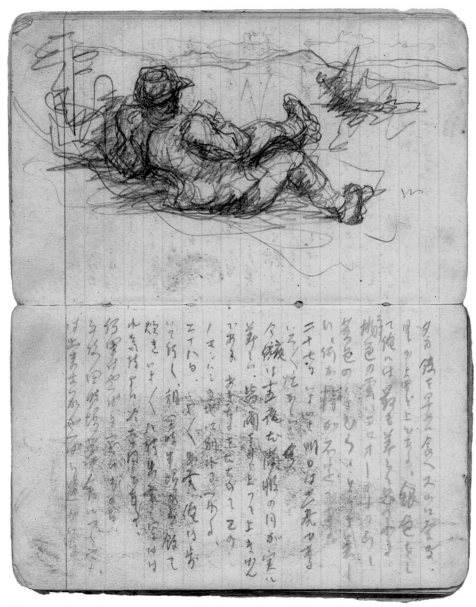

"A man cannot travel a thousand miles in one day; his spirit can easily do so." *Author's collection*.

### The 22nd
Today was good weather and ended without a problem.

### The 23rd
It's been one day since my departure from the battlefield. It was a very fine day. I went to get fodder in the morning, and then went to draw water in the afternoon. I enjoyed the autumn season. Set up a tent and got back directly.

### The 24th
Today was also fine weather and a beautiful morning. We returned the army flag and that was it for

### The 25th

I have been dealing with the dead bodies. They were filled with the emptiness of life. I went outside to wash up in the afternoon.

### The 26th

I ran to the top of the hill. The morning sun began to shine. A man cannot travel a thousand miles in one day; his spirit can easily do so. There was nothing but the hill-like desert as far as the eye could see: hills, covered with grass, and beautiful. The dappled hills seemed to be covered by the skin of a leopard. I looked at the sky above the hill and was overwhelmed with emotion by memories of desire and the dream of a triumphant return. Although I tried to sleep, it was difficult because of the heat. In a dream I saw what I thought were two white horses approaching. Then they turned black and I felt sick. I often have these kind of dreams. I wonder why I get this listless feeling after napping in the countryside. I would rather feel exhausted from a hard day's work than feel like this. I must leave the day after tomorrow. There will be a march! And then what is waiting for me? Of course, my parents are worried about me. I am sure of this. I have been out of contact for two days. Everyone might be enjoying the harvest soon. How is Aman-kun doing? I want to see him first when I return home. My grandparents are old and wait for my return. Oh, look at that cloud and how free it is. What a genius! I ate dinner early in the evening and went to the hills again. Very high! I think silver is the most beautiful color. The light pink cloud, yellow ocher hills and yellow grass. It looks lonely. Something is missing.

### The 27th

Finally, tomorrow is departure day. I was very busy all day. Today was a full moon. The moon of Manchuria became full and it was beautiful. Everybody was happy because the rain stopped. We enjoyed the fall weather and bade farewell to this land, Nomonhan.

### The 28th

Left here at last. I went on foot. Cooked rice at around 4:30 in the morning and left at 8:00. It was a clear sky and the wind was cool. Marching is always good. I arrived at camp at around 4 p.m. with many blisters on my feet. I am a lucky man.

*This ends the Nomonhan portion of the diary.*

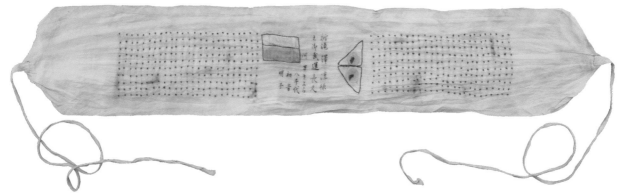

Translation of Atsushi Takizawa's *senninbari-haramaki*: "We wish long-lasting good luck in battle for Atsushi Takizawa. Signed: Kiyora, Yachiyo, Hatsune, Akio, Aman." *Senninbari-haramaki* ("one thousand-person-stitches") take several forms, but were most often a strip of cloth, measuring six inches high and three to four feet in length, with strings at each end that were used to tie the belt around the waist. Senninbari were decorated with 1000 stitches, collected by the man's mother, sister or wife, who would stand near their local temple, train station or department store and ask any female passerby to sew in a stitch. When one thousand stitches were collected, a senninbari was believed to possess special powers to protect the bearer in battle. *Author's collection.*

Cleon Stewart

# KING RAT

Cleon Stewart's Changi Prison POW tag. It was worn attached to a button on his shirt. *Author's collection.*

On 10 November 1941, the 2nd Battalion, 131st Field Artillery Regiment detached from its parent unit, the 36th Division, and traveled by train to San Francisco Bay. There they boarded the USS *Republic,* sailed to Hawaii, and joined a convoy[1] enroute to a secret destination, code-named PLUM.[2]

A week into their voyage Commander Clark made an announcement over *Republic*'s intercom: "Attention all hands, a state of war exists between Japan and the United States. Pearl Harbor has been attacked. Good Luck."[3] As the convoy prepared to defend itself, it was ordered to put in at Suva in the Fiji Islands for the purpose of awaiting further orders. On 12 December the convoy's destination and mission was made clear: redesignated as "Task Force South Pacific," it was ordered to Australia where it would become United States Forces in Australia (USFIA), a supply organization supporting the Philippines, which was under attack.

On 22 December the convoy arrived in Brisbane to cheering crowds along the banks of the harbor. The troops debarked on the 23rd and were taken to temporary quarters while Australian stevedores reloaded supplies aboard MS *Bloemfontein* and USAT *Holbrook*, the two fastest ships, bound north for the Philippines.

On 28 December the 2nd Battalion, 131st Field Artillery Regiment boarded *Bloemfontein* and departed with *Holbrook* for Manila, but on 2 January Manila was declared an open city to avoid its destruction and occupied by the Japanese. Rapid advances elsewhere by the Japanese in the Dutch East Indies made it impossible for the convoy to get through, so *Bloemfontein* and *Holbrook* were ordered back and put in at Port Darwin, on the northern coast of Australia.

The men spent the night there aboard the

1 The USS *Republic* was one of seven ships sailing individually from San Francisco to Hawaii. In Hawaii they formed a group, the *Pensacola* Convoy, that departed for Manila on 29 November 1941. This convoy included the USS *Republic*, USS *Chaumont*, USAT (U.S. Army Transport) *Willard A. Holbrook*, USAT *Miegs*, MS (Motor Ship) *Bloemfontein*, SS *Admiral Halstead,* and SS *Coast Farmer*. Its escorts were the USS *Pensacola* and USS *Niagara*.
2 PLUM stood for Philippines, Luzon, Manila — the code-name for General MacArthur's build-up of U.S. Army forces in the Philippines prior to World War II.
3 Lida Mayo, "United States Army in World War II, The Technical Services, The Ordnance Department: On Beachhead and Battlefront," Center of Military History, United States Army (Washington, D.C., 1968), 35-37.

*Bloemfontein*, nervously watching the sky in the wake of a rumor that Port Darwin had recently been bombed by the Japanese. While *Holbrook* unloaded its cargo, *Bloemfontein* received new orders on 9 January to deliver the 2nd Battalion, 131st Field Artillery to Java, the largest Dutch island still in Allied hands. Once there they would reinforce Australian, British and Dutch forces.

The *Bloemfontein* arrived in Surabaya on 11 January, guided by a Dutch harbor boat through a maze of partially-sunk ships and Dutch mines. The men unloaded their equipment, boarded a train to Malang, and settled into an airfield and Dutch military post called Camp Singosari.[4]

On 27 February 1942, Japan's Eastern Invasion Force with its naval escort gathered to attack Java. Rushing to intercept them was the American-British-Dutch-Australian Strike Force made up of destroyers, cruisers and heavy cruisers.

The ensuing battle raged intermittently from mid-afternoon to midnight. The Strike Force suffered heavy losses, broke off its engagement and turned south, covered by a smoke screen laid down by four destroyers. It then turned west and north in an attempt to surprise the transports, but instead ran into the enemy escort once more. In a devastating torpedo attack, two Dutch light cruisers were hit and sunk within minutes.

The Strike Force, low on ammunition and fuel, was ordered to disperse, and on its own initiative return to Surabaya. HMAS *Perth* and USS *Houston* retreated west to Tanjung Priok, the port of Batavia (Jarkata), where they took on all available fuel and ammunition. As the two ships were attempting to withdraw on the evening of the 28th, they made a chance discovery of the Japanese landing underway on the northwest tip of Java near the entrance to Sunda Strait. They fired upon ships shielding the transports, and in a ferocious action that ended after midnight, *Perth* and *Houston* were sunk. Of *Houston*'s original 1,061-man crew, 368 survived and swam to shore.

Meanwhile, the 588 men of the 2nd Battalion, 131st Field Artillery Regiment had been playing a hopeless game in the defense of Java under Dutch command. They used their artillery and .50-caliber machine guns salvaged from wrecked B-17s to support an Australian Pioneer Battalion which arrived in Java just prior to the Japanese landing. They also provided mechanics, ground crews and aerial gunners to the U.S. Army Air Corps' 19th Bombardment Group which had escaped from the Philippines with a few B-17 bombers.

On 8 March 1942, the Dutch surrendered Java to the Japanese. Most of the men from the 2nd Battalion, 131st Field Artillery Regiment surrendered and were imprisoned together with survivors from *Houston* at the 10th Battalion Bicycle Camp, a former Dutch Army installation at Batavia. From there men were transported to Singapore by ship, confined like cattle in the lower hold.

Of these 902 prisoners, 668 were sent to work on the Burma-Siam "Death Railway," the building of which is portrayed in the film *The Bridge on the River Kwai*. Others were sent to Japanese-controlled Asian countries to work as slave laborers in coal mines and shipyards where they suffered physical and mental torture, starvation and disease. A few stayed behind at various camps where they worked as day laborers for their Japanese masters. What happened to the men of the 2nd Battalion, 131st Field Artillery Regiment and the survivors of the USS *Houston* remained a mystery to the United States government for most of the war. Cleon Stewart was one of those men. This is his story.[5]

## *Japan Attacks*
### Cleon Stewart

We left San Francisco on November 21, 1941. Our first stop was Honolulu and I was sick all the way. There was only 583 of us in the 2nd Battalion.

---

4    Travis Monday, "W. F. Matthews, Lost Battalion Survivor," 2004, 26-27.

5    As edited from Stewart's transcript in the University of North Texas Oral History Collection. Interview ID # OH 0911 (18 March 1993).

Other units were on the ship as well but I don't know who they were. It was a loaded and crowded ship. We were near the Gilbert Islands when we received news that the Japanese hit Pearl Harbor. It made me very, very angry of course and I was ready to do something about it. Our ship spent the next three days going in a circle. We were told that we were headed toward the Fijis to refuel and get supplies. I didn't actually know where the Fijis were located. I didn't know if they were 100 miles or 500 miles or how many miles they were from Australia. But that's where we were headed. When we got there we didn't get off the ship. We just refueled and re-supplied our ship and took off for Australia

We got to Brisbane on December 22nd and left shortly thereafter on the 27th[6] when we took off on the MS *Bloemfontein*, a Dutch Ship. From Brisbane we went to Port Darwin and sat there in the bay in 100-and-something heat. We had to sit and wait for somebody to make a decision, or for the corvettes[7] that were going with us to get there, I didn't know which.

We left Port Darwin, weaving in and out of the islands between Australia and the Indonesian islands, as they are referred to now. We were weaving in and out of those islands to keep from being attacked by submarines. Periodically, the corvettes would take off. We figured they were headed to pick up some enemy somewhere. Then, later, they'd show back up.

We arrived in Java, I think — was it the 1st of January? Maybe it was the 11th. At this time I was still the number one radio operator with our firing battery and so I rode in the car with the commander, Captain Cates. We got off the ship at Surabaya, put one foot on the ground and immediately went into a passenger car and pulled all the curtains. Then we went inland for fifty miles to a town called Malang. We arrived there around midnight because everything was just as black as could be. There wasn't a moon out or anything. We were stationed outside

Malang at Singosari.

There was a little barracks adjacent to an airfield. It was there that I saw some B-17s from the 19th and 22nd Bomb Groups. I'd never seen B-17s before. The airfield appeared to be in pretty good shape until the Japanese started bombing it. We were told to help in any way we could because their ground crews were left in the Philippines. We refueled the aircraft and helped them to reload the guns but I didn't go out on any missions.

The first Japanese air strike occurred on February 3rd. It was like a hail storm and you don't know where to go. The Japanese were in a "V" when they came over. As a radio operator, I was never trained as a crew member of a firing battery. I was in the dining hall line when this air raid siren came on and I headed out toward the jungle. In doing so, I came by a 75 mm that was set up. I don't remember exactly who the sergeant was, but he said, "Get in here and help me!" So, I got in there and helped as best I could. We cut those fuses at twenty-one seconds and fired them. Stories got back to us that we knocked three of them out of the air. Japanese Zeros strafed the field next to us that had B-17s on it. The attacks continued. I don't remember whether it was daily or if it was every other day, but when they came you could bet on one thing—you were either in the dining hall or in the chow line getting something to eat. People would grab a piece of chicken and head to the bush. You never would get used to the raids because you never know where they're aiming. During the second raid they bombed where we had a gun piece on the first raid. So, they were pretty accurate with their bombing. Our guns never got hit because we moved them before the next raid. Had they been left where they were, they'd all have been destroyed.

On February 27th the 19th [and] 22nd Bomb Groups evacuated to Australia. They took some of the field artillery people with them. I didn't get upset knowing they were leaving and we were staying. I knew that when we went into action, the Japanese would be no obstacle to us. Our field artil-

---

6   Stewart misremembers the date of departure, which was 28 December.
7   A corvette is an easily built patrol and convoy escort vessel.

lery unit was selected to do eighteen months' garrison duty because we were good. I was cocky, not having any idea of what good soldiers the Japanese were. I had no idea at this time how much they had accomplished already. All I knew was that once we encountered the Japanese, we were going to win. There wasn't any question in my mind about that. The next day the Japanese landed during the night.

Our unit split into two groups and left Singosari. E Battery went to Surabaya while we headed westward into the island of Java. Along the side of the road every morning we'd see the Dutch stop to have a pot of tea, and here we were, with one battalion heading to the front lines to fight their battle and they were sitting on the side of the road having tea. We pulled our battalion, what was left of it — three firing batteries — into a rubber plantation. And it would rain! It rained cats and dogs. We set up some artillery pieces on a ridge four or five miles down from where we set up camp. We were in action a day-and-a-half before being told to move out because the Japanese were advancing. Our orders were to head towards the south side of Java where the USS *Houston*, USS *Marblehead* and the Australian light cruiser *Perth* would pick us up and deliver us to Australia. As we were heading in that direction the commander was notified that the ships were sunk and that we were to surrender because the Dutch government had surrendered the island. This made me most unhappy. I figured the Dutch were just trying to prevent their stores from being bombed out. They surrendered to keep their property intact and to keep anything from happening to the civilians. Here we are over there fighting for them and they were not putting out any effort. I now know that the Japanese landed with 150,000 troops, and there was two battalions of Americans and Australians on the island; we didn't stand a chance. But in our minds at the time we knew good and well that the Japanese didn't have a chance once they encountered us.

We destroyed most of our equipment and headed toward Gareot. After we had destroyed all

Java: The Dutch surrender. Source unknown.

the vehicles and the weapons, Captain Cates called us all together. He told us that we could either surrender with the unit, or as individuals we could head for the hills and try to find a way to escape. I was still with Captain Cates and I had not received any transportation other than the command car, so I started looking around for a new means of transportation. An Australian said, "There is a motorcycle back over on the other road, but the front wheel is damaged." Well, I worked on bicycles. I thought a motorcycle wasn't much different. So, I went over there and looked at the motorcycle; it had an oblong wheel. Then another Aussie truck came by. They told me, "Back up the road there is one with the back end knocked out of it." So, I went back up there and got me a front wheel and from that I got the first bike put together. I was in real "high cotton" then. A guy named Griffen was going to go with me. He had a motorcycle given to him and he didn't have to do anything but fill it up with gas. He said, "Hold on, Stewart! Just wait until I get the gasoline in it!" So while he was filling it up with gasoline I cranked mine up. I should have waited, I guess, instead of hurrying him. I cranked up my motor and headed south. When I looked back I saw his motorcycle engulfed in flames. After he put gas in it, the whole thing caught on fire, so he wasn't going.

I drove that motorcycle and headed for the beach. Every time the Aussies would stop, I'd go on as far as I could around them. It was raining up a storm but I think I was wetter from sweat than from the rain. It was about one o'clock, I guess, when I finally decided to chuck the bike. I punctured the gas tank and the tires and threw it over a cliff. I took my rifle and a pistol and got on the back of this lorry, the end gate is what it was, and dozed off. That was at one o'clock. At around three-thirty somebody came walking along the side of the lorry.

I said, "Hey, Aussie, what are you doing?"

He replied, "Well, I just had me a pot of tea, and I'm headed to the front."

I said, "Where is that tea?"

He replied, gesturing with his hand, "Back about four lorries. We got some Canadian bacon and some tea."

So, I went back there and got me some tea and bacon. I then thanked them and took off to the front line, just where he was going. Every time those cars would move up I'd ride one until it stopped. When it stopped I'd get off and keep on walking. I don't know how many cars I had ridden or how far I had gone.

The next morning I got down to the place where they were destroying their vehicles. They were throwing them over the cliff. They took everything out of them before running them over the cliff. Their weapons were all stacked over at the side. Anyway, out of the pile of weapons I got me a Tommy gun. Now I had the rifle, the Tommy gun and the Smith and Wesson .38 pistol. Just the ammunition alone would weigh a few pounds. I put the ammunition inside my ditty bag filled with clothes and rations and made my way to a rubber plantation near Pameungpeuk. There I was greeted by twenty-seven Australian sergeant pilots and one flight officer. One of the twenty-seven sergeant pilots was a Canadian. They called him "Tex." Everyone welcomed me with open arms because I was the first Yankee they'd seen. I wasn't a Yankee.

I was a Texan. But, anyway....

They had sent out four Catalina flying boats that morning to Australia. The commander of the Catalinas was supposed to get two other Catalinas to come back and pick them up. They told me that I was welcome to go with them. I wanted to go and get off the island of Java and get back to civilization. We had signal equipment so that if the aircraft ever arrived they would know where we were. They told me, also, that I had to get rid of all my weapons except the pistol. If the Japanese came, they didn't want to make them think that we were setting up a resistance.

We traveled by night. From Pameungpeuk we rode a bus as far as we could and then we started walking. We could hear the ocean from where we were and went down to see what was happening. We were all dead tired and laid down and slept on the beach. I don't know how we slept at all because of all the rocks we were laying on. Then someone said, "We better get off the beach in case the Japanese fly over! They'll see us!" So we did.

The pilots and myself rented this dwelling. There were several little houses. We don't have anything like it. It's a village, but it's not a village; it's a family unit. During this time we wandered up and down the beach trying to find some seagoing vessels but we found nothing.

I better back up a little bit. When we left Pameungpeuk, we came by a rubber plantation. It was run by an Australian woman and a Dutchman. Their name was Hildebrand. We sat down and talked with them and told them what we were planning. He said, "My wife has got quite a few sheets, and she'll sew them all together. I have a ten-horsepower motor, 300 liters of petrol and all the latex you need to put the boat together and seal it." He then added, "And she will cook some hardtack, and I'll get a fifty-five-gallon barrel of rice if you let her and I go with you." Our program of escape appeared to him to be pretty logical. We accepted their offer because of the latex rubber and the motor.

Anyway, we finally gave up on the aircraft

coming back and went inland, trying to find some boat builders. We found some boat builders, and for $500 they'd build us a boat. Fine! In the meantime an RAF wing commander[8] and a flight officer came strolling into the area where we were. They were pushing a bicycle and had some luggage on their backs. This flight officer was an electrical engineer. He had a generator and the bicycle was to generate electricity so he could put a radio to work. Anyway, this group captain . . . a group captain in the RAF is a "bird" colonel in the U.S. Air Force, and a wing commander is a lieutenant colonel. Both of them was stationed in Singapore prior to the overrunning by the Japanese. They had escaped and got to this point. The group commander had 5,000 guilder in his money belt, which enabled us to do a lot of things we wouldn't have been able to do otherwise — and that is to hire help. So, we got the natives to cut the bus we had been driving down to about the level of a table and bring it down to the river. The roof of the bus was going to be the bottom of the boat. We had diked up the water so that when we got the boat ready, we would blow up the dike and ride the stream of water going down and out to the ocean.

One day I was working on the boat with Ronald Ramsey-Rae, the group leader there. He was a good guy. After we got through working we went down to the beach. One of us would go into the water while the other stayed on the beach to stand watch over whatever money and clothes we had. We noticed the natives up on the hill watching us swim. We had no idea why they were doing this because we'd just paid them off that morning for the work they'd done.

While I wondered what the natives were up to, Ramsey-Rae said, "Stewart, if we get put in a prison camp, we won't see each other much, you being an enlisted man and me being an officer. Why

don't you come in an as officer?"

I said, "Because I will come across my unit and they would know what my rank is."

"But a Pfc, they won't even know what that is," said Ramsey-Rae.

"No," I said, "But the unit does."

"Well, let's make you a sergeant before you get put in prison. As a sergeant, we'll get to visit with each other more than we would if you were a private." I agreed to that.

After we finished swimming we walked up to where the dam was. We were going to take a dip and wash off the salt from our swim in the ocean but couldn't because a water buffalo was there. So we went back and started walking up the zig-zag path up to our lean-to. We were no longer staying at the little village house, having moved to a lean-to that we set up near to where the boat was being built. We headed up the path and there was a big log you had to stand on just before reaching the top of the trail. We both stepped up onto the log at the same time and there at the top waiting for us were four Japs with four bayonets pointing at us. They yelled, "Kuru! Kuru!" which meant "Approach! Approach!" We didn't know what they meant at the time but it was said in a very aggressive tone. They also had the boy who was the cook for the RAF officers. He was from Colombo, Ceylon and he spoke both fluent English and fluent Malayan — when he wasn't excited. When he was excited he didn't speak anything. He was one that would really get excited and didn't tell us until a day later that one of our men had been shot. The Japanese brought us over to our lean-to so that we could get our clothes on. I couldn't even find my shoes because the natives went through all our clothing and food. They had stripped our place after collecting the bounty for turning us in: $10 a head.

The Japanese were on horses and we were on foot and they did not allow us to slow down for anything. These particular Japanese weren't unpleasant. They got us some watery soup to eat before we went to bed, and they gave us a mat to lay

---

8    Stewart is referring to RAF Wing Commander Ronald "Ron" Allen Ramsey-Rae and RAF Chief Armament Officer Thomas Howell. At times Stewart uses US Army and RAF ranks interchangeably, but there were no colonels in the RAF (a wing commander would be the equivalent of a lieutenant colonel in the US Army Air Corps). In ascending order, Royal Air Force ranks are as follows (with their US equivalents): flight lieutenant (captain), squadron leader (major), wing commander (lieutenant colonel), and group captain (colonel).

on. The next morning we got up and headed back to Garoet. They put us on a flatbed truck and drove us around the town to let people realize that they were the boss.

At Garoet we were brought before the commandant of the camp, who was a real "hard ass," so to speak. In broken English he asked Colonel [*sic*] Ronald Allen Ramsey-Rae why he did not turn himself in. The colonel told him that he wanted to go back to his family. Then he asked why, as the senior officer, he didn't encourage us to turn ourselves in. The colonel said that we were individuals, and as Americans we all thought for ourselves. Anyway, the Japanese commandant didn't like his answer. He was playing pool, and he took that billiard cue and broke it right over the Ramsey-Rae's head — just bigger than life! I came to realize that the Wing Commander was the only one he was going to beat on because he was a senior officer and he was a big man. This Ramsey-Rae was about another inch taller than I am, and very well built. This Jap was small of stature, but he was very, very cocky and wanted to show his authority.

The Japanese put us in solitary. My place was made of wire, like a kennel. It was a cage about 7 by 2 by 3 feet wide and not tall enough to stand up in. They confiscated everything I had. I had a bunch of quinine; they confiscated all that. That was the reason I didn't have malaria while I was on the beach. But the next day in solitary I came down with malaria and I'm telling you, I didn't know whether I was going to live or die. One day you'd be freezing and the next day you had a 104-degree fever. Then you had chills. I had BT malaria. It's not as severe as some of the other malarias.

On the eleventh day of solitary they let us out and we were put into an Australian prison camp. My possessions were practically nil. I was put in with the Australians. The Australian is a real, real nice guy, and those diggers,[9] well, as a matter of fact, this Ronald Allen Ramsey-Rae was from Sydney. The wing commander was an Englishman. His name

was Howe.[10] We were at the camp in Garoet before being sent to Batavia Bicycle Camp. Ramsey-Rae got the commander of the prison camp to write an order promoting me to sergeant. The work camp had just the bare necessities. A rope bed, a thatched roof, and the structure had no sides on it, just open. We didn't stay there very long, maybe a month after surrendering on the 29th of April. All I had was my clothing. Everything else was taken. My mess kit was gone as well but I got one from an Englishman later on.

## *Batavia Bicycle Camp*

I spent June, July, August and September in Garoet. The Japanese had the rules laid down the first day. Not to strike a Japanese, not to do this, not to do that. You can't have a camera, you can't have a gun or a weapon of any kind. If they caught you with a gun or a camera you'd be sentenced to death. Be in your bed at curfew. If you tried to escape you would cause the death of ten people. The camp had a couple thousand prisoners when I arrived . . . not Americans, mainly Dutchmen. The American prisoners that were there earlier had already been moved out just before I arrived. All were gone except for six that were left behind because they were sick. Later on a lieutenant and a Sergeant Hess arrived. George Hess was put in the sun for three or four days, I forget, without any cover. He was just put out there with no clothes except for a G-string in whatever the weather might be while he withstood it, day and night. His crime was not turning himself in. He evaded capture just like I did and this was his punishment. They told us this: that if we did not surrender like the rest of the men, then we would be treated as Japanese prisoners of war, as compared to the others that would be treated as

---

9    A military slang term for soldiers from Australia.

10    Stewart misremembers the name and rank of RAF Chief Armament Officer Tom Howell in telling his story. After the war Howell held various senior appointments in the Ministry of Aviation and the Ministry of Supply; he was made CBE in 1961, and completed his RAF service in 1967 at the rank of Air Vice-marshal (the equivalent of a two-star general officer in the US military).

"guests" of the Japanese. I don't know what this term was, but I guess it was "guests of Nippon." But after we became prisoners-of-war, I don't think we were singled out for any particular type of punishment as they indicated at first.

If you was going to address one of them, not necessarily report to him but just ask a question, you'd salute him or bow to him. Anytime you was reporting, you had to bow. They considered the bow as a form of saluting. The Japanese demanded respect from their subordinates — the same treatment you, as a prisoner, had to show them. In other words, a sergeant expects his soldiers under him to respect him as though they were prisoners, also, I mean, in the form of saluting, bowing, scraping, and all of this. If a subordinate did not show proper respect to a superior he would be punished. Depending on the severity of the violation, punishments varied from death to beatings with encased sabers. I've seen both. It was amusing to me to see them punish their own. I've seen an officer, for instance, working a sergeant over. He'd knock him down and that little sergeant would jump up and say something of acknowledgment. Then he'd be knocked down again. The officer worked him over, I guess, for five minutes — knocking him down just as fast as that man could get up. What he had done I don't know. Their treatment of us was barbaric but they were barbaric with their own as well.

At Bicycle Camp they hadn't got down to the real bad food at this point. We had gardens there, just outside the camp, and we were allowed to grow some vegetables. We were fed rice and some fish. The food was not ample, but the variety was pretty good. In other words, we weren't suffering from malnutrition because of the lack of vegetables. It offered the best conditions we would experience as prisoners-of-war.

We would go out on work details with the Japanese to do odd jobs. At the Bicycle Camp the work was not too bad. I was a pretty strong guy. You'd sleep well at night. I mean, it was hard, but not more than I could stand. The treatment by the guards was a little bit abusive but not as bad as later.

The Dutch women would ride their bicycles in our opposite direction, giving us information about how well the war was progressing, giving us food, and things of this nature. I admired the Dutch women. Even when the Japanese would break the spokes out of their bicycles they'd be back the next day. There was a lot of grit amongst those Dutch girls. Here, these women are risking their lives just to give us information. I feel that if the Dutch men had as much fight in them, well, the war would still be going. They would not have surrendered.

In Bicycle Camp I had something to eat out of which I disposed of in Singapore because I got something much better, and I still have it. I also picked up some clothing, some shoes and went on work details. At this time I had not acquired the black market attitude that I got later on. Buying and selling and swapping, and things like that. I didn't know that this went on. I hadn't got down to the fact that I needed to steal at that point. When I got to Singapore it had developed real fast. We were in Bicycle Camp for less than a month.

The trip to Singapore was a nightmare! Water was coming through the walls of the boat. That was down underneath the main deck. Water was seeping through rust spots all along the sides and all through the boat. Really, you could drive your fist through it, I'm sure, because it was that thin.

It was very unsanitary. The racks that we slept on were big pallets about thirty or forty inches high. You couldn't sit up in it. You were allowed 2 feet by 48 inches long. You couldn't even lie down. You just sat with your knees folded up if you could keep your head from hitting the ceiling. The food wasn't very much of anything. After about five days, we landed.

Changi Camp was a collection several prisoner-of-war and internee camps, occupying an area of approximately 25 square kilometers. Its name came from the peninsula on which it stood. Prior to the war the Changi Peninsula had been the British Army's principal base in Singapore with an extensive and well-constructed military infrastructure, including three major barracks – Selarang, Roberts and Kitchner – as well as many other smaller camps. Cleon Stewart and Les Carpenter were housed first in either Roberts Barracks or Kitchner Barracks before being moved to Singapore's civilian prison, Changi Gaol (Changi Prison).

## Changi Camp

I arrived at Singapore in October/November 1942. At the Camp there were three-story military barracks. It was a British military camp prior to World War II. It was really nice. I arrive and to Colonel Tharp[11] I tell the whole story. He took down my story and let me keep my service record because he said, "I'll try to get you back over here, but I can't guarantee it." It was a big camp and although it was easy to walk inside the camp to contact Colonel Tharp, I couldn't rejoin my old unit; but I could do it on paper. The Dutch was here and the road would lead back around over there to the Americans.[12] So, I just walked over there and talked to the people in my unit. This was at the battalion level. There were all kinds of stories that they'd heard — that I had gone over a cliff, that I got caught in the barrage of Japanese gunfire, or any number of stories that they had heard about me

11  Lieutenant Colonel Blucher S. Tharp was Commander of the 2nd Battalion, 131st Field Artillery.
12  Stewart was housed with the Dutch at this point.

getting killed. I said, "Well, I hope not because I'm still here!" Getting back in contact with my unit made me feel very good. I believed that our colonel would be able to get me back with the men, and I just felt stronger and healthier around American people.

It was at Singapore that I had it made as a prisoner-of-war. I was real lucky — honestly! I had the ingenuity to negotiate one item for another item for money within the camp, and so I paid to have someone make me a kapok mattress from some discarded mattresses that were there when we arrived, and in that mattress I had my service record sewed in it. Unfortunately, there were a lot of bedbugs at the Camp and unless you got them out, you're going to have bedbugs the next week, next month and next year. The Japanese would not supply us with bug spray of any kind, so the only way you can actually get rid of them is do it by heat. I'd get a wire hot and run it down in there and try to kill them. I'd also bounce the bed and they'd come out of it, some of them. But then the eggs would hatch and you'd have another layer of bedbugs coming in.

The work at Changi Camp was all pick-and-shovel work. They had a blueprint the British had left for making an airstrip there on Singapore. The British had figured it would take them ten years to build that airstrip there. So the Japanese undertook it and in two years they had this strip operational — by using POW labor. We'd work mornings until night, daylight to dark. The guards put pretty good pressure on us at this time. They wanted to get it done. The Japanese officer would put a quota on the guard and it was his job to see that we did it. If we didn't make the quota, the officer would whip the guard and the guard would take it out on us the next day. If the guard wanted to keep in good with the colonel, he'd keep ahead of him and beat us to see that we overdid the work assigned to us. The beatings came about most of the time because of lack of understanding. If he'd tell you what he wanted done and if you didn't understand him, he'd beat you into knowing what he said. This was one of the biggest handicaps and it caused a lot of beatings.

As you marched out of the camp you'd always salute the little yellow bastards. You'd pump them up a salute and go on. We'd come back in and we'd salute again. This particular day, this lieutenant was standing in the back of the guardhouse. He grinned. He didn't say nothing. He was an American-educated Jap. That afternoon we came in and he said, "From this day forward all commands would be given in Japanese. All your counting, all your military formations and everything would be done in Japanese." So, I said, "Well, if I'm going to learn that much, I'll learn enough so that it will do me some good." So here I was, a buck sergeant, and I acquired a certain amount of the Japanese language. Before long, everyone wanted to go on my work detail because they didn't get whipped. They didn't get beat because the Japanese in charge would tell me what they wanted done and in turn I told the work crew.

My black market activities started as a result of somebody trying to buy something out in the field. I saw what the possibilities were like if you had something they wanted. So after acquiring a certain amount of the Japanese language and a certain amount of Malayan, I tried my luck at communicating with the outside world. While I was out on a detail I visited a little grocery store or whatever you call it, a little store, and I got the Japanese to let me do that because I communicated for him with the troops to get work done to please his supervisor. I also got the Jap to agree to me selling Chinese merchandise that I'd bring from the camp.

I'd also sell the guard things that I'd brought from the camp. I'd sell him a watch occasionally. You see, I got to where I worked on watches. If it broke a balance, I'd cut it off, raise the jewel so it would still run by putting a wax on it. Until that wax melted, well, it would run. Those watches would run today until it got hot. But the Japanese guard wouldn't know what happened to it after I'd sell it to him. It was a twofold matter — privilege and a

Robert's Barracks is the only barracks still standing from Changi Camp. It was in one of these three-story barracks that Cleon Stewart and Les Carpenter began their black market trading. Photo: Tristan Moss.

Changi Guard, painted by Changi inmate Des Bettany, 88th Field Regiment, Royal Artillery. Bettany, like Stewart, worked clearing an area for an air strip which still exists, but has grown into Changi International Airport. Reproduced with kind permission of his family. www.changipowart.com.

Above and on the opposite page: Cleon Stewart's prison mess kit and spoon, English Army issue ca. 1939. The ornamentation on Stewart's mess kit is called zig-zag engraving. It was done with a hand-made burin shaped like a tiny flat chisel, called a wiggle tool. Zig-zag engraving is a feature element on Western-style cowboy gear, often as backbones in bright-cut scroll work. *Author's collection.*

Opposite Page Bottom Right: Stewart's prison darts minus feathers. 3 3/4 inches long. *Author's collection.*

Opposite Page Bottom Left: Stewart's prison identification tag to be worn around his neck. 1 3/4 x 2 inches. *Author's collection.*

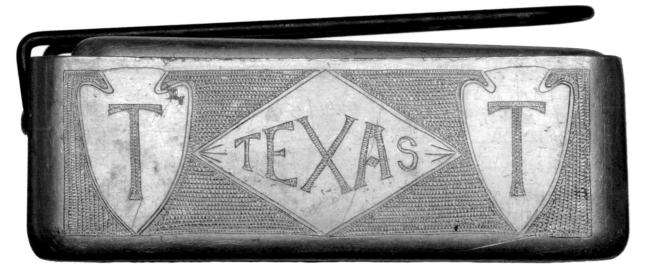

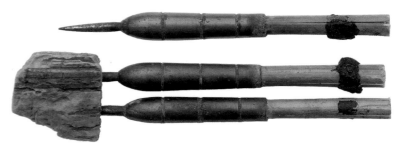

good price. In other words, I'd get the privilege of doing such and such that I wanted to do in exchange for a watch.

I then asked the Japanese guard, "Let me go buy something for the men." The men in camp would get paid something like fifteen cents a day. There was a canteen in the Camp, but they never had what we wanted. Okay, so, I would buy things for them from the store — cigarettes, candies, anything that we wanted — and bring the things back in the camp. Sometimes I lost them at the gate when one of the other guards searched me. If they caught you they would beat you. But searches were very random. If I brought in food items, I might have some friends and sit down and have a nice meal. Our food at this time wasn't as great as it should have been or could have been. It was a very poor grade of rice with weevils. We had herring that was boxed in 1907 and it was full of maggots that you had to scrape out.

So, these are little things, and it got bigger and bigger and bigger. The men gave me money, watches and rings for me to sell. I would ask the prisoner in the camp, "How much do you want for the ring?" And he would give me a price, "I want five ounces of Javanese tobacco." Well, if I get that price, I'm going to charge him 10 percent of that price for my selling it and taking a chance. I would then sell the ring to a Chinaman who ran the store. Five ounces of tobacco is about a dollar and it is bulky, more so than money. Anytime I had to carry items other than cash I charged extra because it increased the chances of me getting caught and beaten. My cut was 10 percent, unless I reappraised it and got more for it. I would give the man with the ring his tobacco minus my 10 percent. Anything I got over that I would keep. I did this for a while and before long, I have a lot of money. I was living better than average. I buy everything I want. I buy clothes, pants, shirts, and help other people.

Leslie Carpenter was the man I was closest to in prison. He was also with Battery D. I helped him the most. One day, Les didn't want to go on work detail. I said, "What's wrong with you, 'Buttercup?'" He said, "Oh, that bunion down there is acting up. I'll go to the hospital to have it removed." So, he went to the hospital to have his bunion removed, and while he was there he got an appendicitis, and he had to have his appendix removed. When the English gave you an operation for appendicitis, they jacked your legs up. He got a thrombosis of his leg, the left leg. And while they were treating him for that and before he got released, he had amoebic dysentery. So, this 6' 2" man went into the hospital weighing 210, and he comes out of the hospital weighing 135 pounds. He was really in sad shape. He didn't have anything but the shorts he stood up in. This man lacked two hours having his college degree in petroleum engineering when he was drafted at Texas A&M. I knew his girlfriend's name, Lena,[13] whom he later married. So I took him under my wing and told him what I was doing. I had a camera, I had a radio. Both meant a death sentence. He was being placed on light duty so I made an agreement with him. I showed him what to do and how I did business. You see, I made Less Carpenter my partner. So it was his job during the day, because he wasn't going out to work, to acquire merchandise for me to sell on a work detail. Les had a footlocker. If you'd seen the movie *King Rat*, why, you'll see a footlocker at the foot of his bed. That's where we kept a lot of our stuff.

At night was when we'd use the radio. I could only pick up broadcasts from New Delhi, India. That was the only news station. We just turned it on only for the news and then we'd turn it off immediately. We used an earphone that you stuck in your ear. I didn't tell anybody and nobody knew we had it. Well, one of the radios was hidden in the bottom of a chair. The other was in the false bottom of a canteen. There were a lot of English people in the communications squadron and they had canteens with false bottoms that they had built with vacuum tubes, and they put them in the bot-

13   Lena was in fact Nina. Stewart misremembers her name in his story.

tom of the canteen. I purchased it from them. I got cameras from people there that had stashed them. You see, Changi Camp itself was a military installation, and the English were there prior to the war and they stashed away things where they could later dig them up. They kept coming up with crazy things like pistols and cameras. Where this one man got all the parts to put that radio together that we hid under the chair beats me.

The camera and the guns I sold, but not the radio. The radio was to my own benefit because I got things out of it that kept me and others informed of where the war was going. You see, we'd go out on a work detail and in the sand the Japanese would make a picture. He'd draw a picture of Australia. He'd say, "Australia! All Nippon." He'd tell me how much of Australia they'd got. Then, the next day he'd come around and say, "Nippon! All Australia!" They were always telling me that. I would hear it on the radio and I'd know what in the heck the story was. But one time we got as far as to the United States and I said, "Oh, really?" You had to be real gullible with them. I came in one day after the work detail, and Les had that Japanese in there sitting right there on my radio. It was right under the chair, and he was sitting on it. I just didn't like this at all. I said, "Man, that thing costs too much money to throw away and you're taking a chance of getting killed because that's the death penalty to have it!"

## Changi Prison

The whole Camp was closed down and I moved into the Changi Prison sometime in 1943. Meanwhile, most of the 131st was already moved up-country to work as slave laborers on the Burma-Thailand railroad. Changi Prison was an ominous-looking place. I was not actually inside the jail itself. We were in billets outside the camp. It looked like a tent, but it was a thatched roof with a floor in it. We also had a level for sleeping. Your sides were on arms that you could lower or raise, and it had an opening at each end. It would hold fifty men. Some from the 131st were left behind at Changi Prison because of sickness. "Quaty" Gordon's shoulder kept jumping out of place. There were others that had bad stomachs.

It was while we lived in one of these thatched-roof billets that the Japanese came out with an order that the dogs in the camp were getting too much of the food that was intended for patients at the hospital. What the dog was getting was the broth of any foods left over from a person that was very sick and didn't eat it. But the Japanese came out and said we had to kill the dogs and that if we wouldn't kill them, they would get rid of them the next day. The dogs were friends of everybody. I took this dog, a Boston terrier, and put her under my bed. Every time I moved that dog would wag her tail. I mean, it was just really making it bad on me. She was just as friendly as could be and it was really hard for me to kill her the next day, to be truthful. She was under my bed and the next morning, pretty early, we put a stick in her mouth and dumped her into a five-gallon bucket of water and drowned her, and cut her throat, too. She bled right there in the bucket. We gutted her right there, too.

I told Colonel Howe [sic] that I'd gotten hold of some goat from some Chinaman, and I asked him if he'd like to come over and eat some.

He told me, "Fine, just as long as I did not feed him any dogs."

And I said, "Okay."

Allen Ramsey-Rae wasn't there at the time; for what reason, I don't remember. The squadron commander and the flight officer was there too, as well as all the Americans. Anyway, we got us a meat grinder and made us a bunch of doggy burgers.

This squadron commander, who had eaten dog in Russia, said, "Cleon, this dog tastes better than any dog I had all the time I was in Russia!"

He shouldn't have said that because Tom Howe, who asked me not to feed him dog before, heard him and said, "What?"

Cleon Stewart's Tobacco Box: 3 1/2 x 2 3/4 inches. It was a Christmas gift from Stewart's cellmate and black market partner, Corporal Albert Carpenter, who took the name of his father, Leslie, while in prison. *Author's collection.*

I said to Howe, "This was goat, not dog."

The squadron commander said, "I can tell dog when I eat it."

I told Howe, "This was goat!"

The commander said, "You can tell him what you want to, but I know what it is."

So, this Tom Howe then started working on this squadron commander. He said, "Was that dog, or was it goat?"

The squadron commander said, "Oh, it's dog." Tom Howe never spoke to me again. He didn't. Absolutely never! But, anyway, the doggy burgers turned out to be real good.

There were about thirty of us all together. I was still with Les Carpenter and we were still involved in black market activities. I was living better than average. This caused some resentment only in the fact that we had better clothing than most of the others —"Buttercup" and I did. Les had better clothes than the base commander, the English commander inside the camp. He had better food than he had. He acquired sake from the Japanese. We were still in Changi Camp when he acquired all this stuff.

At Changi Prison I eventually left him because he would not give up trading with the Koreans. I say left him; I volunteered for a work detail to get

away from him because he was dealing with this one Korean that I didn't trust. I didn't trust the Korean because I had seen him beat up people and I didn't want to have anything to do with him. I sure didn't want him to make any money off me. Also, Les was doing something that I didn't think was right. He said he had contact with a man at night but I can't see how he did it. I think he was bound to have had it with the Japanese. What I was doing was within the law. What he was doing . . . I didn't want to negotiate with the Japanese because if he'd turn on you, you're the one that's going to be hurt. So, I rode it just as long as I could. Then, six months before the war ended I took off on a work detail because I no longer wanted to work within the vicinity of Les Carpenter. He hadn't got to the big stuff yet. Leslie made some big, big, deals. After the war, I never accused him personally of being

Inside the box was the inscription; "To My Bestest Partner, From Les." When Stewart died on 11 July 2004, the box was still filled with tobacco and cigarette papers made from pages of a Bible. *Author's collection.*

A billet outside Changi Prison, September 1945. Australia War Memorial Photo # 019189.

"King Rat," but everybody tells me he is — that he's the one the book refers to.

I got out of Changi on a work detail. We'd break down to two camps. What it was, we went down to the first camp and we worked out of there a little bit, and then we went on to another camp and worked out of there. The Japanese were having us digging a command area there in Singapore in case of an attack. When you go inside a mountain like that, you go this way and zig-zag in case of an attack. That way the blast would not just go straight in to them. It was very tough work. We were boarding up with railroad ties and had to climb up with one on the shoulder every morning. Every man had one. Then you drilled by hand with a sixteen-pound

hammer into that solid granite rock, and then we would blast and carry out the rubble. Yes, you did that from morning to night and you were pretty tired. The food was very poor. Quite poor. The amount of work you did had no bearing on the kind of food you got.

One day I told a Korean guard, "Tomorrow is my birthday," in Japanese. I told him how old I'd be and he said, "Well, tomorrow you can have free tea all day!" I said, "Thank you." So, the next day I filled everybody's canteen up and then when he came by in the evening, he didn't have any tea for his officers and they got on him badly. So he gets on me badly for getting too much tea. He worked himself hard trying to knock me out with a piece

Mess kit, bottom view. *Author's collection.*

his tea. You would have to be there to understand, I guess. We had one faucet for 500 men and it was used to cook with, eat with, bathe with, everything. You had them boil the water. That's why I gave everybody tea: because it had already been boiled and ready to drink. He said I could have it so I took it. But I didn't see where he had any right to beat on me. I turned in his name and he was punished very severely at the war crimes trials.

With the war over, I was very elated over the fact that I was headed home. I didn't think in terms of money, just the fact that I was thrilled to get out of that situation. The Americans flew in and took us out. The British had told us that it would be six months before we could eat any western-type food. So I got on this airplane and asked the flight surgeon, "How long will it be before I can eat a big ol' American steak?" He said, "Well, it's about 12:00 now. Is midnight too long?" I craved steak the most. That plus vegetable juices and what-have-you. They put us in the 142nd General Hospital in Calcutta. They had a section at the end of the room with all kinds of vegetables and fruits and everything else. We could eat twenty-four hours a day.

I got home by October 9 and was discharged on March 10, 1946. I didn't have any problems adjusting when I got back to Texas but I was unhappy by the fact that I could not buy a car. I couldn't even get my name on a decent list. I was 150 down on the list and so I bought a secondhand car instead. The vets who arrived ahead of me had stamps of all kinds. I had no stamps. I had nothing. I tried to buy some tires in Tyler, Texas. Because I didn't have coupons, I couldn't get tires and the manager of the Food Control Board up there said, "Don't you know there's a war on?" I said, "No!" He said "Yes! Everything is under control," and I said, "I haven't had any of it for four years. I merely asked you for a tire." He said, "I can't give you one. You have no stamps." You know where I got that tire? Hope, Arkansas.

of wood. He beat me on my head for about fifteen minutes trying to knock me out, but he never made it. I still got scars. I have scars on my hands where I caught the board when he would swing it. I've got a scar on the back of my head, too. He finally wound up by just throwing the wood down because he wasn't knocking me out.

In August they said the war was over and I was just jubilant about it and we had a real feast during the night. The next day we went to the next camp level and there was the Korean who gave me that awful beating on my birthday. He was looking for me. He wanted to see me and to give me all the stuff he could give me. I was still pretty mad at him but I realized also that I was at fault. I shouldn't have done what I did. I shouldn't have given everybody

End and side views of Cleon Stewart's engraved mess kit. *Author's collection.*

## Epilogue

### My Search for The King

Cleon Stewart's mess kit was discovered at a Texas estate sale. His story was discovered eighteen months later at the University of North Texas, in one of 150 Lost Battalion interviews conducted by Professor Ronald E. Marcello, professor of history and director of the University of North Texas Oral History Program. After reading Stewart's story one question lingered: who was Les Carpenter?

Professor Marcello did not interview Les Carpenter, and his name is not on the Lost Battalion roster. Further checking led me to a 1973 Marcello interview with Roy Offerle in which he mentions an Albert L. Carpenter who went by the nickname "Buttercup." This confirmed in my mind that Stewart's Les "Buttercup" Carpenter and Offerle's Albert L. "Buttercup" Carpenter were likely the same man. But I could not be 100% certain until I had established that "L" stood for Leslie, since Stewart never referred to Carpenter by the name Albert.

I made a request for Carpenter's military personnel file at the National Archives. This was a long shot: nearly all U.S. Army files, housed at the National Personnel Records Center in St. Louis, were destroyed by a catastrophic fire there in 1973.

Somehow, Carpenter's file was one of only a few to survive the fire intact. In it I learned that "L" stood for Lewis, not Les or Leslie. Digging deeper into the file, I discovered that Carpenter's father's name was Leslie. Could he have adopted his father's name while at Changi Prison? And what about Carpenter's connection to James Clavell and *King Rat*? These questions would take a bit longer to figure out.

James Clavell was a young gunner in the Royal Artillery when he was taken prisoner by the Japanese. He spent most of the war at Changi. In 1962 Clavell published his first novel, *King Rat*; in 1965 the novel was made into a film by director Bryan Forbes. *King Rat* is a major piece of post-war fic-

tion. It describes the struggle for survival of four central characters held captive by the Japanese at Changi Prison. Some critics viewed the novel as an indictment of uncontrolled American entrepreneurism. Former Changi POWs took a different view, believing that the book more accurately represented the unique trading skills that led to the survival of many at the camp.

In 1993 Robert C. Doyle, an American academic researching prisoner literature, asked Clavell if there had been a real King Rat and if so, who it was. Clavell's reply was somewhat vague: "The happenings in the novel happened. At least as I remember them . . . Not all . . . occurred in Changi, some in Java and elsewhere, most I saw, the rest came from eyewitnesses, the living and the dead."[14]

Doyle pursued the matter further and discovered that Clavell's commanding officer in Changi had been RAF Air Vice-marshal, Thomas Howell.

> I wrote to Howell and learned from him that Clavell formed Sam King as a composite character consisting of elements from three Americans: Eddie MacArthur, a merchant seaman captured by a German raider in the South Atlantic and deposited in Singapore; Bob Martin, a crewman from the sunken cruiser USS *Houston*; and Albert L. "Buttercup" Carpenter of Battery F of the New Mexico [sic; in fact Texas] National Guard. Remembering that Carpenter was a deal-maker and a dominant force in Changi, Howell recalled, "He was by no means so sinister or selfish" as Clavell's character in the novel, "but he became a skillful operator" and, as a result of using profits for the benefit of other prisoners, he was an instrument in saving many lives at risk.[15]

Howell's response confirmed to Doyle that Carpenter was regarded by the British as someone who shared some of the characteristics that Clavell fashioned into the figure of Corporal King.

With Carpenter's connection to Clavell's central character in the novel confirmed, I attempted to find his family and ask for an interview. In July

---

14    Roger Bourke, "Prisoners of the Japanese: Literary Imagination and the Prisoner-of-War Experience" (University of Queensland Press, 2008), 92.
15    Robert Doyle, "War Through a Looking Glass: Who was the Real King Rat?" in Wolfgang Gortschacher and Holger Klein (eds), *Modern War on Stage and Screen* (New York: Edwin Mellen Press, 1997), 435.

2015 I was able to locate Carpenter's son. When I asked if his father had written about his wartime experiences, Dr. C. Leslie Carpenter replied:

> He never wrote down his experiences and not once did he talk about Changi with me. I asked him about it several times but he steadfastly refused. I did hear somewhere the story that he was one of three men Clavell based his character King on, but I know nothing more than that, really.

When asked about his father's nickname, "Buttercup," he said, "I only learned of that nickname two years ago and I do not know its origin." Dr. Carpenter also mentioned that "Most of what we learned was from our mother. My father was a stern disciplinarian. After WWII, he married my mother and completed his college education at Texas A&M as a petroleum engineer. My father hated the Japanese, and anything made by the Japanese, as did my mother." When I asked Dr. Carpenter where he thought "Les" came from he replied, "Leslie was my grandfather's name, so I am intrigued by my father's apparent use of it while a POW."

In a subsequent interview with Carpenter's eldest daughter, Belinda, I asked about her father.

> My father never talked about the war voluntarily. If I asked him a question he would answer, but would never elaborate. I learned that he had his appendix removed at Changi, and he told me how he made a kind of fermented delicacy eaten by the indigenous people of Singapore. He would roll shark entrails in banana leaves and buried it until it turned — Daddy said it was a clear amber color — and he would slice off some and eat it, or smear it on rice when he had rice. He would sell it because it was pure protein. He said it saved his teeth and his hair from falling out.

I then shared what Robert Doyle had learned about her father's activities as a POW. Belinda had never heard these comments before, but mentioned that she kept in touch with the daughter of one of her father's friends from Changi who was from England. I asked if she remembered his name. She replied, "His last name was Howell." This was RAF

Albert "Les" "Buttercup" Carpenter, 1946. Photo printed with permission from Rebecca Carpenter Heindel.

Air Vice-marshal Thomas Howell, the man whose words I had just quoted to her.

Belinda and her husband generously arranged an opportunity for me to interview Howell's daughter, and through her I learned of her father's unpublished diary. Several entries in the diary confirm much of Stewart's story and provide additional insight into Carpenter's black market activities.

Thomas Howell had arrived in Singapore in October 1941 to join the armament staff of the RAF's main Far East aircraft depot and maintenance facility, No. 151 Maintenance Unit, at RAF Seletar. After the Japanese invasion of Malaya on 8 December 1941, Howell's unit made desperate attempts to service as many aircraft as possible and ready the few crated Hurricanes that arrived as replacements.

On 29 January 1942, ninety Japanese bombers inflicted heavy damage on the airfield at Seletar. Four days later the men of No. 151 began evacuating to Java. By 10 February, the unit effectively ceased to exist. The men reinforced the few remaining flying units on Java until Allied resistance in the Dutch East Indies ended on 8 March. Howell, meanwhile, joined a group of Australian and American men, including Ronald Allen Ramsey-Rae and Cleon Stewart, at a remote spot on the southern coast of Java. They started to build a large raft with the intention of sailing for Australia. With the raft near completion, Howell left the site to find some rubber for use as a sealant. During his absence the Japanese discovered the men at their encampment. After a brief skirmish the survivors became prisoners-of-war. Shortly thereafter, RAF Wing Commander Ronald Ramsey-Rae and Cleon Stewart were captured, as is described in Stewart's story.

Howell was listed as missing but remained at large, seeking refuge with the natives and darkening his skin with natural dyes to be less conspicuous. During regular bouts of malaria he was cared for by the natives, but after many months, the combination of increasing malnutrition, further bouts of malaria and a deep concern for the safety of those sheltering him compelled him to surrender to the Japanese on 2 May. Three days after his capture Howell was locked in a prison cell, "And next door," wrote Howell in his diary, "was none other than Ron,[16] Stew,[17] Bill,[18] and Dubbo![19]"

In late 1943 these five men were transferred to Changi Camp where Howell shared a cell with James "Jimmy" Clavell. The men were then transferred to Changi Prison where Howell acquired new roommates.

Clavell, Stewart, Carpenter and others appear in Howell's diary.

**Tuesday, 16th May – Wednesday, 31st May 1944**
Many plans and changes of plan all through the fortnight and all activity concerned with moving to the Gaol [Changi Prison], into which the remains of the RAF got in on 30th and 31st. I share a coolie quarter[20] with Col. Max-Crumb & Maj. Brocklehurst — not too badly off but it gets very hot indeed on fine days and sleeping is a sticky business. Our last few days in the old area occupied with many trailer parties carting stuff to the Gaol and eating chicken dinners, the last being one with Hank, Robbie and Bish. Friend Carpenter got himself well and truly in the shit over trying to sell a camera to a Nip and caught by their police. Chinese continues and occasional poker game in evening. Troops crowded but cool.

**Thursday, 16th November – Thursday, 30th November 1944**
A few more alarms but nothing like the first show, though we saw one B-29 cruise over at about 17,000, but since then nothing much. Gardening and swimming take up my physical exuberance and Chinese and Spanish and some poetry reading have been enough to satisfy my mental desire for nourishment. In the camp all goes on as usual, food being the main topic, and it is not so bad at present though we officers are fortunate in being able to supplement the diet. On 19th Robbie, Jimmy and I had a monster feed with Stew, Carpenter and Ben Keith. The odd spot of towgay[21] daily is also very welcome, and Robbie makes a good supper every so often. What with that and the chickens, I ain't got no kick. The latest rumour is that 'all field officers into the Gaol.' Another Jahore, or real this time?

**Saturday, 16th December – Sunday, 31st December 1944**
Rumours of moves up country and overseas the chief topic of the period, apart from Christmas and what there was going to be to eat. In our mess, like all the rest, there was plenty of 'doovers'[22] of every shape, form and content, more than enough, particularly for me as I was led astray by Chris Holmyard and others on Christmas Eve on returning from midnight mass! Yes, the locally distilled 'hooch' is no good stuff and in any case outrageously expensive. On Christmas day Les Carpenter appeared with some 'Hungarian' samshu,[23] ice and lemons! That certainly was better. And on New Year's Eve John Olley[24] produced some Singapore-made sake, and that was not so bad either. So the festive season passed as it should. The usual bathing, gardening, wood-sawing and various studies pass the time in the usual way, and now 1944 is over all our hopes and belief are that we'll be free within the year.

---

16   Wing Commander Ronald Allen Ramsey-Rae.
17   Cleon Stewart.
18   RAF Sergeant pilot Bill Betford.
19   A Ceylon native Stewart refers to on page 31.

20   A coolie is an old term for an unskilled native laborer in India or China. Coolie quarter refers to their cramped living quarters.
21   Bean sprouts.
22   Hors d'oeuvres (appetizers).
23   Samshu: an alcoholic drink distilled from millet or rice. Similar to Sake.
24   Flight Lieutenant W.W. Oliver.

**Monday, 1st January – Monday, 15th January 1945**
Another big eating day on New Year's Day and ever since for one reason or another there seems to have been an abundance of food. We have had several good curry tiffins,[25] inviting guests and Robbie has done his inimitable best on several occasions. Sold my watch for $459 during the period which will keep me going a bit.[26] Also cashed a cheque for $600 and another for an as yet uncertain amount. There seems to be plenty of cash about and you certainly need it!

A second interview conducted in 2016 with Belinda provided new information about her father.

When it was announced that the war had ended, my father took revenge upon a particularly cruel guard at Changi. My father told me he killed him — he bashed his brains out — and I have no doubt that he did, and then he took his sword.

After the war everyone thought my father was dead. When he returned home, he secretly went in through the back door of his parents' house where he found his mother at the kitchen sink. Quietly, he walked up from behind and wrapped his arms around her. She looked at him. He said, "Mama, aren't you going to speak to me?" She fainted in his arms.

My father soon learned that Nina, his fiancee from before the war, believing he was dead, met and married a U.S. Army flier. They were married for only two months before his plane went down in the South China Sea; strange things happen in war. My father and Nina were later married.

I couldn't have been over four or five years old when I discovered that my father had been in prison. It was over the shoes, the yard shoes. My father had a pair of shoes that looked like the bottom part of wooden clogs with a strap over the instep. They now have a leather strap, but originally they had straps made of canvas webbing. I liked them because I could roll up on my

The *nihonto* Carpenter took from the Changi Prison guard he killed at war's end. *Carpenter family collection.*

toes and feel like I was on stilts. He became very upset when he found me playing with them. He said, "They weren't a toy." I said, "I know, they are shoes." He said, "You don't understand, they saved my life." And I said, "When?" He said, "When I was in prison." And of course to a young child, for their father to say he was in prison, I didn't understand it was in the context of the war. He told me "When I was in prison, it wasn't because I did anything wrong." When I was older he told me that you needed shoes to survive, to keep from getting infected with hookworms and other diseases.

I know that my father had letters from James Clavell, but my mother must have thrown them out because I never found them when she died. When the movie *King Rat* came out, it had the scene where they took a soldier's dog and made stew out of it. That was a true story and my dad was in on that. My dad went to see the movie and afterwords I asked him "What did you think?" He said, "Too many clothes." He said they mostly went around in loincloths.

My search for The King came to an end at the Oak Knoll Cemetery in Bellview, Texas. Albert Lewis "Les" ("Buttercup") Carpenter, U.S. Army serial number 38-050-412, died in Prescott, Arizona on 12 September 1983.

---

25  An Indian English word for a light midday meal, often consisting of rice, curry, vegetables and spicy meat.
26  Cheques may be IOUs issued by black marketers like Carpenter who then settled up after the war. Roy Offerle, another former Changi inmate, mentions money owed to Carpenter in his oral history interview, preserved in the University of North Texas Oral History Collection. Interview ID #0H 0457 (1973). "I would like to mention here my gunnery corporal who was 'Buttercup' Carpenter—I mentioned him before — who at that time had appendicitis, and the English operated on him. He was still sick when we left, and he stayed behind, and he was in Singapore all during the war. I wouldn't swear to it, but if you saw the movie or read the book *King Rat* — if you haven't, get it. I think 'Buttercup' was *King Rat*. 'Buttercup' got to trading with the natives. When I met him after the war, he had several hundred pounds and several more owed to him. He had an English boy collecting money for him. He had lived like a king, even though he had gotten beat up and this and that. He made a lot of money in prison camp. I would almost swear that he was the American sergeant that they were talking about in the book and in the movie. I talked to him about that, but he didn't elaborate too much."

# USS McFarland AVD-14

USS *McFarland* DD-237, 1932. She was named after John C. McFarland, an American Civil War sailor who received the Medal of Honor for his actions in the Battle of Mobile Bay.

The USS *McFarland* was one of 156 destroyers of the 1,190-ton *Clemson*-class built between 1918 and 1922. Destroyers of *McFarland*'s type remained state-of-the-art until the early 1930's, but by the end of the decade destroyer designs changed and the old four-pipe flushdeckers were converted into minesweepers, fast transports or other auxiliary craft. Fourteen were made over into seaplane tenders — among them the *McFarland*. Her masts were cut down, stacks shortened and the twelve triple-banked torpedo tubes removed to make room for fuel storage tanks, a big crane, repair shop and other essentials required to transform *McFarland* into a mobile, floating seaplane base.

While waiting for her seaplanes to be manufactured and crewed, *McFarland* was sent to Hawaii. On 7 December 1941 she was performing temporary escort duty near Maui when the Japanese attacked Pearl Harbor. After the attack *McFarland* was fitted with a depth charge rack and ordered to conduct anti-submarine patrols in the waters off New Caledonia.

On 2 August 1942 *McFarland* received her PBY Catalina seaplanes and went to the Solomon Islands. There she helped keep sea lanes open for the planned 7 August assault on Tulagi, Gavutu, Tanambogo and Guadalcanal by U.S. Marines. Later that month *McFarland* and her Catalinas returned to Guadalcanal to assist the Marines. As the situation there grew more desperate, *McFarland* returned twice more — not as a seaplane tender, but as a transport bringing in fuel, bombs, and aerial torpedoes for the Marine aviators at Henderson Field.[1] In October, while delivering supplies to Guadalcanal, *McFarland* nearly met her end.

The following story begins with a first-hand account from Paul Helmke, *McFarland*'s last surviving crew member. At age 92 he is alert and active, still bowling in a league twice a week. I told Paul about *McFarland*'s Presidential Unit Citation flag, Captain Alderman's medals, and the telegram from Nimitz that were in my possession, and that I was gathering information for a story. Paul was eager to help. The story was further developed with help from a cache of documents that was sent to me by Sande McLaughlin, the daughter of *McFarland*'s Chief Engineer, Norman Chalmers.

---

1 The airfield originally built by the Japanese on Guadalcanal was later renamed Henderson Field by Allied forces. The fight over its possession (23 October - 26 October 1942) was one of the historic battles of the Pacific War.

USS *McFarland AVD-14* after her overhaul that included a newly-added depth charge rack; Pearl Harbor, 16 May 1942. National Archives photo # 19-LCM-AVD14-018691.

Above: USS *McFarland AVD-14* pictured after refitting at Pearl Harbor on 17 May 1942.

## USS *McFarland AVD-14*

"I was a boat coxswain aboard the seaplane tender *McFarland*," said Paul Helmke, who joined the Navy at 17 and reported to boot camp in San Diego on 26 June 1941. "After training, several of us raw recruits were sent aboard the aircraft carrier USS *Saratoga* for transportation to Pearl Harbor. When we moored at Ford Island, six of my good buddies were sent to the USS *Arizona* and another six to the USS *Oklahoma*. I was put on a motor launch and hauled around to the other side of Ford Island to the USS *McFarland AVD-14*, which in Navy speak means seaplane tender 14. I thought *McFarland* was just a boat that would take me to my ship. But no, she would become my new home.

"In Hawaii, *McFarland* performed temporary escort duty until our PBY Catalina Seaplanes arrived. On 6 December we steamed out of Pearl Harbor to rendezvous with two of our submarines. I had the mid-watch that night and reported a flare to shore command which no one could identify. It was later thought to be from a Japanese mini-sub assisting the attack. Most of the crew never gave it a thought. News of the Japanese surprise attack reached us the following morning and it was a frantic time at General Quarters stripping our ship for action. We met our subs that evening and proceeded to Hilo, challenging every ferry and fishing boat we encountered.

"In Hilo, we moored to a pier behind a warehouse, out of sight from the harbor entrance. A Jap sub lobbed a few rounds into the harbor one night while we were there but hit only water. When we were finally allowed back into Pearl there was still a heavy black oil slick for miles out to sea, and the harbor was in a rotten mess. I remember being so jealous visiting my buddies on the *Arizona* and *Oklahoma*, comparing their big beautiful battle-wagons with my little rust bucket. That jealousy ended when I learned that ten of my twelve friends had died that day.

"We were given new orders to patrol for enemy submarines in the South Pacific until our PBYs could be manufactured and crewed. To prepare for our new mission, we went into the Navy Yard where we got sonar gear, 20mm guns to replace the water-cooled .50-caliber machine guns on the galley deck house, and new 3"/50-caliber dual-purpose guns to replace the old 4"/50 surface guns fore and aft. Sockets were welded to the tops of lifeline stanchions along the main deck to receive the swivel mounts of the spare aviation .30-caliber machine guns stowed on deck lockers aft of the galley. We also got a depth charge rack and 'K' guns.[2] Radar was too new and scarce to be installed in *McFarland*.

"After outfitting, we steamed south for Noumea, New Caledonia in company with the USS *Curtis AV-4*. En route we dropped depth charges one night on the mid-watch which exploded just as the general alarm sounded, waking everyone with the immediate thought that we had been torpedoed.

"An overnight stop in Pago Pago, American Samoa, found a huge reception committee on the pier as we tied up. The skipper, sure it was meant for him, walked proudly down the gangway, only to be totally ignored. The turnout was for Gerald Graham GM-1c who had been stationed there for several years and was wed to the local chief's daughter.

"We arrived in Noumea, a French possession which had never acknowledged the Vichy government. There were a lot of Jap subs off Noumea and in July we sank a big mine-laying sub.

"From Noumea we went off to set up an advance base at Ndeni to service our patrol wing of PBY Catalinas. We were the only ship to stop there in over a year. Ndeni consisted of two main islands. The natives from the larger island paddled out to our ship when we first anchored, their dugout outrigger canoes loaded with coconuts, fruits and things to trade. A small piece of rag, scrap of rope or bit of soap would buy a whole canoe full of goods. Many of the islanders had teeth filed down to points, which were black from chewing betel nuts. One of our old chiefs aboard ship had false teeth. He pulled them out and began clacking them at the natives who back-paddled so quick that one fell overboard. Well, as the natives cautiously came closer once more to the ship, we could see several of them trying to pull their own teeth out!

"The natives on the smaller island didn't get along with those on the larger island and they had a couple of wars that we watched from aboard ship. Only a couple hundred yards of waist deep water separated the two islands. The theft of a pig brought out a large group from each side down to the beach brandishing clubs, spears and rocks.

A PBY-5 Catalina seaplane refueling from seaplane tender *Williamson AVD-2*. The designation "PBY" was determined in accordance with the U.S. Navy aircraft designation system of 1922: PB representing "Patrol Bomber" and Y being the code assigned to Consolidated Aircraft as its manufacturer. PBYs were used in anti-submarine warfare, patrol bombing, convoy escorts, search and rescue missions (especially air-sea rescue), and cargo transport. National Archives Photo # 80-G-20627.

2   'K' guns fire one depth charge at a time and are mounted on the ship's deck.

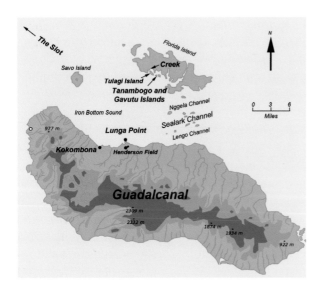

They always quit fighting as soon as the first minor injury occurred. Too bad the rest of the world isn't that smart!"[3]

On 2 August *McFarland* received six PBY Catalina seaplanes and their crews. They had orders to scout north in and around the Solomon Islands where the Japanese were constructing a seaplane, ship refueling and communications bases on Tulagi and the nearby islands of Gavutu, Tanambogo, and Florida. Allied concerns were also directed towards a large airfield under construction on Guadalcanal. These bases were to become part of Japan's southern defensive perimeter and a stage for attacks against supply and communication routes between the U.S., Australia and New Zealand.

On 7 August the U.S. Marines attacked at Tulagi, Gavutu, Tanambogo, and Guadalcanal. Surprised by the successful Allied offensive, the Japanese made several attempts by land and sea to retake the airfield on Guadalcanal, now renamed Henderson Field by the Americans.

By mid-October the Marines were beating back the Japanese counter-offensive but were running low on fuel and ammunition. *McFarland* was quickly re-purposed as a supply ship. Her big aviation gas tanks were filled with fuel and her deck loaded with bombs, ammunition and aerial torpedoes for delivery to Guadalcanal. Each trip was filled with danger. Her cargo had transformed the ship into a floating bomb with a fuse of gasoline, and both the sea at Skylark Channel and the passage leading to Guadalcanal from the north, known as the "slot," were controlled by the Japanese.

On their fateful 15 October supply run, *McFarland*'s crew spotted a Japanese carrier plane; an Aichi 99 had emerged from a cloud with a big fat torpedo slung under its belly. "No firing unless we are attacked," ordered Captain Alderman. He watched as the Aichi ducked in and out of the clouds, coming as close as 2,000 yards off *McFarland*'s starboard beam; after ten or fifteen minutes the Japanese pilot must have decided the ship wasn't worth the torpedo he carried and retired northeast in search of larger game.

By afternoon the *McFarland* was approaching Guadalcanal and at first daylight the island lay dead ahead. Everything had gone well on the dangerous passage and the ship was about to begin her run for Lunga Point, a thumb of land jutting out from Guadalcanal, near Henderson Field, where supplies would be unloaded.

Lieutenant Commander Alderman was in sight of his goal and understandably anxious to unload his combustible cargo when the radioman came to the bridge and delivered a message. It warned of intense enemy activity expected and instructed all ships in the area to depart immediately for a specific longitude and latitude to the south. Alderman called a meeting with his officers and informed them about the order to return, but added that the Marines on Guadalcanal were in desperate need of *McFarland*'s gas, oil and supplies. "Hell," said Alderman. "What's the use of running away and then having to come back and do it all over

---

3    Telephone interview with Paul Helmke, 10 October 2015. Email interview 9 June 2016. Additional quotes taken from Paul Helmke's letter written to E. Andrew Wilde, 14 May 1995, in which he describes his experiences on the USS *McFarland AVD-14*.

again?"[4] He sent a message ashore that he was going in.

They cruised inside Sealark Channel, ducking in rain squalls and hiding from anything hostile that might be in the neighborhood while searching with binoculars for the all-clear signal to go in. On Guadalcanal there were two kinds of signals: "all clear" and "enemy planes overhead." They received the "all clear."

As the *McFarland* headed in at high speed, Alderman noticed flashes of light coming from the water ahead. Through his binoculars he could see that the flashes were coming from artillery shells splashing into the water. The target was a small Yippie stuck on the reef. It was being shelled from the jungle-covered hills near Kokombona, west of Henderson Field.

Yippies were tuna-fishing boats from California fitted with machine guns and depth charges. Yippies may have looked warlike to civilians, but to a Japanese warship they looked like pushovers: too weak to fight and too slow to run. They were essential to the Marines in the early days of the Guadalcanal campaign and the Japanese would not rest until each one was destroyed.

This particular Yippie still had a fishing license tacked to the bulkhead. It was commanded by chief Bos'n Banyon, an old retired Navy man. Banyon stood on his afterdeck wig-wagging signal flags to *McFarland*.

### SHOTGUN THINKS HE'S GOT ME. STAND OFF.[5]

Shotgun, also known as Pistol Pete, was a single Japanese gun crew with a rusty 4-inch fieldpiece that was just within range of Lunga Point. When it was safe, the Japanese would roll it out of its cave and lob shells into the American-controlled sector. Alderman grinned and waved,

hoping that Banyon on board the *YP-239* could see him. He was tempted to go in close and talk to the man waving the signal flags. There was little danger. Pistol Pete never seemed to hit anything. Another signal came from the Yippie.

### WILL FLOAT HER OFF AT HIGH TIDE. GETTING OFF NOW.

The McFarland turned back away from the west side of Lunga point to a new position 500 yards east and approximately 300 yards from the beach. She then sent a signal to the Higgins boats waiting ashore that it was safe to come out and receive her cargo. As soon as the men arrived from shore they began moving cargo off *McFarland* like farmers hurrying to make hay before a storm. Hoses with shut-off nozzles, like the kind found at gas stations, transferred aviation fuel from *McFarland*'s thirty-thousand-gallon reservoir into fifty-gallon drums that lined the deck of a Higgins boat. A detail of 17 Seabees brought out a pontoon barge loaded with empty fuel drums, tied it up on the *McFarland*'s starboard side and began to pump fuel into the empty drums. Torpedoes were lowered into a waiting Higgins boat with *McFarland*'s deck crane. Once loaded, the Higgins boat cast off and roared away to the sandy beach as an empty boat waiting alongside slid in to replace it.

The unloaded boats returned from the beach carrying a combined total of 60 walking wounded Marines squeezed between the empty drums. Several of these ambulatory patients were suffering from battle fatigue and were being sent back for hospitalization.

The afternoon light of 16 October faded as *McFarland* finished unloading her cargo, and transferring the remaining two-thirds of her aviation fuel into drums on the barge. Along the shore cooking fires were beginning to glow yellow and red against the darkening jungle when a message was signaled out from the beach: a periscope had been sighted in the channel.

4   James F. Lowery, "Tender Now at Pearl Harbor" *Honolulu Star Bulletin* (31 December 1942).
5   Charles Rawlings, "The McFarland Comes Home" *Saturday Evening Post* (March 13, 1943).

The *McFarland*, dead in the water, was a perfect target for the sub, even at long range. She hoisted anchor and churned away with the barge loaded with fuel-filled drums still in tow. It was early evening. Soon the ship would be safely sheltered in darkness and her remaining cargo could be unloaded.

Suddenly, and without warning, the first of nine carrier-based Aichi Type 99 Japanese dive-bombers fell screaming out of the sky in a dive. This Aichi released two 130-pound bombs that appeared to grow in size as they plunged toward their intended target. Both hit the water a hundred yards to port, their thudding detonations serving as a call to general quarters. "I watched geysers of water exploding on the portside just long enough to be startled by more explosions on the starboard side," recalled communications officer Lieutenant Frederick Dean. "There was little possibility to maneuver, for the barge was alongside and its mooring lines were made taut by the movement of the ship, making it difficult to cast off."[6]

The second Aichi came in and missed, but the bombs were closer this time. The explosions showered the bridge with shrapnel and knocked two men off their feet.

*McFarland*'s 20mm guns were manned and drawing their aim when the third Aichi peeled off and came down. A round was fired from one of the *McFarland*'s three-inch guns and met the Aichi head on at 100 yards, felling the Japanese bomber like a shot-gunned mourning dove.

Three converging streams of fire from *McFarland*'s 20-mm gunners shot down the fourth bomber. Men were still struggling to release mooring lines to the barge when the fifth and sixth Aichi began their attack. Several battle-fatigued Marines were seen trying to dig foxholes into *McFarland*'s steel deck as the two planes dropped their bombs, each missing its mark.

As the planes pulled up from their dives and joined into formation they were met by the unex-

pected sound of distant machine-gun fire. Lieutenant Colonel Joe Bauer had been circling Henderson Field in his F4F Wildcat. He had just finished leading a group of 26 planes on an over-water ferry flight of more than 600 miles from Espiritu Santo. As the last of his group was landing, Bauer, still flying overhead, saw black smoke rising from the *McFarland*. Seeing she was under attack and undaunted by the odds against him, he flew alone, low on fuel, in the direction of the Aichi bombers. As the surviving Aichis climbed out of their dives and joined in formation at 200 feet, Bauer came in from behind and dropped them one-by-one before returning to base with his fuel tanks empty.

The last three Aichis to deliver their bombs did not falter, and began their attack. *McFarland*'s 20-mm guns stopped the first two, sending them smoking low over the water. The ninth and last Aichi dove and dropped two bombs as the rear gunner leaned out of the cockpit and tried to hit *McFarland*'s deck with a hand grenade. The first bomb fell astern. One of the Marines cut the line to the pontoon barge as the second bomb struck *McFarland*'s stern rack of depth charges, each charge filled with several hundred pounds of TNT. The explosion detonated the depth charges and ignited fuel aboard the barge, incinerating several Seabees in a massive fireball that burned several hundred feet into the air. The violent explosion heaved *McFarland* upward and nearly out of the water, hurling everyone in the forward half of the ship off their feet. Amidship, all hands were vaulted into the air, landing in a pile of ship fragments while suffering shrapnel wounds and flash-burns. Everyone aft of the deckhouse was blown into small pieces, their flesh and bones driven down into the torn metal remnants of the ship where the scent of dead flesh would cling to the torn metal for months.

Twelve of *McFarland*'s crew were killed or missing, eleven were wounded and an unknown number of Marines were killed outright. "The near misses knocked us around plenty, so when

6  Frederick S. Dean, *Going Back to Tulagi*, unpublished, 1987.

the real thing came along, few of us realized what had actually happened," recalled Chief Engineer Norman Chalmers. "Only when the ship didn't answer to the rudder did the captain go back to investigate."[7]

Although the ship had lost its lights, fires from the burning barge provided plenty of illumination for Captain Alderman to estimate the damage. He slid on deck in grease and blood while examining the dark hole that had once been his ship's stern. Thirty feet had been blown away. The rudder was gone and the steering engine-room had disappeared in the blast.

Chalmers went for the engine throttles and waited for the opening howl of his turbines that would tell him his propellers were gone, but there was none: "Some miracle had saved both screws and what was more miraculous, the stern shaft bearings."[8] His second engineer, Charles Clarkson restored the lights — the concussion had blown every fuse.

Alderman hurried back to the bridge. The port throttle, blown off by the explosion, was feeding steam equivalent to about 1/3 ahead into the turbine, making the ship hard to handle. "With the ship swinging uncontrollable to starboard I gave the order to back on the port engine. By putting more steam on the stern turbine than was pulling ahead and by backing the port engine, we were able to keep from going on the beach [in enemy territory].

"We got turned around by steaming full ahead on the starboard engine and backing hard on the port engine. Thus we set out for Tulagi, about twenty miles away.

"When we got about halfway, the water was coming in badly aft. Meanwhile a lot of things were going on at the same time. The executive was helping remove the dead and wounded, and

John C. Alderman. *Author's collection.*

since we were settling by the stern and taking on a heavy list, we put them all on the forecastle. We rigged pumps and kept the water from rising inside. We still had enough flotation to keep the ship afloat. Well, then we had a fire aft, which we thought was in the magazine. We flooded the magazine but later found that the fire was in the crew's mattresses."[9]

The bilge pumps howled as they cut in one by one. The list slowly disappeared and the stern lifted. Yawing like a drunken sailor, the *McFarland* — minus thirty feet of her stern — tacked and skidded her way north across Iron Bottom Bay. Then steam no longer fed to the port engine. The ship was dead in the water about five miles south-

---

7   "Jap Supplies Repaired Crippled U.S. Destroyer, Lieut. Chalmers Tells of Hardships of 4000 mile Voyage." *The Sunday Republican*, [dateline Waterbury, CT] n.d. Norman Edward Chalmers' collection, courtesy of his daughter Sande McLaughlin.

8   Charles Rawlings, "The McFarland Comes Home."

9   Robert Trumbull, "Destroyer With Makeshift Stern Reaches Hawaii From Solomons," *The New York Times* (31 December 31, 1942): 1,4. Norman Edward Chalmers collection, courtesy of his daughter Sande McLaughlin.

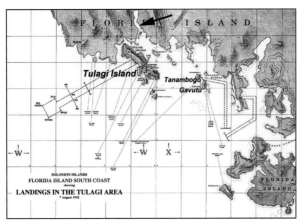

"The arrow points to where *McFarland* was moored, up where the channel narrows, on the east bank. Just to the north, on the west bank, a converted yacht moored as a PT Boat tender. I don't recall the name, but it was a beautiful craft." — Paul Helmke.

west of Tulagi. "It was dark when we came near Tulagi. We sent a visual signal for help, and lay to," said Alderman. "The wounded were transferred to boats from Tulagi and then PT boats made an unsuccessful attempt to take *McFarland* in tow."[10]

Shortly thereafter, chief Bos'n Banyon's Yippie came alongside. "Stand by for a line!" hailed Banyon, who was in the act of freeing his ship off the reef when the attack fell upon the *McFarland*. Knowing there was nothing else around big enough to tow 1,200 tons of crippled destroyer, he hurried out to help. "Shotgun didn't get me!" he bellowed. "Tulagi-bound, I guess, but God'lmighty couldn't be sure, from watchin' that course you're steerin'."[11]

The Yippie prepared to take *McFarland* in tow while Captain Alderman and the other officers gathered that evening and made plans for the following day. With the ship in tow and not all reports yet in, *McFarland* sent message No. 161345 to command:

CANCEL MY 160600 X SHIP UNDERWAY WITH BARGES ALONGSIDE AVOIDING SUBMARINE WHEN ATTACKED BY MANY

DIVE BOMBERS  X  SHOT DOWN ONE AND DAMAGED ONE  X  STERN BLOWN COMPLETELY OFF AFT OF AFTER DECK HOUSE X  SIX ENLISTED MEN MISSING AND FIVE DEAD MANY WOUNDED  X  SAME BOMB BLEW UP BARGE WITH TWENTY THOUSAND GALLONS GASOLINE  X  SHIP NOW ANCHORED TULAGI HARBOR  X  ENGINES OPERATIVE BUT NO RUDDER  X  PUMPS KEEPING WATER DOWN IN AFTER FLOODED COMPARTMENTS  X  MORE COMPLETE REPORT OF DAMAGE TOGETHER WITH RECOMMENDATIONS DISPOSITION OF SHIP TOMORROW.[12]

A few miles from Tulagi was a no-name creek with a wide mouth and deep water. The sheer banks of both Florida and Tulagi Islands dropped straight down one hundred feet or deeper and battleships could moor to the islands without danger of going aground. *McFarland* was towed to the creek with no name and moored tight against the eastern bank under the cover of dense mangroves that lined each side each side of the creek. The crew would have to build a new rudder in their jungle repair yard, but out of what, nobody knew.

At first light, the dead were buried in makeshift graves and the wounded were moved to the Marine Corps field hospital on Tulagi. Message No. 170645 was then sent to command:

THIS IS SENT BY MCFARLAND TO COMAIRSOPAC INFOR TO COMSOPAC XX BOMB APPARENTLY EXPLODED ONE OR MORE DEPTH CHARGES  X  ALL COMPARTMENTS AFT OF AFTER FUEL TANKS FRAME 137 FLOODED  X  AFTER CREWS COMPARTMENT AWASH, PUMPS HOLDING THEIR OWN BUT CANNOT DO SO INDEFINITELY X ENTIRE SHIP MISSING AFT OF FRAME 164 X PROPELLERS PRACTICALLY UNDAMAGED BUT STRUTS SHAKY X PARA X CONSIDER

10  Loc. cit..
11  Rawlings, "The McFarland Comes Home."
12  U.S.S. *McFarland AVD-14* War Diary, 16 October 1942 entry.

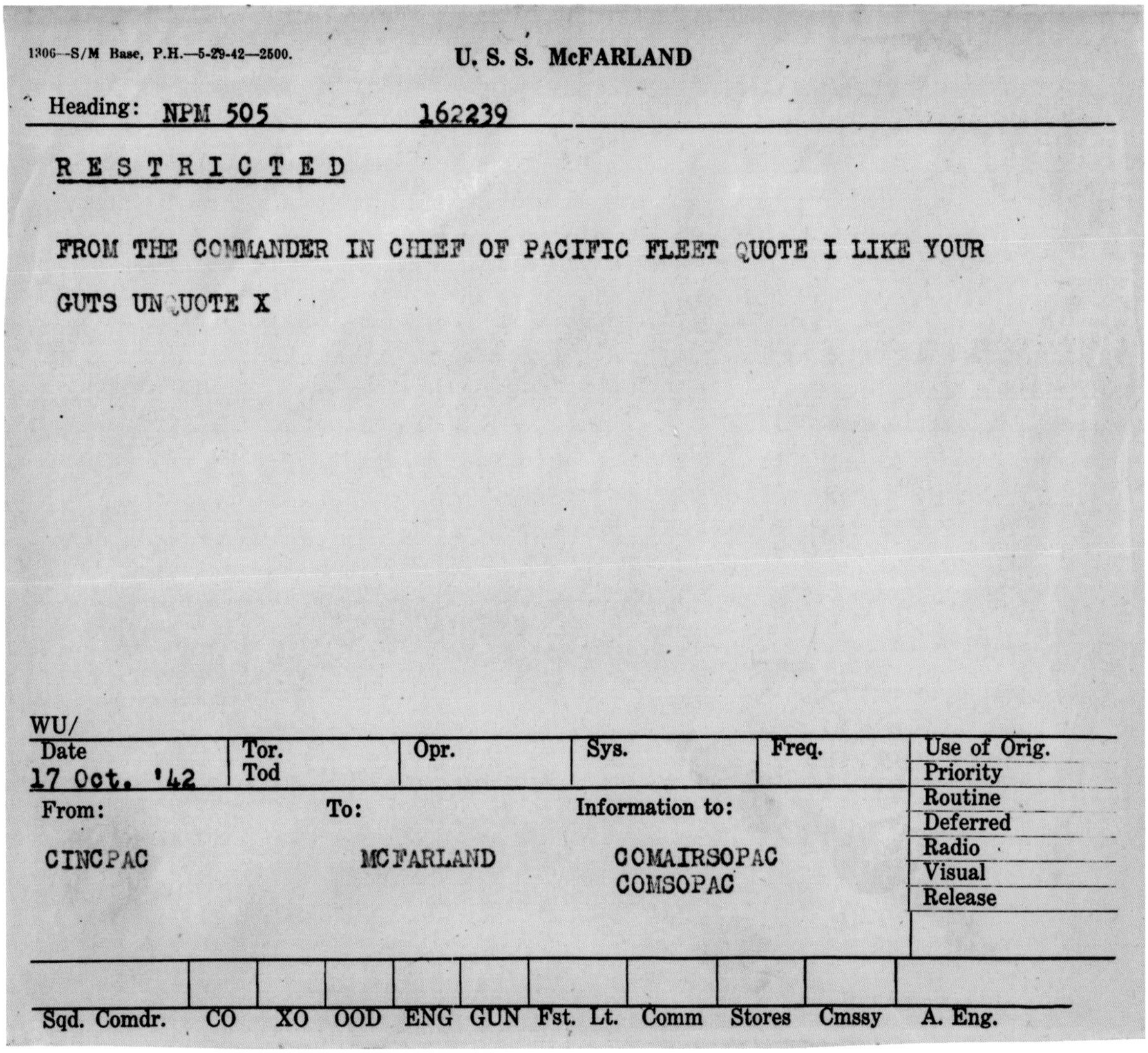

1306--S/M Base, P.H.--5-29-42--2500.    U. S. S. McFARLAND

Heading:  NPM 505            162239

R E S T R I C T E D

FROM THE COMMANDER IN CHIEF OF PACIFIC FLEET QUOTE I LIKE YOUR

GUTS UNQUOTE X

WU/

| Date 17 Oct. '42 | Tor. Tod | Opr. | Sys. | Freq. | Use of Orig. |
|---|---|---|---|---|---|
| | | | | | Priority |
| From: | To: | | Information to: | | Routine |
| | | | | | Deferred |
| CINCPAC | MCFARLAND | | COMAIRSOPAC COMSOPAC | | Radio |
| | | | | | Visual |
| | | | | | Release |

| Sqd. Comdr. | CO | XO | OOD | ENG | GUN | Fst. Lt. | Comm | Stores | Cmssy | A. Eng. |
|---|---|---|---|---|---|---|---|---|---|---|

Admiral Nimitz's 17 October 1942 message to *McFarland*: "I Like Your Guts." *Author's collection.*

THAT SHIP CAN BE REPAIRED BY SALVAGE TUG IN ABOUT ONE WEEK SO THAT SHE CAN PROCEED UNDER OWN POWER WITH JURY RUDDER  X  PARA X SHIP NOW SECURED ALONGSIDE BANK IN BACK CHANNEL TULAGI HARBOR AND IS SECURELY CAMOUFLAGED AGAINST AIR ATTACK X PLACE CONSIDERED IDEAL FOR SALVAGE OPERATIONS XXXX.[13]

Admiral Chester Nimitz, Commander-in-Chief of the U.S. Pacific Fleet, sent the *McFarland* this reply:

FROM THE COMMANDER IN CHIEF OF PACIFIC FLEET QUOTE I LIKE YOUR GUTS UNQUOTE X[14]

---

13  U.S.S. *McFarland AVD-14* War Diary, 17 October 1942 entry.

14  See above photograph of Nimitz's message.

The entire ship was camouflaged with mangrove brush to conceal it from enemy aircraft while repairs were underway. A brush-cutting detail was organized. They went into the mangrove in small boats, armed with butcher knives, machetes and fire axes. Paul Helmke described the scene: "As coxswain, I was part of the brush-cutting detail. For the next 42 days we renewed the camouflage, which quickly wilted under the tropical sun. Every time Jap planes were sighted in the area we would run the boats deep into the mangroves to avoid being seen. Weeks later, a First Lieutenant asked me why all the boat compasses were getting rusty. I wonder if he ever figured out it was because of the salt water we used to replace the alcohol which went down so good with wild pineapple juice.

"When not cutting brush we stood watch around the clock. The first few nights were unnerving. You didn't know if the jungle was full of Japs or not. At 18, that was a scary thing. During the day watch I saw frequent dog-fights over the channel while archer fish came to the surface of the creek and gunned down their prey, shooting six-foot-long streams of water, knocking bugs off their perches and into the water to be eaten. They didn't get enough bugs, however, because I soon came down with a raging case of dengue fever. In a matter of days I dropped from 165 pounds to 110 pounds."[15] [16]

Communications officer Red Dean was moved ashore to Tulagi with all the radio equipment to supplement Guadalcanal's radio base. Over the next few weeks, Dean would often listen in on the chatter between Marine fighter pilots Marion Carl, Joe Foss, John Smith and others during their mêlées above Iron Bottom Bay. "At night the conversation dropped to sea level," said Dean. "Our Small Boys often chased enemy landing barges and also got in the way of the Big Boys during the Savo Island contests.[17]

"At least four PT Boats left Tulagi each night just to patrol Iron Bottom Bay. Their crews were often tired and depleted by malaria or dengue fever. We soon discovered that riding around in a speed boat with the probability of getting to shoot at something was great fun. Many exchanges of duty for night watch became commonplace. The best part of a PT patrol came just before dawn. Morning twilight found the PT boats approaching our customized latrines erected on pierlets over the calm harbor water. When high tide and dawn coincided, a PT Boat could kick up a bow wave that would really wash down an unsuspecting squatter."[18]

On 19 October the *Navajo*-class fleet tug USS *Seminole* arrived at Tulagi and moored to the island. Aboard the *Seminole* were Navy divers Edward Raymer and Moon Mullen, fresh from a salvage operation on the sunken *Arizona* at Pearl Harbor. They were now serving with *Seminole*'s five-man salvage team. Years later, Raymer wrote about their arrival: "We had just secured the last line when the Captain of the USS *McFarland*, John Alderman, and the engineering officer, Lieutenant Chalmers, came aboard and asked for the assistance of our salvage unit to help with repairs. Holes and split seams in the underwater hull section of the ship needed to be repaired so that *McFarland* would stay afloat."[19]

The *Seminole* pulled up alongside *McFarland* and with *Seminole*'s crane, the crew removed much of *McFarland*'s deckhouse. One of the three-inch guns was also removed to lighten the ship's stern. Raymer and Mullen filled shrapnel holes and repaired the split seams in the underwater hull section. "Visibility under the ship and in Tulagi Harbor was only fair," recalled Raymer.

15   Dengue fever, also known as "The Devil's Disease," is a mosquito-borne tropical illness cause by the dengue virus. Symptoms may include a spiking fever, searing muscle and joint pain, blood seeping through the skin, shock and possibly death.

16   Telephone interview with Paul Helmke, 10 October 2015, and email correspondence 9 June 2016. Additional quotes taken from Paul Helmke's letter written to E. Andrew Wilde, 14 May 1995.

17   Small Boys were PT Boats. Big Boys were destroyers.

18   Cdr. Frederick S. Dean, *Going Back to Tulagi*, unpublished. 1987.

19   Cdr. Edward Raymer, *Descent into Darkness, A Navy Diver's Memoir* (Presidio Press, 1966), 150-152.

"I had been underwater for an hour when Moon signaled that he was bringing me to the surface. I came up and asked why. He pointed up the inlet between Tulagi and Florida Islands with a look of fear on his face. About one hundred yards upstream were two of the biggest crocodiles I had ever seen, lying on the bank sunning themselves. We suspended diving for the day."[20]

While Raymer and Mullen made their repairs, six men from *McFarland*'s mechanical department boarded a motor launch and headed for the nearby island of Tanambogo in search of materials to build a new rudder. Each man weighed more than 230 pounds and together they were referred to by *McFarland*'s crew as the "Big Six."

The Japanese had started a seaplane base on Tanambogo which they hastily abandoned following the American invasion on 7 August 1942. The Big Six soon found fuel storage tanks supported by steel I-beams set into concrete bases. The I-beams were just what they were looking for. Oxygen for welding and cutting was in short supply so they preheated the steel I-beams with gasoline blow-torches before finishing the cut with oxygen.

From the I-beams the Big Six fashioned two out-rigger struts that would hold the rigging blocks, giving the tiller ropes leverage. They also found creosote-dipped telephone poles that the Japanese left behind. From these they would fashion *McFarland* a new rudder. The telephone poles were cut flat on one side and butted up tight against one another. The new twenty-five foot long rudder was held together with special bolts turned on the ship's lathe in the engine room. The biggest piece of I-beam was welded like a stern-post to *McFarland*'s torn aft end. The rudder was swung by steel-cable tiller ropes attached to the double-drum deck steam winch, so turning in one side turned out the other. The bottom and sides of the ship's hull were patched using a large steel plate taken from another part of the ship.

When welding the I-beam sternpost, *McFar-*

USS *Seminole*. National Archives photograph #19-N-22658.

*land*'s stern was raised out of the water by shifting all ballast forward. It was then that they saw how the screws had been saved from the blast. About six feet of the keel had been spared. Attached to that stump were plates that held the shaft struts. It was that solid construction that held the ship afloat while her plates were peeling off her sides on the run from Lunga Point to Tulagi.

On 25 October, while repairs on *McFarland* were still underway, two World War I four-stack destroyers named *Trevor* and *Zane* arrived in Tulagi from Espiritu Santo. They were carrying a cargo of 300 drums of aviation fuel, ammunition, four howitzers and 100 Marines. The cargo and men were quickly transferred to the *Seminole* and the *YP-284* for delivery to Guadalcanal. The two ships were nearly finished unloading off Lunga Point when they were ordered to return to Tulagi with all possible speed. Three enemy destroyers, part of a larger force of eight enemy ships, were sighted rounding Savo Island, heading for Guadalcanal. As *Seminole* and the Yippie neared mid-channel, the Japanese ships changed course in their direction. Realizing that they would be cut off, the two ships set a new course for Lengo Channel.

Meanwhile, *Trevor* and *Zane*, both uncamou-flaged and fearing that they might attract attention

20  Loc. cit.

to the vulnerable *McFarland,* charged out of Tulagi Harbor steaming south at twenty-nine knots. The enemy destroyers immediately gave chase and opened fire at a range of five miles.

*Zane* was hit by a 5-inch shell, knocking out one of her guns and killing three men. The four-stack destroyer's best chance for survival was to attempt a high-speed transit of shoal-studded Ngela Channel. Seeing this, the Japanese destroyers broke off their engagement and headed back for *Seminole* and *YP-284.* The Yippie was hit with a salvo of 5-inch shells and sank almost immediately while *Seminole* ran a new course parallel to the beach, hoping that she was not seen. Navy diver Raymer described what happened next: "The enemy ships headed straight for us, firing as they came. At first, the distance was so great that I watched the shells lose their spiraling motion and tumble end-over-end over my head before falling harmlessly into the sea. Hiding behind drums of aviation gasoline and watching shells flying overhead made Moon and I wish we were back in Pearl Harbor. We grabbed life jackets and used them as shields as we peered through the armholes at the fireworks. Strangely enough, even this completely useless protection gave me a feeling of safety."[21]

Three salvos pounded the *Seminole* in her forward area. At least fifteen armor-piercing shells tore through her thin hull plating without exploding. Another shell hit and then exploded. "I heard a cry and saw a seaman drop dead from a shrapnel wound," said Raymer. "Moon, the ship's chief carpenter's mate, Henry Buhl, and I were huddled on the open fantail, expecting the ship to reach shore. We looked over the side and to our surprise, saw members of the crew floating by in life rafts and life jackets. 'What the hell's going on?' yelled the chief carpenter's mate to the life raft crowded with men. 'Abandon ship. Get the hell off there!' came the answer. We were surrounded by fires. The boat deck was burning fiercely and gasoline drums were exploding. The forward part of the fantail was ablaze and the flames were licking at our heels as we hurriedly donned life jackets and jumped over the stern."[22] When the *Seminole* was two-hundred yards downwind from Raymer and the others it exploded with a thunderous roar.

News of the attacks on the four-stack destroyers and the sinking of *Seminole* and *YP-284* alarmed COMSOPAC,[23] prompting it to send message No. 242334 on 25 October:

ACTION MCFARLAND FROM COMSOPAC X DESTROY ECM [Electric Coding Machine] AND ASSOCIATED PUBLICATIONS X DESTROY ALL OTHER UNNECESSARY PUBLICATIONS X RETAIN CHANNEL 104, 106, 135, 136, CSP 1270, 1286, 1312 THROUGH FOX X REPORT DESTRUCTION DIRECT TO ME.[24]

On 26 October *McFarland* reported back that, with the exception of a few cryptographic aids named by COMSOPAC to be retained, all other secret and confidential publications, correspondence, files and charts were burned in the ship's boilers. The situation looked grim as Red Dean remembered: "Guadalcanal could have easily been a failure had the enemy known how weak the American position was. We all knew that damaged American ships had been abandoned in the Philippines. We, too, might be left to rust. Shore duty in the miserable Solomon Islands inspired our engineers to design and build a jury rudder good enough to get us safely back south into the New Hebrides."[25]

With torch and trip-hammer *McFarland*'s crew labored. By Thanksgiving Day their work was complete. The engine room could now reliably operate the damaged engines. The throttle of the port turbine blown off during the attack was feeding steam. To make way on a steady course, more steam was admitted to the astern turbine

---

21  Loc. cit.

22  Loc. cit.
23  Commander South Pacific.
24  U.S.S. *McFarland AVD-14* War Diary, 25 October 1942 entry.
25  Dean, *Going Back to Tulagi.*

while backing off on the port engine by two-thirds-together with full ahead on the starboard engine.

*McFarland* steamed from her hiding place, passing through the southern end of the Sealark Channel to Torpedo Junction and into the open sea. From there she sailed to Noumea where a shipwright made additional repairs and gave her what he hoped was a better rudder than the jungle-conceived contraption. Chief Engineer Chalmers was highly critical of the new rudder, insisting that his own invention would have taken them to Pearl Harbor just as well. He may have been right.

On 17 December *McFarland* set a course for Pearl Harbor. Things went well for a time, but the new heavy jury rudder gave them trouble in a gale and twisted. "The cable broke several times," said Chalmers, "and then, 1,200 miles from Pearl Harbor, we discovered that the keel had warped and that it was disrupting the steering. Fuel hoses, chains and finally the ship's anchor were thrown overboard to act as a drag to offset the drift caused by the damaged keel. The anchor trailed 40 fathoms of chain. Only a single screw turned over and our speed was fifteen knots to nothing."[26]

The crew joked that the *McFarland* might not make it back to Pearl Harbor before the war was over. Together they composed a sea song called *"The Return of the Rudderless Mac."*

My name is Jack Alderman
I'm skipper of the *Mac*.
When going gets tough,
On all engines I back.

I lost my ass end
They gave me a spare
Everything hokay till in my ass
I get a wild hair.

To de fantails I go
And take off the pants,
I'm barrin' my all
For national defense.

The crew's all mad
The gold braid is too
Because they *Mac*'s
Going on only one screw.

Chalmers says this
Raidline says that,
Gemmill says nothing
He just come and sat.

Chalmers says fuel line
So over she goes,
Where that will drag us?
God only knows.

Raidline and his gang
In a huddle do go,
And over the side
A hawser they throw.

Gemmill still says nothing,
But his face it sags,
When nobody's looking
His anchor he drags.

Old Nimitz, he stands
Alone by the pier,
And down each cheek trickles
One large tear.

The medals are rusty,
His head is all grey,
He keeps on saying,
"Is the *Mac* in today?"

The war is all over,
The Axis is beat,
They hold Victory Parade,
Down on Market Street.

The reserves have come,
The reserves have went,
And the people have chosen,
A new President.

Tokyo has fallen,
Berlin, it has too,
The *Mac*, she's still comin',
On only one screw.[27]

On the evening of 29 December 1942, *McFarland* entered the blacked-out shoreline of Pearl Harbor to a chorus of cheers. She moored and her crew disembarked to converse with a reporter who had been waiting on shore. Chief Gunner Red

---

26  "Jap Supplies Repaired Crippled U.S. Destroyer," [dateline Waterbury, CT].

27  Sea song: *Norman Edward Chalmers' collection.*

USS *McFarland AVD-14* pictured at Pearl Harbor, 31 December 1942. National Archives Photo # 80-G-36082.

Admiral Nimitz, far right, inspecting the *McFarland*'s damage and subsequent repairs. National Archives Photo # 19-LCM-AVD-14-BS110219.

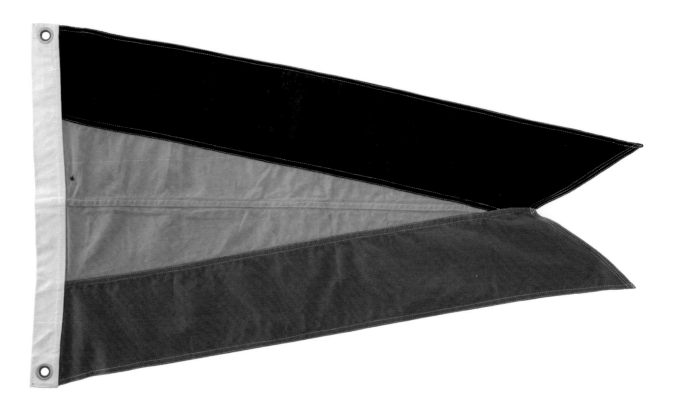

Harp summed up things best when he said to the reporter: "Here we are, and mister, you tell'em it feels right good."[28]

Two days later Admiral Nimitz pinned the Navy Cross on Lieutenant Commander John Alderman. As a tribute to her officers and men, the USS *McFarland AVD-14* was recognized with a Presidential Unit Citation, the first ever awarded to a ship.

For the remainder of the war, *McFarland* went on training exercises with carriers off the California coast. At war's end *McFarland* was struck from the Navy register and sent to Bordertown, New Jersey, where she awaited the cutting torches that would tear open her sides. The USS *McFarland*, her decks once red with heroes' blood, was sold for scrap in 1946 to the North American Smelting Company.

---

28  From an unidentified period newspaper clipping. *Norman Edward Challmers' collection.*

Top: USS *McFarland*'s Presidential Unit Citation Flag, 33" x 19". *Author's collection.*

Above: Alderman's Navy Cross (left): "For extraordinary heroism and distinguished service in the line of his profession as Commanding Officer of the Destroyer USS *McFarland* while on special missions in the Solomon islands area during the period 8 August 1942 to 18 October 1942. On repeated occasions, Lieutenant Commander Alderman courageously entered the Solomon waters to assist in the task of protecting the valuable supply lanes to Guadalcanal, in support of our land and sea defenses of that island. With utter disregard for his own safety, he exposed himself to the ever-present danger of hostile air attacks. On one occasion, his ship was so damaged by enemy fire that it was almost lost. By his perseverance, determination and technical ability, he made the necessary repairs to his ship, under the most adverse conditions, so that she was able to continue in the service of her country. His heroic conduct was in keeping with the highest traditions of the Naval Service." *Author's collection.*

Frank Schwable

# NIGHT FIGHTER

*Night Fighter* takes the reader to North Africa, England, the United States and the Solomon Islands, where events set in motion one of the lesser known episodes of the Pacific War.

The stage was set in September 1939 when war erupted in Europe; twelve months later Italy invaded Egypt and Germany began bombing London for 57 consecutive nights. In response to the Blitz, the RAF deployed the world's first capable night fighter, the Bristol Beaufighter. It was equipped with the AI Mark IV, a breakthrough in miniaturized radar, that enabled the British to intercept and destroy German aircraft flying night missions.

When U.S. involvement in the war seemed imminent, the Marines sent several officers as observers to North Africa and England. Among them were Captain Edward Dyer, Lieutenant Colonel Lewis Merritt, and Captain Frank Schwable — three experienced aviators who were qualified to understand the methods and technical details being developed by the British to defend their airspace. They were instructed to pay special attention to British facilities, logistics[1] and tactics.[2]

Captain Dyer, a degreed radio engineer, left for his tour in May 1941. When he returned from England in October, he brought with him the technical details of the British AI Mark IV radar.

On 10 November 1941 Captain Schwable flew from Washington D.C. to Honolulu, where he met with Lieutenant Colonel "Griff" Merritt. From Hawaii the two men journeyed to North Africa, and from there to England.

In mid-March 1942 Colonel Merritt returned to the United States while Schwable stayed in England for an additional five weeks. Merritt gathered much from his tour in the way of technical and tactical information, but it was Schwable's time in England, both at the Fighter Director school at RAF Stanmore Park, and as an observer with the Royal Air Force night fighter squadron at RAF Coltishall, that had the greatest effect on the future of Marine Corps aviation.

Schwable returned to the United States in May and submitted his *Warfare Operations Report A16-3*. The North African portion of his report was filled with interesting observations, while his descriptions from England about night fighting and the AI Mark IV were purposely vague because the information was secret. The missing details were recorded separately in his notebook and revealed during his debriefing by the Bureau of Aeronautics.

The lessons learned during his warfare operations tour would exert their full measure of influence when he was called upon by the commandant to create the first night fighter squadron in United States military aviation history.

---

1  The organization of moving, housing, and supplying troops and equipment.
2  Methods for using weapons and military units to engage and defeat an enemy in battle, or gain an objective that is a part of a broader campaign strategy.

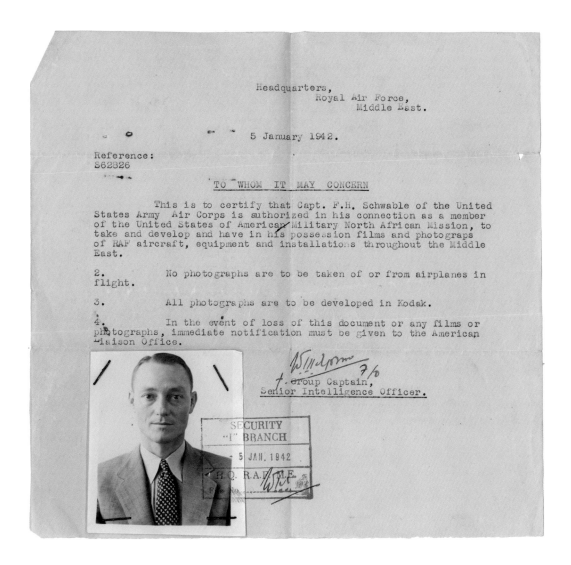

Headquarters,
Royal Air Force,
Middle East.

5 January 1942.

Reference:
S62326

## TO WHOM IT MAY CONCERN

This is to certify that Capt. F.H. Schwable of the United States Army Air Corps is authorized in his connection as a member of the United States of American Military North African Mission, to take and develop and have in his possession films and photograps of RAF aircraft, equipment and installations throughout the Middle East.

2.    No photographs are to be taken of or from airplanes in flight.

3.    All photographs are to be developed in Kodak.

4.    In the event of loss of this document or any films or photographs, immediate notification must be given to the American Liaison Office.

Group Captain,
Senior Intelligence Officer.

SECURITY
"I" BRANCH
5 JAN. 1942
H.Q. R.A.F. M.E.

## Warfare Operations Report A16-3

The flight across the Pacific took me to many of the islands that would soon figure in the news. Unfortunately, Pan American's schedule does not leave many daylight hours at these overnight stops in which to see very much. On Wake Island there was time for Major Devereaux to take us for a quick drive around the island. There was a considerable amount of construction activity at both Midway and Wake and there was a pronounced atmosphere of tension and hurry at both islands. This same tension was in evidence at Guam. I saw no aircraft at any of these islands, though the advanced ground party for a Marine squadron at Midway and Wake had left Pearl Harbor by ship a few days before I departed from Pearl Harbor. I did, however, see some Navy patrol planes at Cavite.

I was at Singapore from November 29 to December 5, two days before hostilities broke out, during which time I was able to visit the RAF Far

Above: Schwable's warfare operations tour RAF Security and Identification travel document. All of the Schwable artifacts that appear in this story were sold at auction by the Schwable estate on 26 August 2000. *Author's collection.*

Eastern Headquarters at Sime Road, the main air-drome at Seletar, the large troop barracks at Changi and the municipal airdrome at Kallang. The latter field had been taken over by the RAF for use as a fighter airdrome. There were only two squadrons of fighter aircraft at Kallang, and they consisted of our American Buffaloes.[3] At Seletar there were several squadrons of rather old Albacores,[4] and at the sea-plane facilities there were six Catalinas — our Con-solidated PBY flying boats and six Dutch Dornier[5] flying boats that had just arrived to reinforce the British. During my last few days at Singapore a great deal of activity and tension was in evidence. Local civilian volunteer organizations were being mobilized, officers were required to remain at their messes at night instead of going home, officers making visits to town carried side arms, and aircraft on the airdromes were being dispersed. The arrival of the *Prince of Wales* and the *Repulse* appeared to have quite a salutary effect upon the morale of Singapore. All along the coast, seaward, I saw line after line of barbed wire running in rows starting about 50 yards out into the water and running up to several hundred yards inland — also many con-crete machine pillboxes that were open only on the seaward side.

From Singapore, I flew to Cairo on the BOAC,[6] via Rangoon, Calcutta, Karachi, and Basra, in addi-tion to numerous short intermediate stops.

It was at Rangoon that I experienced my first blackout; it was one that was very definitely black, too. At that early stage of experimental practice blackouts, the Rangoon system seems to have been simply to throw the main switch at the power house and that put everything in complete darkness. You can imagine what this was like in a country where even the natives are a vary dark color.

At Karachi, in West India, there were excellent dock facilities with numerous storehouses, railroad sidings, cranes, etc., which appeared to be quite new and modern in comparison with such ship-ping centers as Rangoon. We had just left Karachi, and I'll never forget this, there was an Australian general, General Blamey, who was the head of the forces in Libya; he was sitting right across from us when it was announced over the internal radio that Pearl Harbor had just been attacked. He leaned over towards Colonel Merritt and I, looking like Santa Claus, round face, reddish, a little white beard and moustache. He leaned over and said, "I'm so sorry for you, but I'm so glad for us."[7]

On December 9, I reported to the Naval At-tache in Cairo and shortly thereafter I took a trip to Alexandria to see the RAF reconnaissance group stationed there. At Alexandria I witnessed my first exhibition of anti-aircraft fire against a real, not training, target. I was somewhat disappointed. The first burst from a 4-gun 3.7-inch battery detonated about 1,000 yards behind a German reconnaissance plane flying at 25,000 feet on a slightly curving course, and thereafter, all remaining bursts for a period of at least three minutes trailed the Hun pre-cisely along his line of flight at exactly the correct speed of advance, still at about 1,000 yards behind. It appeared as though no effort was ever made to correct the 1,000 yard lag and the German plane continued on its course obviously disregarding the anti-aircraft fire.

On December 19, one month after the push in Libya started, I joined Battle Headquarters in the desert. These Headquarters consisted of the 8th Army Headquarters commanded by General Ritchie and Advanced Air Headquarters commanded by Air Vice-Marshal Conningham. Battle Headquar-ters was then at Sidi Bu Amud but two days later advanced to Tmimi. By this time the Axis forces had withdrawn to the vicinity of Benghazi, leav-

---

3 The Brewster F2A Buffalo was an early fighter aircraft built by the Brewster Aeronautical Corporation. It was largely obsolete when the U.S. entered World War II.

4 The Fairey Albacore was a British single-engine biplane used for scouting, dive bombing and as a torpedo bomber.

5 A three-engine flying boat of German design used for marine patrol and search and rescue.

6 BOAC: British Overseas Airways Corporation.

7 General Blamey's remark was not included in Schwable's final version of his Warfare Operations Report. Benis Frank, *Oral History Transcript, Brigadier General Frank H. Schwable* (History and Museums Division, U.S. Marine Corps, 1983), 86.

ing only small roving patrols and stragglers to be wiped up, plus the strongly defended but isolated forces at Bardia, Sollum and Halfaya Pass. These later forces, however, necessitated detaching one of General Ritchie's two corps, the 30th, to contain them. It was expected that these garrisons would soon fall of their own weight but, partially due to the German's success in supplying them nightly by aircraft, it was finally necessary to storm the garrisons to force them into submission.

At Battle Headquarters I learned that coordination between the ground and air forces was accomplished solely by cooperation. The RAF's mission in this campaign was to support the 8th Army by any and all means. The amount and type of support for operations was agreed upon by the GOC and the AOC.[8] On inquiring what the procedure would be if these two officers disagreed, I was told that the matter would have to be referred for decision to Middle East Headquarters, 685 miles back in Cairo, to General Auchinleck direct for the Army, and through Air-Marshal Tedder for the RAF.

In carrying out its mission, the RAF had three primary objectives: (1) to gain and maintain air superiority, (2) to give direct air support to ground forces, and (3) to carry out long-range bombing and reconnaissance missions against distant bases such as Benghazi for a while and later Tripoli, and against ship-borne supply lines. The RAF was successful in accomplishing its first objective. It gained and maintained unquestioned air superiority; nevertheless, German and Italian aircraft carried out numerous bombing and strafing missions and considerable aerial reconnaissance. Four times during my two-week visit to the desert I saw German aircraft far behind the front lines, and I heard Tobruk, 12 miles away, being heavily bombed one night. Another night an enemy aircraft flew overhead for at least an hour as it dropped flares around the Tmimi area. Incidentally, these flares were very bright and burned for at least four minutes.

8  GOC: General Officer Commanding. (R)AOC: (Royal) Air Officer Commanding.

The RAF's second objective consisted of two different forms of support, (1) direct bombing and strafing and (2) aerial reconnaissance. In order to coordinate the direct support of ground forces, a unit was established at battle Headquarters called Army Air Support Control. If a brigade or the Forward Air Support Liaison officer, all called the forward tentacles, desired air support against a specific target, a request was made to Corps Headquarters. The Corps would coordinate requests between adjacent units and then ask for support from the Army Air Support Control Unit at Battle Headquarters and at the same time the Corps would notify the bomber and fighter wings of this request. AASC would submit the request to the AOC and GOC for a decision, and if it was decided that sufficient aircraft were available, that the target was suitable and that neither officer had more urgent plans for the planes involved, AASC would notify both the Corps and the bomber and fighter wings of Headquarters for approval. By this time the bomber and fighter pilots had been briefed and the aircraft armed, warmed up and ready to take off. The system appeared to be quite satisfactory, except for the time lag — about 40 to 50 minutes from the time the brigade made the request until the aircraft were over the target, by which time the situation had often changed considerably. In fact, I was told that several times friendly troops had been bombed by mistake in fast moving situations as a result of this time lag. Part of the delay was the result of the long flights the bombers had to make due to the distances they were based behind the lines. Later on, the bombers used to fly up to one of the forward airdromes each morning about 9:30 already bombed-up, there to await assignment of targets. Considerable time was saved by this arrangement. It was planned that AASC, when more thoroughly experienced, would be given the authority to approve requests for aerial support without reference to the AOC or GOC, in which case the time lag would be correspondingly reduced. At the time of my visit, AASC consisted of one squadron leader and one flight-lieutenant for the RAF, and one major and one captain representing the Army.

The second form of aerial support consisted of reconnaissance flights under the immediate direction of the Corps Commanders. One Army cooperation squadron of 12 operating Hurricanes[9] and several Lysanders[10] was assigned to the 13th Corps and was employed as directed by the Commanding Officer of that Corps without reference to the RAF. The Hurricanes, 3 of which were equipped to take photographs, operated individually. They avoided all combat where possible. The squadron commander stated that credence was always given to his reconnaissance reports covering the rear areas but action was seldom taken on his reports of front line movements until confirmed by the forward ground forces, by which time the situation had often changed materially and the advantage of early information was thereby lost. This squadron had its own mobile photographic laboratory. This unit stated that they had tried out both trailer and prime mover photographic laboratories and that the trailer had proved useless, they would not stand up to the strain of being towed around the desert.

While at Tmimi I experienced a typical desert dust storm. As soon as the wind reached a fairly high velocity, the air was so thick with fine dust that it was impossible to distinguish objects 15 feet away. The dust gets into everything, no matter how well protected. You eat, breathe and taste dust. It gets into all of your clothes, in between papers and into equipment and during the height of the storm it is almost impossible to accomplish anything out in the open because the visibility is so reduced. The dust gets into your eyes so that you can't see and into your nose so that it is difficult to breathe. During such a storm the British practically ceased all operations, but the Germans continued their withdrawal on several occasions during dust storms. As soon as the wind dies down, the dust settles very

rapidly and the atmosphere clears remarkable fast. It is several days, however, before the dust stops sifting through from tent flies, blankets and so forth. All aircraft, tents, office vans and in fact everything is filthy inside with dust.

In connection with the office vans or lorries, the entire advanced air operational Headquarters was housed in one large specially constructed lorry with a small canvas lean-to on either side. The entire 8th Army was controlled from a similar lorry. There were, of course, additional lorries or offices to house the camp commandant, signal units, supply departments and so on. These lorries are similar to a small moving van with doors on each side. At each end is a large desk with drawers and map cases, and the sides of the van are provided with shelves and large boards upon which to post maps, orders, availability charts, etc. The vans are provided with electric lights, fans and numerous field telephones. The canvas lean-tos were equipped only with large wooden tables and benches. Incidentally, a typewriter is not standard equipment and I did not see a single one in the desert, hardly any in the Middle East headquarters and very few at the RAF stations in England. Paperwork is reduced to the barest minimum. Paper itself is saved as much as possible, especially in England, by using "China graph" pencils and thin transparent celluloid composition for such things as scratch pads or memorandum pads, map tracings, plotting boards, and certain order forms. The "China graph" lines can be easily wiped off with a rag similar to wiping chalk off of a blackboard. Using this transparent celluloid sheet secured over a wall map provided an extremely economical and very handy means of recording all day-by-day troop movements or positions, or for demonstrating or planning operations.

A visit to the desert is quite impressive from the dispersal point of view: everything is well dispersed — tents, aircraft, ammunition and supply dumps, and motor vehicles, both on and off the road, either parked or under way. One of the greatest difficulties in getting around in the desert is to

---

9    A British single-seat fighter aircraft that accounted for 60% of the RAF's air victories in the Battle of Britain, and served in all the major theatres of WWII.
10    A British single-engine aircraft with short take-off and landing requirements that allowed it to operate from small, unprepared airstrips.

find the unit you are looking for, be it a tent, an aircraft squadron, or any other large or small unit, particularly if the situation is quite mobile. Very little use is made of sign-posts and there is practically no standardization in setting up camps. It is surprising how difficult it is to find your own little pup tent on a black night on the flat desert even though you know the way perfectly by day. Had it not been for a small compass I carried, I would have walked clear out of the camp any number of dark nights trying to find my tent. Even at that, the compass did not prevent me from falling into a shallow slit trench that I had well-spotted.

On the way up to Derna I saw a sight that convinced me of the need for dispersal of vehicles on the road. Ten Italian lorries loaded with ammunition and gasoline had been parked very close to one another in a little wadi[11] fourteen miles beyond Tmimi. They had been surprised and hit by bombs and the whole convoy must have exploded at once and then burned — there were Italians and parts of Italians scattered over the whole area. The lorries were completely demolished and the road covered with bits of parts of men, machinery and ammunition. Had they been properly dispersed, only those suffering direct hits, or possibly near misses, would have been destroyed. On the other hand, wide dispersal in camps has the disadvantage of resulting in almost a complete lack of personal contact between units.

Because of the distances involved and the lack of transportation, complete dependence is placed on the field telephones, with the result that the personnel of units cooperating in the field or air do not see enough of one another to foster the spirit of teamwork. It was most difficult to obtain intelligent directions from one unit to the other. At Msus, where ten fighter squadrons were located, I found that one squadron on one side of the field did not even know what squadrons were operating from the other side of the same field. All field telephone lines are laid directly on the ground, even where they cross the roads. While the wires appeared to stand up very well under the heavy traffic passing over them, nevertheless, they were a source of potential confusion where such complete dependence was placed upon satisfactory telephone communication.

Near Derna I passed a temporary prison camp filled with rather miserable looking Italians. Most of them were very shabby and some had no shoes at all, just rags wrapped around their feet. Their uniforms were generally badly worn or torn. The Italians were not too reluctant to surrender after a face-saving effort at resistance. There is one instance that I know of where a British Short Sunderland flying boat was shot down off of Tolmeita by two German ME110s[12] on December 22. The crew and passengers surviving, numbering 19, made their way back to Tmimi as best they could, mostly by walking for several days. They were completely unarmed but when they were first picked up by the British they had 100 Italian prisoners with them. This is not an exaggeration, it is a matter of record and I talked to the pilot of the plane Xmas night at Tmimi while he ate his first full meal in several days. This tendency to surrender however is not shared by the Germans. There appears to be two distinct types of German prisoners, one the older German, often with world war experience, who, when once captured, has the attitude of having done his best but, having lost, is willing to accept his predicament. The other type is the German youth who has been taught to hate for years — this type when captured is sour, obnoxious, unruly and truculent. Incidentally, the Germans have absolutely no respect for their Italian allies in Libya and little love is lost by the Italians for the Germans.

I was in Derna two days after the Italian forces evacuated the city. The airdrome was littered with German and Italian aircraft of all description, and the entire area was a mass of little ammunition, bomb and gasoline dumps and piles of airplane auxiliary fuel tanks. I was able to observe very

---

11  A valley, ravine, or channel that is dry except in the rainy season.

12  Messerschmitt Bf 110, often called the Me 110, was a twin-engine heavy fighter aircraft.

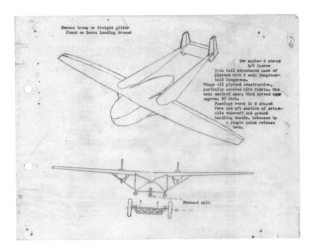

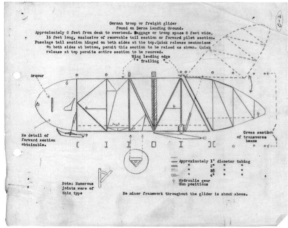

Schwable photographed and made drawings of this Gotha Go 242 German glider while on his desert tour. He would later recall, "In one of my trips in the desert I came across some German gliders, and that was before our military was interested in gliders. I actually have the Iron Cross that was painted on the side of one. I cut that out. The glider was in good condition. As a matter of fact, it must have landed and just been abandoned there. And they were darn good, efficient designs. I am a little handy with paper and pencil, so I drew some very good drawings of that thing. That's one bit of information that I picked up and brought back to the States." *Author's collection*.

closely six new German Gotha 242 Gliders that had recently been flown to Libya. The gliders were quite interesting from a design point-of-view, in that they were so arranged that the tail section of the fuselage or gondola could be raised while on the ground, giving a clear loading space eight feet wide and six feet high, thus permitting very rapid loading or unloading. By pulling one small lever, this entire section would drop off so that parachute troops could jump out three or four at a time. These gliders had a capacity of twenty-one completely equipped troops. The material and workmanship on

these gliders, and in fact on all German equipment that I saw, was excellent. I also saw some of the Ju 52 transport airplanes that had landed several days before not knowing that the airdrome had just passed into British hands. These planes, which were loaded with German engineers and technicians, were allowed to land and were then destroyed. Several others, however, sensed the situation upon seeing the first one attacked and managed to escape.

The road to Derna, like so many others in the desert, was lined on either side with motor transport vehicles, some of which had been destroyed

The Iron Cross Schwable cut from the German Gotha Go 242 glider. *Author's collection*.

by bombs or gunfire and others had just been abandoned where they broke down. The desert is very hard on tires and literally hundreds of tires lie about that to outward appearance look almost brand new, but upon closer examination show large splits in the casing where the jolt of a heavily laden lorry striking large stones has been too much for the tires to stand.

From Derna I proceeded to Benghazi via Barce, arriving at Benghazi four days after the 4th Indian Division had moved in. The main highway running generally along the coast from Tobruk around to Benghazi is extremely vulnerable in three places: where it winds down off of the escarpment into Derna, then back up again onto the escarpment further along to the west and, finally, near Tocra where once again the road twists back and forth with sharp bends down a steep embankment. The road had been destroyed near Tocra about 1/3 of the way down the escarpment and heavy motor vehicles were held up several days before getting through. I was able to proceed only by sliding through the mud down a very steep incline in the comparatively light Ford desert car in which I was riding. The Italians had tried several times to destroy the road into Derna but had not succeeded in disrupting traffic. In approaching Benghazi, I passed through miles of scattered ammunition and gasoline dumps. While the gasoline drums and carriers were generally empty, a huge amount of ammunition apparently is in excellent condition.

Benghazi, like Tobruk, showed the results of very heavy and prolonged bombing, though Benghazi was not in the complete shambles I had expected to see. In fact, with all the bombing it has sustained over a long period of time — in addition to the fact that it has changed hands numerous times — the power house was still in operation and I enjoyed the first electric lights and running water that I had seen since coming to the desert. I also had my first bath in a tub in ten days.

The dock area had been very thoroughly bombed and the harbor was filled with ships that were either grounded, turned turtle, half submerged, or blown to bits. At Berca airdrome, the field just outside of Benghazi, there were many Italian airplanes, the closest of those to town having been burned, but those further away from the city not having been touched in the Italians' haste to withdraw — except for the clock and compass, which are the two items of aircraft equipment that are *always* stolen. In this connection, it was found that many damaged aircraft — which could otherwise have been easily repaired — were rendered almost useless by souvenir hunters, of which there were many. All units had this fact brought forcefully to their attention, but many a good Tomahawk or Hurricane was nevertheless reclassified from a minor to a major repair job by our own troop's carelessness.

The troops had also been warned against souvenir hunting from the standpoint of personal safety. The Germans were notorious for leaving behind enticing looking cameras, pistols, field glasses, thermos bottles, fountain pens and other bits of equipment that are military souvenir hunters' masterpieces. But many of these articles were purposely abandoned, and prepared, to form the well-known booby trap where you swap a hand, leg or an eye for what you thought would be a nice little trinket to have. In spite of repeated warnings, there were a number of troops who couldn't resist the urge to get something for nothing — some of them got away with it and some didn't. There was one instance where an abandoned German aircraft had the control wheel, rudder bar and numerous valves and levers all wired up to an explosive charge. People will always climb into these planes, sit in the cockpit and do a little synthetic ground flying. Fortunately the battery for operating the charge had been left in an exposed position and the first souvenir hunter on the spot, a truck driver, needed a new battery for his personal radio set. When he started to walk off with the battery, he noticed the peculiar system of wiring and then the fact that the battery was not stowed in the normal position and thus he exposed what might have been a very serious booby trap.

Further out from Benghazi I visited Benina airdrome which was the same story — a field littered with wrecked aircraft, inevitable little piles of bombs, ammunition and gasoline drums every fifty yards or so, and at this field, some eight hangars partially destroyed. It gives one a rather odd feeling to walk around a completely deserted airdrome with all sorts of equipment from small but very fine hand tools to a complete and almost brand new Ju 88[13] and Me 109[14] airplane just lying around, unattended, unguarded. Having spent about an hour and a half climbing in and out of the more complete aircraft in the hangars without seeing a soul, I felt rather relieved when I started back to town.

At Benghazi I ran into a rather interesting difference of opinion as to the best location for headquarters units. The 7th Brigade of the 4th Indian Division was the first unit to move into Benghazi and on the theory of first-come-first-servd, the Brigade had taken over several of the biggest, roomiest buildings in town. They established their headquarters and barracks in the comparative comfort and warmth of four solid walls with roofs and cement floors. They had running water, electric lights, stoves, toilets, and good paved streets outside for rapid communication, all of which improved the morale and efficiency of the unit. But they knew, as well as everybody else, that sooner or later Benghazi would be bombed. They felt it was worth the chance. I drove out to the site picked out for Battle Headquarters; the advanced party had already established themselves. They were out in the cold, wet, windswept open, five miles from town with their pup tents and office vans dispersed over several miles of almost impassable mud. I am not prepared to say which of the two types of camp sites is preferable, when considered from all angles.

From Benghazi I proceeded south to Chemines and then back inland to the east of Msus which was the forward airdrome for all the fighter squadrons that were then supporting the British forces attempting to take Agedabia about seventy miles away. Just outside of Soluch the RAF pilot officer from whom I was bumming a ride lost track of what little road there was so we drove the next 30 miles just following a compass course. In this part of the country the road is merely that part of the surface that has less rocks on it than the surrounding countryside and where the brush is worn down a bit more. The British forces are fortunately relieved of the necessity of building and maintaining roads in the interior of Cyrenaca, but striking out on compass courses restricts one's speed considerably because of the many rocks scattered all over the Western desert.

My whole automobile trip from Tmimi to Msus was possible only because I was able to beg, borrow or steal two or three gallons of German gasoline at a time. It was during the first part of this period that almost every tactical reconnaissance flight reported heavy German motor vehicle columns withdrawing towards El Agheila, but there was not sufficient gasoline in the forward areas about Christmas time to send out effective bombing and strafing missions — though it was reported that there was ample gasoline in the supply depots in Cairo. One could not help but feel that splendid and rare opportunities for creating considerable losses in General Rommel's supply system were being lost to incomplete planning for supplying forward areas with sufficient fuel.

When I left Battle Headquarters at Tmimi the day after Christmas, it was anticipated that Headquarters would move to Benghazi in a day or so. At the time, there was not even sufficient motor gasoline to move the Headquarters' trucks. When I left Msus two days after New Year's, Headquarters was still in Tmimi, about 250 miles behind the fighting line, and I believe it remained in Tmimi until the recent retreat started, though certainly there must have been other considerations involved.

I had been in Msus only fifteen minutes when a German Me 110 flew directly overhead on a recon-

---

13  Junkers Ju 88 was a German Luftwaffe twin-engined medium bomber combat aircraft.
14  Messerschmitt Me 109 was the most widely produced German fighter aircraft during WWII.

naissance flight and the anti-aircraft guns put up a heavy barrage. I, as did everyone else, watched the show out of pure curiosity. It was most interesting until someone noticed little puffs of dust springing up all around us. By the time I could look around, I found myself standing completely alone amid numerous falling bits of anti-aircraft shell fragments; the other officers had all disappeared into their tents to get their steel helmets. The desert offers remarkably little natural cover from such things. Incidentally, shortly afterwards the station commander issued an order requiring all personnel to wear their steel helmets whenever the anti-aircraft guns first started to fire. Practically no one, with all of their experience, had worn his steel helmet that day.

No. 3 Fighting Squadron of the Royal Australian Air Force at Msus had just been equipped with the new Kittyhawk — our Army P-40E.[15] They were extremely pleased with it and much preferred the six .50-caliber guns to their old Tomahawk's two .50 and four .30-caliber machine guns or the Germans' Me 109F with its one cannon and two machine guns. They considered the Kittyhawk superior to the Me 109F under 10,000 feet, equal to it at 15,000 but inferior to it above 15,000 feet; however, for the tactics employed in that area, the Kittyhawk was ideal. Most daylight bombing raids were carried out just below the prevailing cloud level, 6 to 7,000 feet, which was the level at which the Kittyhawk escort had its greatest performance advantage. If the Hun wanted to intercept the raid he had to come down to the altitude at which he was at a disadvantage, and if he didn't come down, the bombing mission was carried out and nobody worried about the high-flying Hun fighter.

In connection with the bombing, the British always bombed in formation using a horizontal bombing attack and releasing bombs in salvo. The Germans used dive bombing, one plane following the next. Ground officers who experienced both types of bombing disliked the dive bombing much more in that it was continuous over a period of time during which there was always the fear or annoyance of being hit, where as with the horizontal salvo bombing, there would be one terrific explosion and then it was all over.

In visiting the various RAF messes I noted considerable variation in the food situation. The basis of all meals is cornbeef or "bully beef" as they call it, hardtack, tea or coffee and jam. Some stations were able to have a few extras. The biggest difference in the messes was the variety of preparation shown by some, and the utter lack of imagination by others. Just cold bully beef day-in-and-day-out is very uninteresting, but cold bully beef one day, hot the next, a stew the next and an occasional bully beef pot pie, adds considerable zest to one's meals. A cook with imagination is almost a necessity in the desert where everything is dreary enough anyhow, especially in wet weather.

I was disappointed to find how little gunnery practice fighter squadrons had both in Libya and England. The value of this type of training was appreciated but the time and facilities were apparently lacking. As a result there were usually only two or three consistently good gunners in a squadron and these few gunners accounted for the vast majority of the Huns credited to the squadron. One squadron leader told me that he had fired his entire load of approximately 2,100 rounds of .50-caliber ammunition from close range and from an almost ideal position at a closed formation of 6 Ju 88s without hitting a one. This occasion, however, was his first actual combat in Libya and he admitted that he was overly excited, however he did state that he had almost no gunnery training in Australia before coming to Libya. At a Spitfire Operational Training Unit I visited in England, where pilots are given advanced training in the type of aircraft they are to fly operationally, the students are given only six firing runs against a towed sleeve, and all those runs are made from the easiest firing position, nearly astern the target. At one night fighter OTU, no gunnery

---

15   Kittyhawk P-40 was an  all-metal fighter aircraft variant of the American-built Curtiss P-40 Warhawk.

practice whatsoever took place.

In moving unit bases forward, the so-called "leap frog" method was used in Libya; that is, squadrons at the forward airdrome would carry out all operations while squadrons to the rear were moving to airdromes still further forward. This system obviated squadrons having to operate while they were packing up, moving and getting settled at the new airdromes and, at the same time, there were always a certain number of squadrons established and settled at airdromes to the rear, which, in the event of a retreat, could take over operations and cover the withdrawal of the forward squadrons.

There are a surprising number of tanks of various types scattered throughout the desert. Nearly all of those that I was able to examine had been thoroughly burned inside, many of them showing comparatively little exterior damage. It appeared that one of General Rommel's secrets of success was his highly-efficient tank repair and salvage units. Time and again evening reports made to Headquarters indicated that a number of German tanks had been knocked out of action, yet when morning came it was found that many of these tanks had been hauled away by the salvage units.

At El Adem I had a brief opportunity to hurry through an RSU.[16] These units go out into the desert and haul crashed airplanes back to their base where the aircraft are repaired, unless they are major crashes (in which case they are sent back to the maintenance units behind the lines). This particular unit did practically all of its work out in the open. I watched one mechanic, standing out in a light rain on a very cold, windy day, try to fit a bolt in the engine mount of a Tomahawk. The bolt wouldn't fit so he took a hammer and drove it through. On trying to fit a nut to the bolt, he found he had stripped the threads so he had to force the bolt back out again. A second one fitted more easily. I mention this fact only as an indication of the type of work I saw. Frankly, I did not have an opportunity to see enough of this unit to judge whether that

was a representative standard of workmanship or not. Certainly the working conditions under which these men labored was none too good and was not conducive to careful, painstaking workmanship.

On flying back to Cairo from Msus, I was most impressed by the difficulties of transporting supplies up to the forward areas from the dumps 100 to 600 miles behind the lines. At one place, flying about 1,000 feet in the air, I saw a supply column of over two hundred lorries that stretched from one horizon to the other in a long, well-spaced line. It raised a perfect sheet of dust that was visible for miles. Each of the supply lorries was required to carry sufficient gasoline, oil, water, food and spare tire equipment to make the complete round trip, so naturally the useful load was thereby considerably reduced. One of the first things that Air Vice-Marshal Conningham told Colonel Merritt and me when we joined Headquarters was that, if given 200 large transport aircraft, he would no longer be restricted by supply difficulties and could carry out his mission one hundred percent. About Xmas time, when the forward areas ran short of gasoline, and at other times when ammunition and spare parts were almost exhausted, one could appreciate the benefit of having a quick means of supply that could keep up with the very rapid advance. As it was, there were only five old Bombay bombers[17] of very slow speed and quite restricted carrying capacity available for this type of utility work, including ferrying personnel from El Adem and Msus.

Back in Cairo I visited the main central ammunition dumps and one of the principle maintenance units that was just being set up for overhauling aircraft engines. The British have a perfect location prepared for them hundreds of years ago — they are using the tremendous limestone caves at Ma'sara. It is from these caves that the large limestone blocks for the pyramids were produced. These caves provided perfect bomb-proof cover and unlimited floor space, only, however, after very laboriously

---

16   RSU: Repair and Salvage Unit.

17   The Bristol Bombay was a British troop trasnsport capable of carrying 24 troops or the equivalent load of cargo. It was also used as a medium bomber.

clearing out the rubble that accumulated during the past few centuries. These caves were being cleared by hand, hundreds of tons of broken-up stones being carried out one-by-one by a steady stream of Egyptian laborers that weave back and forth like a trail of ants. The foremen actually carried long whips with which they occasionally urged some of the ten-year-old laborers on to greater speed.

The size of these caves may be imagined by the fact that one cave housed three complete parallel engine stripping and assembly lines. Engines due for overhaul were delivered to the entrance of the cave. There they were disassembled and given a rough cleaning. The parts moved down one of the three lines depending on whether the engine was an Allison, P. & W. or Merlin. After cleaning, gauging, etc. the parts moved further down the line where they were assembled to form the complete engine by the time the rear end of the cave was reached. It was estimated that over 90 overhauls per month could be handled in this one cave as soon as the personnel was available. Incidentally, the fact that these caves were being used was kept secret.

Shortly after I returned to Cairo, Colonel Merritt was a passenger in a British Wellington bomber that was shot down by German anti-aircraft fire and I believe that convinced him (and I do not blame him) that we had seen enough of the Middle East, so on January 14, we left Cairo by BOAC for Khartoum in Egyptian Sudan.[18] There we boarded a Pan-American transport that flew up to Freetown [Sierra Leon] via Lagos, Accra and Takoradi, that is, along the trans-African ferry route. Pan-American was progressing fairly rapidly in establishing suitable facilities along this route, with their Headquarters being at Accra. Barracks and BOQ[19] for some 500 men were fairly well under way at Accra. At Khartoum we saw many Blenheims[20] that were being held in reserve for the Middle East, and at Takoradi there were many Hurricanes and Blenheims being assembled for the ferry flight across Africa.

Freetown was most impressive from the point of view of the tremendous number of ships lying idly at anchor awaiting the formation of convoys. There were 45 ships of all kinds in the harbor the day we arrived and before we left thirty more came in, making a total of 75 ships in the harbor at one time, with a lot of room to spare. We made the trip from Freetown to Glasgow, Scotland, by ship in eleven days. On this trip we were on a 20-knot troop transport so we were unescorted the entire way. We were on the ocean by ourselves and it scared the hell out of me because German submarines were all over the place.[21]

While in Scotland, I visited the Combined Training Center in Inverary with Colonel Hart. There I saw the various type landing craft the British were using and watched their three principal types of tank — the heavy, forty-ton Churchill, the medium Valentine and the light Matilda — operate. I watched the trials of a newly-developed gear for overcoming barbed wire entanglements on the beach. A Bren Carrier [22] was rigged up with a large spool device protruding in front of it, upon which was wound about 25 yards of canvas slightly wider than the Bren Carrier tracks. When the carrier neared the barbed wire, the spool was permitted to rotate, unwinding the canvas strip which then acted as a carpet under the Bren Carrier, forcing the barbed wire down to the ground and helping it clear of the Bren Carrier's caterpillar tread. In addition to getting the Bren over the barbed wire, the canvas provided an unobstructed path for troops to use. On the day the demonstration was witnessed, a strong cross wind was blowing and the canvas streamed up in the air directly behind the Bren instead of remaining on the ground. Eventually the canvas, Bren Carrier, and barbed wire became thoroughly entangled in one another. I believe Colonel Hart

---

18    Colonel Merritt was the only U.S. Marine shot down by German aircraft during WWII.
19    BOQ: Bachelor Officers' Quarters.
20    The Bristol Blenheim was a British twin-engine light bomber aircraft.

21    "We were on the ocean by ourselves . . . ." This anecdote was not included in Schwable's Warfare Operations Report.
22    Britain's Universal Carrier, also known as the Bren Gun Carrier, was a light-tracked armored vehicle used for transporting personnel and equipment, and was used as a machine-gun platform.

has covered this subject in a written report.

At the combined Training Center, a limited number of army tank units are being given considerable training in the new method of embarking and disembarking on beaches from TLCs (Tank Landing Carriers). Practically all such training up to the time of my visit had been conducted around Inverary and Toward Castle, near Dunoon, where the beaches are steep and the TLCs could approach almost up to dry land. It was planned to establish facilities in the near future at some locality where a long gentle-sloping beach could be found, thereby introducing entirely different problems for all type of landing practices.

While in Scotland, I also visited No. 32 Army Cooperation Wing which is organized to give close support to the Scottish Command troops. The chain of command for this unit is very similar to that used in the Middle East with a similar Army Air Support Control attached directly to Army Command. This unit, which was responsible for both tactical reconnaissance and for local bombing missions, felt that the bombing should be done by other RAF squadrons in that the reconnaissance required a high state of specialized training with the ground forces, but the bombing could be carried out by almost any bombing squadron as was done in Libya. This procedure would permit withholding both aircraft and pilots for the type of duty in which they were most highly trained and specialized. On the other hand, by having the bombing squadron assigned directly to the Army Command, the undesirable time lag existing in Libya between the time the bombers were requested and the time they appeared over the target was appreciably reduced.

As a matter of demonstration, one of the photographic planes took a picture of the field as it passed overhead, and about five minutes after the plane landed and stopped at the parking area, the finished photograph was placed in our hands, the developing and printing having been done in their mobile photographic lorry.

I noticed that in arming one of the Blenheim squadron attached to this Wing, the method of hoisting the 250 lb. bombs into their racks consisted of two men lifting the bomb onto a third man's back, the latter then straightened up, shoving the bomb into the rack — a bit crude but, as they said, it was the quickest method of handling a bomb that size.

*Major Schwable[23] then traveled to London, and upon his arrival at the U.S. Embassy he received a letter from the Division of Aviation with new instructions.*

> Look into the question of night fighters. In general, get all the information you can on the organization and operation of night fighting squadrons, paying particular attention to the operational routine, squadron training, gunnery and tactical doctrine. . . . We would also like to get your opinion on single-engine, single-seat operations vs. other types for Marine Corps operations.[24]

While in England, I was able to cover briefly day-and night-operational fighter squadrons, a night bomber squadron, operational training units for both day and night fighters, Coastal Command and Fighter Command Headquarters, a free gunners' school, and the fighter control systems. Most of my attention was devoted to radio-location devices or RDF,[25] operation room procedures and controlled interception methods. In fact, I spent three weeks at a controllers' school learning about these subjects.[26]

The subject [of night fighting] is a bit involved

---

23   Promoted to Major 1 January 1942.
24   HMQC, Division of Aviation letter AA-203 mj to Major F. H. Schwable, dated 31 January 1942.
25   A radio direction finder (RDF) is a device for finding direction, or bearing, to a radio source. RDF was used as a radio navigation system for aircraft.
26   Schwable does not elaborate in his report about his time spent at the fighter director school at Stanmore, but later described how "they rode around on tricycles with a hood around you so you couldn't see, and you had to do things by compass and by radio, just like you were flying. They would tell you how fast to go, and there was a metronome that ticked back and forth. If they said you were going 80 miles an hour, then you set this thing to 80 and pedaled to keep up with the pace of the metronome. It worked. That's the way they taught all of their fighter command people."

Royal Navy WRENs on their ice cream tricycles, guided by vectors transmitted through their headsets by student Fighter Direction Officers. (Trustees of the national Museum of the Royal Navy. Fleet Air Arm Museum; Yoevilton, England, Image #YEORNE03476/0001.)

Night Fighters - Squad 68

work, then it is turned over to station repair shop, if latter can not do it, civilian contractor is called in. Major overhaul at 240 - wings don't come off. Requires 5 to 6 weeks. Crew goes to overhaul with plane.

Wind screens require particular care in cleaning before night flight.

Tactics - Dawn + dusk patrols mentioned previously. Good night maybe six planes ordered up, two doing GCI intercepts, 2 on CHL intercepts and two on patrol line, all available for operational interception. Plane should be brought by GCI to within about 2 to 3 miles within 30° below and 20° to either side of target. AI operator must immediately close range in order to keep blip away from ground return. Must give slight changes of course and then come back to bombers course to avoid starting large swing. Steady down on bombers speed with bomber dead ahead, then close at about 20 MPH. Must be very careful not to over shoot. Pilot normally makes visual from slightly underneath - also identification from exhausts best from below. Must duck quickly after firing to avoid bits of bomber.

Personnel C.O. has had 14 months at it and still quite fit. He + other pilots insist you have to want to be night fighter. It is no more strain than day fighting, though routine more monotonous because of regularity of flights and lack of huns.

Secret operational details about Britain's night fighter program were omitted from Schwable's *Warfare Operations Report A 16-3.* They were instead recorded within the pages of his personal notebook. *Author's collection.*

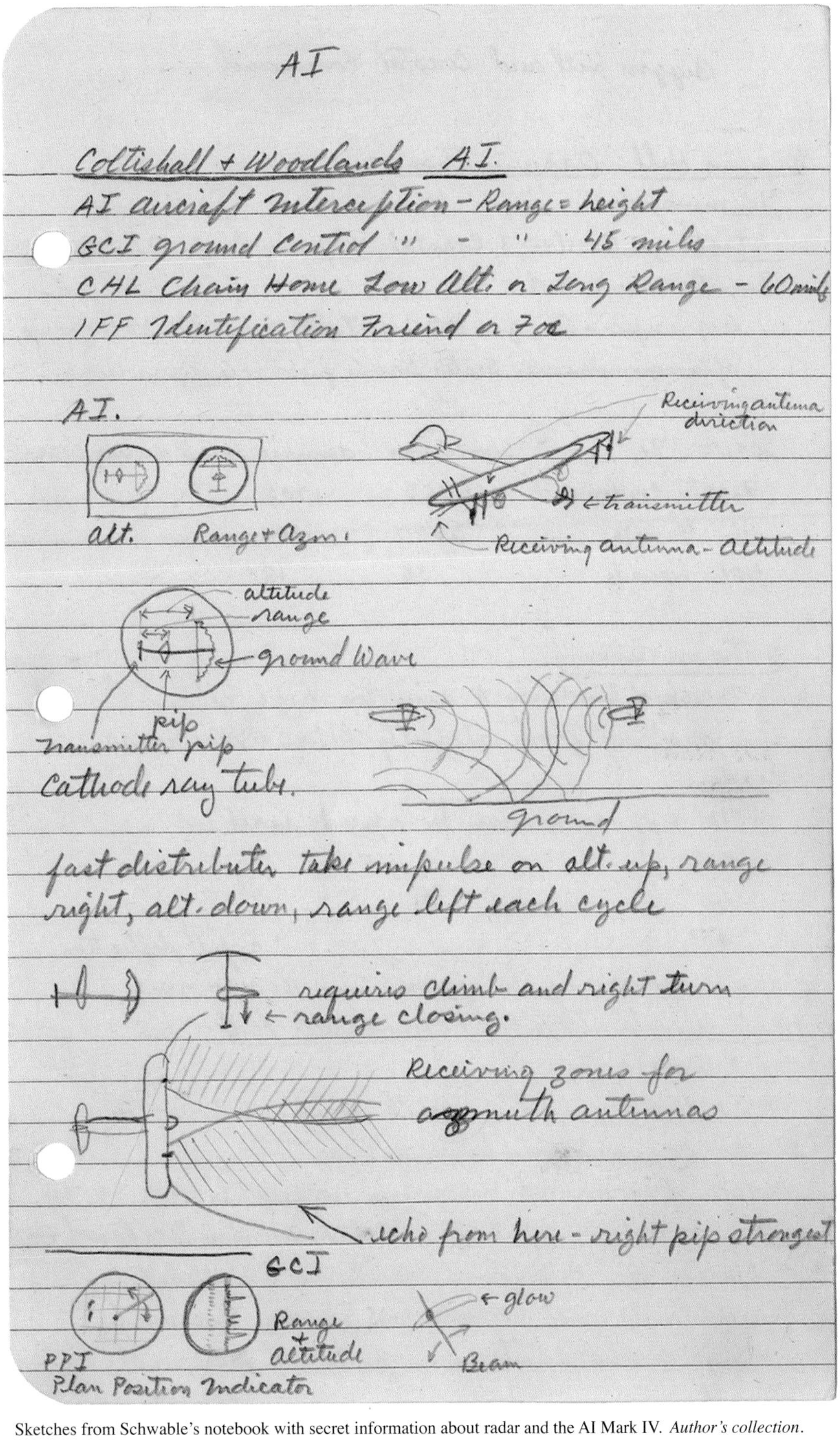

*AI*

Coltishall + Woodlands  A.I.
AI aircraft Interception - Range = height
GCI ground Control  "  -  "  45 miles
CHL Chain Home Low Alt. or Long Range - 60 miles
IFF Identification Friend or Foe

A.I.

alt.    Range + Azm.

Receiving antenna direction
← transmitter
Receiving antenna - Altitude

altitude
range
ground wave
transmitter pip
pip
Cathode ray tube.

ground

fast distributer take impulse on alt. up, range
right, alt. down, range left each cycle

requires climb and right turn
← range closing.

Receiving zones for
azimuth antennas

echo from here - right pip strongest

GCI

PPI
Plan Position Indicator
Range + altitude
← glow
Beam

Sketches from Schwable's notebook with secret information about radar and the AI Mark IV. *Author's collection.*

to cover at this time but, briefly, the defense of England against aerial attack is based on radio devices which emit impulses that are reflected back to the transmitting stations by aircraft, and their objects, thereby giving an indication of the range, bearing and a fair indication of the height of the aircraft. All such data are plotted on large sector, group and Fighter Command operation room plotting boards. This information is supplemented by Observer Corps reports and direction finder plots, when available. Fighter squadrons are then dispatched to intercept the plotted raids. The fighters are coached into the correct position by the controller until a "tally ho" or visual contact is made, at which time the squadron commander takes charge and attacks the raid. The procedure at night is somewhat the same for single night fighters, except they are equipped with specialized radio devices that give them further indications of the enemy's location.[27] I am purposely being somewhat vague about the details of this equipment because some of it is still classified as secret, and also because it is a bit involved.

There are, of course, other systems for dealing with night raiders. There is the new Turbinlite[28] system whereby a night interception aircraft of the twin-engine type makes contact with the enemy through the normal ground control means and then exposes a very brilliant searchlight in its nose, illuminating the target which is then attacked by two or more normal day fighters that have been flying formation with the control plane. The advantages of this system are: the control plane can proceed from one interception to the next without having to land and rearm; the target is brilliantly illuminated, during aiming and firing; more than one aircraft can be used for the actual attack; recognition is simplified; and only the Turbinlite aircraft requires the specialized detection equipment, the fighters being normal day fighters. This system had not yet been tried out on the Germans, but had worked very well in practice excepting under heavy haze or smoke conditions in which case the light diffused by the haze blinded the attacking pilots. This system is still classed as secret.

Another method of combating night bombers is by means of the so-called searchlight boxes — areas of forty-five miles long by sixteen miles wide, with lights so spaced that an enemy aircraft within this area will always be within range of one or more searchlights. The normal day fighters then make a visual interception upon the illuminated enemy aircraft in accordance with mathematical schemes that have been worked out. A number of searchlight boxes are located next to one another to form belts across certain parts of England. Strange as it may seem, the searchlight batteries in the southeast of England have six Huns to their credit without a shot being fired. On six occasions very low flying German aircraft have suddenly been caught in the full beam of searchlights, head on, and have been so blinded by the light that they have momentarily lost control and have crashed. The searchlight and anti-aircraft battery units operate in very close cooperation with the RAF, both units having representatives in the RAF operations rooms to follow aircraft plots, both enemy and friendly, and it is by this means that anti-aircraft fire is controlled or searchlights exposed at just the right moment to give the RAF the maximum assistance.

The night fighters greatest difficulty is in recognition. The responsibility for shooting down a friendly aircraft rests entirely upon the night fighters shoulders regardless of the fact that he is coached into position by the ground controller who will have stated that the raid was either unidentified or definitively hostile. Various recognition devices have been tried but there is always the chance that these devices may have been damaged while the bomber was over enemy territory and that they are not operative. Often the night fighter has to forfeit his advantage of position and surprise to definitely

---

27    Schwable is referring to Britain's top secret AI Mark IV radar.

28    A 2,700-million candlepower searchlight, fitted in the nose of an aircraft drawing current from a large generator in the nose of the fuselage. The Turbinlite system was later tested extensively in combat conditions in England without a single successful enemy interception.

identify the target.

When identification has been established, however, if the night fighter can get into a good position, there is little question of the outcome if the fighter is a Beaufighter[29] because the four 20mm cannons and six 30-cal. machine guns simply blow the German to pieces. I took a practice flight in a Beaufighter during which all the guns were fired and I can assure you that firing that weight of metal is a terrific shock even to the firing aircraft. To counteract the night fighters responsibility for identification, he is relieved of all worry about navigation because he is told by the ground station what courses to fly, so the ground station can tell him how to get home. The controller can get an RDF position on him, a DF[30] bearing, or the pilot can find his way back by his own specialized direction devices.

Night Fighter Operational Training Units first train their pilots to fly at night by use of a special set of goggles equipped with several lenses of varying darkness to represent moonlight or black night conditions. These lenses will pass the light emitted by yellow sodium lights that are used to mark out the runways. By this means the pilot sees only as much as would be visible to him at night but the safety pilot has full daylight vision. Practice can thus be carried out both day and night.

All of the installations I visited in England used camouflage to a considerable extent. The camouflage in general was limited to painting all buildings dark green, brown and black wavy lines, no effort being made to reduce shadows or symmetrical outlines. Certain areas, like automobile parking spaces at some stations use chicken wire covering with bits of green cloth interwoven in it. Almost all airdromes had black, slightly irregular lines painted across them that, from the air, made them look as though they were fenced off into numerous small farmyards similar to the surrounding countryside. Several large factories that I saw from the air were camouflaged to look like many small adjacent houses. I saw one such factory from 2,000 feet in the air and I found that I had to fly by at least 1,000 feet to make certain that it was really one long building.

The RAF is spoken of as a united airforce [that] amounts to six separate and distinct commands: the Fighter Command, Bomber Command, Coastal Command, Army Cooperation Command, Flying Training Command, and Technical and Experimental Command. In addition there is the Fleet Air Arm under the Navy. Each command is responsible for an entirely separate mission, both on the offensive and defensive; their aircraft are entirely different; their division of England into administrative groups is entirely separate; there is very little interchange of personnel excepting between operating and training units; there is considerable rivalry between commands and a very definite difference in the order of priority between them for delivery and development of equipment. It is even carried to the unofficial, personal point where it is a Fighter Command pilot's privilege to wear the top button of his blouse unfastened and the Bomber Command pilots rate to undo his bottom blouse button. More or less as the result of the Battle of Britain, with the heavy requirements for fighters, the Fighter Command has been supreme with the Bombers a good second and Coastal Command a very poor third.

I visited an RAF fighter station the day after the German battleships *Scharnhorst*, *Gneisenau* and *Prinz Eugen* sailed through the Straits of Dover. I have never seen such a disgusted, demoralized group of British pilots before or since. It was my personal impression that this event, followed so closely by the fall of Singapore, was a great shock to England. They were definitely not complacent about those two events. At the same time everyone was talking about General MacArthur's successful resistance, expressing a general attitude of "If he can do it why can't we," and again, "If the Japanese can sink our *Prince of Wales* and *Repulse* so easily by air power, why couldn't we sink the German

29  Like the Bristol Blenheim, the Bristol Beaufighter was a twin-engine aircraft, but with better speed and firepower than its predecessor.
30  The act of measuring the direction of a radio source is known as radio direction finding, sometimes more simply referred to as direction finding (DF).

ships in the narrow 20 mile Straits of Dover with the whole RAF available, in spite of the adverse weather?"

The only item of aircraft equipment that I am going to mention at this time is the parachute Type K Dinghy with which all fighter pilots are furnished. It is small, compact, [and] acts as a parachute seat cushion. I was told by any number of fighter pilots who fly regularly over the Channel that it gave them a tremendously increased feeling of personal safety to know that, if they have to abandon their aircraft over the water, they will land with their little boat with them, not in the airplane. They said it was indispensable.

British pilots and gunners spend considerable time on aircraft recognition, especially in their schools. Every pilot's ready room in the operational squadrons is equipped with many aircraft models, the walls are plastered with aircraft silhouettes and the tables are covered with intelligence reports indicating enemy aircraft performance and design characteristics. They consider instantaneous recognition essential for fighter pilots. I saw several rather good synthetic trainers used in teaching recognition but I shall not take the time now to describe them. The training units also insisted on considerable cockpit drill to thoroughly familiarize pilots with the aircraft controls before they even get into an advanced type airplane. Alertness can also be tested by this means.

The women take a large hand in certain types of work in England. I was most impressed with the military snap, the quiet, calm, efficiency and especially the seriousness with which these women do their jobs, particularly the chauffeur and the many women who perform tedious plotting tasks for long hours in the Fighter Command operations rooms. They are almost indispensable in the Ops. rooms.

*Schwable's report went on to describe fighter sweeps over France and high altitude bombing with fighter escorts for another two pages before it concluded.*

Seeing all of these things gives one a much fuller appreciation and insight into the vastness, the difficulties and the organizational and material developments of these operations which now extend around the entire globe.

*—End of Report—*

Not included in Schwable's report were his observations as a passenger aboard an RAF night fighter based at Coltishall on the east coast of England. On a typical mission, the aircraft took off and climbed in darkness towards a prescribed altitude, loitering in long lazy circles "on station" while men on the ground searched the sky for German intruders with help from a British invention called GCI (Ground Control Interception) radar.

Introduced in January 1941, GCI radar had many features now recognized as modern innovations. It had an antenna that spun on its vertical axis, providing a 360° view of the sky around the station. This was a major advancement over earlier radars which could only detect aircraft in front of a fixed antenna.

Another identifying feature of GCI was the Plan Position Indicator. The PPI display was laid out as a polar diagram with the radar's rotating antenna represented at its center. The 360° circular display was ruled off in 10° increments, just like a compass. Range (the distance from the antenna to a target aircraft), was ruled in concentric circles separated by 10 miles.

As the antenna rotated, it sent out pulses which bounced off various targets. These returning signals, called echoes, were received by the antenna and appeared on the PPI display as blips of light.

When a bogey[31] was detected on the PPI, the GCI operator (called a controller) used radio voice communications to relay a series of directions, called vectors,[32] to the pilot.

---

31   Any unidentified aircraft. Bogey means "ghost" in old Scottish.
32   Vectors were measured in degrees clockwise from 0° north on a magnetic compass. Imagine the plane as a movable needle on a compass. If the pilot is

The controller's objective was to vector the night fighter into a position below, behind, and within two to three miles of the bogey, which was the range of the night fighter's onboard Airborne Interception Mark IV radar.[33]

Once the radar operator detected the bogey on the AI Mark IV, communications with ground control ceased and he took over the interception. The radar operator guided the pilot closer to the bogey, communicating to him by voice while tracking the bogey on his AI Mark IV radar displays called scopes. The pilot, meanwhile, tried to establish visual contact with the bogey, which might reveal itself as a silhouette against a starry sky, as a black shadow against clouds, or by light coming from the bogey's exhaust ports which could be viewed from below. When visual contact was made, and the bogey was identified as an enemy aircraft, the pilot moved the night fighter in for the kill.

It was a dangerous business. The night fighter crew was totally dependent upon ground control to guide them safely through darkness. Once contact was made with the enemy, they then stood a good chance of being shot down by the enemy's rear gunner despite their advantage of stealth and surprise. It took a very cool set of characters and many hours of training to produce controllers and crews with the specialized skills required for an effective night fighter team.

## The First Night Fighter Squadron
### A Chaotic Beginning

While Schwable was in England, the Marine Corps studied the situation in Europe. Air operations there indicated that as British day fighter

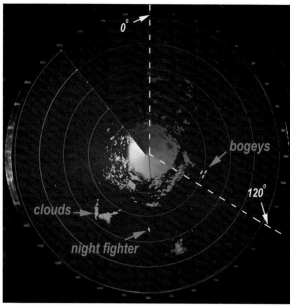

Above: A PPI scope is showing one friendly, and three bogeys. The bogeys are on a heading of 120° traveling south east. Heading is the direction the aircraft's nose is pointing, and is measured in degrees clockwise from 0° north on a magnetic compass. (Courtesy Christian Wolff.)

superiority was established, the Germans resorted to bombing at night. In order to meet a similar situation in the Pacific, on 28 March 1942, the Marines authorized the formation of eight night fighter squadrons, of 12 aircraft each, to be commissioned by 30 June 1945.[34]

Major Schwable returned to the United States in May 1942 and delivered to the Bureau of Aeronautics (BuAer) his 38-page *Warfare Operations Report A16-3*. What Schwable witnessed as an observer in England had turned him into a staunch advocate for the development of night fighters and, with BuAer's approval, he began building a night fighter program. Schwable recalled, "They more or less turned the night fighters over to me, saying, 'Here, you start it,' and left me alone. I was to organize the Marine night fighter program and Dyer always was behind everything. He pushed it and was a tremendous help."[35]

---

issued a vector of 120°, then he turns the nose of his aircraft until it is pointing at 120° on the compass, and flies in that direction (heading) until the controller issues him the next vector. The pilot's course is described by a series of vectors, in connect-the-dot fashion.

33  The night fighter was positioned below and behind the bogey because the pilot's view in front and above the cockpit was relatively unobstructed, whereas the nose of his own aircraft obstructed the view below when flying level, which, unlike day fighters, was how night fighters pursued their prey.

34  CNO letter OP-12F-dcr over (sc) A21-1 To All Bureau and Offices of the Navy Dept. dated 28 March 1942, Subj: 27,500 Plane Program.

35  Benis Frank, *Oral History Transcript, Brigadier General Frank H.*

With a sense of urgency, Lieutenant General Holcomb, the Commandant of the Marine Corps, moved the night fighter program forward, recommending on 12 June 1942 that one or more night fighter squadrons be established between January and June the following year.[36] The Chief of BuAer endorsed Holcomb's recommendation by approving the advanced commissioning of a single squadron.

BuAer's endorsement was largely the result of several conferences it had with Schwable and Dyer. It was evident from these conference, however, that the Navy was not yet fully committed to full-scale night fighter training. Until that happened, the Marines would have to form their own night fighter squadron and train them at their own facilities. It was also evident that finding a suitable aircraft would be problematic. The Navy was developing a night fighter version of the F4U-1 Corsair, but it would not be available until early 1943.[37] The Army's version of a night fighter, the XP-61,[38] was not expected to be ready until the summer of 1943. Schwable and Dyer would have to settle for what they could get — a twin-engine, low-altitude scouting plane called the Vega Ventura PV-1.

While Dyer fought bureaucratic battles over aircraft and personnel procurement at BuAer, Schwable worked on organizational matters. He approached the Director of Aviation and proposed that personnel and equipment be assembled beginning 1 October. This was approved. He then wrote the Table of Organization for the first Marine Corps night fighter squadron and sent out a barrage of requests to man and equip it.

By November, Lieutenant Colonel Schwable[39] had enough men and equipment to begin operations for night instrument training at the Corps' new air station at Cherry Point, North Carolina. "We started with nothing," he recalled. "In fact, we were the first combat squadron to move into one of the new hangars there. When I moved into the office there were three packing crates — one was my desk and another was my chair. We had to get all the squadron equipment including jeeps and trucks and, well, everything that an outfit needs because we started with nothing, absolutely nothing."[40]

Although Schwable was free to organize the procurement of equipment and devise tactics, he did not get to choose his own pilots. "I don't think anybody had more than 500 or 600 hours of flying time," said Schwable, "and here they were, put in twin-engine airplanes that they weren't used to flying, or flying at night which they weren't used to, really, I just had a bunch of kids."[41]

The only experienced pilot, besides himself, was his executive officer, Major John D. Harshberger. The two men would dedicate much of their time teaching new pilots how to fly on their instruments. Few were qualified to make even short cross-country flights, as exhibited by the number who became lost attempting to do so. Until the new pilots were taught the fundamentals of flying at night, their instruction in the complexities of radar-directed night fighting and gunnery would have to wait.

While all this was going on, the First Marine Division landed at Tulagi, Gavutu and Guadalcanal in the Solomon Islands on 7 August, marking the beginning of an island-hopping campaign designed to cut off Japan's major forward air and naval base at Rabaul on the Island of New Britain. Rabaul was the hub of Japanese air power in the South Pacific, and a stopping point for planes coming from Truk — home of the Japanese Combined Fleet in the south central Pacific. Until Rabaul was neutralized the Allies could not attack Truk from the south.

By October the Marines at Guadalcanal faced a steadily mounting Japanese counter-offensive. By day, the hard-pressed Marine aviators managed to

*Schwable* (History and Museums Division, U.S. Marine Corps, 1983), 97.
36  Major William Moore, USMC, *Under the Cover of Darkness: A History of the First Night Fighter Squadron of World War Two* (the Marine Corps Command and Staff College Education Center, Quantico, Virginia. May 1981), 6.
37  Loc. cit.
38  The first American combat aircraft designed specifically for night fighting.
39  Schwable was promoted to Lieutenant Colonel on 12 August 1942.

40  Benis Frank, *Oral History Transcript, Brigadier General Frank H. Schwable*, 97.
41  Ibid, 105-106.

provide sufficient air cover for the landing of reinforcements and supplies. By night, without naval support, there was little the Marines could do but watch as Japanese warships loaded with troops and supplies steamed unmolested into the area shrouded by darkness, landing troops and artillery on either side of the Marine perimeter.

Flying above it all was a solitary Japanese airplane dubbed "Louie the Louse," dropping flares off Lunga Point to aid the naval gunners shelling Marine positions.

During lulls in the fighting another aircraft dubbed "Washing Machine Charlie" dropped bombs on the exhausted Marines, robbing them of their much-needed sleep. The Marines tried to shoot down Charlie with anti-aircraft guns and even attempted a night combat sortie flown in an F4F-4,[42] guided by anti-aircraft searchlights, but neither approach yielded positive results.

All through October the Marines fought off heavy ground attacks. In November, with the arrival of additional aircraft, the daytime situation improved but the night situation remained unresolved, prompting Admiral Halsey to put out this urgent request:

> Current night nuisance raids over CACTUS[43] are lowering combat efficiency of our troops through the loss of sleep and increased exposure to malaria during the hours of darkness spent in foxholes and dugouts. Recommend that a minimum of six night fighting aircraft with homing radars and personnel now undergoing night fighter training plus ground equipment be dispatched CACTUS earliest time. Best available altitude determining interceptor radars with night fighter directing personnel should accompany.[44]

Halsey's dispatch was relayed to Headquarters by Brigadier General Ross E. Rowell, the Commanding General of the Marine Air Wings (Pacific), with the additional comment:

Above: The Ventura PV-1 was built by the Vega Aircraft Company division of Lockheed. In 1922 a new aircraft designation system was adopted. The "P" stood for patrol, to identify the basic purpose of the aircraft. The designation system recognized two classes of aircraft: airplanes were identified by the letter "V," and airships lighter-than-air were identified by "Z." The number one in PV-1 indicated that it was the first version of the aircraft. United States Library of Congress photo #fsa.8e01506.

> Refer COMSOPAC[45] 250449 request information states night fighter aircraft, equipment and personnel. Strongly request small unit be made available immediately for overseas duty. Advise.[46]

On 1 January 1943 the Marine Commandant sent the following reply to the commanders in the Pacific:

> Night fighting aircraft not now available. Other equipment procurable in limited quantities. One squadron under initial training but without suitable aircraft. Night fighter program being expedited but no date availability can be given.[47]

To Schwable the message was clear. Prepare your men the best you can, as fast as you can, and work out the details in the combat zone.

His personnel began arriving at Cherry Point in greater numbers, all housed in a new brick barracks that was heated by steam from an ancient locomo-

---

42   A Grumman F4-F Wildcat, a carrier-based single-engine fighter aircraft.
43   CACTUS was the code name for Guadalcanal.
44   Major William Moore, *Under the Cover of Darkness,* 7.

45   COMSOPAC: Commander South Pacific.
46   Lieutenant Colonel P. D., Lambrecht, USMC, *Employment of Night Fighter Aircraft* (Written for Amphibious Warfare School, Senior Course 1948), 11.
47   Loc. cit.

tive parked on a nearby railroad siding.[48]

While waiting for the squadron's PV-1 aircraft to arrive, Schwable and Harshberger trained their pilots with the only aircraft available — a pair of SNJ-4s[49] acquired from the Navy. The pilots practiced night landings using only runway lights, rather than the usual flood lights or wing landing lights — floodlit airfields in the combat zone would be an invitation to enemy bombing.

They practiced night attacks by following a blacked-out target plane. This was an important skill because the final identification and gun attacks against an enemy aircraft were done visually.

By the end of January more aircraft arrived. The six SB2A-4s[50] were part of a contract the Brewster Company signed with the Netherlands East Indies for 160 aircraft in 1942. They were purchased by the Navy from Brewster after the East Indies fell to the Japanese.[51] The SB2A-4s were immediately put to use training pilots in night instrument flying.

Unfortunately, the Brewsters had several shortcomings: they were restricted to airspeeds below 200 knots, had machine guns that wouldn't fire due to electrical shorts in the firing circuits, and were not outfitted with radar. Without radar, there was no way for night fighters and GCI controllers to practice airborne interception (AI). Exactly when the radar-equipped, combat-ready Ventura PV-1s would arrive was anyone's guess.

By February, two of six PV-1s ordered were delivered but not yet available for training purposes at Cherry Point. One was at the Naval Operational Training Unit at Quonset Point having VHF[52] radio, IFF,[53] and Airborne Interception SCR-540 radar installed, which was an exact copy of the British AI Mark IV. The other PV-1 was at the Aircraft Armament Unit at Norfolk, Virginia where six fixed .50-caliber machine guns were being fitted into the specially fabricated sheet metal nose alongside the radar antenna. Additional work that needed to be completed included the installation of oxygen equipment, the design and installation of flame dampers, and the testing of flash hiders[54] for the six .50-caliber nose guns.

Still hoping for a better aircraft, Schwable and Harshberger flew to Washington on 24 February to test-fly a British de Havilland Mosquito.[55] They thought it might provide an alternative to the less-than-desirable PV-1, which was slow and had a low 15,000-foot flight ceiling. The Mosquito was a twin-engine aircraft laid out so that the radar operator sat alongside the pilot for optimal communication between the two men. Schwable recalled "It was a beautiful airplane to fly and for my purposes it would have been excellent, but the Navy wouldn't buy any and so naturally we didn't get any."[56]

Even if aircraft availability had improved it was unlikely that much night AI training could have taken place. Their VHF radio and GCI SCR-588-A radar station at Cherry Point were finicky and operated only intermittently.

Another problem was that Schwable's rookie pilots were not yet qualified to solo in twin-engine Ventura PV-1s. Time was running out. Unless he began receiving pilots pre-qualified to fly the PV-1, he wouldn't have any pilots ready to receive advanced instruction in the specialized skills of night fighting before the squadron departed for the Solomon Islands. He later lamented the lack of progress in his report to the Division of Aviation at Marine Corps Headquarters.

In endeavoring to combine organizing and equipping a new combat unit with developing a new technique, conducting basic training, experimenting and testing new equipment and aircraft, this squadron has made only

---

48    First Sergeant James L. Sankey USMC, Interview with Colonel Charles Quilter I., dated 19 November 1943.
49    A single-engine trainer aircraft built by North American Aviation in 1936.
50    The Brewster SB2A Buccaneer was a single engine scout/bomber aircraft.
51    The date of Dutch capitulation was 8 March 1942.
52    Very High Frequency.
53    Identification Friend or Foe was an radio operated identification system that enabled ground control to determine the bearing and range of an aircraft fitted with a transmitting IFF radio device. Its name is a misnomer; IFF can only identify aircraft that carry a functioning IFF device.
54    Flash hiders (flash suppressors) hid the flash of light that appeared over the muzzle of a firing gun. Muzzle flash caused the operator to temporarily lose his night vision, making it difficult to see the target in darkness.
55    A British multi-role combat aircraft with a two-man crew.
56    Benis Frank, *Oral History Transcript, Brigadier General Frank H. Schwable*, 98.

mediocre progress in any one of the above considering the four months the squadron has been organized.[57]

Meanwhile the squadron's GCI SCR-527-A radar, which was a mobile version of their GCI SCR-588 ground station at Cherry Point, was going into production at the General Electric plant in Schenectady, New York. It was a copy of the original British GCI, but instead of having an antenna that was rotated by sweating airmen on a bicycle-driven contraption, its antenna was powered by electricity.

Production delays with the GCI SCR-527-A were just some of the headwinds Schwable faced, and the squadron's overall slow pace of progress was a disappointment to him. Headquarters, however, was encouraged, considering the obstacles encountered during such an unprecedented endeavor, and on 1 April 1943, Marine Night Fighter Group 53, known as MAG(N)-53,[58] was officially commissioned. It was responsible for the training of all future VMF(N) squadrons and Lieutenant Colonel Schwable was designated its commanding officer. Major John Harshberger took over command of VMF(N)-531,[59] the first squadron of MAG(N)-53. When VMF(N)-531 was sent into combat, Schwable would once again take over as its commanding officer.

On 16 April the first operating AI SCR-540 radar-equipped PV-1 became available for training. It would remain the only functioning radar-equipped PV-1 with which to train 15 pilots and 15 radar operators in AI techniques until late May. The following week Schwable reported improvements:

> With all [radar] equipment working much better lately, the project is reporting very good results. The new controllers are making very rapid progress and have taken over a large percentage of the work. Training of AI operators is also giving very promising results.[60]

An SCR-527-A GCI mobile radar installation in the Philippine Islands. VMF(N)-531 used this same set-up in the Solomon Islands, although it was dismantled and transported by water rather than on land due to the lack of roads. National Archives photo # 342-FH-3a30479-A60778AC.

On 15 May, in anticipation of the squadron's imminent deployment to the Solomon Islands, the radar section led by Lt. Colonel Bisson departed from Cherry Point by rail with a small group of maintenance men, four intercept controllers and their GCI radar. After arriving in California their instructions were to set up, operate and train with their equipment.

Schwable, meanwhile, mailed Dyer a seven-page memorandum on 28 May. He listed, item per item, the personnel and equipment problems that the air group was encountering. The work performed on their PV-1s at the Naval Aircraft Factory in Norfolk was found wanting. Guns seldom fired simultaneously and when they did the gun sights vibrated so violently that accurate shooting was impossible. Antennas were installed upside down, and the instrument panel cut-out-design prevented the pilot from reading his altimeter from 0 to 2,000 feet. Schwable concluded his memorandum with this pledge:

> If it is the desire of the Bureau to have this unit proceed to the combat zone in an airplane that is admittedly makeshift for the job, with guns that may or may not fire and with instruments that are difficult to read and

---

57  Commanding Officer, VMF(N)-531 letter 0006, A3/FHS-ees to Division of Aviation, HQMC dated 16 March 1943, subject: "General Summary of the Progress Made by VMF(N)-531 Since Commissioning."
58  MAG(N)-53: Marine Air Group (Night Fighter)-53.
59  V designates "fixed wing" (from the French *voloplane* — an aircraft sustained in the air by lifting surfaces as opposed to a hot air balloon or Zeppelin). M stands for Marine; F designates fighter aircraft;  N stands for night fighter.
60  Marine Night Fighter Squadron 531 Squad Log 16 November 1942 - 25 June 1943. Entry: 16 April. *Author's collection.*

radar that so far has an average of one out of three work-ing, this unit will plan accordingly, and accept without comment, the experimental installations furnished. [61]

On 8 June 1943, orders to depart for the Solo-mon Islands arrived. The following day the last of six combat ready PV-1s were delivered. By weeks end, the squadron's ground troops had boarded a train for California.

On the 28th Lt. Colonel Schwable was back in command of VMF(N)-531 as he and Harshberger each led a section of three PV-1s, taking off from Cherry Point and arriving at El Centro, California on 3 July.

For the next two weeks the PV-1s were flight-tested and checked while crews practiced AI with their GCI unit. Meanwhile, Schwable contemplated having the PV-1s repainted from black to their original colors. BuAer delivered the PV-1s in black paint like the night fighters in England, thinking that a black airplane would be harder to see at night. Schwable felt that might be true if the aircraft was only viewed looking down into a black water background, but when coming from above against a lighter sky, a light color would be best. He also noticed that under a hot California sun a black PV-1 quickly turned into an oven with harmful effects to the electronics.

The issue was decided when a flight of one regular and two black PV-1s flew over and he could not see the lighter one. Acting on his own authority, Schwable got the overhaul shop in San Diego to repaint their airplanes the standard color — light, almost white, underneath and dark blue on top.

The squadron's personnel and equipment departed from California for the South Pacific in separate groups. The ground section departed on 16 July aboard the USS President Polk.[62] The GCI section departed aboard the USS Hammondsport on 30 July.[63] Both groups were to be off-loaded at Espiritu Santo. The Flight Section had their PV-1s craned aboard the USS Long Island and set sail for Hawaii on 1 August, where upon their arrival the PV-1s would be unloaded and then flown to Espiritu Santo.

On their first day out to sea Schwable got his flight crews together and said, "Each one of you get a monkey wrench, a screwdriver and a hacksaw. Go through those airplanes and tear out everything we don't need and throw it over the side." He would later remark, "De-icers. Now, can you imagine go-ing to the Solomons with de-icers on your wings and all the machinery that goes with them? And navigation equipment — a big navigation table with lights with all kinds of heavy brass joints. We weren't going to use it, we didn't even have naviga-tors. I don't know how many thousands of pounds of weight we eliminated but the PVs climbed better because of it. While I never fought the Bureau of Aeronautics about that, it was one of the sug-gestions we made that just got passed over. The Bureau would say 'You can't take the deicers off; they are part of the airplane.' I figured — and for-tunately I was senior enough to get away with a lot of things — I figured what the hell, we don't need them. I can justify their non-use."[64]

While Schwable's men stripped the aircraft, he voiced concerns over the PV-1's slow speed and low flight ceiling to Dyer in a letter dated 2 August 1943.

It is only if the Japs are more stupid than anybody thinks they are, and come down to 15,000 feet, do we even stand a chance to knock them down — if we can go fast enough to catch them! If we lack speed, expert vectoring may put us in a position to do some good, but if the Japs fly thousands of feet higher than our planes can physically be pushed up to, there's not one damned thing on God's green earth we can do about it.

On 8 August the USS Long Island made port in Hawaii and Major Harshberger was there to wit-ness the unloading of the aircraft. "When we got

61  Commanding Officer MAG(N)-53 Memorandum to Lieutenant Colonel E. C. Dyer, USMC, Division of Aviation, Headquarters Marine Corps, dated 28 May 1943, Subject: Comments RE — Night Fighter Program.
62  4 officers and 147 men.
63  6 officers and 26 men, along with equipment and supplies.
64  Benis Frank, Oral History Transcript, Brigadier General Frank H. Schwable, 109.

to Hawaii, they docked us at a little dock that was just about wide enough to fit a PV on lengthwise. They had a caterpillar tread crane that grunted and groaned and finally picked up the first PV, swung-it over the side and started to lower it, missing everything by a matter of feet. When they got down near the ground they found that they couldn't lower it all the way because of it hitting the cab of the crane, so at that point they lowered the boom a little. The PV tipped the caterpillar crane up on one tread, bounced up on the railing around the dock, and nearly went over the side. It took us six hours to unload six planes by that system."[65]

From Hawaii the flight west went smoothly, despite the fact that the over-water navigators temporarily attached to the flight section had only recently graduated from navigational school. The first leg of the trip took them to Johnson Island, a speck of land 800 miles southwest of Hawaii. Not wanting to take any more chances than necessary, Schwable had the six PV-1s spread out on a line as far as possible, hoping it would increase their chances of spotting the tiny island. They made landfall right on course, to everyone's relief. After a few more stops they arrived at Espiritu Santo on 25 August, the day after the GCI section had been off-loaded.

Unfortunately, the *President Polk* disembarked the ground section at Noumea on 3 August, where they remained stranded for nearly two months. Not until 10 October would VMF(N)-531 be together again as a complete unit.

During the interim, on 11 September five of six PV-1s flew from Espiritu Santo to their new base on Banika, the second largest of the Russell Islands.[66] On Banika the flight section flew familiarization flights by day and, in the absence of their own GCI

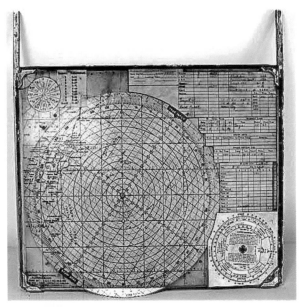

The A-type oscilliscope (left) was used on radar sets like the Signal Corps Radio Model 270 (SCR-270). Readings from the oscilliscope were interpreted by a technician while another man marked the readings with a grease pencil on a summary plot (above) from which the controller would issue vectors. The plot shown above was carried by daylight fighter pilots to mark down vectors. FDOs sometimes used this type of summary plot in the early days of the war.

unit, attempted to cover the Russells by night using Banika's SCR-270 radar outfitted with an oscilloscope and plotting table. As expected, the exercise proved to be a waste of time.

Non-GCI radar like the SCR-270 served well in the Solomons as an early warning radar and for directing day fighters, but was useless for directing night fighters. Radars like the SCR-270 had a rotating antenna, but lacked a PPI. In its place was an A-type oscilloscope which required two operators — one to interpret the image and another to track the results with plots marked with a grease pencil on a plotting table. Interpreting the image on an oscilloscope was more art than science, and time delays in plots and plotting errors were not uncommon. Day fighters could manage such shortcomings, compensating for plotting errors and delays visually as they approached their targets.

---

65  Lt. Colonel John, D. Harshberger, USMC. "The First Marine Night Fighter and GCI Activities." Interview by the Air Intelligence Group, DNI, 7 July 1944. (On file at Quantico Marine Corps Aviation Museum). This document, a brief firsthand account of VMF(N)-531's activities in the South Pacific, could not be found when the author inquired, and appears to have been lost when papers were moved from the Aviation Museum to a new location around the year 2000. They are also referenced in Moore, *Under the Cover of Darkness*, 20.

66  The sixth PV-1 was slightly damaged in a collision with a coconut tree while taxing at Espiritu Santo. It would rejoin the group after repairs.

This system, however, could not provide the accurate, instantaneous and continuous flow of bogey information required for night fighting when pilots flew blind in darkness, and when a lag of thirty seconds could lose the interception.

The flight section also flew AI exercises under the direction of a New Zealand GCI unit at Guadalcanal using the call name "Kiwi Control." On 16 September Lt. Colonel Schwable and Lt. John Mason were practicing airborne interception with Kiwi Control when a condition red necessitated postponing the practice. Schwable radioed to Mason, suggesting they practice AI west of the Russells. Mason agreed and Kiwi Control gave Schwable a vector back to the Russells. Then all communications with Mason stopped. Schwable landed on Banika at 2020 and requested that searchlights be turned on but Mason never returned. After sixteen separate air searches neither wreckage nor crew was recovered.

On 5 October Schwable flew to Munda on the island of New Georgia for conferences with Navy and Army personnel, and then flew the squadron's first patrol from Munda airfield.[67]

On 10 October Schwable's GCI and flight unit finally arrived at the squadron's base on Banika. Four days later, the GCI unit departed by sea for Liapari Island at the southern tip of Vella Lavella. It was up an running by the 18th, but the site did not provide full coverage to the north toward Rabaul from where the threat would come, so Schwable requested and received authorization to have the unit moved again, this time to Pakoi Bay on Vella Lavella's northwest coast.

Although their GCI was on wheeled transports, roads in reasonably good shape on Vella Lavella were nonexistent and so, on 25 October, the GCI unit at Liapari was dismantled, packed up, loaded aboard two landing craft and transported five hours by sea to the uninhabited bay.

Setting up the GCI equipment was relatively easy. Calibrating it to make accurate altitude readings was not. Lt. Colonel Bisson, the squadron's senior radar specialist and officer-in-charge of the radar section, initially had difficulty calibrating GCI in the Solomons. The topography there differed greatly from that in England, which provided the basis for the majority of available technical literature.

According to this literature, an ideal GCI site was one free of heavy vegetation, having gentle sloping terrain on all azimuths for at least 1.5 miles with no masking hills. But in the Solomon Islands, except for grassy areas on Guadalcanal, the dense jungle canopy absorbed so much radar radiation that little usable range could be obtained through it. The only clear sites were on the beach but the British warned of the impossibility of calibration with water as a reflecting plane due to changing tides. If a night fighter was at a range of 50 miles, a one foot tide not accounted for would build a 5,000

U.S. Marine Corps map.

---

VMF(N)-531 staff and pilots on Banika, in the Russell Islands. Front row, left to right: Capt. Jack Plunkett, Lt. Col. John Harshberger, Col.Frank H. Schwable, Capt. Duane R. Jenkins. Second row, left to right: 1st Lt. Clifford Watson, Warrant Officer William Lane, 2nd Lt. Robert Carvell, 1st Lt. Frank Abegg. Third row, left to right: Lt. Thomas Finch, Capt. Robert Barry, Capt. Howard Cross, Capt. Harold Torgerson, Capt. Thomas Baker. Jenkins, Watson and Torgerson were killed in operational or combat missions. *Author's collection.*

foot altitude error and almost guarantee a missed interception.

Bisson conducted a number innovative experiments to adjust for the changing tide.[68] He arrived at a simple set of altitude corrections for tides based on 1° per foot of tide, and determined that a correction of 100 feet (in night fighter altitude) per mile (distance the night fighter was from the radar set) per foot of tide was required — a formula that was to be crayoned over the chart at the height/range tube[69] operator's position. It was a brilliant solution

68    Charles Quilter II, *A History of Marine Fighter Attack Squadron 531* (History and Museums Division Headquarters, U.S. Marine Corps, Washington D.C. June 1987), unpublished working draft, 32-33. *Author's collection.*

69    The height and range of an aircraft was not determined on the PPI. This was done separately on a height/range oscilloscope. The SCR-527-A antenna was divided into two sections, with the upper section having twice as many lobes as the lower. Although both sections would transmit, only the lower half received. When a pulse sent from the top half of the antenna struck an aircraft and returned to the antenna, a blip would appear on the scope. When a pulse from the bottom half of the antenna was sent and returned, a second blip appeared. By comparing the distance between the two blips, the altitude of the aircraft was determined.

to a complex problem and greatly streamlined the lengthy calibration process.

Within three days of their landing at Pakoi Bay, Bisson had the GCI radar up, running and directing night fighters. The site's call name was Moon Base, and it was an ideal location that provided excellent coverage of the approaches to Vella Lavella and part of the routes Allied ships would use for the planned 1 November landings at Bougainville. After two frustrating months it seemed as though the squadron would finally get to function as a trained team in an area well-populated with enemy aircraft.

Instead, Command assigned the flight section to almost exclusive assignments covering various Naval task units and groups[70] due to the long flight endurance of the PV-1. These missions would be controlled not by their own GCI team, but by ship-based controllers called Fighter Direction Officers (FDOs) who were not trained to direct night fighters.

Unlike GCI controllers who focused their attention on one single purpose — directing night fighter interceptions — FDOs acted more like air traffic controllers, juggling vast amounts of information about many types and number of aircraft, both friend and foe. They were managers of many assets and could not focus on any one aspect of the situation for fear of losing track of the big picture.

FDOs were trained to direct day fighters towards their targets with altitude advantage onto a collision course. When pilots were within four or five miles of their targets, they were expected to make visual contact with the enemy and adjust by eye for any irregularities in vectored course or speed.

At night, however, the picture changed. A night fighter was flying blind and needed to be continually coached, not just to an area, but to a pinpoint spot one-and-one-half to three miles from the bogey, and not onto a collision course, but at the proper speed into a position behind and slightly below the bogey. Daylight trained FDOs failed to understand that night fighter pilots required considerably more detailed bogey, course, speed and altitude information than their day fighter counterparts. Without this information a successful night interception was next to impossible.

A night fighter also needed to know that he would be brought home safely after each mission. FDOs sometimes failed to plot every change in course and, through inexperience, let the night fighter not only get out of radar range while being vectored around, but out of communication range as well. Night fighters sometimes ended their Task Force patrols 200 miles away, on black nights, usually out of sight of land and often with one or more thunderstorm areas between them and their base. Schwable described the squadron's poor results under the direction of FDOs in one of his report to the Commandant, Headquarters, U.S. Marine Corps.

> None of the FDOs in this area, with the exception of several Army controllers at the Guadalcanal GCI station, had ever controlled night fighters. They were not familiar with the special problems involved, had no training or experience in this work and had no appreciation of the necessity for complete, accurate, instantaneous and continuous flow of bogey information required for night interceptions.... Until the FDOs are schooled or given more than a helping suggestion or two over the air by pilots of this squadron, the problem of night interceptions over Task Units or shore bases without GCI and trained night fighter controllers will depend on too great a measure of luck.[71]

In his report Schwable recommended that night fighters operate under the control of their own GCI unit as the *only* means of hunting down Japanese aircraft, arguing that it was essential for night fighter pilots and controllers to know and trust one another, and be trained and operate together as a team. He also expressed the need for coordination between night fighters and ship/shore based anti-aircraft (AA) batteries. He wondered why AA would give way to day fighters, but not to night fighters who

---

70   A task unit was comprised of 3-5 ships; a task group 4-10 ships; a task force 2-5 task groups; and a fleet was comprised of several task forces.

71   Report of Marine Night Fighter Squadron 531 Operations in the South Pacific, 25 August - 25 November 1943. Schwable's report to the Commandant, Headquarters, U.S. Marine Corps (25 November 1943), 3.

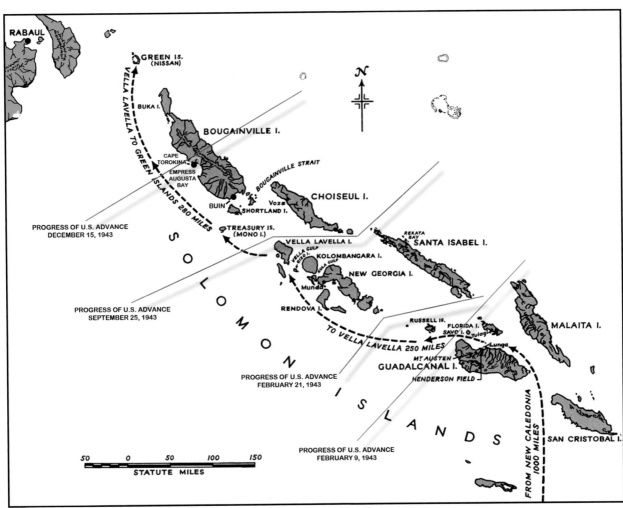

Island hopping in the Solomons. "The Perimeter" at Cape Torokina, Bougainville is marked in yellow.

were directed to stay outside of AA searchlight range or be fired upon.

> The procedure is then to watch the Jap drop bombs on or float lights around the ships, observe the anti-aircraft bursts with their wide variation in altitude and azimuth and then frantically endeavor to catch the bogey on his low altitude, high speed retirement after accomplishment of his mission.[72]

To top it all off, night fighters had to deal with AA from airfields as they returned to base.

Schwable recalled, "We had trouble for the first couple of months when we came in at night. The anti-aircraft people would shoot at us, small caliber stuff — .50-caliber machine guns, things like that. But that's not very comfortable when you're tired, it's late at night and your coming in for a landing and they're shooting at you. That was particularly so at Munda. But finally we were able to get the word out that there was such a thing as night fighters."[73]

---

72  Ibid, 7.

73  Benis Frank, *Oral History Transcript*, 114.

The above photograph of Corporal William Duffey (right) was taken on Vella Lavella, where the humid jungle plagued men with malaria, open sores, and rashes so often associated with jungle rot. In a letter written after the war Duffey described Vella Lavella as "a malaria infested hell." I interviewed Duffey's son, Walter, by telephone on 26 November 2014: "My father died in 1986. He did not talk much about the war. He did suffer from malaria, and I do remember him talking about the attack on Pearl Harbor. He was on top of Diamond Head on Sunday morning. I don't know why he was on Diamond Head or what he was doing up there. All I know is that my father said that from atop Diamond Head he watched the entire attack unfold. The ships were on fire. The surface of the water all around was covered with oil and was on fire. The boys on those ships were trapped — there was no place to go. After the attack he was assigned to a group responsible for collecting and identifying bodies. My dad said that he stacked them up like cord wood, there were so many." The 4th Defense Battalion was re-deployed from Hawaii to Espiritu Santo in March 1942. In July 1943 it was moved to New Zealand and then briefly to Guadalcanal before landing at Vella Lavella in August 1943 to support the 1 Marine Amphibious Corps (I MAC). Circumstantial evidence places Duffey's damaged helmet (opposite page) on Vella Lavella. Camouflaged helmet covers were not issued until mid-1943. Duffey was stationed on Vella Lavella from August 1943 until April 1944 when, suffering from malaria, he was sent back to San Francisco. Duffey spent the duration of the war stateside where he served as an instructor until his 3 October 1945 discharge. Photo provided by Walter Duffey.

## Operation Cherry Blossom

In late October the Allies set in motion Operation Cherry Blossom — the seizure of Bougainville. The attack began on 1 November when Task Force 39, composed of light cruisers and destroyers, shelled Japanese airfields on Buka Island to the north and the Shortlands to the south. This kept the enemy off balance while Task Force 31, carrying most of the 3rd Marine Division, entered Empress Augusta Bay to begin their amphibious assault.

Days before these operations took place, there were two other landings — one on the Treasury Islands, and the other at Choiseul.

On 26 October Schwable covered the landings at Mono and Stirling Islands, the largest of the Treasury Islands. The purpose of these invasions was to set up SCR-270 radar on Mono Island, and establish a staging area on Stirling for the assault on Bougainville. No bogeys were sighted under the direction of the destroyer-based FDO.

On 27 October Schwable covered the diversionary landing at Choiseul. The size and location of Choiseul would suggest to the Japanese that it was being taken to support an attack on the east rather than west coast of Bougainville. During the landing, Schwable was vectored toward a bogey which turned out to be a Black Cat.[74] A second bogey was detected but the FDO could not get good plots.

On 31 October at 1845, Captain Jenkins went on station over Task Force 39 as it traveled north along the southwest coast of Bougainville to shell Buka Island. A Task Force FDO with the call name "Trick Base" vectored Jenkins towards a bogey over Mono Island, but as Jenkins approached, he came under attack from anti-aircraft guns and quickly retired. The FDO was unaware that he had just vectored Jenkins over the island's recently-installed Allied anti-aircraft batteries.

The FDO then vectored Jenkins towards two new targets, ten miles away on a heading of 130°.

---

74    A Navy night fighter PBY-5A seaplane painted black.

Jenkins then saw two lights from an aircraft and gave chase. He followed the lights for five minutes but the chase led him too far from the Task Force and he was ordered back.

Next, the FDO mistakenly vectored Jenkins *in front* of one of two bogeys. Jenkins was told to orbit, and came around into a position beside and slightly above one of the bogeys. The turret gunner spotted the bogey but was unable to communicate this to Jenkins because of a design defect in the PV-1's interphone, which allowed FDO and interphone communications to be heard inside Jenkins' headphones simultaneously, rendering the overlapping voices unintelligible. Nor was he able to suppress his guns sufficiently to fire. Because of the night fighter's unfavorable position, Jenkins was unable to see the bogey, the AI operator could not find it on his scopes, and the bogey flew away unharmed.

The FDO then gave Jenkins a vector home that brought him over the Shortlands. There he was met with enemy anti-aircraft fire, but at an altitude of 6,000 feet he was out of range, and the shots landed short and trailing. He was later fired upon by friendly anti-aircraft batteries at the southern tip of Vella Lavella, and again north of Barakoma, before landing.

Captain Plunkett also covered Task Force 39. After arriving on station, he contacted the FDO who was operating under the call name "Dog Base." He saw a white flare and anti-aircraft presumably from the Treasury Islands at about 2240, but the FDO found nothing on his scope.

At 2315, Plunkett saw a light to starboard, 12 miles northwest of the tip of Vella Lavella. He turned toward the light but Moon Base told him there was another night fighter on it. He later saw a second light, and as he turned toward it he noticed flames coming out of his left engine cowling. Moon Base gave Plunkett a vector home and told him to hurry because a bogey[75] was following close behind. Plunkett put on full speed and crossed Vella Lavella

Above: The anti-aircraft guns of the 4th Defense Battalion were concentrated near Barakoma's harbor, shooting down 42 Japanese aircraft during 121 raids. Duffey's helmet was believed to have been damaged during one of these raids. Through Duffey's service records I learned that his hometown was Brownsville, Tennessee. A man at the Brownsville County Clerk's office remembered the family and directed me to Duffey's son, Walter, who I later interviewed. *Author's collection.*

Duffey's name is stenciled inside his helmet liner.

Above: Defense battalions used large anti-ship and anti-aircraft guns, searchlights, and small arms to defend coastal bases in the Pacific during the war. In the above photograph, mud-spattered men of the 4th Defense Battalion on Vella Lavella tend to their equipment after a Japanese raid. Duffey's helmet was likely damaged in one of these raids while hanging from equipment, as illustrated in this photograph. Schwable makes frequent reference to night fighters being mistakenly shot at as they made their approach to Barakoma airfield on Vella Lavella. It was the guns of the Marine 4th Defense Battalion that were doing the shooting. Eventually, communication with gun crews improved and the night fighters could make their approaches unmolested. National Archives photograph USMC 58419.

75   The bogey may have been a Japanese Gekko night fighter. Gekkos operated without AI and the pilots were selected for their excellent night vision.

## Operation Cherry Blossom and the Isolation of Rabaul

One of the most important Allied military strategies in the South Pacific was to cut off Japan's powerful air and naval base at Rabaul on the island of New Britain. The Solomon Island portion of this strategy began on 1 August 1942 with the capture of Tulagi and Guadalcanal. From there the Allies leapfrogged north, capturing the Russell Islands in February 1943, New Georgia and Vella Lavella in August, followed by raids on the Treasurys and Choiseul in October. Sitting to the north of these islands was Bougainville, the largest of the Solomon Islands and the key to neutralizing Rabaul. The plan for Bougainville was not to occupy the entire island, but instead to seize enough flat land on which three airfields could be built and surround them with a strong defensive perimeter. From these airfields would come the final air campaign against Rabaul.

The attack on Bougainville began on 1 November, when an American naval task force shelled and bombed Japanese airfields on Buka to the north of Bougainville, and Shortland Island to the south, keeping the enemy off balance while the 3rd Marine Division entered Empress Augusta Bay. Cape Torokina was selected as the landing site because the Japanese were not there in large numbers and thick jungle and mountain ranges to the east would prevent a major counterattack for months, by which time a robust defensive perimeter could be established.

Japan reacted by sending a force of cruisers and destroyers to attack the American troop and supply transports in Empress Augusta Bay. In the naval battle that followed, known as The Battle of Empress Augusta Bay, two Japanese ships were sunk and the others were forced to retire.

With the beachhead still vulnerable and with news of more heavy cruisers arriving in Rabaul, Admiral Halsey sent out a carrier task force with orders to damage as many warships there as possible. On 5 November, aircraft from Task Force 38, which included carriers *Saratoga* and *Princeton,* inflicted enough damage to convince the Japanese to withdraw their heavy cruisers. Halsey would later say that the threat posed by the cruiser force at Rabaul to his landings at Bougainville was "the most desperate emergency that confronted me in my entire term as ComSoPac."

During the night of 6-7 November, four Japanese destroyers eluded American warships and landed 475 troops northwest of the Marine beachhead at Cape Torokina. Captured documents indicated that the Japanese intended to put 3,000 men ashore in three echelons, the landing force of 475 being the first. Additional troops never arrived and their effort to retake the beachhead ended in defeat.

By mid-November the Marines had landed 34,000 men, established a small fighter airstrip near the bay at Cape Torokina, widened the beachhead perimeter inland through dense jungle, and had a bomber strip under construction, dubbed Piva Uncle. The perimeter was then expanded to acquire higher ground suitable for the building of an escort fighter strip, dubbed Piva Yoke.

25 November marked the naval Battle of Cape St. George where Allied

ships sank three Japanese vessels out of five filled with troops to reinforce Buka, at the northern tip of Bougainville. Meanwhile, the Marines pushed the perimeter inland along the Piva River, destroying the Japanese 23rd Infantry in the Battle of Piva Forks. This was the last major effort of ground resistance put up by the Japanese until March.

In mid-December, the U.S. Army's XIV Corps relieved the 3rd Marine Division on Bougainville. When all three airstrips in the Torokina Perimeter were operational, Marine Major General Ralph Mitchell, Commander of AirSols (Allied Air Units, Solomon Islands), moved his headquarters to Bougainville to direct the final air campaign against Rabaul. Within a month, Rabaul was rendered ineffective. By the time Nissan Island was captured in February, Rabaul was no longer capable of sending air power to interfere with Allied operations.

On 9 March 1944, a force of 15,000 Japanese troops led by General Haruyochi Hyakutake counter-attacked American positions. Known as The Battle for the Perimeter, Hyakutake's men made a three-sided assault against the American horseshoe-shaped perimeter surrounding the airfields. Hyakutake's men traversed a deep ravine towards Piva Yoke airfield and succeeded in penetrating the perimeter at one point, but the Americans sent in tanks and infantry to drive them back. The Japanese attempted twice more to penetrate the perimeter but were driven back both times. The final counter-attack came on the night of 23-24 March. After suffering heavy losses, Hyakutake's forces retreated deep into the interior and to the north and south ends of Bougainville.

Encouraged by reports from Halsey about his naval success in the Central South Pacific, General MacArthur moved up the invasion of the Philippines from January 1945 to October 1944. With the perimeter around the airfields at Cape Torokina secure and the sole objective for the Bougainville campaign complete, MacArthur withdrew Griswold's XIV Corps and replaced it with the Australian II Corps. Because the war was expected to continue until at least 1946, General Sir Thomas Blamey, commander of the Australian Army, chose to take a much more aggressive approach on the ground with the aim of freeing up Australian manpower for future operations. After Japan surrendered, he was criticized because the costly engagements had little if any affect on the outcome of the war.

For the Japanese, the Bougainville campaign was one of deprivation, desperation and defeat. In the most extreme instances, men resorted to cannibalism. Of the 65,000 Japanese troops stationed on Bougainville when the Marines arrived, only 23,800 remained when combat operations ended on 15 August 1945.

Above: A Japanese helmet found recently near Buin, south of the Hongorai River at the southern tip of Bougainville. *Author's collection.*

over Barakoma, losing the bogey before landing at Munda airfield on New Georgia Island.

After Plunkett landed, an F4U went off the runway on takeoff and struck his PV-1 broadside behind the wing, splitting the night fighter in two. Fortunately, Plunkett had left the aircraft before the incident. Salvage value was for spare parts only.

After midnight, Schwable covered Task Force 31 into Empress Augusta Bay where the Bougainville landing took place. He was vectored by a Task Force FDO within a few miles of two bogeys, but with negative results. He then circled at 10,000 feet and watched as twelve transports and escorts approach Torokina Point and shelled the shore, lighting up the darkness below. He departed at 0710 when day fighters arrived, just as the last boats of the assault wave were clearing the ships.

Ironically, while VMF(N)-531 Marine night fighters Jenkins, Plunkett and Schwable spent hopeless hours chasing bogeys under the direction of inadequately trained FDOs, Major Hicks, their own fully-trained GCI controller at Moon Base directed one of their rivals, an F4U-2 from Navy Night Fighter Squadron VF(N)-75 (commissioned six months after VMF(N)-531 and flying out of Munda since September), into the first night fighter victory of the Pacific War. It was a textbook interception. Had Schwable's Marine night fighters been allowed to operate using their own controllers from the beginning, they undoubtedly would have been the first to score.

The Japanese wasted no time reacting to the Bougainville landing. On 2 November they sent a powerful naval force from Rabaul to disrupt the assault operation underway. Waiting for the Japanese at the entrance of Empress Augusta Bay were light cruisers *Montpelier*, *Cleveland*, *Columbia* and *Denver* from Task Force 39. They were almost invisible under the dim moonlight. Only the occasional burst of heat lightning silhouetted their shapes that otherwise remained hidden in darkness.

At 0230, the light cruisers made radar contact with the enemy ships and a spirited sea battle began.

Captain Jack Plunkett's PV-1, cut in half after landing at Munda airfield, New Georgia Island. Note the red arrows pointing to the lower wing AI antenna. National Archives Photo # 80-G-208557.

Circling high overhead was Lt. Colonel Schwable, watching as hundreds of flashes from naval gunfire lit up the sea below. Only after landing at Barakoma airfield did he learn that Japanese ships under the command of Admiral Sentaro Omori had been forced to withdraw.

For the next eleven nights the squadron covered Cherry Blossom task ships under the direction of their FDOs, and controllers at the SCR-270 radar installation that went ashore on the first day of the landing. In 29 combat night patrols they were directed against 29 bogeys, including a flight of ten torpedo planes. There were three AI contacts — two impossible head-ons and one distant visual, none of which led to successful interceptions.

## The Squadron's First Victory

Captain Duane Jenkins scored the squadron's first victory in the early morning hours of 13 November. He was covering Task Force 39 when it came under attack by Japanese G4M1 "Betty" torpedo bombers. The Task Force was west of the Treasury Islands covering the forward movement of Task Group 31.5 as it steamed towards Empress Augusta Bay to support the landing there. Leading the attack was Sergeant Major Seiji Sekine. His firsthand account[76] begins at midnight, 11 November.

### *Seiji Sekine*

My mind and body were worn out from the previous night's mission. As I went to bed after midnight, the sensations of being battered by enemy gunfire were still with me. I was deep asleep when I heard, *Raigeki-tai, prepare! Raigeki-tai, prepare!*[77] I shook my head two or three times, trying to wake up, wondering if I was still dreaming. The sun was already high in the sky as I jumped up and rushed to the command post and said, "Let me fly with the Raigeki-tai today!"

The commander of the mission, Major Genzo Nakamura, would fly with Second Lieutenant Maruyama and myself, as I was the most experienced pilot from the 702nd Air Corps. We would lead a formation of six torpedo bombers into battle.

The pilots from last night's attack gathered to review the events from yesterday. We also heard from our scout aircraft. It had been up searching since well before dawn, trying to locate the aircraft carrier that we were unable to attack yesterday. He radioed that the ships were spotted near Mono Island, the largest of the Treasury Islands. In fact, the scout reported that he had seen two groups of ships — an aircraft carrier group and a separate group of battleships.

Preparations to begin our mission went quickly. It was impressive to see everyone working together so diligently on our behalf. After the meeting I rushed to my favorite airplane — the No. 321. It was all set to go. "The torpedo test drop went well," said one of the mechanics. Even so, I felt a little uneasy not being able to execute the test myself.

I finished my checklist just as a wall of black clouds approached from the west. Huge drops of

rain began to fall and soon the rain came pouring down. I covered my plane just in time and ran back to the pilot shelter.

We tried to stay dry but the roof on the shelter was full of holes from the B-24 attack that we had a few days earlier. The shed was packed full of an elite group of pilots from one of our aircraft carriers. They were fighting with us here in Rabaul ever since they had lost half of their planes ten days ago in hard fighting. I was happy to see that among the survivors was Mizukoshi. He was a classmate of mine.

Air Sergeant Major Fujimoto was busy with calculations and wrote enemy positions on an aerial chart as he prepared our strategy. Air Sergeant Major Kida, his co-pilot, sat beside him sleeping. "Sleep well," I thought. "Dream of visiting your mother because tonight is an important mission and you may never see her again."

At 1400, after an hour's delay, the heavy rains let up, the sky cleared and black storm clouds began their journey east toward tonight's battlefield. The planes and pilots from the aircraft carrier were the first to go, splashing through the muddy runway as they took off on a heading north toward Truk.

Then there was a strange order — *Attack group, line up!* Our faces were tense as we lined up together and then saluted Commander Kuno who said, "The first attack target is the aircraft carrier and the second is the sea convoy. The third attack target is the battleships. Mission Commander Nakamura and Air Sergeant Major Sekine will fly lead. Two Gekkos[78] will provide radar disturbance." Commander Kuno then ordered, "Take off immediately."

We all knew that the enemy ships would be

---

76   Seiji Sekine, *Hono-o No Tsubasa* (Konnichi-no-Wadaisha, 1976), 264-277. This first- ever English translation was made for the author by Kazunori Tanoue.
77   Raigeki-tai: torpedo attack squad.

78   The Nakajima JINI *Gekko* (Moonlight) was the Imperial Navy's reconnaissance and night fighter aircraft. It was nicknamed "Irving" by the Allies. Gekkos were used in local air defense at Rabaul, using searchlights without AI or ground control radar. In May-June 1943, a Gekko pilot Aviation Chief Petty Officer Shigetoshi Kudo, flying out of Lakunai Airfield near Rabaul, became the first night fighter ace of the Pacific War on either side, shooting down six B17s as confirmed by USAAF records. Gekkos also flew with bomber attack groups, providing interference on Allied radar by dispensing metal foil strips cut to the wavelengths of allied radar. The metal strips, known as "window," flutter down and reflect a disproportionately large signal that can flood radar scopes with return signals, obscuring real targets. Window was first used by the British against the Germans on 24 July 1943.

protected during the daylight hours by an umbrella of fighter planes. The elite pilots from the aircraft carrier had tried once before to break through this umbrella and were eaten alive. Our six torpedo-laden IchiShiki-Rikujo Type One attack bombers would lumber through the sky defenseless, unable to maneuver with such a heavy load. We would never arrive at our target without a fighter escort and I paled at the thought of a wasted death. In support of our formation, we had two Gekkos that could provide radar interference, which is useless in daylight but very useful at night. If we delayed our attack time and waited until evening, then we could take advantage of the darkness and our radar jamming capability. Perhaps Commander Nakamura was thinking the same thought. I was soon convinced this was the commander's intentions and my spirits lifted.

When the test run of all the airplanes was finished, we boarded and taxied into position. I took off my flight cap, put on my *hachimaki*[79] and saluted in the direction of the command post. Both engines made a roaring noise as I started my take-off. Dozens of men were lined up on both sides of the runway, waving their caps and swinging back and forth a large flag of the Rising Sun as I made my take-off. It was a great sight to behold.

We finished making the formation and turned the nose of our planes to a point south, far from the enemy fleet. Although the sun was low in the sky, it was still too early to attack. We would bide our time until the enemy's umbrella of fighters returned to their base for the evening.

Cumulonimbus clouds were gathering in the wide bay region to the south. I was relieved to see them because of the cover they would provide. Unfortunately, the sky cleared about an hour later. The sun was now setting but it was still too early to attack. We flew south, far away from the enemy.

When the sun set and we were sure that the

Ground crew preparing a Mitsubishi G4M1 "Betty" for action. Seiji Sekine flew with the 702 *Kokutai* (air group) based at Vanakanau, Rabaul.

enemy planes covering the ships had returned to their base, we started north toward the battlefield. All of our planes were flown by combat veterans and everyone was anticipating action.

When we approached the southern-most area where we expected to rendezvous with the enemy ships, they were nowhere to be seen. What had happened? Did we miscalculate the enemy position? Was there a navigational error? Even if there was an error, the enemy has a large presence, three groups in all. I went to the east for a while, waiting for the ships to appear. I thought if I went ten more minutes east I should be able to see the enemy.

I was becoming anxious over our situation — it was my responsibility to locate the enemy ships. Earlier I worried about arriving at our target too soon. Now I worried we would run out of time before finding it! Wondering if I had made a navigational error, I said, "Commander, I am sorry. I will go north to Bougainville Island and check our position. Then I will approach the target again." "That will do," replied the commander.

Darkness fell as we moved north. The evening mist was hanging over the water and visibility was getting worse. After flying north for 40 minutes I spotted Mt. Bagana rising from the center of Bougainville Island. I checked our position. There was

---

79  *Hachimaki* is a stylized headband, similar to a bandana. It was usually made of red or white cloth, decorated with inspirational slogans, and worn as a symbol of perseverance or courage by the wearer and as a charm against evil spirits.

an error of approximately 30 nautical miles made during our two-hour flight. When I discovered my error I couldn't believe it. I panicked inside and felt like I would lose my composure. I reported to the commander who was sitting next to me, "Commander, our position has been determined. I will fly on course from here on." The Commander, who was a kind man replied, "You do not need to rush. We will go after the enemy at Torokina."

I led the nose of the airplane to Empress Augusta Bay which was covered in evening mist. Although the enemy was deep in the bay with two or three searchlights shining, there was no shooting from their ships. "It seems that there were few enemy transport ships inside the bay," I said. "Well, then, we will go south towards the enemy fleet," said the Commander.

I turned southwest and then looked back to check our formation which was illuminated by the pale moonlight. After ten minutes I turned south, feeling both anxious and confident at the same time. Then I felt relieved when I saw a tiny black spot in the distance. It was the group of cruisers we had seen the previous night. I grinned and said, "I found the enemy. Let's pass through right above them and scout carefully, then go further to the south and look for an aircraft carrier." Major Nakamura replied in a calm voice, "So you found them at last. Let's do as you suggest." Both Petty Officers Ogasawara and Minamiyashiki wore perfect smiles. Only Air Chief Hamada, the co-pilot, was fearful; he was shaking all over.

As we continued south past the outermost destroyers of the enemy's ring-shaped formation. I wondered to myself why I was no longer receiving reports from the other aircraft. Just then the central enemy cruiser fired its guns. Two shots drew a red arc in the night sky and then fell into the south sea. I leaned over as I followed the salvos. I thought to myself, "Was it shooting at our fleet? No, we have no fleet here. Maybe one of our two Gekkos was the target."

We flew south a little more but could not see any sign of an enemy aircraft carrier. A rain cloud was hanging to the west. I said, "Let's attack the cruisers." Commander Nakamura who was searching in all directions nodded, "Let's circle left, skirt around the enemy's back and attack from the north."

After I transmitted the attack order I turned around to see if the other planes were following. "Ahhh!!" I shouted. No one was there! Without my knowledge, the others had already thrown away their extra fuel and had gone in to attack, splitting off into two groups. I hadn't noticed any of this because we were flying in the lead position. When the men at the back of our plane learned that we were the only plane not yet attacking they stomped their feet and roared, "Sekine, you fool!"

\*    \*    \*

United States Naval Task Force 39 was 50 miles southwest of Treasury Islands, covering the forward movement of Task Group 31.5 as it steamed toward Empress Augusta Bay. The Task Force had been followed by a snooper[80] for quite some time. The snooper had been on the job before. It remained out of gun range but within the ten-mile circle which by force doctrine a night fighter could not cross without being fired upon. At sunset, in anticipation of a night air attack, the ships aligned themselves in special formation Jig Three.

Exasperated by the persistent snooper, the Task Force Commander gave the FDO unit aboard USS *Columbia* permission to direct a night fighter inside the ten-mile circle.

Captain Jenkins, circling on station over Task Force 39, was vectored from a position northeast of the Task Force to one south in order to start the interception of the bogey, which was 23 miles away. After the vector had been given, a larger group of bogeys was picked up at 0300 on the FDO's PPI scope on a course of 140°, speed 160 knots at an elevation of 6,000 feet. The group was visually picked up as well by Jenkin's turret gunner,

---

80  A snooper was a Japanese surveillance airplane. In this case it was a Nakajima JINI Gekko.

Above: Air Sergeant Major Seiji Sekine flying his favorite — the No. 321 Mitsubishi G4M1 Type One attack bomber. The "Betty," as it was known to the Allies, was envisioned by the Imperial Navy in 1937 as a new long-range bomber with a maximum speed of 247 mph, a range of 2993 miles, a 1764-pound payload and crew of nine. Such requirements were very difficult to achieve. By comparison, Germany's Henkle He11B carried twice the bomb payload but for only 565 miles. Kiro Honjo, who led the Mitsubishi design team, concluded that a four-engine design was the only way to meet the Navy's requirements. Before the first planning conference between Mitsubishi and the Navy, Honjo sketched his design on a chalkboard. Upon entering the room and seeing the sketch, Rear Admiral Misao Wada was enraged; "The Navy will decide matters of operational need! Mitsubishi should just keep quiet and build a twin-engined attack aeroplane in accordance with navy specifications. Erase the drawing of the four-engined aeroplane on the blackboard at once!" Honjo did as he was told. But where to put 1294 gallons of fuel into a twin-engine bomber? His solution was to use integral fuel tanks, with the sealed inner surface of the wing's outer skin serving as the upper and lower walls of the fuel cells. Honjo explained to the Navy that his design would deliver the range they demanded, but the lack of conventional fuel tanks, fully internalized within the airframe, would make the G4M1 extremely vulnerable to enemy fire. Consequently, the G4M1 tended to explode or catch on fire in battle and was nicknamed the Flying Hamaki ("Flying Cigar"). To Allied pilots the Betty was also known as "The one shot lighter." If, however, it did not catch fire after being hit in the wings, G4M1s were quite capable of remaining airborne despite being badly damaged. Osamu Tagaya, *Mitsubishi Type I Rikko "Betty" Units of World War 2* (Osprey Publishing, 2001), 8.

who saw a group of six in the moonlight far off to starboard. Jenkin's vectored course intersected that of the larger group of bogeys, which were the better target, so he was maneuvered against them instead of the snooper. Undaunted by the odds against him, Jenkins pursued the group as they traveled south.

Within minutes, at a distance of 30 miles from *Columbia*, all planes disappeared from the screen. Captain Jenkins was vectored back towards the Task Force formation and, almost simultaneously with his reappearance on the FDO's PPI, five bogeys reappeared close aboard[81] at one o'clock, three miles distant. Jenkins was vectored 270° on their tail; later, at 300°, the blips merged on the FDO's PPI scope. The fighter was vectored 270° to sepa-

rate the blips and was told the bogeys were to his starboard.

At 0400, the tension increased between the FDO aboard *Columbia*, call name "Horse Base," and Jenkins, call name "Crystal 51."

Horse Base: Bogey still two miles on port bow.
Crystal 51: We'll fix that
Horse Base: Bogey one mile fine on starboard bow.

At a range of 4,000 feet a bogey appeared on the night fighter's AI scopes, going from right to left. A moment later the bogey came into sight and Jenkins recognized a Betty. Although the night fighter's radar operator had made AI contact, the FDO continued to call out intermittent instructions.

Crystal 51: Roger
Horse Base: Dead ahead.
Crystal 51: Roger.
Horse Base: Merge Plot, Merge Plot.

---

81   There is a discrepancy between Sekine's and *Columbia*'s account. Captain Jenkin's Action Report states that his turret saw six Bettys flying in formation heading south. In his story, Sekine said five of the six planes dropped their extra fuel, turned and attacked without his knowledge as he continued south in search of other targets. *Columbia*'s Action Report says that four, not five, aircraft reappeared on the PPI shortly after vanishing from the scope. It is likely that the bomber formation obstructed the view of the fifth Betty from the FDO's PPI. This detail may never be resolved with certainty.

Crystal 51: Roger.
Horse Base: Look down.
Crystal 51: Roger.
Horse Base: Still together.
Crystal 51: Roger.
Horse Base: Together.
Crystal 51: Owwff![82]

51 from Horse — Do you have a tally-ho?[83]

There was no response as lookouts aboard *Columbia* saw tracer fire high in the night sky followed by a small ball of flame which increased in size as it fell, comet-like. The plane struck the water and flames shot high into the air. The FDO, not knowing which plane had fallen, screwed up his nerve to ask the next question.

Horse Base: Hello Crystal 51, Hello Crystal 51, Are you alright? Are you alright? Over.
Crystal 51: Hell yes — we just got a Betty. Where are the rest of them?

Jenkins had just made the squadron's first kill, and it was the first successful interception by an FDO. The FDO then reported two more bogeys in the same area; as Jenkins was vectored he had a momentary AI contact, but the bogey was immediately lost.

At 0430 the *Columbia* fired two shots at one of the snoopers. The snooper retired. Then at 0433 the group of Bettys came to within 6,000 yards of the port side of the Task Force and several ships opened fire as they approached the outer ring of destroyers. The Bettys were difficult to detect at their low altitude and a visual sighting was made almost simultaneously with radar contact. The formation then withdrew without attacking.

At 0445 the Bettys were picked up again on the FDO's PPI, as was a solitary bogey — Sekine — flying north from the southwest, preparing to attack.

### Seiji Sekine

I turned the nose of the plane toward the center of the enemy ring formation. The altitude was 2,000 meters. Sergeant Ogasawara said, "Captain, let's attack the large one in the center." Minami-yashiki said incredulously, "That? That big one?" Then Jibiki came from the rear of the plane, shoved the others aside and said, "Captain, please attack the big one in the center." We all wanted a meeting of minds just before dying, and so a decision was made — the one in the center would be our target.

Going after the ship in the center of the ring-shaped formation [*Columbia*] meant that we were likely to be shot down by the enemy's heavy fire. I thought to myself, "Now we go!" I didn't care about the wall of fire we were heading into, "Go ahead and shoot me!"

I dove down to an altitude of 50 meters. As we approached a destroyer in the outside ring formation, a great pillar of fire rose with a roaring sound from the back side of a battle cruiser located behind a destroyer. I could see the ship now painted in red light from the explosion. "One of the others must have hit his target," I said. The destroyer moved to the left and approached the damaged warship. I could have reached out and touched its mast directly below and wondered why the enemy did not shoot. Then I saw a pillar of fire from the destroyer at my back! Then a glowing red projectile arched like water from a garden hose toward our plane from the battle cruiser to the front right! Then, our target cruiser fired its gun! I could not make sense of who shot what from then on as the enemy put up a heavy wall of fire.

We were flying at an altitude 20 meters, 5,000 meters from our target. The sea surface was full of bubbles from the impact of the torpedo that struck the cruiser. I had to get closer, to within 1,000

---

82    *Columbia*'s FDO wrote in his After Action Report: "'Owwff,' it appears, is a night fighter's abbreviated equivalent for 'Tally-ho, one Betty, eleven o'clock.'"
83    Tally-ho means that visual contact was made with the enemy aircraft. It is a British phrase that originated from the activity of hunting with hounds, shouted when the rider following the hounds sees the fox.

meters! Our altitude was now 10 meters. 3,000 meters ahead was the black silhouette of the target ship. "Azimuth angle of 90 degrees. Enemy speed is more than 20 knots. Ready." It was Second Lieutenant Maruyama's calm voice. I said, "Wait, wait, wait, 900 meters, wait, wait." At the moment of dropping the torpedo I had to be sure I was flying horizontally. Tilt to the right or left would make the torpedo rotate, causing an error. Second Lieutenant Maruyama, who was grasping the control lever, looked severe. I called out, "800. . . 750. . . Yes!" "Stopwatch started," said Maruyama.

The airplane floated gently upward once the heavy torpedo was released. The side of the enemy ship appeared like a high wall as we closed in. I caught a glimpse of the torpedoed cruiser [*Denver*] which was now beginning to list. As we flew above the target ship its massive tower-like bridge nearly clipped our left wing. There was an enormous array of guns — two gun turrets and another battery with three cannons directly under us. "Stopwatch stopped," said Maruyama. The enemy shots were like rain. Bang, Bang, Bang, Kaboom! The red light from their guns illuminated the inside of our plane. My mind was free of thoughts as my eyes filled with red, yellow and various colors from their guns. The noises were terrible. I watched to the right as my body naturally lurched to the left, away from the gunfire. Although I wanted to confirm the torpedo hit, we were now caught in crossfire of the enemy guns. I wanted to cry out — "Help me!"

\*     \*     \*

With the enemy threatening attack, the cruiser formation made an emergency turn. The ships had just changed course again when a group of three Japanese Bettys was seen coming in low out of a small rain squall. *Denver* opened fire with her 5-inch guns just as the Bettys launched their torpedoes. The planes were flying low and so it was necessary to check fire frequently to avoid hitting other ships. One Betty disintegrated with a direct hit. The other two turned east coming under con-

The rear gunner for a G4M1 Betty.

centrated automatic anti-aircraft fire from *Denver* and a nearby destroyer.

*Denver*'s Captain Briscoe ordered "Hard left rudder!" *Denver* swung fast as a fourth Betty approached from abeam, very low and close. The Betty dropped its torpedo at a range of 700 yards before pulling up toward *Denver*'s bow to escape, but *Denver*'s forward guns sent it crashing into the sea off the port bow.

*Denver*, still swinging to port, was boxed in by torpedoes approaching from two directions. The first torpedo struck *Denver*'s starboard side, nine feet below the waterline, and a huge geyser of water shot up one hundred feet into the air, showering the entire aft section of the ship with water as the blast tore a forty-foot hole in her hull. Several compartments were flooded, knocking out all power and communications. The hatches were sealed and twenty sailors trapped inside were either dead from the blast or doomed to drown.

The severe force from the blast knocked everyone off their feet. Gunners strapped to their 40mm guns felt the deck being driven upward. Captain Briscoe on the starboard wing of the open bridge got to his feet just in time to see the starboard torpedo pass parallel to the ship at a distance of 75 yards. The navigating officer saw a torpedo wake passing parallel to port.

Wounded, *Denver* listed rapidly to 7°. Shipfit-

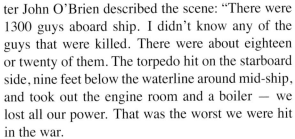

"I'm surprised the Japs never came after us. Over the radio, Tokyo Rose announced that we sunk. They knew our names and everything." A quote from an interview with John O'Brien, USS *Denver* Shipfitter Seaman SSRF. Photograph provided by his son, Paddy O'Brien.

Above:  On the back of this photograph John O'Brien wrote, "The *Denver* herself. Some people claimed she is not the best in the Navy but they haven't convinced me of it." Photo provided by Paddy O'Brien.

ter John O'Brien described the scene: "There were 1300 guys aboard ship. I didn't know any of the guys that were killed. There were about eighteen or twenty of them. The torpedo hit on the starboard side, nine feet below the waterline around mid-ship, and took out the engine room and a boiler — we lost all our power. That was the worst we were hit in the war.

"As a shipfitter, I was involved in the temporary repairs. My job was welding and so I was active in damage control. I helped build a temporary coffer dam with quarter-inch plates on the third deck around the damaged area. I know I worked 24 hours straight before I got any rest. Back in Washington they built a model of the ship and simulated the same damage in it — the model rolled over. But their test did not account for the actions of the crew. We had a big diesel up on deck that generated power

for the portable electric submersible pumps. One of the crew acted quickly. I don't know his name, but I know he was a drunk . . . who became a hero. He was the one who kept the ship from sinking by redistributing fuel and ballast to control the ship's 12-degree list caused by the off-center flooding. After that he could do whatever he wanted. They called him the 'Oil King.'"[84]

### *Seiji Sekine*

We had succeeded at last and withdrew far to the South. Maruyama's first words since the attack were, "Did I drop it too far back?" "But if it runs, it surely must hit the target," I said as I folded up

84    Videotaped interview with John O'Brien, 2000.

the targeting device. It took three minutes for the approach, three minutes to escape. It was a total of six minutes that seemed to me more like ten years in passing.

I looked out at our wing. There were two holes as big as the Rising Sun and the flaps were heavily damaged. "Captain, please give me water" came from one of the many wounded on our plane. Then suddenly ten quick shots were fired to our lower left. Damn it! I jumped out of my seat surprised, and gave a bitter smile. It was those annoying picket warships and their surprise attacks!

Although I wanted to return high above the enemy fleet and check the success of our strikes, my love of airplane No. 321 kept me from pushing her any harder. She was waddling due to the damage from the attack. I put us on a safe course for home.

We debated for the next half hour about exactly which type of ship we had attacked. "Sekine-kun, is this it?" said Commander Nakamura pointing to a table of ship types. "No, this one," I said. "It had two gun turrets with three cannons. I'm sure of it." "No, it was surely a remodeled *California* type," said one of the other men. On and on went the debate. No one could recall if our torpedo actually hit the target. Upper Maintenance Staff Sergeant Ogasawara thought he saw a column of water go up, "But I was distracted by the amount of enemy fire." Then Air Staff Sergeant Minamiyasiki said, "The enemy fire was so beautiful, I can't . . . ." There he sat, scratching his head.

When I asked, "Did anyone shoot their machine gun as we flew over the deck of the ship?" Jibiki, the rear tail gunner did not respond. "Where is Jibiki?" He was still at his gun and appeared to be hit. I said, "Hey! Jibiki! Come here, even if you have to crawl." He stirred and came on all fours, dragging his left leg. I left the cockpit and held him in my arms at the center of the plane. There were countless wounds all along the right side of his body. He was bleeding everywhere and there was a deep wound big enough to stick my finger in on the right of his neck. Blood was flowing like

a little fountain. Although I tore away his uniform and put on a bandage, the wound was difficult to treat. Petty Officer Minami-yashiki, who had no duty because the radio was shot through, applied a bandage and held him. "Jibiki," I said. "Did you see the torpedo strike?" Jibiki replied weakly, "I don't remember anything after I was hit. Please give me water, water. Water!" I would not give him water in his condition and Jibiki looked at me with disapproval. If he died I knew I would regret my decision the rest of my life. "It's only an hour and a half to Rabaul. Be patient," I said.

I could not look after the injured forever and returned to the cockpit. My beloved plane was flying poorly due to the damage and could not gain speed no matter how much I tried. The duralumin skin was beginning to peel off in places. Fortunately, both engines and the No.1 and 2 tanks on both wings were undamaged. Our transmitter and receiver were shot-out and useless — we were deaf and dumb. There was no way to know the condition of the other planes.

Halfway back to Rabaul Jibiki began to act strange. He closed his eyes and his breathing was labored. "Stay with us," I said, "Rabaul is so close." Jibiki whispered, "So cold . . . it's hard to breathe. How much longer till we get back to base?" Jibiki had lost a lot of blood. His uniform was torn and it was as though he was half naked. Everyone's flying jackets were gathered together and put over Jibiki to keep him warm. I tried to encourage him, "We'll arrive in 30 minutes — we're almost there." It was going to be much longer than that but I did not want him to lose hope. I looked up at the full moon. It sat so lonely in the sky.

We finally arrived at Rabaul in what was left of our airplane. "Call the ambulance! He needs a transfusion immediately," I shouted. Three of the other planes from our mission had already landed. The others had not yet returned. I hastily reported to command and then rushed to the sickroom to donate blood. I couldn't help thinking about Jibiki, who might already be dead.

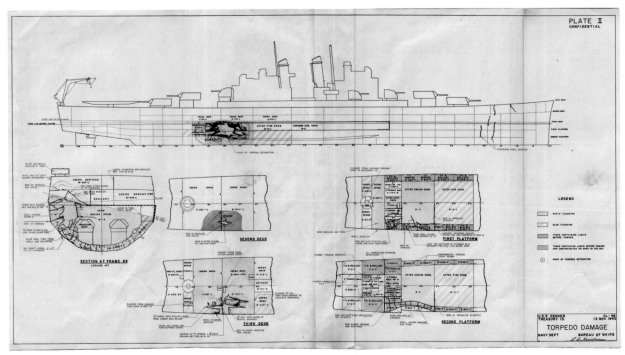

USS *Denver CL-58*; Treasury Island, 13 November 1943, Navy Department, Bureau of Ships. Plate II.

I rushed into the sickroom, out of breath. Sitting on a chair and completely covered in bandages was Air Chief Jibiki. The surgeon smiled, "Hello, I've heard it was a terrible battle. The injured are all doing well." When I heard this I felt a great sense of relief and my darkness parted like the clearing sky after a typhoon.

The following day I went to my airplane and found it surrounded by a large crowd of men. I heard one of them say, "Hmmm . . . they returned in this?" I counted 380 flak holes in my beloved Rikujo. The maintenance chief said it was a total loss. "It's scrap," he said. My beloved No. 321 would never fly again.

\*    \*    \*

USS *Denver* CL58. Length: 10 ft.; beam: 66 ft.; displacement: 11,744 long tons; draft: 25.6 ft; propulsion: 4 geared turbines; speed: 37.4 mph. National Archives Photo #NH84397.

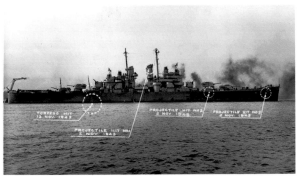

The left circle marks the torpedo strike. Also identified are three 8" shells that struck *Denver* but did not detonate during the Battle of Empress Augusta Bay. Navy Department Library Photo # 0405822.

Gunner's Mate Leonard Lofton "Red" Martin manned one of *Denver*'s 5-inch guns during the attack. Photograph provided by his son, Robert Martin.

By morning, *Denver*'s crew had pumped the starboard tanks, the list was under control and *Denver* was in tow. All submersible pumps were on and the holes and leaks were plugged. Water seeping through the cable runs shorted out the steering control panel, and the loss of steering caused *Denver* to ride out on the tug's port quarter, making towing difficult. Emergency power was then fed directly to *Denver*'s steering motors and steering control was restored.

By midday there were 24 planes flying cover over *Denver* and anti-aircraft batteries on the attending ships were kept on alert into the evening. Why the Japanese never returned to finish her off remains a mystery — an angel rode *Denver*'s yard arm that day.

The cloudless brilliance seemed to have no end as *Denver* was towed into the semi-friendly area southeast of Treasury Island. *Denver* tried to keep hidden, passing as close to Simbo and Remdova as she dared, relying on charts from the early 1900s that could not be trusted to avoid reefs that would happily split open her hull. By day's end *Denver* entered a rainstorm and slid into the darkness until early morning.

No ship's company was ever more thrilled to be cold and wet than was *Denver*'s when she arrived safe at Purvis Bay on the morning of the 15th. Her tow line was cast off and sentries posted to the damaged areas. USS *Denver*, the "Dirty D," had been in combat for fifteen days.

*Denver* was then towed to Espiritu Santo and put into dry dock for repairs. On 28 November, water from the flooded compartments was pumped out. Someone would have to go in and retrieve the bodies. Gunner's Mate Leonard "Red" Martin drew the short straw: "The smell was overwhelming. The men had been soaked in warm seawater for over two weeks. I'd grab hold of an arm and it would come right off." One of the dead, a chief gunner's mate, still had his pipe clenched tight between his teeth. "It was the worst duty I ever had."[85]

USS *Denver* after repairs. National Archives Photograph.

85  Interview with Robert Martin (Leonard Martin's son): March 14, 2014 – April 24, 2014

## Repairs and Maintenance

For the weeks leading up to Jenkins' victory, and for the rest of November, the squadron flew an average of three combat patrols per night under the direction of ship-based FDOs — with no resulting victories. The squadron also flew a similar number of administrative and transport flights, stretching crews and their planes to the limit. A 6,000-mile supply line resulted in chronic parts shortages, and forced maintenance crews to perform minor miracles. Many of these repairs went unrecorded for fear of incrimination. For example, a fractured wing spar at Banika was repaired by carefully welding metal straps around it. Sergeant Albert Barker, who served as one of VMF(N)-531's mechanics during the squadron's entire combat tour, recalled, "It flew, but I had more faith in the pilot than the wing." Years later, Harshberger recalled how an entire nose section, including radar and guns, was grafted onto a PV-1 bomber by an ad hoc team of Marines and sailors.

These activities did not occur in a vacuum, and an intricate system of barter using beer and booze as currency evolved. This was institutional theft — theft for benefit of the unit rather than the individual. The unofficial suppliers for PV-1 parts were Navy patrol squadrons, while AI radar parts came from the USAAF's 6th NFS.[86] Other acquisitions included an abandoned Grumman F4F-4 Wildcat and a pair of F6F-3 Hellcats, both of which were used for search-and-rescue missions.

When the squadron's ground crews found themselves denied rations from the Army-run mess at Banika due to the unit's round-the-clock maintenance operation, the Marines located the desired cases of rations with field glasses by day and "delivered" them by night.[87]

## The Squadron's First Combat Death

On the night of 3 December, Captain Jenkins took off from Vella Lavella to cover Task Group 31.6 and its Destroyer Squadron 23 as they steamed towards Empress Augusta Bay. At 2000 the destroyers came under continuous attack from 30 to 35 enemy aircraft, described by Japanese historians as the 6th Air-Sea Battle of Bougainville.

At 2211 an Army GCI unit with the call name "Dane Base"[88] observed a plane shot down by an aircraft transmitting a friendly IFF signal.

They then tracked the night fighter as it pursued a second a bogey, watching on their scope as the two blips merged before fading from view. Jenkins, who was freelancing,[89] was credited with a kill but never returned to base.[90] How he and his crew met their end is not known, but a mid-air collision or a collision with pieces of the disintegrating enemy aircraft are likely explanations.

Meanwhile, on the ground the Third Marine Division consolidated their perimeter on Bougainville while Seabees operating within the perimeter constructed Piva Uncle, the first of two parallel-running air strips.[91] Setting up next to Piva Uncle to control night fighter operations was a New Zealand GCI unit with the call name "Tiki Base."

In his most recent progress report to Headquarters, Colonel Schwable[92] wondered why his own GCI unit had not been selected for the job. Moon Base at Pakoi Bay had little to do and could easily have moved, set up, and been running within days. In either case, bringing GCI to Bougainville this late in the operation was viewed by Schwable as a mistake. He noted in his report that during the first day of the landing and for three weeks afterwards there was heavy bogey activity over Empress Au-

---

86   USAAF NFS: United States Army Air Force Night Fighter Squadron.

87   *Rescue and Maintenance* was sourced from Charles Quilter's 82-page unpublished draft manuscript, *A History of Marine Fighter Attack Squadron 531.* It was given to Schwable for review and is part of his group of artifacts. Most remarkable in the manuscript are quotes taken from interviews that Quilter made in the 1980s with former members of VMF(N)-531. *Author's collection.*

88   Dane Base had been set up next to the fighter strip along the shore at Cape Torokina, Bougainville since 10 November.

89   Freelancing is patrolling without GCI control. Records do not indicate why Jenkins was freelancing.

90   Two G4Ms of the 751 *Kokutai* (air group) went missing that night.

91   Piva Uncle (Piva Bomber Strip) and Piva Yoke (Piva Fighter Strip) were situated on high ground three miles inland from Cape Torokina.

92   Schwable was promoted to Colonel on 5 November.

gusta Bay, but little effective night coverage. The endless hours that he and his pilots wasted chasing bogeys under the direction of FDOs could have been avoided had his GCI unit gone ashore with the 1 November assault echelon. Schwable recommended that, for future landings, the squadron's GCI unit be put ashore early so that night fighters could provide effective coverage during those first critical nights when bogey activity was heaviest.

He found it ironic when Fighter Command then requested several of his controllers at Moon Base be sent to work at Tiki Base, which was not yet operational.

Three days after Jenkins' death, Lt. Colonel Harshberger took off from Barakoma and checked in with Dane Base. His call was greeted by the familiar voice of Captain Hines, who was one of the controllers sent from Moon Base to assist the still not-operational New Zealand GCI station.

Hines vectored Harshberger towards a bogey coming in from the west. A minute later AI operator Sergeant Kinne had the bogey on his scopes straight ahead. Harshberger closed too fast, the bogey turned and went off Kinne's scopes to starboard. Kinne called for a sharp right turn and then re-established AI contact. As Harshberger closed he saw a Jake[93] begin a flat "S" curve, but otherwise it gave no indication of evasive tactics. Harshberger fired one burst from a position slightly below, and the burning Jake fell into the sea, marking the first victory under one of the squadron's own controllers.

---

93  During the first year of the Pacific War, Allied personnel struggled to quickly and accurately identify Japanese aircraft. Several code systems were tried but added to the confusion. In mid-1942, Captain Frank McCoy, assigned to a U.S. Army Air Intelligence Unit in Australia, devised a simpler method. Together with Technical Sergeant Francis Williams and Corporal Joseph Grattan, McCoy divided the Japanese aircraft into categories. Fighters and single-engine-float planes were given men's names. Women's names were given to bombers, transports and reconnaissance aircraft. Bird names were given to gliders and tree names to trainer aircraft. McCoy gave many of the aircraft hillbilly names, such as Zeke, for the Mitsubishi A6M Zero, a long-range fighter plane, and Rufe, the Nakajima A6M2-N single-engine float plane — all names he encountered while growing up in Tennessee. Others were given names of friends or people he knew personally. The Mitsubishi G4M twin-engine bomber, with its large gun blisters, was named Betty in homage to a busty female friend of Williams. Irving was the Nakajima J1N Gekko (Moonlight), a twin-engine aircraft used for reconnaissance, kamikaze missions and as a night fighter.

## Vindication

By early January 1944 the Piva Uncle and Piva Yoke airstrips were complete. With these new airstrips came the increased risk of friendly fire. The need for caution was confirmed by Schwable when he took off from Piva Uncle on 9 January, was vectored towards an inbound bogey, but refused to fire under AI guidance alone. As Schwable closed he made visual contact with a U.S. Army B-25 bomber flying with its IFF turned off!

This was not an isolated incident. "As a matter of fact," recalled Major Hicks, "we had contacts [with] B-24s and Black Cats that were running around without their IFF on. One night, Lt. Colonel Harshberger almost got a B-24 over the Shortlands. He chased him for 70 miles, started after him at 6,000 feet and ended up at 12,000 feet — the fellow kept climbing. He had his finger on the gun button ready to go when those twin tails popped up in front of him. We would have shot down quite a few if we had shot directly from the AI scope."[94]

On 12 January Schwable was airborne under the direction of Captain Baker, one of his controllers working at Tiki Base, the now-operational New Zealand GCI unit set up next to Piva Uncle.

The first vector of the evening was towards two bogeys which showed up on the AI scopes directly ahead, up 40°. Schwable closed rapidly, and sighted two single-engine aircraft flying in close formation directly above at a range of 1,000 feet. To check his speed he attempted an "S" turn, but lost altitude so rapidly that he had to pull out of the interception just as the bogeys flew into a cloud and AI contact was lost.

Schwable describes what happened next in his third person narrative that appeared in the report *Combat Experiences of VMF(N)-531, The Pioneer Twin Engine Night Fighter Squadron in the South Pacific. Serial #00347 13 November 1943 - 13 March 1944.*

---

94  Major William Moore, *Under the Cover of Darkness,* 37.

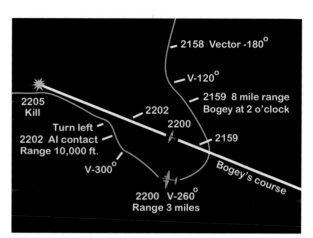

2158 Vector -180°

V-120°

2159 8 mile range
Bogey at 2 o'clock

2205
Kill

2202

2200

2159

Turn left
2202 AI contact
Range 10,000 ft.

V-300°

Bogey's course

2200 V-260°
Range 3 miles

This illustration is a tracing of Colonel Schwable's hand-drawn diagram that descried his 12 January interception (*Combat Experiences of Marine Night-Fighter Squadron 531 In the Solomons. 13 November 1943 - 13 March 1944*). The Nakajima B5N Kate that Schwable shot down has since been identified as tail code 2/46D of the 42nd Shotai from the carrier *Zuikaku.*

At 2156 a bogey appeared suddenly at a point 40 miles from Torokina heading N.W. The fighter was vectored towards it on a vector of 180°. At 2158 he was vectored to port 120° at a range of 10 miles. At 2159 the bogey was eight miles away at 2 o'clock and coming from port to starboard. The fighter was vectored 260° to starboard. At 2200 the range had closed to three miles and a minute later to two miles, at which point the fighter was well below the bogey who was at 10,000 feet. The fighter was vectored 300° on its tail.

At 2202 an AI contact was made, with the bogey showing to the right 30° up and at 10,000 foot range. It was closing fast to the left, and when it was at 5,000 foot range the Radar Operator called for a hard left turn. The range closed to 3,000 feet and then opened to 5,000 feet showing to the left, and still up. As the fighter completed the turn, it came in behind the bogey.

After a few seconds, the turret gunner saw a single engine monoplane 80° up and about 3,000 feet from the fighter. He communicated with the pilot who nosed up and fell in behind the enemy, and then closed. As he was closing, the bogey slipped slightly to the left, and the fighter followed, giving a two-second burst at less than 500 feet. The turret gunner opened up at the same instant. Immediately the Jap plane exploded and burst into flames. To avoid the wreckage the pilot swung hard left and felt a scorching heat as the right wing just cleared the flaming mass. It was 2205. He continued to orbit, watching the plane [a Kate] settle towards the water and was seen from shore as it plummeted toward the sea, exploding again just before it hit the water. It

had taken just nine minutes from start to finish.[95]

It was Schwable's moment of vindication. With only four vectors in seven minutes, the bogey was identified and brought down. His After Action Report offered forceful proof to Marine Corps Headquarters that interceptions could be easily made when properly trained pilots, crew and GCI controllers worked as a team.

What Schwable was able to achieve with his GCI controller made the poor performance of ship- and shore-based FDOs all the more apparent. For the situation to improve, someone would have to train them.

The opportunity came during a liaison visit to the fleet in January 1944. Schwable sent his senior controller, Major Hicks, to meet with Navy Lieutenant Reginald "Reg" Dupuy, who represented the FDOs of Task Force 31.[96]

Hicks explained to Dupuy the night fighter's need for a steady and continuous supply of information, particularly in regard to indicated air speed, altitude, and magnetic course vectors. Together they discussed ways to remedy the problem.

Dupuy explained to Hicks the FDO's point of view, and the limitations of space and equipment imposed upon a destroyer-based FDO. This helped Hicks understand some of the stark differences that he observed between GCI and FDO control.

Hicks then spent three weeks aboard various ships, presenting lectures on night fighter interception techniques. He also brought up another thorny issue — that a properly guided night fighter was more likely to shoot down a bogey than was their inaccurate anti-aircraft fire. Hicks would never forget the response he received from the first destroyer he visited. "I was introduced to the captain and they told him what I was going to do and he said, 'Well, we like to shoot the guns; that's what we're here for and we like to shoot the guns,' but two weeks later

95 "Combat Experiences of VMF(N)-531, The Pioneer Twin Engine Night Fighter Squadron in the South Pacific." 28 April 1944. United States Pacific Fleet, South Pacific Force, Intelligence Division, 5-7.

96 Major William Moore, USMC, *Under the Cover of Darkness,* 39.

Above: Schwable's PV-1, named "Chloe," was Bureau of Aeronautics aircraft number 29854. November 1944, Bougainville. *Author's collection.*

even he was of a mind that it was probably better to go along and not be observed and not shoot the guns than to shoot the guns and be bombed."[97]

As January came to a close, the squadron's flight and maintenance section moved to Bougainville, Moon Base was relocated north to Treasury Island, and five more PV-1s arrived, increasing the squadron's total combat strength to eleven planes. Unfortunately, not one of the pilots who arrived with the aircraft was qualified to fly alone at night, and the five radar operators were not ready for combat.

The squadron did the best with what they were given, scheduling the replacements as co-pilots on combat missions and letting them fly daylight logistical runs.

## *The Art of Airborne Interception*

With the Bougainville beachhead secured, Admiral Halsey planned the next step to isolate

Rabaul — the taking of Kavieng, the largest town on the island of New Ireland.

To serve as an advance air base for the proposed assault, Halsey chose Nissan Island, the largest of the Green Islands. Nissan was close to Kavieng and could easily be supported with aircraft from Bougainville.

Plans for the 15 February amphibious landing on Nissan Island included eleven of the squadron's GCI technicians, and three of its controllers. They were assigned to Argus Seven, the Navy's GCI unit scheduled to land with the first assault echelon. Once ashore they would set up and operate under the call name "Mongrel Base," directing night fighter patrols supporting the landing. The Nissan landing marked the first time since arriving in the Pacific that the squadron participated in an operation from the beginning under the direction of its own GCI controllers. While preparations were being made for the landing, Schwable scored his second kill.

On the night of 6 February, a bogey was picked up by Tiki Base. It was sixty miles to the northwest, flying at an altitude of 15,000 feet on a course paralleling the Bougainville coast. Lieutenant Guy, an

97    Major T. E. Hicks, USMC, "Marine Corps Night Fighters" (Interview by the Air Intelligence Group, DNI, 3 May 1944), 4-5.

A copy of an AI Mark IV indicator, made by Norman Groom (Pitstone Green Museum. Pitstone, Bucks, England). Like the original, it has two cathode ray tubes: elevation tube on the left, azimuth tube on the right. It is nearly identical to the AI SCR-540, the American copy of the AI Mark IV carried aboard PV-1s.

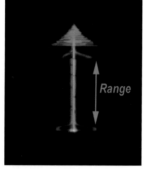

Above are simulated signals on Sergeant Ward's elevation scope (left), and azimuth scope (right). The Christmas-tree shaped ground returns register on each scope at a range of 15,000 feet (the same distance the night fighter is above the ground). The bogey is on the time trace at a range of 12,000 feet, 20° up (elevation scope) and 20° degrees starboard (azimuth scope). The large signal at the far left on the elevation scope's time trace, and on the bottom of the azimuth scope's time trace, is from the night fighter's transmitter bleeding into the system. The Mark IV had two types of aerials: one for transmitting and others for receiving. The transmitting aerial looked like a barbed arrowhead protruding approximately eighteen inches in front of the nose of the aircraft (see photo on page 111). To pick up return echoes, a pair of aerials were placed on the central upper surface of both wings (for the azimuth plane), and the lower surface of both wings (for the elevation plane), as seen in the photo on page 97. If a bogey was flying above and to port, then the aerials on the top surface and on the port side (left side) of the wing would pick up stronger signals. By measuring differences in signal strength received by the aerials, information in elevation and azimuth could be determined.

experienced Army controller at Tiki Base, vectored Schwable into a prolonged tail chase which led the two aircraft off his PPI scope. Schwable caught up

with the bogey sixty miles south of Torokina where his radar operator, Sergeant Ward, made AI contact with the bogey.

The bogey appeared on Ward's AI SCR-540 (Mark IV) radar as blips on two separate displays, called scopes, each located at the end of a cathode ray tube. They required frequent adjustments in tuning and gain control that affected the brightness and clarity of the picture.

On each scope was a luminous green line known as the time trace. The scope on the left front face of the unit displayed radar returns in relative elevation, telling Ward if the bogey was above, below, or flying at the same altitude as the night fighter (in which case the bogey would be centered on the elevation time trace). The azimuth[98] scope on the right indicated whether the bogey was to the right, left, or straight ahead (in which case it would be centered on the azimuth time trace).

The bogey's range could be determined from either scope. The further up from the base of the time trace the bogey appeared, the further away it was from the night fighter. The distance scale on the time trace was imprecise and Ward estimated the target's closing distance by eye, passing on the information verbally to Schwable by interphone.

When the bogey first appeared on Ward's scopes, it was at a distance of 12,000 feet on the time trace, 20° above center on the elevation time trace, and 20° to the right of center on the azimuth time trace. Ward relayed this information to Schwable by interphone, "Bogey 12,000 feet ahead, 20° up, 20° starboard."

By continuously tracking the movement of the blips on his scopes, Sergeant Ward could determine not only the position of the bogey, but also which way it was moving.

The bogey was not the only blip on Ward's scopes. Returning echoes from the ground also appeared, although they were proportionately much stronger. These ground reflections are called

98    Azimuth is the horizontal angular distance from true north — east = 90°, south = 180°, west = 270°, north = 0°.

"clutter" or "noise" and appeared on Ward's scopes as a Christmas tree-shaped disturbance on the time trace at a point equal to the night fighter's absolute altitude.[99] Schwable had climbed to at an absolute altitude of 15,000 feet, and so the ground returns appeared on the time trace at a range of 15,000 feet.

The closer the night fighter flew to the ground, the further down the time trace the ground returns moved, spreading over more of the scope. At altitudes below 2,000 feet the Christmas tree shaped ground returns filled the entire time trace and blotted out all other signals, rendering the AI SCR-540 useless for tracking bogeys. Because of the "Christmas tree effect," the performance of the Mark IV depended largely on the height above the ground the night fighter was flying. This limitation was overcome as radar technology developed, but for users of the Mark IV, it was something that had to be accepted.

The large return at the base of each time trace was caused by the transmitter system bleeding a small amount of signal to the receiver.

Tasks were divided aboard the night fighter; Sergeant Ward monitored the scopes and called out directions while Colonel Schwable searched the darkness for a silhouette of the bogey. This division of labor saved Schwable from staring at the illuminated scopes and ruining his night vision, which would have made it difficult for him to establish visual contact with the bogey, but at the same time it put great reliance on teamwork between pilot and radar operator.

The blips on Ward's time trace were at a range of 7,000 feet (two kilometers away) when turret gunner Fletcher suddenly made visual contact with the bogey in the moon lit sky — an amazing feat of visual acuity. Most sightings were made well under 2,000 feet.

Schwable instructed Ward to leave the scopes, keep the bogey in sight through the cockpit window, and direct him towards it while he adjusted his course and speed, all the while focusing his attention on the dimly-lit instrument panel.

When the range closed to about 3,000 feet, Ward returned back to his scopes and read ranges to Schwable over the interphone until the night fighter was within 800 feet of the bogey, 600 feet being the AI's minimum operating range. At a distance of 700 feet Schwable visually identified the bogey as a Betty[100] and brought the PV-1 below and directly behind it.

Schwable pulled up slightly and fired four long bursts as Fletcher opened up with his turret gun. Hundreds of incendiary bullets flashed brightly upon impact as they pierced the Betty's fuselage.[101] The Betty wavered, then turned slightly to starboard and Schwable and Fletcher gave it a second shorter burst, incendiary bullets again flashing as they struck their mark. After a final burst the Betty fell off into a steep vertical spiral to starboard. Now out of sight, Ward turned to his radar and followed the Betty on his scopes as the blips drifted and then faded from view.

### Iron John

On 9 February the weather was almost below flight minimums at Barakoma when First Lieutenant Watson and his crew boarded their PV-1. Shortly after take-off, in heavy rain, their plane plunged into the water at the south end of the airstrip. The crash boat quickly arrived on the scene but found no survivors.

After a four-and-one-half hour delay due to Watson's crash, Lt. Colonel Harshberger took off at 0145, circled on station over Empress Augusta Bay,

---

99  Absolute altitude is the height above the ground. True altitude is an aircraft's height above mean sea level. Before GPS there was nothing in an airplane capable of measuring true altitude. Instead, pilots used indicated altitude as the next best thing. This is the reading that a pressure altimeter gives — the greater the altitude, the lower the pressure. An aircraft flying at a constant indicated altitude could experience wide variations in absolute altitude, which would decrease as it flew over a mountain, and increases as it approached a valley.

100  One of eight such aircraft of the 751 Kokutai that departed Rabaul at different hours to search Dampier Strait and bomb Mono Island.
101  In this encounter, the nose guns fired a total of 520 rounds. The turret guns fired 78 rounds.

and reported to Dane Base.[102] No bogeys appeared, but before returning to Barakoma, Harshberger had some unfinished business to attend to.

Although bombing runs were a secondary priority, PV-1s were now armed with two 100-pound bombs. Before arriving on station he orbited over an area where the Japanese were known to be operating. He dropped flares, and several moments later he dropped his bombs. Now on his way back to base, he circled over the same area and dropped flares again, but no bombs. He altered this pattern nightly to keep the Japanese on edge, leaving them wondering if they would or would not be bombed on each visit.

Harshberger enjoyed his bombing runs. He was a man driven with desire to bring destruction to the enemy. His courage and aggressiveness were well-respected and he pushed himself beyond normal limits, making as many as five flights every night.[103] These qualities earned him the nickname "Iron John Harshberger" and "The Iron Duke."[104] His abrupt demeanor sometimes invoked a third nickname — "Harsh John Ironberger."

Later that night he was scrambled once more, this time at 0145 by Tiki Base to meet an inbound raid. Harshberger spent the next ninety minutes chasing a bogey but lost it due to poor controlling.

Lieutenant Guy, a more experienced controller, took over at Tiki and at 0329 had Harshberger on a fresh vector. Sixteen minutes later AI operator Sergeant Kinne picked up a larger than usual target on his scopes. At a range of 4,000 feet the blip separated, forming two distinct blips. Turret gunner Tiedeman then sighted a pair of Bettys flying in formation.[105]

Harshberger had just closed to within 1,500 feet when both Bettys opened fire with their tail guns. Harshberger attacked the Betty to the left with the night fighter's six .50-caliber nose guns, putting a burst of incendiary bullets into her belly. Turret gunner Tiedeman attacked the Betty's tail section but was temporarily blinded by muzzle flash which appeared above both barrels of his .50-caliber guns as a white light three feet in diameter. The effect wore off quickly and, believing that Harshberger had the first Betty in hand, swung his guns towards the Betty to his right. Sergeant Kinne, meanwhile, had just left his scopes to watch the fight unfold when the radio compartment was hit by enemy gunfire, knocking the Aldis lamp[106] loose which fell and struck him on the head. Enemy gunfire then struck the PV-1's nose, destroying five of her six guns.

Iron John did not falter and attacked with his one remaining gun while Tiedeman put a burst into the Betty to his right, which then peeled out of range to starboard. Tiedeman swung his guns back to help Harshberger and together they fought the Betty, which began to glow internally.

The intensity of the glow grew, and the Betty's bullet-riddled fuselage took on the appearance of a brightly colored sieve. Harshberger brought the night fighter to within 150 feet, allowing Tiedeman to get in another burst, but Tiedeman considered the plane a dead pigeon and began looking for the other Betty which by now was out of sight. Fearing Tiedeman was hit, Harshberger sent Kinne to investigate. As Tiedeman motioned to Kinne that he still had plenty of ammunition, the burning Betty slowly descended before breaking into a steep nose dive.

Harshberger dropped back "to watch the flaming Nip go down" when Dane Base vectored him towards the second Betty. He gave chase but Lieutenant Guy lost the Betty off his PPI. Running low on fuel, and with his radio damaged in the attack, Harshberger broke off his pursuit of the Betty.

When he returned to Torokina and attempted to land, Piva turned on their searchlights and anti-aircraft guns did their best to shoot him down. The

---

102    The Army GCI unit set up next to the fighter strip along Empress Augusta Bay at Cape Torokina, Bougainville.

103    Charles Quilter II, *A History of Marine Fighter Attack Squadron 531,* unpublished first draft manuscript, 26, 65 and 70. *Author's collection.*

104    Major William Moore, USMC, *Under the Cover of Darkness*, 32 - 33.

105    The Bettys belonged to the 751 Kokutai (abbreviated as the 751 *Ku*). They were on a mission to bomb American positions on Mono Island.

106    The Aldis lamp, named after its inventor Arthur Aldis, was an optical communication device (signal lamp) used to transmit Morse code.

night fighter was finally recognized as friendly and landed safely with just 70 gallons of fuel. Climbing out of his plane Harshberger's only comment was, "Never had so much fun in my life."[107]

## *Citizen Sailor Dupuy*

Schwable's third victory was directed by FDO Reginald Dupuy, a 39-year-old realtor who enlisted in the Navy in 1942. By war's end, "Reg" Dupuy would become one of the war's innovators in shipborne fighter direction.

Naval Fighter Direction Officers were a rare breed. They were self-confident, with a natural ability to work at peak efficiency while sifting through vast amounts of information. FDOs monitored huge amounts of changing information and could quickly arrive at a correct opinion, directing pilots with well-defined orders radioed in a clear, calm speaking voice.

As a ship-based FDO, Dupuy worked in the Combat Information Center — a darkened room full of electronic gear and illuminated tables. In the center of all this gadgetry was a chair, known to the men who worked inside the CIC as "the madhouse." This was where the FDO sat and directed fighter operations.

In front of the FDO was a Plan Positioning Indicator (PPI) along with push-buttons and controls that allowed him to listen and talk to every key post on the ship or in the sky.

A six-foot vertical circular Plexiglass window called the vertical summary plot dominated the CIC. It was an enlargement of the picture seen on the PPI and was marked out with identical bearing and range lines. A man standing behind the plot used a grease pencil to mark mirror-image symbols representing the various aircraft as they appeared on the PPI, creating a tactical picture for the FDO. Dupuy wrote in his training notebooks,

Dupuy, seated left, in the darkened room of a ship's CIC somewhere in the South Pacific. On the reverse side of the photograph, Dupuy writes, "Yours truly, on the left with earphones on, radar to my right, board shows tracking of bogey and friendly aircraft." *Author's collection.*

The FDO shall maintain continuous plots of all pertinent information, record flight operations of our own forces, and shall evaluate plots and originate appropriate "alerts" of impending air attack.

To distinguish between friend and foe, the FDO used the intermittent signals transmitted from a special Identification Friend or Foe system (IFF).

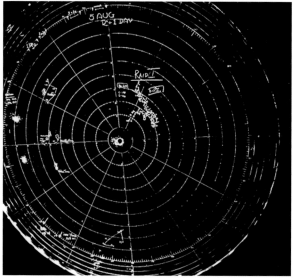

Plots marked with grease pencil on a vertial plexiglas summary plotting table.

---

107   Robert Sherrod, *History of Marine Corps Aviation in World War II* (Presidio Press, 1980), 168.

The system had several components. The interrogator was a radio that interfaced with the ship's radar, transmitting "A signals" between pulses. Aboard each friendly aircraft was a device called a transponder. Upon receiving a signal sent from the interrogator, the transponder responded automatically, sending back a coded signal which could be switched in form and duration for specific missions. The ships responder received the returning signal and processed it for display on the IFF oscilloscope.

If an FDO wanted a pilot to identify himself on his PPI, he would contact the pilot by radio and ask him to press a button that caused his transponder to transmit a special signal (a "G signal") which would show up the PPI as a row of blips next to the blip of light representing his aircraft. The response would remain on the PPI for as long as the pilot pressed the button.

Failure to use his IFF could cost a pilot his life. If he was lost or his plane was damaged and he could not make it back to base, he would be asked to transmit a G signal and the FDO would then give the pilot his location along with any last minute instructions. Dupuy wrote in one of his notebooks,

> If a pilot was hit and was going down, I need to quickly be able to tell him where enemy ships or shore bases were. If I could get him headed toward friendly territory, he'd be my friend for life.

The FDO used high-frequency radio transmissions to communicate with his pilots. Keeping the FDO's radio circuit secure was essential. The enemy must not be tipped off by unusual FDO activity in advance of a landing. In the drive for Vella Lavella during late September 1943, Dupuy designed and tested a new tactic to keep the fighter director radio circuit more secure. The tactic proved to be so successful that it was adopted by the entire Pacific Fleet. It is described in Destroyer Squadron 22's secret letter of 5 September 1943, (FC4-22 / A16-3, Serial 0012).

The various bases ashore are given fighter director calls. These calls have been in use for some time and no doubt the enemy knows where each base is located. When a strange call comes on the circuit, and this call comes on only when a convoy was noted approaching Barakoma, it won't take the Jap long to figure out what is happening. It is suggested that the call assigned the convoy fighter director unit should be used every day and not just when that particular unit is in the area. This could be done by having the call of the convoy fighter director unit used by each base in succession every day for certain specified hours, thus keeping the call on the air all the time. On days when a convoy is in transit all bases could be notified and on those particular days the convoy fighter director unit would be the only base using the convoy fighter director call.

Reg Dupuy was not only a clever tactician, he was an expert controller. On 1 November, Vice Admiral T. S. Wilkinson's Third Amphibious Force was landing at cape Torokina, Bougainville. Dupuy's Fighter Director Unit was aboard the destroyer USS *Conway*. The first Japanese counterattack against the Amphibious Force came from Rabaul at 0735 when 9 Vals[108] and 44 Zekes[109] approached just as the last boats of the assault waves were clearing the ships. Admiral Wilkinson ordered all transports to get underway while Dupuy expertly vectored 16 fighters from Munda and Vella Lavella, preventing all but 12 of the enemy planes from getting through. Those that got through met with limited success: a near-miss on USS *Wadsworth* that killed two men and wounded five.

At 0930 unloading resumed and was again interrupted for two hours when, at 1300, a group of 85 Japanese carrier planes approached. They were savagely attacked by AirSols' fighter planes — all under FDO Dupuy's direction. Reg won a commendation from Admiral Halsey that day.

On 11 November, Lieutenant Dupuy was promoted to the staff of Vice Admiral Wilkinson where he served as Force Fighter Director for South Pacific campaigns for the Third Amphibious Force.

As Force Fighter Director, Dupuy helped de-

---

108    The Allied reporting name for the Aichi D3A carrier-borne dive bomber. It was the primary dive bomber of the Imperial Japanese Navy.
109    Mitsubishi A6M Zero-Sen carrier fighter aircraft.

Top: Dupuy kept this piece of the Rising Sun cut from Japanese Zero shot down under his direction during the drive for Vella Lavella. It was during this drive that Dupuy tested a new tactic that he devised to keep the fighter director radio circuit secure. *Author's collection.*

Above: It was this Japanese helmet, camouflaged with communications wire, that led me to Dupuy's story. I acquired the helmet from fellow collector Jeremy Severn. Jeremy put me in touch with Dupuy's stepson, Kyle Lemons, from whom he acquired the helmet. From Kyle I arranged to purchase Dupuy's personal papers, notebooks, a diary, photos, and an envelope with a piece of the Rising Sun (top of page). A year later I discovered Dupuy's connection to VMF(N)-531. *Author's collection.*

Above: Dupuy on Leyte beach holding the helmet pictured at right. *Author's collection.*

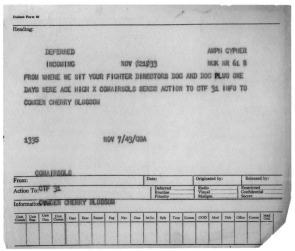

Dodert Form 90

Heading:

DEFERRED                                    AMPH CYPHER
INCOMING              NOV ∅21∅33           NGK NR 61 B
FROM WHERE WE SIT YOUR FIGHTER DIRECTORS DOG AND DOG PLUS ONE
DAYS WERE ACE HIGH X COMAIRSOLS SENDS ACTION TO CTF 31 INFO TO
COMGEN CHERRY BLOSSOM

1335                  NOV 7/43/GBA

COMAIRSOLS
From:                                    Date:        Originated by:        Released by:
Action To: CTF 31                        Deferred     Radio                 Restricted
                                         Routine      Visual                Confidential
                                         Priority     Mailgm.               Secret
Information To: COMGEN CHERRY BLOSSOM

"From where we sit your fighter directors Dog and Dog Plus One days were ace high." ComAirSols (Major General Nathan Twining, Commander Allied Air Units Solomon Islands) congratulating Dupuy and his Fighter Director Unit for their service during the 1-2 November 1943 landing at Bougainville. *Author's collection.*

velop techniques that became standard in amphibious fighter direction and assisted in the preparation of air defense and fighter direction plans. He also exercised tactical control over fighter aircraft protecting surface forces and beachheads during the amphibious assaults at Green, Emiaru, Manus, Guam, Peleliu, Leyte and Luzon Islands.

In the early morning hours of 15 February, Dupuy was in command of a two-man FDO unit operating with the call name "Cocker Base" aboard the destroyer USS *Wadsworth*, which was en route to Nissan Island as part of a task unit that would make the first landing there.

Flying over the task unit at 9,000 feet was Colonel Schwable. Dupuy was on mic when radar contact was made with an enemy reconnaissance aircraft sent down from Rabaul to observe the landing. Dupuy vectored Schwable towards the bogey. On the PPI he could see the bogey erratically changing course as it circled to drop flares on the task unit. Its constantly changing geometry would present him with a challenging interception.

As Schwable approached the bogey, 20 miles west of Nissan Island, Dupuy's difficulties in deter-

mining bogey altitude almost scotched the interception. At one point he had Schwable searching at an altitude of 2,000 feet, flooding the night fighter's AI scopes with interference. Schwable asked Dupuy to control him into visual contact with the bogey. This was tried and failed. The bogey was there, but no one knew its altitude. In a moment of inspiration, Dupuy sought help from four different ships, asking them to assess the bogey's altitude which he then averaged at 7,000 feet.

Colonel Schwable began climbing to 7,000 feet and at 0455 was put in a tail chase. As the night fighter closed, Dupuy switched from magnetic compass vectors to clock-code vectors,[110] periodically calling out adjustments in course — "11 o'clock — 1 o'clock — Dead ahead . . . ."

At 0500 AI contact was made at a range of several thousand feet, full right, 10° up. With only a few AI directions necessary, Schwable closed to within 2,000 feet and the bogey suddenly came into view, slightly above, crossing slowly from left to right with distinct blue exhaust flames visible under its fuselage.

Schwable continued to close, and at 1,000 feet the silhouette of a Jake[111] stood out with its twin floats clearly visible. Schwable flew closer. At 700 feet he positioned himself slightly below and directly behind the Jake, then eased up to its level. He set his sights and fired one short burst of 13 rounds from each of his nose guns, followed by a short burst from Sergeant Fletcher's two .50-caliber turret guns. A small cherry red glow appeared in the enemy engine accessory compartment which rapidly grew in intensity and size.

Due to the excess speed of the PV-1, Schwable pulled off slightly above and to the right of the Jake where the large rising sun was plainly visible on the top of the wing. The Japanese aircraft then fell off into a slow, easy left-hand diving turn. As the Jake was falling away, Fletcher got in another good

110  Clock-code vectors direct the pilot using positions of the clock, with the nose of the aircraft pointing at 12 o'clock, and the tail at 6 o'clock.
111  An E13A floatplane assigned to the 958 Kokutai on a scouting mission to locate American transport ships.

Above: Notes from Dupuy's January meeting with VMF(N)-531 contoller Major Hicks (see page 110). The two men discussed the problems night fighters were having with ship-based FDOs. Scribbled at the center-bottom-right of the lower spine Dupuy writes "Wants 3 things: 1. Indicated Air Speed 2. Altitude (indicated) 3. Magnetic course." *Author's collection.*

burst with his turret gun. "I was in the best position I had ever experienced to get in an ideal shot," said Fletcher, "I saw the Jap pilot and he seemed so close that I could have hit the Jap over the head with the butt of my gun."

Oil from the damaged Jake spewed onto the PV-1, covering the cockpit windshield. The Jake's glow became a flame as the airplane fell into a steep dive. Schwable watched from his side window as the Jake plummeted toward the water. After watching the Jake hit the water, Schwable radioed Dupuy who reported back that personnel on the bridge had witnessed the kill.

At the end of the war, Lieutenant Commander Reginald Dupuy was awarded the Legion of Merit for his innovations in ship-borne fighter direction, and for his contribution as Force Fighter Director for South Pacific campaigns for the Third Amphibious Force. With nine battle stars on his Asiatic-Pacific Ribbon, and two battle stars on his Philippine Liberation Ribbon, Reginald Dupuy, citizen sailor, returned to civilian life — selling real estate.

| Date | Type of Machine | Number of Machine | Duration of Flight | Character of Flight | Pilot | PASSENGERS | REMARKS |
|---|---|---|---|---|---|---|---|
| 1 | PV-1 | 33254 | .7 | T | Schwable | Ward-Kinneson | Russells - Koli Pt. (Spare Reg AA4XF |
| " | " | " | .4 | T | " | " " | Koli Pt. - Russells |
| 4 | " | 29854 | 1.2 | N | " | " | Russells-Yella- move trunk+gear  Load 1 LCT |
| " | " | " | 1.0 | " | " | " | Yella- Russells. |
| 5 | " | " | 1.1 | U | " | Ward-Fletcher-Barna | Russells-Vella  move gear  Load 2LCT 1LCI |
| " | " | " | 1.8 | U-K | " | " " | Vella-Torokina -Strafed barges for PT boats. |
| 5-6 | " | " | 4.3 | K-1Y | " | " " | Tiki Cover  SHOT DOWN 1 BETTY |
| 6 | " | " | 2.9 | J | " | " " Barna | Search of Torokina for Betty |
| 6-7 | " | " | 4.7 | K-1Y | " | " " | Tiki Cover - negative - 1 practice |
| 7-8 | " | " | 4.3 | K-1Y | " | " " | " " |
| 8 | " | " | .9 | U | " | " " " | Torokina - Vella  Air Ops Vella ASSUMED |
| 9 | |  |  |  |  | Watson, | Lost |
| 10 | " | " | 1.1 | U | Schwable-Pierce | Ward, Fletcher-Levy | Yella - Torokina |
| 10-11 | " | " | 4.7 | K-1Y | " | " " | Tiki Cover - chased 2 bogies (Hunt) |
| 11-12 | " | " | 4.5 | K-1Y | " | " " | " " bad weather - negative |
| 12 | " | " | .9 | U | " | " " " | Torokina - Vella. (Confer Gen. Herman |
| 14 | " | " | 1.2 | U | Schwable | " " Barna | Vella- Torokina. |
| 14-15 | " | " | 5.3 | K-3Y | " | " " | Cover Task Force 38 (Camel) |
| 15 | " | " | 2.2 | K-3Y | " | " " | " Green Island Landing  DOWNED JAKE |
| 15 | " | " | 1.1 | U | " | " " | Torokina - Vella. |
| | Total time to date, | | 44.4 | | | | |

Above: Schwable's flight log showing his 6 February kill, Watson's death on 9 February, and his third kill directed by FDO Dupuy on 15 February. *Author's collection.*

## *Relieved of Command*

During the 15 February 1944 amphibious landing on Nissan Island, Japanese dive bombers tried to break through to the amphibious Task Force at daybreak. They were met by Corsairs. Six Vals were destroyed, and the others were driven away with their bombs still slung under their bellies.

By mid-morning all troops and their supplies were safely ashore. With them came Argus Seven, the Navy's GCI unit and the squadron's detachment of controllers and technicians under the command of Captain Hines.

Nissan Island was bombed again that night but the night fighters were ineffective because Argus had not yet finished setting up.

Argus had "Mongrel Base" up and running by the afternoon of 16 February and the squadron put six overlapping patrols over the island that evening — Schwable had the third patrol. Shortly after 0330, Hines vectored Schwable to the nearer of two inbound bogeys. It was a head-on set-up and AI contact lasted only ten seconds before it was lost.

Hines then vectored Schwable towards the second bogey. What followed was nearly a copy of his victory two nights before. Schwable's score was now four enemy planes destroyed, making him and his crew the leading night fighter team in the Pacific at that time. One more and he would become the first Marine Corps night fighter "Ace" in history.

Hines vectored Schwable towards another bogey. He gave chase but after running low on fuel he was forced to disengage and returned to base.

Lieutenant Plunkett relieved Schwable and, at 0315, Hines vectored him towards a "highly maneuverable bogey" ten miles west of Nissan Island. Plunkett's AI operator, Staff Sergeant Pulham, got the bogey in his scopes at a distance of 4,000 feet and notified Plunkett to slow down from 160 knots and lose altitude — a difficult combination — which Plunkett did with S-turns (full flaps and throttles cut completely back).

At 400 feet and still closing at 90 knots, Plunkett saw the silhouette of a Jake making violent S-turns. Losses during the last few days had made the Japanese pilots very wary indeed.

At 350 feet, and with the PV-1 still closing, Plunkett quickly aimed and fired a short burst at the enemy cockpit. There was no fire or explosion. The Jake simply rolled off to the right and dove straight into the water.

The next morning at breakfast, Colonel Schwable was called over to sit with Major General Ralph Mitchell, Commander of Allied Air Units in the Solomons. Schwable's hands shook as he lifted his coffee cup.[112] Mitchell saw and understood. After struggling to organize the first night fighter squadron and then flying 269 hours in combat in 72 missions, spending six or seven hours every night in the sky for a total of 421 hours in the combat zone, Schwable had driven himself to exhaustion.[113] Mitchell ordered him to take a month's rest before reporting for duty as Operations Officer, Fighter-Strike Command, Air North Solomons, directing daily airstrikes against Rabaul.

Stunned into disbelief, Schwable pleaded with Mitchell to let him stay on a little longer "to get a

Top row, left to right: Frank Schwable was awarded the Legion of Merit with Combat "V" for his pioneering work with VMF(N)-531, the first night fighter squadron in U.S. military aviation history; a Gold Star added to his LOM in lieu of a second award for service as Commanding Officer, Strike Command Operations from 6 March to 1 November 1944; a second Gold Star added to his LOM in lieu of a third award for his service in Korea from 25 April to 8 July 1952 as Chief of Staff of the First Marine Aircraft Wing; the Distinguished Flying Cross with three Gold Stars in lieu of four Distinguished Flying Crosses for heroism, awarded for his work with VMF(N)-531 in the Solomon Islands; the Air Medal with two Silver Stars in lieu of a ten Air Medals, awarded for his work with VMF(N)-531 in the Solomon Islands; the Nicaraguan Campaign medal; and the American Defense Service Medal with Base Clasp. *Author's collection.*
Bottom row, left to right: the European-African-Middle Eastern Campaign Medal; the Asiatic-Pacific Campaign Medal with four bronze stars; the American Campaign Medal; the World War II Victory Medal; the United Nations Korea Service Medal; and the ultra-rare Nicaraguan Cross of Valor. *Author's collection.*

few more planes," but Mitchell refused.

Schwable's friend, Colonel Clayton Jerome, put him aboard the next flight to Australia. "It takes a strong man to cry," recalled Jerome, "There were deep tears in his eyes. He wanted to stay right there and fight."[114]

112   A quote from Maude Schwable, Frank Schwable's mother, *The Evening Tribune* (San Diego), 11 March 1954. *Author's collection.*
113   Charles Quilter II, unpublished manuscript, 69. *Author's collection.*

114   Raymond B. Lech, *Tortured Into Fake Confessions, The Dishonoring of Korean War Prisoner Col. Frank H. Schwable* (McFarland & Co. 2011), 26.

## *The Squadron's Last Days*

When several Japanese floatplanes traveled south from Rabaul under a crescent moon to harass a task unit en route to Nissan Island, Lt. Colonel Harshberger, the squadron's new commander, was on station. Captain Hines directed him towards a bogey 25 miles southwest of Mongrel Base. After a ten-minute chase, turret gunner Tiedeman spotted two bluish-white lights coming from the bogey's exhausts. As the PV-1 closed to 1,000 feet, the silhouette of a Jake stood out plainly against the star-filled sky.

Sergeant Kinne called out the range from his scopes and when the PV closed to 800 feet, Tiedeman took over, calling out the range by eye while Kinne left the scopes to watch the ending unfold. Harshberger closed to 300 feet, took 40 seconds to draw a bead, and gave a short burst of ten rounds from each of his six nose guns, followed by a burst from Tiedeman's turret gun. The Jake burst into flames, bringing the squadron's tally to ten.

When Harshberger returned to base he learned that Lieutenant T. M. Banks and his crew had not returned from a barge hunting mission. Harshberger refueled, took off and searched for the missing plane. Two more PVs joined the search at daybreak. The only wreckage discovered was 15 miles south of Nissan Island — a few parachutes and a wheel floating in the water.

Five more pilots joined the squadron in the last week of February. The Japanese, meanwhile, had given up on the Green Islands.

By March, Rabaul had been cut off from re-supply and the once powerful 100,000-man Japanese fortress was rendered useless. Flights from Rabaul dwindled, and the few float planes that continued to operate did so cautiously and at low altitudes to avoid detection in areas patrolled by night fighters.

Lt. Colonel Harshberger saw the only action that month. On 2 March he took off from Piva Uncle on a cooperation mission with PT boats. At 2200 he located several Japanese barges off the south coast of Bougainville. He dropped float flares and notified three PT boats that were operating a few miles away about the barges.

The PT boats radioed back that a Jake was dropping flares over their position and requested he come and chase it away. The Jake must have been flying very low because neither ground radar nor the night fighter's AI could pick it up on their scopes. The floatplane got away and contact with the moving barges was lost.[115]

That same night, Harshberger was patrolling along Bougainville's southern coast when he spotted five barges unloading troops and supplies. The Japanese were beefing up General Hyakutake's 15,000-25,000 troops as they prepared for what would become their unsuccessful three-pronged counterattack against the Marine perimeter protecting Piva Uncle and Piva Yoke airstrips.

After repeatedly assuring the PT boats that he was targeting five Japanese barges and not three PT boats, Harshberger was urged to strafe the barges while they sped toward the scene. Sergeant Kinne threw out float lights to mark the location of the barges, and at a higher altitude he dropped parachute flares. When the barges were well silhouetted, Harshberger strafed them with hundreds of rounds from the night fighter's nose guns.

While waiting for the PT boats to arrive, he returned to Piva Uncle for more flares, causing a delay of nearly an hour. Before take-off he radioed the PT boats, "be ready for my return." Harshberger found the barges, dropped flares, and the PT boats let loose with a chain of fire along the shore as Harshberger flew off, retiring for the evening.

On 13 March Harshberger scored the squadron's eleventh victory, a Jake from the 958 Ku.

The following day two PV-1s were lost to accidents. One crashed while taking off from the Russells on an logistics flight. Another was dam-

---

115   Not long after this encounter the squadron conducted experiments using PT boats equipped with radio and radar equipment to see if they could control night fighter interceptions with low-flying bogeys.

aged beyond repair at Henderson Field after it was caught in prop wash from a B-26, lost control, and crashed. For Harshberger these accidents were indicative of the poor training received by the latest group of pilots to arrive.

Two more PV-1s were lost on 21 March. Lieutenant Notestine had taken off from Piva Uncle at 0520 and patrolled until 0630. He then started for Barakoma and was joined by Lieutenants Pierce and Birdsall, all three flying in formation. At 0650 Pierce's PV-1 burst into flames after clipping Birdsall's wing. Birsdsall went into a spin and both night fighters crashed into the sea.

Notestine circled low over the wreckage and radioed for help. Harshberger led the search effort in an F6F-3 Hellcat assisted by Capt. Wehmer in the F4-F Wildcat, but there were no survivors. This accident by more experienced pilots highlighted the dangers inherent in flying at night in formation. VMF(N)-531 was back to its original strength of six PV-1s with little chance of getting replacements.

With Rabaul no longer capable of sending air power to interfere with Allied operations, and with all eight Marine night fighter squadrons now in commission, Harshberger felt that there was little point keeping the technically obsolete and worn out PV-1s in combat much longer.[116] What the Corps needed most from Schwable's night fighting experiment were its combat-tested controllers and pilots for training new crews. With this in mind, Lt. Colonel Harshberger put in a request that the squadron be returned to the United States.

Fighter Command agreed. On 6 May Harshberger handed command of VMF(N)-531 over to Captain Wehmer before returning to the U.S. with seven pilots, three ground officers, 678 men and all but three of the radar controllers. He had flown an amazing 756 hours in the theater, 433 hours in combat and 100 combat missions.

The squadron added one more victory before leaving the Solomons. Lieutenant Notestine was freelancing on 13 May — flying without GCI due to distance and terrain 20 miles north of Rabaul. At 0345 he spotted anti-aircraft fire coming from PT patrol boats. He radioed the patrol which reported back that a low flying floatplane had recently attacked their craft. Notestine executed a cat's eye search at an altitude of 400 feet for almost an hour before he saw a bogey flying straight at him with its navigation lights on.

As the floatplane passed 200 feet below it made a 90° left turn and lined up for a landing at Rabaul's harbor. Realizing he would overshoot the bogey if he turned right, Notestine made a hard 270° turn left and rolled out directly behind the target. Using the bogey's tail light as a target he fired a short burst. The Jake exploded into flames and fell towards the water.

Flying through the smoke, Notestine continued along the water's edge before climbing to a higher altitude. As he flew back over the burning Jake, a bright-red flare shot out from shore, followed by explosions from three anti-aircraft guns that lit-up the night fighter's darkened cabin. Notestine gained altitude and flew out of range, stooging until sunrise when he spotted an oil slick where the Jake had gone in. It was the squadron's twelfth and final victory and the only one without the use of radar.

From here on the missions were routine — occasional bogey chases, barge hunting missions and bombing runs. On 14 July 1944 Lieutenant Arnold Loken flew the squadron's last combat flight of the war — a dusk patrol over Rabaul.[117]

---

116   Night fighters from eight Marine squadrons claimed 107 victories during the war, 93 of which were made by squadrons flying Hellcats.

117   In October 1944 the squadron was reorganized as a replacement training squadron.

# 2nd MARINE DIVISION

*Five Marines tell their stories about the 2nd Marine Division as it worked its way across the Pacific: from Tarawa to Hawaii, Saipan, Tinian, Nagasaki and home again. The story ends with a reunion of three men, two of whom tried to hunt down and kill the third in the jungles of Saipan.*

## *Tarawa*

*Don Jones*[1]

We went over the side of the ship at pre-dawn and labored down the rope nets. So far, it was as it should be. We had all seen enough war movies to know what it would be like. It was always the other guys, the supporting cast, who were hit. And the bad guys always lost. Amphibious tractors milled in the black water. With dawn, they aligned themselves in long rows: the first three waves to hit the beach. Swooping Hellcats and Helldiver torpedo bombers strafed and bombed in the first light. "They're all dead or shell-shocked," we reassured each other. We sat on the edge of our tractor and watched the first wave, 100 yards ahead of us, move toward the distant palm tree. We were the first of 20,000 men who would start ashore. A twinge of

fear went through all of us when the order came: *Fix bayonets!* I, for one, had no intention of letting the enemy get that close.

Then something went wrong. Geysers of water rose in the air around us: we could see small spurts of water rising around the tractors of the first wave; the man on the starboard machine gun fell back into the crowded tractor, a bullet hole in his forehead; another stepped up to take his place. The sound of the tractor, explosions, fire from the guns and aircraft all blended into a single roar. Geysers of water rose in the air around us. Bursts of ack-ack immediately above us rained shrapnel into the craft. Crouched now, in the far rear port side of the tractor, I watched a growing circle of blood slowly spread over the back of the man in front of me. He didn't move. Two more machine gunners died of head wounds. Now we were afraid.

We were on the reef. The tractor lurched and bounced. The tops of palm trees appeared and grew closer. The sound of machine-gun bullets ricocheting off the tractor blended into the noise of explosions, the returning fire of our guns, and low-flying aircraft. An exploding shell rocked the tractor, spraying us with water and coral fragments. But we kept going.

Then the bouncing stopped. We were on sand. The palms moved past us — twenty yards, thirty yards. Machine-gun fire raked us from all sides.

---

1  Excerpts from a 1991 letter to George Pollard from Don Jones, printed with permission of the Don Jones Trust, courtesy Ms. Bonnie J. Lawless. The story was revised and appeared as "We Weren't Yet Afraid," *Leatherneck*, (November 1993): 38-43.

"Get back to the beach!" an officer yelled at the driver. "We can't get out here!" In his fright, the driver stalled the tractor.

We listened to the grinding whine of the starter. I knew it was only a matter of moments until they began lobbing grenades into the tractor. I was going to die! With that realization, and the loss of any chance of survival, I also lost my fear. The tractor engine caught. The driver headed back to the beach, then, once in the water, swung around until the tractor was again angled toward the shoreline. The noise of exploding shells and machine-gun fire merged into a constant roar, but we heard someone shout "OK, let's go!"

We went over the side, half on the right, the rest of us to the left. Those of us on the port side landed in knee-deep water in the lee of the tractor. We didn't learn until later that the other half had leaped into the direct fire of machine guns.

We huddled behind the tractor for several seconds, looking at the 20 feet of water to the shoreline. Someone again yelled "Let's go!" and we ran. Some of us got to shore, others did not. I was aware of men dropping, and I saw water spurt between me and the man ahead. A shell hole ten feet from the water's edge was our mutual objective. One by one, seven of us reached its protective cover. But only seven. The 28 others who had been aboard the tractor were dead.

His mission completed, our tractor driver headed back to sea with his cargo of dead and wounded. Other tractors could not. They studded the reef and beach. Bodies of Marines bobbed in the shallow waves where our tractor had been. Most were face down. Only their packs and entrenching tools were clear of the water. We hugged the bottom of the two-foot-deep crater. Automatic fire cracked above and around us.

The only officer to have made it ashore in our tractor was Lt. Wayne Sanford, a tall and tanned, soft-spoken executive officer of F Company, to which I was attached as an intelligence scout from Second Battalion headquarters of the Second

Marines. At the edge of the water, ten feet from us, a young Marine lay on his back, groaning and breathing in gasps. Lt. Sanford looked at him, "Is that Jones?" I looked. There was a resemblance, but it wasn't. "No sir, I'm here," I replied.

Then, I remembered that one of my duties was to keep the company commander informed of our position. I looked at the pier to our left, then at my map. "We're right here on Red Beach Two like we're supposed to be, sir," I said to the lieutenant. He peered at me rather strangely, then glanced away. "Thanks," he answered. Sanford, a laconic man whose bearing earned respect, was the only man in the hole I knew by name, except for our radio man, Courte. In New Zealand, I had trained with G Company, but my assignment had been changed to F Company aboard ship. The others in the hole were strangers.

When I told Lt. Sanford I was not the dying man on the beach, a Navy corpsman — short, pudgy, bespectacled, and the last guy you'd expect to be a hero — jumped from our hole and ran to the Marine. He had no more than knelt at the man's side when machine-gun bullets tore into both of them. Now we were six. Courte had fallen in the water when he jumped from the tractor. His radio was useless. We could see no other Marines ashore and had no means of contacting anyone.

The fourth wave was in trouble. The Higgins boats couldn't clear the reef. Someone had screwed up on the tides. They were walking in from 500 yards. Their heads and shoulders were above the water. Some held their rifles above their heads. A couple hundred men, 40 from each boat, began the long, slow walk to their deaths in the area directly in front of us. Water spurted around them. Gradually, one-by-one, they disappeared. One of them was our battalion commander, Lt. Col. Herbert R. Amey, Jr.

We laid in our hole for about 20 minutes watching boatload after boatload of men die in an effort to get ashore. One, a radioman, was within 50 feet of the beach when he went down. Our last hope of communicating with anyone died with him. As far

George Pollard captured this rice painting at Tarawa. It was folded like a *hinomaru* inside the uniform of a Special Naval Landing Force soldier. The writing is a three line Japanese proverb: *Oni Ni Kanabo* ( "A rod to the ogre"); *Oni Ni Kanabo* ("A rod to the ogre"); *Tora Ni Tsubasa*, *sousi* ("Wings to the tiger"). The ogre in this case represents an American and the tiger represents the Japanese soldier. In Japanese legend the tiger goes on the prowl for 1000 miles before returning home safe from the hunt, thus the tiger became an important lucky charm for Japanese soldiers going off to war. *Author's collection.*

as we knew, we were the only six men ashore. Six, against some 5,000 Imperial Japanese Marines who were sweeping our position with machine-gun fire. Fires raged just inland from our hole and the noise of explosions of gunfire was overwhelming.

Then Lt. Sanford issued what I considered at the time to be the most stupid order ever given: "Hell, we're not doing any good here, let's go on in!" They had trained us well. After all, we were Marines. I shed my pack and entrenching tool. If I had to run, I wanted no extra weight to slow me down. Sanford already was crawling over the edge of the crater, heading inland. At the edge of our hole was a gasoline drum with both ends blown out. I crawled through it. If I had ever doubted, it was confirmed that we were fighting Japanese. A foot, shod in a rubber, split-toed shoe, was at the other end of the drum. The man attached to the shoe was dead and motionless.

Shattered palm trees were strewn over pillboxes of five-foot-thick concrete walls reinforced with coconut logs and steel, and covered with several feet of crushed coral and sand. Shells and bombs had simply exploded on top of them. We got up and ran, each man for himself, plopping into shell holes. Rifle and machine-gun fire was everywhere, but the enemy was nowhere. He fired from inside bunkers that looked like mounds of sand.

Within ten minutes and 50 yards from the beach, two snipers were trying to kill me — one in a palm tree to my left, and the other from a tree somewhere behind me. I pawed frantically at the sand in a corner of a shell hole. "Gotta get deeper!" Their bullets thudded into the sand inches from me. Dominick Vanditti, top sergeant of F Company, dropped into the hole beside me. But he stopped on his hands and knees! He'd probably told a thousand Marines that when you hit the deck, you go flat. But he stopped on his hands and knees! "Get down! We're pinned down!" I said. Blood gushed from Vanditti's mouth. He was dying. I reached to pull him closer. I felt the impact in his body as another bullet entered it. He stopped bleeding in less than a minute.

The sniper behind me stopped firing. The one to his left fired every forty-five seconds, exactly. I located him in a palm tree and put three rounds into the brown frond from which I saw the sniper's rifle protrude. I watched. The rifle emerged again. I ducked, and the sniper fired. Then I put three more rounds just above where I had fired before and he fell. The sniper fell; not far, only about three feet. He was tied to the tree and his rifle to him, which dangled in the air below. I got the son of a bitch! I wanted to jump up and shout with joy but I didn't. I rubbed sand into Vanditti's blood stains on my dungarees.

A few minutes later the guy behind me began firing again. I didn't know where he was, but I was willing to wait out the war in that hole, digging deeper into its side. But someone was dropping heavy mortars to my left, walking them in a line straight toward me. Time to move!

Two or three holes later, I found a shattered foundation of a one-room building, protecting about a dozen Marines lying in a 360-degree defense. At one end of the foundation, a sand-covered bunker provided some protection. I took a position between two Marines and began to feel a little strange. "Hey, wake up! What the hell you doin', sleeping?" The Marine on my right was shaking me. I awoke, but with the next blink of my eyes, I was asleep again, and with vivid dreams. Adrenalin sharpens the senses, but too much can have the opposite effect.

We continued to run, shell hole to shell hole. We weren't killing the enemy, just running through them. From one hole I killed a sniper who was hiding inside the broken fuselage of a plane on the fighter strip.

By late afternoon, I found myself with about 50 Marines in a 30-foot-square hole that had been used to store gasoline drums. Its six-foot depth gave us the best protection we had all day. We crossed the fighter strip, and now faced the bomber strip and the last 100 yards of the island.

For the first time since we left the beach, except

for the brief sleep period, I wasn't alone. Even Lt. Sanford was there. Rumors that we were pulling off the beach circulated, but were not really believed. The trouble was, we couldn't contact them, and they didn't know we were three-quarters the way across the island.

We stood 25 percent guard that night. Shadows jumped back and forth under swinging parachute flares lighting up the night sky. I lay in a shallow pit ten feet from our protective hole. A nearby body, and I couldn't tell its nationality, seemed to move with every flare. If the Japanese stayed in their bunkers all night we had a chance. If they came looking for us, that chance was slight. If they counter-attacked in force, we'd had it. A lone Japanese plane dropped some bombs about midnight, but otherwise nothing. At daybreak, another 15 or 20 Marines made it to our hole. I wonder now at the terror each must have felt alone in a hole all night.

We still had no communication with the beach, or with anyone else. I had pinpointed our location on my map. The far beach was just beyond the 100-yard-wide bomber strip. Lt. Sanford, the only officer there, made the decision. We would jump off at 11 o'clock. Small arms fire was everywhere as the Japanese continued their fight from inside bunkers and pillboxes. "Let's go!" someone shouted and a moment later 70 Marines, rifles at port, ran yelling across the bomber strip.

Beyond the strip, and only feet from shore, we jumped into a deep tank trap — a 100-yard ditch paralleling the waterline. This was the beach the Japanese had expected the Marines to assault from the sea. We were the first to make it across the island, but we had no way to communicate with the beach, or anyone else.

Snipers in nearby trees kept us close to the wall of the ditch. It didn't take long before the Japanese pulled a heavy machine gun to the left end of the tank trap. The machine gun opened fire, sending a river of bullets along the length of the ditch. Dead and wounded fell the entire way. Frantically, we dug into the wall of the ditch, scraping with whatever we had. I used my helmet. I saw the man next to me using his entrenching tool and I wished I hadn't thrown my backpack away. It was a good ten minutes before Marines closest to the machine gun silenced it with grenades.

One of my duties as an intelligence scout was to obtain information about the enemy. I decided to go through the pockets of one of the dead enemy machine gunners. I rolled to my left side and as I pulled the dead machine gunner into the trench a concussion grenade exploded, peppering the area with match-head-size shrapnel. I couldn't stop shaking. I knew I was hit. Blood was streaming from a small wound in my right hand. This was pretty much the end of the battle for me.

## Tarawa
### Bud Benoit[2]

I was a corpsman assigned to Dog Company, 1st Battalion, 2nd Regiment, 2nd Marine Division. After six months in New Zealand we were up to strength and were lookin' for a fight.[3] We shipped out November 1st, 1943, zig-zaggin' toward the equator for twenty days. Our destination was Tarawa and as far as I was concerned, it was the only battle I was in and the battle we should have lost.

I started down the cargo nets and that was about as dangerous as going to war! It was very dangerous just getting down to the Higgins boats. You had to hold the vertical part of the ropes or the guy above

---

2  The artifacts for Bud Benoit's story belong to my friend Kurt Barickman. They were given to him by Benoit, who served with the 2nd Marine Division as a navy corpsman. When Kurt told me that he was going to visit Bud, and asked if I wanted to come along, I said "Hell yes!" When we met Bud in Minneapolis, he was wearing a hat and a smart, double-breasted grey suit, reminding me of pictures that I had seen of Harry Truman. At age 93, Bud is vibrant, and tells his story like a man narrating a movie that he can see playing inside his head. As Bud spoke, his voice filled with emotion. The scenes he described were burned into his memory; he cannot forget — even after all these years.

3  The U.S. Marines do not have their own medical department, unlike the U.S. Air Force, Army and Navy. Because they are technically part of the U.S. Navy, the Marines rely on the Navy for their field medical officers, called hospital corpsmen. Navy corpsmen are attached to a Marine field unit to offer medical support during operations and battle. As a corpsman, Bud Benoit was entitled to wear Navy and Marine Coprs uniforms, with a mix of insignia.

you would step on your hand — and down you'd go. The Higgins boats were bouncing around and slamming against the side of the ship, and at some point you said, "This is it," and you jumped in. Just as I was about to go down the nets the island started talking back. A couple of close rounds caused us to up anchor and get the hell out of range.

I went in at Tarawa with a Reising gun that I kept from Guadalcanal. We were attacking right into the sun; even John Wayne knows better than that. Then there was a loud bang and a puff of smoke and a nearby Higgins boat vanished — it was just gone. Our boat was in the first wave that got hung up on the reef 500 yards from shore. I went over the side and waded in through the bullets. The ocean was red from blood. There were bodies floating in the water while others sunk to the bottom. I don't know why some floated and others sank. I walked on top of several dead Marines who had sunk to the bottom of the lagoon on my way to the beach.

The Jap commanding officer on Tarawa was an admiral, not a general. To him, Tarawa was his ship, and he armed it to prevent the enemy from boarding. Other battles during the war reached their climax after the landing — this one almost before. That's the reason some 520 men are still unaccounted for from the battle; the sea claimed them.

On the beach I was all by myself. My outfit was gone and I didn't know anyone. Everybody was dying, dead or wondering what the hell was going on. The Jap Naval Landing Force did not have mortar platoons. They were reserved for their army which was a very fatal mistake, proven by how mortar fire nearly wiped out the 1st Marine Division a year later on Peleliu. Our tiny concentrated beachhead would have been candy for them

Then a lieutenant said, "To stay here is to die. We need to get over the seawall and fight. Get over the seawall and into a shell hole!" I got to a shell hole with six other guys. The pure horror of wading into bullets had knocked all the decency out of us, making us like animals.

This guy was sitting across from me with his

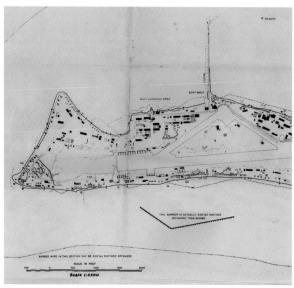

Betio is the largest atoll in the Gilbert Islands and is where the Battle of Tarawa took place. A freak neap tide exposed the reef, which prevented the landing craft from continuing on to the beach. The Marines were forced to wade the remaining 500 yards to shore, approximately the length of the pier (as seen in this map's upper right-hand section) under heavy enemy fire. *Author's collection.*

guts in his hands. So I got his skivvies out of his pack and helped put his belly together. I told him I had to go, but he should wait and someone would come back for him. Another guy in the shell hole stuck his head up and, "thump," he rolled back dead. The guy next to me was all bleary-eyed. I wondered why he looked that way and then I saw some brains hanging out behind his ear. I told the two of them to stay there and that someone would come and get them. We all wore the same uniform and so I suppose they didn't even know I was a corpsman.

Everything was crazy, evening was coming and we just thought "dig in and wait for a bonzai." It never came and later we learned the reason. The head Jap commander was in this big block house. He came out to lead wounded in and someone spotted him, called in a naval strike and killed him. So it was from lack of communication that the Japanese failed to charge the first night.

We were happy to see a sunrise that we hadn't figured on. Though our beachhead was small, they were killing as many on D-1 as they did on D-day. But now we heard some of our guns and we were seeing some dead Japs.

Later that morning I found a guy with his jaw shot off and was surprised how long his tongue was, hanging down and covered with sand. I said, "Are you able to help me if I help you?" He nodded his head so I got him back to a makeshift aid station where I noticed the tide had taken most of the dead in the water out to sea. They were floating out past the transports where small boats were collecting dog tags and weighing down the bodies so they would sink. Anyway, when I brought him in, I stepped on a Marine lying down on the beach and heard him groan. I told the doctor, "Hey, there is a guy dying right here." The doctor said, "The guy has less of a chance of surviving than the others." I sort of mouthed off and said, "I wonder if that's what his mother thinks!" He and I never got along after that.

In returning I ran into a familiar face, my old pal Gunnery Sergeant Reber, a dyed-in-the-wool Marine. Later I would have to watch that great guy die on Saipan. He said, "Ben, we're making history!" His face was all bloody, but the blood was not his. We were pinned down in one hole when a Jap tank rolled up and lowered his gun and waved it back and forth. There were about eight or ten of us in there and of course we all froze. The tanker must have figured we were dead or his gun jammed because all of a sudden he about-faced and rumbled off. We thought "Boy, that's great." While we were catching our breath a grenade rolled in and a Marine rolled on top of it. He was blown all over us. I took his dog tags and later turned him in for the Medal of Honor. When they asked me if I had anyone to substantiate it. I said, "Hell no, I didn't even know the guy who saved our lives!" So he didn't get the medal. The name of that dead Marine had a funny name that I can't remember, it started with a "V."

The next day I saw this guy who was shot below the knee and his leg was shattered. As I put a rifle on his leg for a splint and bandaged him up, a big Jap ran up and said, "Marine, you die!" He should have used his rifle instead of his mouth because I shot him while he was hollering. That's the other thing; when you land on an island like that, bullets are flying all over, people are dying all over and you have no idea who's killing who. But here I was, looking down at this dead Japanese soldier when he could just as easily have been looking down at me. When you kill a man yourself it's an entirely different feeling.

Years later it got to be my private war as it all came back in my dreams. That's why my wife and I slept separate years ago. The dreams come back even now and in a way it's a wonderful thing, you know. Most people think it would be terrible thing, but where else could you go to experience something from the past that was so important?

## *Tarawa*
### *Anthony Karcher*

*On the morning of 23 November, the last day of fighting, Anthony Karcher was with a group of Marines from the First Battalion, Eighth Marines of the 2nd Marine Division as they advanced on a pocket of resistance. Karcher was met by a Japanese soldier whose gun jammed — Karcher shot him dead. Inside the dead man's helmet was a letter which Karcher quickly stuffed into his backpack before rejoining the battle. By noon the pocket of resistance had been neutralized and the island was declared secure at 1300. During the 76-hour fight for an island three miles long and a half-mile across, an area approximately equal to the size of the Pentagon and its parking lots, 1056 Americans were killed and another 2,292 were wounded. Nearly all of the 4,700 Japanese defenders were killed.*

*In 2015 Anthony Karcher's captured letter was translated into English for the first time. It was written by Shigeichi Kinoshita and addressed to his mother via a post office within the 7th Sasebo Naval*

**Captain J. J. "Jack" Wade**

In this famous photograph taken on 23 November 1943, Captain J. J. "Jack" Wade, liaison officer for the 1st Battalion, 10th Marines, 2nd Marine Division, is seen standing center left as he consults a map with Colonel David Shoup, who led the initial 20 November invasion of Tarawa. During the landing Shoup's LVT was destroyed by enemy fire. As he waded to shore Shoup was struck by shrapnel in his legs and received a grazing bullet wound to the neck. Shoup rallied his men on the beach and for the next sixty hours, without sleep, he directed attacks against fanatically defended Japanese positions before Colonel Merritt Edson, the helmeted figure standing in the shadows with hands on hips, took over command on the night of 22 November. Edson was well known for his defense of Lunga Ridge on Guadalcanal in September 1942 — for which he received the Medal of Honor. Also present in the photo is Lieutenant Colonel Evans Carlson, seated front. Carlson is renowned for the Makin Island raid in 1942, for his "Long Patrol" behind enemy lines on Guadalcanal, and is considered the forefather of U.S. special operations forces. Most published examples of this photograph appear with the tag line, "Lt. Colonel Shoup briefing an unidentified Marine officer." Although the identity of the Marine standing next to Shoup has gone unrecognized for over seventy years, this was never the case at Jack Wade's house. His framed copy of the photograph carries the topsy-turvy tag line "Captain J. J. Wade briefing an unidentified Marine officer." Jack Wade, always a true Marine, died in 1993 on the Marine Corps' Birthday, 10 November. Department of Defense Photo USMC 63505.

Top left: Wade's Tarawa dog tags and captain bars.

Above left: A close-up of Captain Wade.

Above right: Wade as he appeared in 1952. Wade was promoted to Captain on 8/43, Major on 9/44, and Lt. Colonel 1952.

*Barickman collection.*

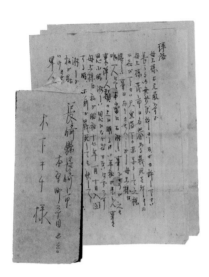

Kinoshita's letter. *Barickman collection.*

*District, suggesting that Kinoshita was fighting with the 7th Sasebo Kaigun Tokubetsu Rikusentai, the Marine component of the Imperial Japanese Navy. They were known to U.S. Marines as the Special Naval Landing Force and Tarawa was their most famous defensive battle of the Pacific War. Kinoshita's mother's address, 3 Chome, 430 Banchi, Motohara-machi, Nagasaki-shi, Nagasakiken, was twelve blocks from what would become ground zero when the atomic bomb was dropped on Nagasaki on 9 August 1945.*

Mother, how are you?

Please excuse me for not writing for such a long time. Mother, I have died an honorable death in battle. Please be happy. As a child of His Majesty the Emperor, there is no greater honor. Although you are probably lonely as you read this please do not despair. When I joined the military on January 10, Shouwa 17, you promised that you would never miss me or cry, even if I am killed in the war. Please don't cry just because I was killed in the war. It was my destiny. Please smile bravely as a military man's mother. I don't know how many soldiers in a one parent and one child family have

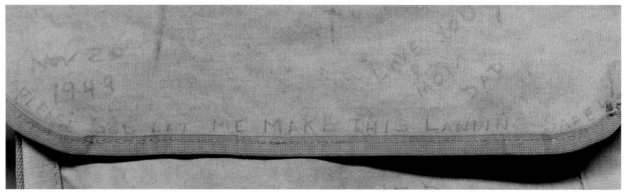

Top right: Private Anthony Karcher stuffed Shigeichi Kinoshita's letter into his pack (top right) and then rejoined the fight. Before the battle Karcher wrote a note on the inside flap of his haversack (above): "November 20, 1943. Please God, let me make this landing safely — Love you Mom and Dad." *Barickman collection.*

been killed in war. If people say that you are lonely and sad, please say that nothing makes you happier than being a military man's mother; this is my last request. Thank you for loving me until now. After I'm gone, please live peacefully with Uncle Takeno Kubo every day. And also get the money from the company and use it for living expenses. If you receive a plain wooden box with my ashes, please place it to the left of father. Please inform Aunt Asako. Mother, please be a person loved by others by doing good things as much as possible. Even if I go to the Yasukuni Shrine and become a God, I will always be at your side to protect you. Please cheer up, work hard and strive for victory. Take care of yourself. I am praying for your health.

Shigeichi

# *Hawaii*
## *George Pollard*

After the battle we were shipped off to Hawaii. The air below deck stank of Tarawa: the smell of burning flesh from Japanese killed by flamethrowers; our dead on the beach, bloated and rotting under the hot tropical sun — it was all too much. It clung to our hair, clothes, everything. From Hilo we went to our new camp near Kamuela, a tiny village in between Mauna Loa and Mauna Kea. The camp was located on the Parker Ranch. I spent my spare time writing letters home and sketching.

Dear Folks,

The reception we received upon our return from Tarawa was definitely a "Sign me up, I'll fight" one. Our ship lists under the weight of the men as they rushed to our starboard — everyone wanted to see the band. It was playing the Marines Hymn — the feeling was wonderful. It was still more wonderful to realize that you deserved it. I couldn't help but laugh at the people fighting for our Japanese souvenirs, as we threw them from the ship's deck to the dock below and every now and then one of them would fall flat on' their face. A barter system was immediately set up: our Japanese souvenirs for anything they had to offer — it was quite fun. Even our officers seemed to be enjoying them-

"After The Battle": Ink drawing by George Pollard aboard the USS *Zeilin*. *Author's collection*.

selves. Despite the fact that part of the time a steady rain fell from an overcast sky, the harbor seemed more beautiful than the one we had just left thirty days previously — Wellington.

Merry Christmas,
George

Dear Mother and Dad —

Nothing much to write about, but here goes. Mail service is real good these days, a week to ten days. Just recently have my Christmas Pks. stopped coming. They all arrived in good order — all practical too.

Did I ever mention Forrest B. Prince. He was one of my very best friends. He got shot through the neck getting out of a landing boat on Tarawa. Just finished writing a letter to his girl in New Zealand, telling her of his death. They had big plans on getting married when

In Hawaii, Pollard sketched drawings of some of the men from the Division who distinguished themselves at Tarawa. The drawings appeared in the Camp Tarawa newspaper *Tarawa Boom De-Ay. Author's collection.*

Above right: Pollard's drawing of Pfc. French as it appeared in *Tarawa Boom De-Ay. Author's collection.*

the war was over.

Hope dad is sleeping these nights. Incidentally, how is the arthritis? You should both take it plenty easy now that you have sold the farm.

My time is occupied mostly by drawing. I believe experience I gain in the Marine Corps will prove most beneficial when I carry on after the war, so don't worry about me, I'll be O.K.

Attended a [Camp Tarawa] rodeo last week. It was just fair. Good attempt by the Marine corps thou'. They try their best to keep the morale of the men high, which is really not difficult. Most men are certain that they will come back or are certain they will die, so either way nobody cares a'lot what happens. You mentioned that you bought some war bonds. It is a relief to know that some of the people back home are supporting the

men behind the guns. Just keep up the work back home and we can't fail. I'm afraid the fellows would be a little itchy on their trigger fingers if they ever sighted in on a few of the men that are on strike.

The time is 22:00, which is 10:00 PM your time. I am writing this letter by the light of kerosene lantern, the same kind we used to milk with - sort of makes me homesick.

Love,
George

## *Saipan*
### *Bud Benoit*

My group landed at Saipan two days behind our division. We were a special group used to plug trouble spots. As we advanced through a wooded area a big mountain gun let go and shaved off the treetops right above us. The next round was even closer. While digging in we found we were sitting on top of an ammo dump! The next one would have been in our pocket but by then the Navy had them spotted and blew the side of the hill out. Hurray for the Navy!

Over the next hill we could hear the Japs approaching. This prompted a frantic search on our part for a bazooka man. We found one, he popped the tank and we took the hill overlooking Garapan town, dubbed "Hill Able."

Keeping it was another story. I'd seen some crazy Japs before but these seemed not only willing but over-anxious to die. They attacked all night and

our biggest advantage was that our hand grenades exploded and most of theirs didn't. They were so close that we had to count down so they wouldn't throw ours back. I thought for sure that there would

"I killed a Jap on Saipan and he had a roll of film on him. I had it developed and this was one of the shots he took." — Bud Benoit.

The flag Bud Benoit captured at the Battle of Saipan. *Barickman collection.*

be some hands missing. Just when you wondered if dawn would ever come, it did, and attacks fell off.

It was always raining on Saipan and so we were always wet. We were drying things out one day while waiting for the 4th Division to catch up. We had just put wet socks and Jap battle flags out to dry when a Navy pilot thought we were a hill full of enemy troops. We'd never seen smoke rings from a plane before but someone yelled, "Hit the deck!" and all hell broke loose. The rocket made small rocks into shrapnel, causing casualties galore. John Bakeman had been sent down for more ordinance and Spike Larson had taken his foxhole. The rocket took all the meat off his leg. He asked me

if it was bad. I said, "Pretty bad," and he rolled his head to one side. Gunnery Sergeant Reber was less fortunate. He should have died outright but he was too tough and ornery. He gave me his prize rifle, a Springfield 03. I wish he could have hung around a little longer. He saw it as a sign of weakness to show affection to anyone, but since my stripes

Benoit's KA-BAR fighting knife, carried on Tarawa, Saipan and Tinian. *Barickman collection.*

matched his, he tolerated me and at times I thought he even liked me. He was a different kind of guy and didn't associate with anybody. He got to like me though. Back in New Zealand, every six weeks or so he would walk into our tent when we were rolling dice. He would only roll the dice once. If he lost, he'd walk out. If he won, he also walked out — but with a lot of money.

A blow-by-blow description of Saipan is beyond my memory. Highlights will have to do. One night I was dueling a Jap from a machine-gun pit when all of a sudden he stopped shooting. I figured he moved on but in the morning he was still there, shot through the neck. He had a novel flag portraying two big Japs making little Japs in the middle of the meatball.

Later, we came upon a defensive position recently evacuated and thought, "Great, we do not have to dig foxholes." During the night we got visitors. The Japs were active at night and so you slept light. They were moving through their old position and must have figured we were still Japs yet. I woke up with someone talking Japanese to me! So I was thinking, "What am I going to do now?" I'm lying on my rifle and I didn't have a pistol. If I couldn't answer him soon, I was going to be gone or he was going to be gone. The Jap continued talking and as he came in low near my foxhole I lunged out and ran him through. He gurgled for a while and then went quiet. In the morning I saw he was an officer. Inside his uniform he had tucked away this novel flag. It had the Bengal tiger jumping out of the meatball. The tiger is supposed to be a good luck thing. The tiger goes out to hunt but always returns home. Well, I fouled that thing up for him. He also had a saber and a *harikari* knife that I later sent home but some censor put the grab on them, but I still have the flag.

As corpsmen we were in the same danger as scout snipers because we were the only ones who would leave the protection of the line to perform our duty. The Japs knew that if they knocked us off it would take a couple of Marines to come off the line

and do our duty. The Japs would yell, "Corpsman!" and when a corpsman would come they would shoot him. For this reason I told my guys to call me Ben, not corpsman. I also told the new corpsmen working with me that when they approached a wounded Marine, move him, because someone has got that wounded Marine in their sight. Get him out of there first and then take care of him. I lost many corpsmen and often they were found dead next to a dead Marine. I would lose four, call headquarters and they would send four more. I would see them going up the hill and later I'd see a cart full of bodies coming back down, their legs dangling. "Who are they?" I'd ask. "Your corpsmen," they'd reply. I lost twenty guys on Saipan alone.

We called for artillery during the terrible banzai charge that spread out for half a mile. The first short round picked me up. I was unconscious and bleeding from my eyes, ears, nose and ass, and they put me in the pile with the dead guys. I woke back up in a field hospital, which started a missing-in-action report that took me months to clear up.

When it was reported back home that I was missing-in-action, my girlfriend, who Mom didn't like anyway, came over and they worked the Ouiji board. It said "Bud's six feet under." I wrote home but Mom was convinced I had written a letter dated ahead so she wouldn't worry. I wrote her, "Since when does a little Catholic mom believe in an Ouiji board?" But the thing I'll never forget was watching mothers throwing their babies off Marpi Point to be bashed to death or drowned and then jumping after them. The Nips had told the natives we had caused all the atrocities that in reality they had committed. All our loudspeakers didn't help. They just kept it up. You never saw such a pile of humanity. Some were dying, some were smothered beneath, all screaming and hollering and beyond help.

## *Tinian*
### *Bud Benoit*

After Saipan we prepared for Tinian. For two weeks we enjoyed the safety of the USS *Bell*, where we were given the run of the ship to sleep, shower and slurp ice cream. Word got out about my flag with the two fornicating Japs and everyone wanted to give me money for it. I said, "Nope." Then an ensign came up and he said, "What do you want for the flag?" I said, "Keep us all pretty well figured out in a little booze until we land on the next island, that will take care of it." He done a good job.

On July 24th, 1944 we invaded Tinian. The Corps split up the island, the 2nd Division driving north and the 4th driving south. Because of the flat terrain the 10th moved in with their howitzers, which was just what the doctor ordered.

I was with Corporal Shultz near the end of the battle when people started walking out of caves to surrender to the both of us. Shultz and I split up to look for more prisoners. As I walked a little bit further this Jap came out of a cave. Many of the soldiers tried to disguise themselves as natives, but this officer was proud and came out in his uniform. In perfect English he said, "I want to surrender my sword, I am your prisoner." I took his sword and him as prisoner. I continued bringing back prisoners and when I'd turn them in they would all bow politely. "Shultz brings us prisoners, Benoit brings us bowers," the Marine in charge would say.

When the battle was nearly over I dug a little guy out of a hole he was hiding in. I didn't know it at the time but a Marine Corps photographer took a picture of me cleaning him up. This little guy followed me around and I loved taking care of him.

Unaware of the photographer, Bud Benoit is pictured cleaning up a Chamarro boy after pulling him from his hiding place on Tinian. National Archives photo #127-GW-866-90441.

I looked after him and he followed me wherever I went. Being a corpsman I could do what I wanted, so I brought him back to Saipan. At Saipan I was in charge of a tent where I made him a little cot. When I went to the chow line I'd bring him back some food; he would never go to the chow line with me. I would say "Stay here," and he would be there waiting when I got back. He ate all the food I brought him. I was thinking of adopting him and wrote to my mother about it. He was Chamorros, not Japanese. The word got out that he was there with me and his relatives came over from Tinian and got him. He was a very big part of my life.

The sword surrendered to Benoit from the English-speaking Japanese officer on Tinian. *Barickman collection*.

## The Occupation of Nagasaki
### George Pollard

*After Saipan and Tinian, the 2nd Marine Division participated in the Battle of Okinawa (floating reserve), and in the initial occupation of Japan.*

Dear Folks,

We are located near the city of Nagasaki on the Island of Kyushu, southern-most of the Japanese Archipelago. On 9 August the second Atomic Bomb fell in the heart of the city. The damage is indescribable. The ultimate in horror has reached infinity. To expedite killing to a finer degree would be impossible. But even so there are many cities and areas surrounding this nucleus of death that have remained untouched to the delight of all hands.

The Japanese people observed us at first with forced reserve because of an unwarranted fear of Marines indoctrinated in them, quite completely, by the Japanese Gov't. The country is picturesque with its oriental architecture, rice paddies, streams and snow-covered mountains. Its inhabitants are quaint and easy to like, even thou' just as easy to kill a few months ago. The climate is invigorating. All war and want of war has left the Marines and uppermost in my mind is coming home. Despite my hopes, the Marine Corps system of rotation STINKS! Actually it's disgusting. Men in the army with a great deal fewer points than I have are already released. This should be in reverse because of the minority of Marines compared to other services. My being home by Christmas is unlikely. Better count on my birthday as the final word. In just a few months I'll be on my way home in a zoot suit with a cigar in my mouth.

Love,
George

Dear Yous, and never mind the grammar —

I am late, I am late again with my letter for the week. Time flies at a speed that is fantastic. It really is unbelievable. Weeks fly by like sign posts.

For the last two hours it has been pouring, similar to standing under Niagara Falls. What were dry gulches are now raging torrents. You step out of your tent and almost drown. This afternoon we were coughing from the dust.

Incidentally, the picture of the Marine was not me. Good guess thou! Keep trying. Fact is I have never been on that island. Don't feel foolish about thinking that was me. Just about every fellow I know over here has had a Mother or sis at one time or another who has seen them in official photos — they are especially prone to recognizing anyone as their son in the news reels.

My resistance must be very low. I have drank two cans of beer this evening and feel inebriated. The food situation stinks. It really isn't food, it's garbage. Boy they really got a good line when they tell you all the food is coming overseas. I am constantly famished 24 hours a day, and I eat in the NCO mess which is a little bit better than the lesser rated men. So draw your own conclusions as to what the average man is eating. Maybe that's why I can't write long letters — I don't have the strength. Seriously, things are worse than I say and censorship regs say you can't talk about it because of civilian morale.

The camp is full of poker games tonight. Also, the crescendo of dice can be heard over the din of laughter, screams and curses. Fortunately I don't have a cent. I left it all riding on the books, arn't I smart!

Well this ends another letter. With my solemn promise to write a longer letter next week. Just wait and see? You know Mother, you always said a man's no better than his word.

Love,
George

*(See his mother's response to this letter on the opposite page.)*

Dear Folks,

It's Sunday afternoon, this is the first time during the war that I have seen Sunday observed in its proper manner. Usually there was work to be done if we were not fighting. Today it was church in the morning and then rest for the remaining part of the day. It's very sunny and warm and the weather seems more like spring than fall. It's truthfully a beautiful day in Nagasaki!

I have just returned from the shopping district in town. Naturally the Japanese don't observe the Sabbath so they don't close their shops. The attitude of everyone seems so docile and unbelievably cooperative that it's hard to think about wanting to kill them, as we did such a short time ago. The Marines and the shopkeepers

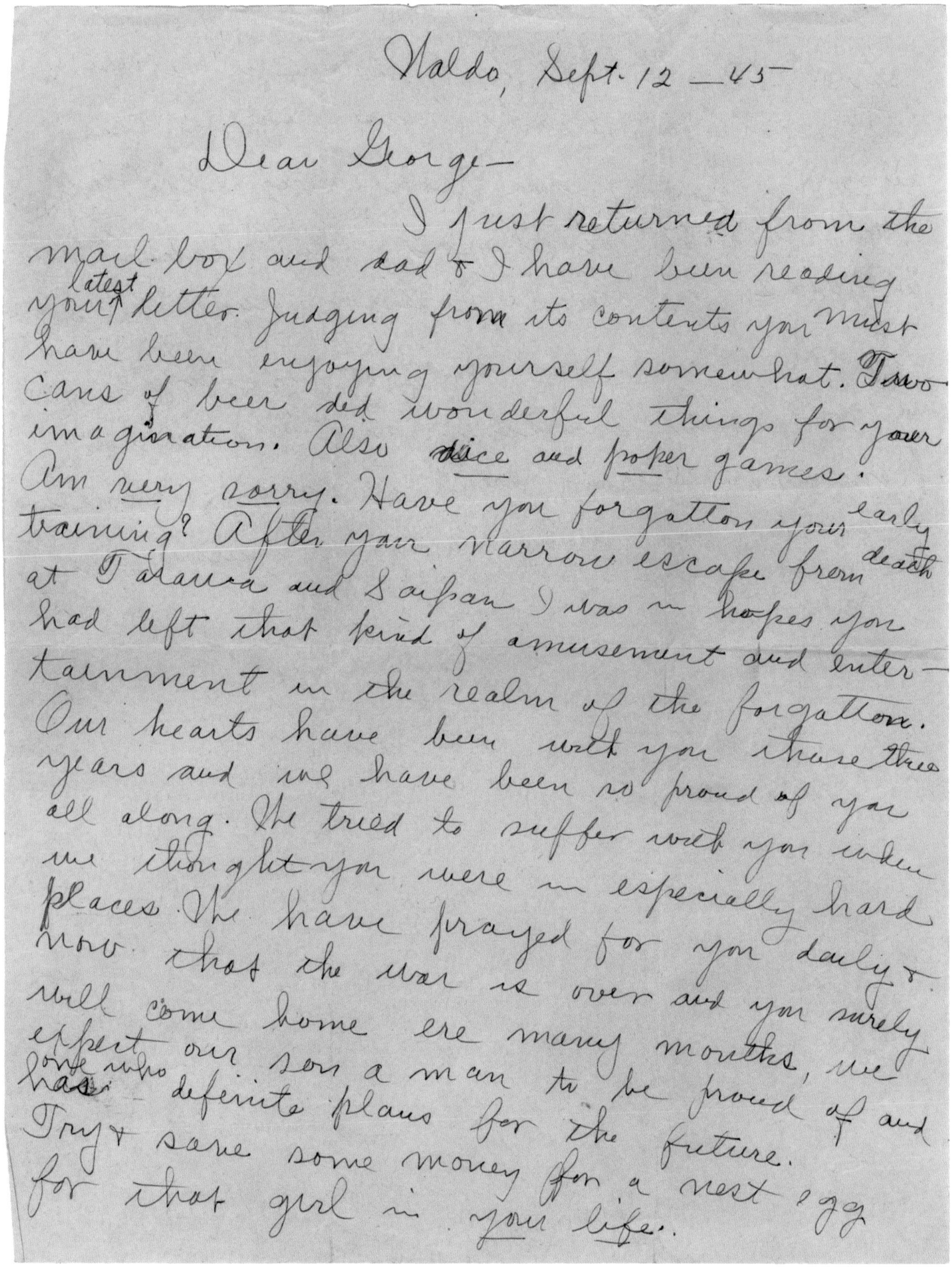

Waldo, Sept. 12 — 45 —

Dear George —

I just returned from the mail box and dad & I have been reading your latest letter. Judging from its contents you must have been enjoying yourself somewhat. Two cans of beer did wonderful things for your imagination. Also dice and poker games! Am very sorry. Have you forgotten your early training? After your narrow escape from death at Tarawa and Saipan I was in hopes you had left that kind of amusement and enter— tainment in the realm of the forgotten. Our hearts have been with you these three years and we have been so proud of you all along. We tried to suffer with you when we thought you were in especially hard places We have prayed for you daily & now that the war is over and you surely will come home ere many months, we expect our son a man to be proud of and one who has definite plans for the future. Try & save some money for a nest egg for that girl in your life.

From Waldo, Wisconsin, Anna Pollard wrote this letter to her son George in response to his letter that begins, "Dear Yous." *Author's collection.*

"Playing Cards," brush and ink drawing by George Pollard. *Author's collection*.

carry on very polite and business-like transactions. The large store (the only one left) that we shop at is very modern with its nice-looking shop girls, elevators, etc. I stopped in the record department and purchased one. Boy, you should hear this Oriental music. If bringing a record from Japan to Waldo without breaking it is possible, I'll show you what I mean. I am not alone with my music critic's attitude. The Japs around camp have the opportunity to overhear our lively Jazz music and they think it stinks (period).

Perhaps you are amazed at some of the things I have told you in previous letters as well as this one, about the friendly way things are going here. Personally I find it rather hard to treat these people like cattle. Not one of them has done anything against me as an individual. The war is over and I am only too happy to forget it. Unfortunately, there are some who don't feel quite that way because of the atrocities that the Nips performed on the Allied troops who were prisoners-of-war here. There were a large number of Aussies who were captured at the fall of Singapore. Some evidence leads us to believe that they were very cruelly treated.

Love,
George

Dear Folks,

It is late evening and I am all alone. From where I am sitting I can look out across the harbor and see the ruins of the city. Out in the bay many of our ships are anchored. It seems so strange to see them without the blackout restrictions. Back here at camp everyone is fast asleep, all except the sentries walking post. The forgotten man, the underpaid, and underfed and overworked Private. He does all the work and gets the least credit.

Tomorrow is another day of patrolling. We will go north of the city, all the way to the bay. The people in the country are much cleaner with a higher standard of living which makes patrolling a most delightful task that is more like a Sunday school picnic than a regular working day in the Corps. Believe me when I tell you that I am really taking it easy. The only order I ever give as sergeant is to "Take it Easy." Naturally, this is a direct violation of Marine Corps policy. They would have us snapping if they could. You might not believe or understand this but it is true. The officers are really sorry to see the end of the war. All the end means to them is lost prestige. The Pvts did all the work while

the officers bathed in splendor.

I have told you about how cute little kids these Nips are. It really is impossible to over-emphasize this. They all are real tiny with big brown eyes and blue black hair. The little girls all wear these pot hair cuts with bright-colored flowers or ribbons in their crowning glory. The kids all possess an obsession of curiosity. They climb all over you and examine everything on your person. Their Mother never sees them from early morn to bedtime which is any time they feel like. The mischief they get into is inconceivable, no kidding. If the average American mother ever saw these kids they would pass out. You used to think the Kasners were a bunch of roughnecks — they were angels. These kids just about die laughing at my Japanese. Evidently, I have an accent that is something like a Polish immigrant. I do speak enough to get by on. Haven't tried my technique on the older babes yet, but most of the fellows are interested in seeing if it is true what they say about Japanese women. (Better have someone else explain that one to you.)

Love,
George

Dear Folks

It's a beautiful day in Japan. We are having a rest from patrolling (about time) and just taking it easy. I listened to the first three games of the World Series by direct broadcast from Detroit. Certainly wish I could be in Chicago to see the series end. Even the Japanese are mildly interested in the game.

All the little Nip shops have opened and are displaying their wares. It's mostly junk, and because of the exorbitant prices they were charging the Occupation Gov't was forced to establish a price ceiling similar to our OPA. They did have a very limited supply of silk kimonos. I priced a bright red one with a satin lining plus some elaborate hand stitching for 2000 yen. I didn't have the money at the time and some one else glommed on to it.

The favorite drink in this country is Saki. It is reasonably priced and very popular among the Marines, as well as the Japs. One thing this place isn't short of is Rice! It is grown on little plots of land called rice paddies. I have never seen such soil conservation, even the sides of the mountains are terraced. When the people go out to harvest the crop it's everyone from the tiniest of infants to the most decrepit of grandmothers. They

Pollard pictured with a local gal on the outskirts of Nagasaki. She is wearing *monpe* (women's trousers). It was considered unpatriotic for women to wear more extravagant *wafuku* "traditional clothing" like *kimonos* "thing to wear" or *yōfuku* "western clothing" during the years of war rationing. *Author's collection.*

work from very dawn to late evening. It is difficult to comprehend the amount of work these people put forth.

The form of Gov't was a direct oligarchy, ruled with an iron rod by the Militarists and the Industrialists who keep the populace in the dark. The average person had absolutely no conception of the situation as it existed during the war. Their only faith is an undying loyalty to his Emperor who they believe to be a direct descendant of the sun god. To commit Hari Kari is part of their national creed — one of the reasons that the Japanese Soldier was such a tenacious fighter. Rather than surrender and bring shame upon his god he would take his own life. More on the far Eastern situation in a few days.

Love,
George

Dear Folks,

Once again I sit down and attempt to think of new and original ideas in presenting the Orient to you. Guess I'll tell you a little about the women. To start with they do all the work. It is not at all unusual to see a woman walking along carrying some huge bundle while her husband walks ahead of her, empty-handed!! Incidentally, this walking ahead of the woman is a custom that is rigidly adhered to. The woman walks about three or four paces to the rear, following very meekly.

Marriage is a strange act in the far east. The man takes her more or less as a slave, as the husband visits Geisha houses and brothels unhidden. It is a common practice for wealthy men to take Geisha Girls as mistresses and have them live in the same house as his wife.

At this point I shall attempt to explain the difference between the Geisha and the common whore. The Geisha is always very beautiful and primarily an expensive, talented entertainer, not necessarily a prostitute. In rare cases her virginity is her biggest asset. You might describe the Geisha as the equivalent to our movie actresses. They can be had under the right conditions and the right price. But even this description is not worthy because they also hold much social prestige, similar to a cross between Congresswoman Clare Boothe, Gloria Vanderbilt, Eleanor Roosevelt and Paulette Goddard — with a Betty Grable thrown in to make her fickle. The red light district is in the same area as the Geisha houses. A washed out Geisha usually turns into a prostitute. I might mention that the Geisha is a very honorable profession, the only woman that is considered on a equal with the men. Time and time again we took Geisha prisoners-of-war. They were always outstanding because of their arrogant appearance. To sum it all up the Oriental woman is very intricate piece of flesh, and just about as hard to understand as the average American gal??? I can just hear the screams that will be put by American mothers when the "Yanks" start getting hitched to these broads. They are getting ideas already.

Love,
George

## The Return Home
### Bud Benoit

It was at Saipan that I got a bad case of dengue fever and was sent home for thirty days to convalesce. Minneapolis was heaven on earth. I didn't see another Marine for 30 days. The people there treated me like I was one of the flag raisers at Iwo Jima.

My next duty station was Pearl Harbor, where I was in charge of corpsmen on LST 208. With a belly full of tanks we headed for Okinawa. We were lucky the kamikazes choose larger targets than us. After doing what a LST does for seven months, we found ourselves in a harbor in Jinsen, Korea, across from China, and WHOOPIE! The war is over!

The LST had come from the States so all aboard had no discharge points except for me. Since they weren't going back, it was time for me to start hitch hikin'. I was broke and found a Dutch ship that would take me, but only if I joined their boxing program to pay for my fare til we got to a rotation center. I had to box every other night til we docked in the Philippines. There I caught a ship back to Pearl, and from Pearl, back to the U-S-of-A and then Minneapolis. This all took about three months, and what a difference — no more welcoming party. The only people who knew I had returned were my family and friends. I received a one-hundred-dollar mustering-out pay and registered for the 52/20 club, where you could receive $20 a week for a year, or until you found a job.

Before the war I had a great job as a delivery truck driver for a bakery. After the war my old boss didn't forget me and wanted me back soon, so all I collected from the 52/20 club was one week — twenty bucks. I bumped everyone back in the bakery one notch and some of the employees might have resented it, but I never heard anything.

After several months I found that the skin condition I developed after Tarawa was from what today they call post-traumatic stress. I just called it bad dreams. I'd wake up just as tired as when I went to bed, and at my job as a delivery truck driver you had to be alert. So I started thinkin' my good job wasn't so good anymore. Then me and the boss's son who had been overseas together with me started a French dressing business, since vegetable oil hadn't been removed from the war ration list but through the bakery we had access to it. The dressing was in such demand that we didn't have to do no delivering. Later, when oil was available we closed up. We had made a lot of money and had a lot of fun evenings while drinkin' beer. Mom knew of my night tantrums so when her and my older sister were shopping for a beer joint, she said, "Join Us." We found a beer joint for sale and when I applied for a license I was told by the official, "You are the youngest person ever to apply, and you picked the toughest joint in town. Can you handle that?" When I told him I had seen Tarawa, he just said, "Sign here."

Three Warriors, left to right, George Pollard, Don Jones and Sakae Oba. Jones and Oba together wrote the book *Oba, The Last Samurai* which was released in the U.S. in 1986. A movie with the same name was released in 2011. When asked what his thoughts were 44 years ago when he learned U.S. Marines had for the first time gone on the offensive in the Pacific, he reflected a moment before answering: "I remember it well, for I thought, 'The Americans are weak. Victory will be ours.' I was wrong." Photo taken by the Author in Kenosha, Wisconsin.

# Epilogue
## Reunion

*It was September 1986. George Pollard, Don Jones and Sakae Oba sat at the dinner table telling stories. Forty-two years earlier the first two were trying to kill the third in the jungles of Saipan. Jones was a 19-year-old interpreter and Pollard was a 24-year-old corporal; both were best of friends serving with the Second Marine Division. Oba was a 29-year-old infantry officer in the Imperial Japanese Army with seven years of combat experience in Manchuria.*

"The Battle of Saipan began on June 15th, 1944," said Pollard. "The Japanese put up a strong defense but were eventually overwhelmed." In early July, having suffered heavy losses and with no re-supply or relief available, the situation appeared hopeless for the Japanese defenders.

Speaking through Jones, who was fluent in Japanese, Oba jumped into the conversation. "When the island was about to fall I prepared to commit suicide. I was to the point where I had the pistol in my hand and had chosen a second when an order came through for me to lead my men in a *Gyokusai* attack on the American lines."[4]

On 7 July, Captain Oba and his men participated in the largest banzai charge of the Pacific War. As the banzai charge struck in one area, Oba and his men battled through the American front line to the middle of the island. Oba survived the assault. Thinking that the Imperial fleet would return and that Japan's victory in the war was inevitable he decided to carry on.

For eighteen months Oba lead a small group of Japanese soldiers who watched over an additional 160 civilians who had retreated into the jungle. The soldiers taught the civilians survival skills and prevented their capture. Oba's men also conducted guerrilla-type attacks, confounding the 45,000-strong U.S. force on Saipan after hostilities were declared over.

"Back then we called Oba 'The Fox' because he was so elusive and refused to surrender even though the battle was lost," said Pollard. "We'd have killed him had we found him. We tried day patrols, night patrols, ambushes; nothing worked. He had his Japanese civilians surrender, but not his soldiers. We whittled them down but we could never get Oba."

Through Jones, Oba said that he was afraid many times on Saipan, "But there is nothing shameful in being afraid," he said. "And any soldier will tell you that."

Then Jones remarked, "We'd learned his name and his rank from prisoners. Oba had over 50 troops and 150 civilians under his command and that they were holed up in an area that was 3 miles wide and 5 miles long."

Jones again interpreted for Oba: "The American

---

4   *Gyokusai* often took the form of a banzai charge, but was not conceived in such raw terms. Its literal meaning, "the shattered jewel," comes from a Chinese proverb: "If we fail, it would be better to fall like pieces of broken jade than remain intact as a worthless tile." One interpretation of the proverb is that it is better to end one's life early with honor than to live a long life with none. In another interpretation, dying gallantly in battle is viewed as ennobling. Shattering oneself in a hopeless battle, rather than surrendering in shame, turned military defeats into moral victories.

troops were very strong and had powerful weapons. They had resources we did not. They were able to call in naval bombardments. But they had flaws. They would not go off the trail. Many times we would be hiding one or two meters from the trail and watch the Americans walk by, searching for us." Oba chuckled.

"He delayed surrendering," Jones added, "because he had been told Japan was winning the war." As Jones and Pollard continued their discussion about Oba's refusal to surrender, Jones paused to translate what was being said. Oba replied, "I felt it was right to resist surrender because I was fighting for my country. Even now, I think it is correct. I was finally convinced to surrender after demanding that my commanding officer on another island issue me orders to do so."

It took Oba time to persuade some of his subordinates who did not want to give up. After his surrender on 1 December 1945, Oba was invited to a U.S. officers club on the nearby Tinian island, where Americans lined up to shake his hand.

Back in Japan his wife, Mineko, had been told that her husband had been killed on Saipan. She held a funeral service for him in 1945.

Oba returned to Japan in 1946. Because of his decision to fight on, many in Japan labeled Oba a coward. In fact, Oba was stripped of his "posthumous" promotion to major which had been awarded in the belief he had died during the Gyokusai.

Jones first contacted Oba in 1965 while working as a foreign service officer in Niigata, Japan. "I wrote to a government locator service for information about Captain Oba. Two weeks later I got his last known address, in Gamagori, near Nagoya. I called information and then dialed his number. A man answered and I asked, 'Is this Captain Oba?' There was a long silence, and I realized that no one had called him 'Captain' in 20 years. I explained that I was interested in his 18-month battle with the U.S. military."

Two days later, Oba and his wife took a train to Niigata where they spent four days with Jones.

They covered his living room with hastily drawn maps, reliving battles they had fought, and formed a lasting friendship. "It was the second time I'd ever seen him. The other time was in a photograph. I was in Chicago being discharged from the Marine Corps in December 1945 when I saw a picture on the front page of a local newspaper." Jones held up a news clipping that Pollard cut out and saved from the same newspaper, now brittle with age, showing Oba surrendering to Lieutenant Colonel Howard Kirgis on Saipan. The heading read "*All Over Now On Saipan.*"

It was not until 1980 that Jones suggested doing a book on Oba's exploits. "He was very reluctant," said Jones, gesturing with his hand towards Oba. "I told him that I thought it would be good for Japan. There are no novels about Japanese soldiers. There have been no novels and there are no heroes. The Japanese do not talk about the war, they prefer to forget. Had he been one of ours, he would have been given the Congressional Medal of Honor." Jones translated what was just said. Oba glanced at his wife; she lowered her eyes, hiding a faint smile.

Pollard clipped this news photo on 9 December 1945 while at Great Lakes, Illinois, awaiting discharge from the Marine Corps. Brittle with age, it depicts Oba surrendering his sword to Lt. Colonel Howard Kirgis on 1 December 1945. *Author's collection.*

# Robert Thompson

# SHANGRI-LA

Thompson's manuscript.
*Author's collection.*

A story here, a story there, Robert Thompson must have felt as if the writing would never end. The experience was too big; he could never tell it all. Thompson's amazing handwritten nine-volume manuscript describes his war years serving as a photographer and photographic gunner with the 4th Photographic Squadron, which flew missions from 1941 to 1945 in South America and in the Pacific.

Volume eight of Thompson's manuscript begins in November 1944 as his squadron heads for the South Pacific to conduct aerial photographic surveys away from the front lines. His story differs from others in this book: it reads like a travelogue, and offers the reader a strangely tranquil portrait of the Pacific War.

## *The South Pacific*

Our first base in the South Pacific was Hollandia, Dutch Guinea. They had trucks ready to take us to our camp, which was about a mile from the airstrip. Our camp was located in what was called "Paradise Plantation in Pom-Pom Valley." Pom-pom was an expression the natives used to describe how men and women made little natives. It sounded reasonable, I thought. Hollandia itself was a few miles away from the ocean. We would spend the next few months mapping the islands in this part of the South Pacific.

Malaria was common here. We took a pill called atabrine with a salt tablet every day before our evening meal. Atabrine turns your skin and the whites of your eyes yellow. As long as you kept taking the pill you would be OK. I was lucky. I had to be, for I roamed the jungle and was around the natives more than any of the guys in our squadron and never came down with the disease.

Glen Hood was a member of the ground crew that set up our camp. We were waiting for our special planes to arrive so we could get started on mapping and reconnaissance work of the islands in the area. Glen was with our group in South America. We had been flying a lot. When we finished mapping the surrounding islands, we were told to prepare to move to Morotai. From there we would continue mapping islands in that area as well.

One of our planes made a test run to see what Morotai was like. When they returned they told us, "Be sure you know where your shoes are when you go to bed. The Japs bombed the part the Allies held of the island every night. Put your shoes on and head for your dugout bomb shelter as fast as you can go." The Allies held one half of the island, the

The Crew. Robert Thompson pictured second from left. *Thompson family collection.*

Japs the other half. The Marines were fighting and the sounds of cannon fire could be heard all night. We figured, no way, they are trying to scare us so we laughed along with them.

From the air, Morotai looked like a lot of other islands we'd seen. We landed and parked our B-24 with other planes on the island. From there we took a truck to our camp which was about half a mile from the airstrip. The boom-boom-boom of the cannons could be heard off in the distance. That part our friends had told us was right. The fighting seemed to be on the far side of the island so it didn't bother us too much. We were told where

our bomb shelter was and to know where our shoes were when we went to bed. We did make a special note of which side of the bed our shoes were on. We finally fell asleep after much discussion about the situation. We hadn't been sleeping long when the sirens started screaming. I couldn't find my shoes. They weren't where I put them. No, they were on the other side of my bed. I must have turned over in my sleep. I quickly put them on and went to the nearest bomb shelter.

The Japs bombed the airfield every night. There was a lot of bang-banging going on and the sky lit up from the exploding bombs. The Japs' bombs hit

#28

"Here I am with the K-18 camera. It is using the mount our welder helped me make." *Thompson family collection.*

the airstrip and then it was over. I returned to bed and spent the remainder of the night trying to sleep. The only casualty was an officer who tripped on his tent guy ropes and skinned his shin.

The next day I went over and examined the bomb shelter. It was made by scooping a hole in the ground. Then a bunch of downed palm trees were laid over the hole. Then dirt was put on top of it all with a hole left in front from which to enter. Inside I saw several bugs with red spots on their underbellies, sort of like a black widow. Now I wasn't sure which was scarier, the bombs or the shelter. From then on, when I went to the shelter I'd stand just outside the doorway. One night I did move inside a ways when the bombs were landing a little too close for comfort.

It wasn't long after that first night that we became used to the nightly bombing. Most nights we would be at a movie when the sirens would go off. On some occasions they would start the movies up again if the raid was a short one. Other times it would take three days to get through just one movie.

One evening we were on our way to a movie when a Jap Zero came in strafing. We went running toward the shelter. I looked back over my shoulder and could see the fire coming from his ma-

chine guns. Everybody was diving into the muddy ditches beside the road. I sure didn't want to hit the muddy ditch and so I kept on running. Lucky for me, about that time the Jap veered off and plunged into the ocean nearby. There was a British Spitfire on his tail and he shot him down. One of our P-38s was in back of the Spitfire.

During the day we would amuse ourselves by lying on our cots and watching the lizards we called Jancos. They would run up and down the sides and tops of the tent. I learned later that they were Chameleons. Most of the time Griffith and I were on the beach or out in the water. George Griffith was our radio operator. We both flew together in South America. Anyway, when we were on the beach we could see far down towards the end of the island. Sometimes we would see men swimming in the ocean. They were Japs. Presumably if we could see them, they could see us. We were shooting at each other at that end of the island and yet we could peacefully watch each other going for a swim in the ocean. It didn't make sense to me.

Griff and I would look for seashells in the water. We'd bury them in the sand and in a couple of days the ants would have them cleaned out for us. These shells were a lot shinier and nicer than the ones found on the beaches. I guess the sand dulled the shine from the shells. There was one special shell we looked for called a cat's eye. Well, it wasn't actually a shell but the end of the animal in the shell. It was what the animal closed the shell's opening with to be more precise. We found a few on the beach. Another GI told us we could find this live shell at the bottom of the reefs out some distance from shore. He said the cat's eye would be a lot better than the ones we found on shore.

We decided to give it a try. There was a two-man life boat that we paddled around in. We got in it and paddled out to the ocean side of the reef. I went overboard and hung on to the boat until I had gotten all the air in my lungs that I could. Then down I went. I was surprised how quickly the water got cooler. I went farther down the face of the reef.

There were holes in the reef. Some were pretty large. I wondered if there might be sharks or barracudas. My imagination got the best of me. I never reached the bottom and came back up in a hurry. When I surfaced I told Griff I'd rather find my cat's eyes on the beach.

Another time we were paddling around in the survival raft from a plane. We paddled out too far and got caught in a current. With a simple one-board paddle we couldn't make any headway back to shore. In fact, we were losing ground. I jumped overboard and started pushing the raft back to shore while Griff paddled. It didn't help. We were going away from our island and getting too close to an island we knew was held by the Japs. I told Griff we'd better try and go sideways to our island. With a lot of padding and feet kicking we finally got out of the current and made our way back to the island. By the time we made it back on the beach we were really pooped and had to rest a while. It was later when we discovered that the island we had been drifting towards in our raft was where the Japs had an airstrip. It was so well camouflaged that our planes never picked it up. I wondered if this was

"Walke and I teamed up in the last tent in the last row of tents near the jungle." *Thompson family collection.*

where they flew from to bomb our airfield at Morotai every night. The Jap airstrip was later bombed and the island taken.

After finishing our mapping flights from Morotai we flew back to our base at Hollandia. After we landed I went to my tent and later returned to the airstrip with my camera. A lot of the bombers had art work painted on the noses and I wanted to get a few pictures. Along the way I had a close look at one of the search lights used to light up the Jap bombers when they came on a raid. Beside the search light was an anti-aircraft gun. The men there said the Japs flew so high that the guns didn't have much effect on them.

The first piece of artwork was "Big Chief Cockeye." I had a seen this picture once before behind a bar at Arrowhead Lake. It looked pretty good on the plane. "Drunkard's Dream" was another good one. A beautiful woman was painted above the nose wheel. Below, on the nose wheel was a painting of a little drunk with a dreamy expression on his face and a big hard-on in his pants. Another was called "Well Developed." One of our photo recon planes had painted "Clique and Shudder" in big tall letters.

We continued with our mapping. On one of our flights we flew over Australia and could see how

hard the Japs had bombed Darwin. We'd heard they'd about wiped it out. What we'd heard was right. There wasn't much left of the place. We'd heard Darwin was a thorn in the Japs' side. One time when the Aussies captured a downed Jap flyer, the pilot was offered a knife to kill himself.

On another of our flights we landed on Los Negros Island to gas up. It was late so we had to spend the night. All the GIs on the island were colored. They put us up for the night in a hanger away from their camp. It was the first time I'd seen a colored GI in the South Pacific. They kept us separate because the coloreds weren't very happy being kept on the island. They were afraid that even the slightest incident might cause a lot of trouble

The 3rd Photographic Squadron was also at Hollandia with us. They lost a plane on the other side of the mountains from Paradise Valley, which was where we were. Three of the crew survived the crash. One was a WAC. The area was full of head hunting natives. The natives thought the plane was from heaven and the three were treated royally, especially the WAC. They called the area Shangri-La. Supplies and a radio set were dropped to the survivors and there was an almost daily accounting of their experiences. It was some time before the army figured how to get them out. The natives in Shangri-La had a complicated irrigation system. Their fields were uniform in the area where the plane went down. It must have taken a fairly large population to keep the fields going. The natives seemed to be somewhat sophisticated in their own way, not like the ones on our side of the mountains. We flew over the area before the survivors were rescued. Our B-24 wasn't really made for buzzing but we flew overhead. Lt. Egan buzzed real close, almost hitting the tops of the palm trees where the survivors were. You could almost shake hands with the girl and two men waving their hands to us. There was some talk of getting them out with gliders.

Down the road from our camp about a quarter of a mile through the jungle was a river. The natives had a trail through the jungle and across the river

"One of the many works of art I had the pleasure of photographing." *Thompson family collection.*

"Someone found this skull in the jungle and stuck it on a pole. Why? I don't know — IT STUNK." *Thompson family collection.*

"These two British New Guinea women are holding little pigs. The Australian soldiers told us the natives regard the pigs as sacred animals, and that they will nurse the pigs. Custom is custom I guess." *Thompson family collection*.

the trail led to their village. My friend Walke and I carried our shoes across so they wouldn't get wet. The village was on a lake. Across the lake from where we stood we could see the village buildings. They are all built on stilts in the lake. When we got to the village we traded cigarettes for six native arrows and a black palm bow. Then we stopped at the missionary's house. He was a native educated by the Dutch. He gathered all the kids into the church and had them sing "Pistol Packin' Mama" for us in perfect English. It was really great. We felt especially honored. The kids speak no English except, "give me cigarette." They learned to sing the song from a record. Their canoes were long hollowed out trees. The kids had smaller versions of their own and would sit at each end. I tried to ride one of the large canoes. Did you ever try to ride a log? It's impossible. The thing just keeps rolling over.

We were invited back to the missionary's house for tea. His wife served us crumpets and cookies made from the flour of a special palm tree. We were the only ones I know of that were ever invited, so it was a real honor. There was a lot of motioning and smiling and it was a good time. We were always welcome at the village. Out of 400-plus men in our camp, only about a dozen ever visited the village and even fewer went exploring the jungle. The kids were all pot bellied from their diet. A lot of the natives had skin cancer and up close their skin had a rough appearance. They all chewed betel-nut and spit globs of red juice every few minutes. I asked one of the natives in sign language if he liked the Japs or the Americans. He motioned that he liked the Japs best. He signed that a Jap officer pom pomed his wife and then he signed, laughing, "I pom pomed him."

McCormick from our camp caught a small lizard; it was about three-and-one-half feet long. McCormick knew Walke and I collected pets so he brought it to our tent and gave it to us. McCormick had been swimming in the swimming hole when he saw the lizard on the bank and threw his shirt over it. He carried the lizard to our tent wrapped in the shirt. I tied a cord around his neck and staked him out in front of our tent. The lizard had a frill on his back that was about three inches high when raised. Its tail was about two-and-one-half feet long and was sharp and very hard. If you bothered him, he'd swing around and try to clobber you with his tail. It would hurt, too. I could never figure out what he ate. I tried feeding him eggs from the mess hall but he wouldn't eat and he kept getting weaker. I decided it was best to let him loose. In a clearing just this side of the jungle I let him loose. When he saw the trees he got up on his hind legs and with his frill raised took off running, just like a small dinosaur. Wish I had the camera.

I always wore my .45 revolver. I always carried it, even when flying. I crossed the big river and instead of going toward the native village like before, I went the opposite way, up the hill. I was

"The Dutch had educated this man (standing left in photo) to be the village missionary. The first time Walke and I visited the village, he invited us into the church and had the native kids sing "Pistol Packin' Mama." They sang amazingly and we really felt honored." *Thompson family collection.*

just wandering about to see what I would see when I suddenly came upon four natives. They had just killed a wild pig and were busy dressing it out. They hadn't noticed my approach and were as startled as I was. They looked at me and I looked at them. The tension between us — you could cut it with a knife. I'd never felt or even knew tension could be so electrifying. I knew I was in the wrong place and had to get out of there. I smiled, motioned to the pig and then to them. I tried to make them feel it was theirs and that I didn't want it. Somehow I had the idea that they thought I'd try and take it from them. Perhaps the Japs did in the past. Anyway, I backed away and then turned and went back toward the river. I had my .45 revolver but I sure didn't want to use it unless I had to. Lucky I didn't. They had only their machetes and maybe spears, but there was four of them and I was sure glad to get out.

Walke went along on one of the flights to Australia and he brought back some canned goods to supplement the lousy meals. The meat he brought back was sure tough. We figured it was kangaroo meat. Walke also brought me back a small green and red parrot. It was a great pet. I kept one wing trimmed so he couldn't fly far. He liked to ride on my shoulder and nibble my ears. When I showered and shaved I'd turn him loose in the high weeds to feed on seeds. He always would come back in the shower, climb up the pipe and watch me shave. He seemed to really enjoy it.

Our squadron had three Australians transferred to us to teach the flying personnel jungle survival in case we were forced down in a jungle area and had to fend for ourselves. They issued us each a $50 gold piece and different Japanese currency to be used to bribe our way out if necessary. Sgt. Goddard of the Australian army split us into small groups to show

"These natives are examining something given them by the Australian soldiers." *Thompson family collection.*

"This native with his two kids wanted to pose with me." *Thompson family collection.*

us how to survive in the jungle. Our first lesson was to protect ourselves from the weather. We learned how to make a platform above the ground and then, with palm leaves, make a rainproof cover above it. Then we were taken into the jungle to learn about plants that were edible and how to get drinkable water from a vine. It was about 3 inches in diameter. You cut the vine and caught the water as it ran out into one of our helmets. Then he cut it again a few inches above the first cut and more water came out again. We learned how to make a simple gadget and weave vines into a rope. You could even make a rope from long grasses. Insects and grub worms were some of the edible insects we learned about. We sure liked our Australian instructors.

Templeton and I made friends with Sgt. Goddard. Goddard told us he was due a furlough and so we asked our pilot, Egan, to see if he could get special permission for him to go along with us to the Philippines. Egan asked around and Goddard was given a three-week vacation to go with us to our new base located at Zamboanga, Mindanao in the southern Philippines.

We started mapping north from the southern

"Here I am sitting on a curb (left) at the waterfront in Zamboanga with our Australian friend Sgt. Goddard." *Thompson family collection.*

Philippines soon after arriving in Zamboanga. We lived in a tent city. Our tent would hold probably 30 GIs but there were only the seven of us in our crew. It was easy to see that Zamboanga City had been a large city before the war. Now, after the bombing by the Japs and then by the Allies, it was a mess. Our camp was practically in town. In fact, it was just a short walk. Many soldiers went to the town but most places were off limits. A lot of GIs had come down with the runs after eating in town. Now there was only one restaurant considered safe to eat at that wasn't off limits. Our meals at camp weren't all that bad but it was more fun to eat in town. We went to the safe restaurant at first but it took forever to get waited on.

From then on we went to the ones off-limits. They would take us into their backyard where they kept the chickens and told us to pick out the ones we wanted, which we did. They would say, "Come back in an hour." They knew their place was off-limits. The meals there were really good, better than expected. I'll never forget how good their fried rice with pieces of beef was. Most of the livestock had been killed by the Japs. We wondered exactly what kind of beef this was — better not to ask. We had eaten like this in Central and South America quite often and figured our systems could handle the native food ok. We were never caught by the MPs.

The waterfront was the most interesting place in Zamboanga. It had been blown to pieces but the natives salvaged what they could and put up a marketplace. The structures were made from pieces of wood, bamboo and tin sheets with palm leaves for roofing. There was lots of bartering and even currency exchanged hands. Life goes on, even in war, and people were carrying on as if things were back to normal. They even smiled and laughed although most had very few possessions left. An odd collection of boats would bring in an even odder collection of fish of all kinds, colors, sizes and shapes to trade.

Many of the natives lived in covered canoes. They all had outriggers in case the wind came up.

I watched a canoe come in with a native who was standing up in the canoe when it docked. He must have been six feet tall, the tallest native I'd ever seen. He was barefooted and I noticed that he had six toes on each foot. I really wanted to take his picture, well, of his feet anyway but felt embarrassed to ask him. His feet were like flippers.

The marketplace was always busy. Where the natives got their money I never quite understood. One family came in from one of the islands that could be seen in the distance. They had come to do some shopping at the market and had two canoes with a platform between them. On top of the platform was dried fish. You could smell it from quite a distance but it didn't seem to bother the natives. You could see natives buying the dried fish. They would make a fish soup. They used the whole fish, heads and all. For us, bartering was the best way to get what we wanted. Cigarettes were high on the list. Clothes came next. The market was a good place for the kids to hang out. You could always find a group of men hanging around as well. Some were busy working but there was always another group just loafing.

Our Australian friend, Sgt. Goddard, and Templeton had gone into town. I was walking around in town when we met. I traded a pack of cigarettes for a sack of avocados that I had been carrying, slung over on my shoulder. Then Goddard and I walked around town together for awhile. We came alongside a GI truck full of GI prisoners. There seemed to be quite a few prisoners in Zamboanga who had broken the law.

This is a picture of our guys with a Philippine girl. It seemed like it would make a good picture.[1] My head is just over her shoulder. I'm still holding on to the sack of avocados. Later we went over to a cocoa grove near camp. I cut one of the pods in half. There are two rows of big seeds and there is a white substance inside. A native who was harvesting the pods had us taste it. It was sweet and quite good. He said the seeds were ground up and

---

1   Photo missing from archive.

#18

#19

roasted to make cocoa. The seeds were awful bitter and we spit them out.

We met up with Lim Hui Hong and his family. Templeton and I were friends with them. Both he and his wife had been educated in the States. They were both teachers here when the Japs took the island. They escaped into the high mountains where they spent two years trying to evade the Japs in the mountain area where the Tasaday tribe lives. The Tasaday lived isolated from the world for generations. They wore no clothes and lived off the land. Hong's youngest child was born in the mountains. Templeton and I tried to help them all we could.

We told some of the guys at the mess hall about Lim Hui Hong and his family. The cooks were very generous and would give us what they could. We also collected clothes and other things from some of the guys. Lim Hui invited us to dinner at where they were living. We were curious what the meal might be like.

The morning we were to have dinner at his place, we took off with another plane on a long mission. Our plane took off first and circled as we waited for the other to get airborne. He didn't show so we circled again and that's when we saw the ball of fire. Both of our planes were carrying a big load

Above: "Lim Hui Hong and his family. The girl on the left was sort of a maid, while the two tall girls are his sisters." *Thompson family collection.*
Opposite Page: "Outrigger canoes in Zamboanga." Thompson's photos were numbered to correspond to numbered passages in his text. *Thompson family collection.*

"Well, at least Swain was ready for action. S/Sgt. Howard Swain was the 1st engineer on our plane." *Thompson family collection.*

of fuel. The plane had hit the top of some palm trees on take-off. It also hit two native huts and about 20 people were killed. We cancelled our flight and flew out over the ocean to jettison our fuel before landing. We circled four hours to burn up more fuel in an effort to reduce our load so it would be safe to land. We finally landed and then went to see what was left of the plane and crew that crashed. The sight was terrible. There were parts still smoking and everything was burnt black. All you could see of the crew were their helmets. What was left of their bodies was unrecognizable. They found dog tags on some of them. It was to be their last flight before going back to the States for a rest. The crew had over 300 combat hours. That evening was the dinner Templeton and I had been invited to attend at Hong's house. We never made it. The next day we apologized when we saw him. He said it wasn't

necessary; he understood.

Every Saturday night there was a big cock fight. The betting would be heavy. They (men only) tied two-to-three-inch razor-sharp knives on the rooster's spurs. The cocks then fly at each other, trying to slice the opponent with their knives. The blood really flies. All the men seemed to have plenty of money to bet on their favorite birds. There is a lot of noise as spectators shout instructions to the bird they bet on. The winner kills the other bird or renders or wounds it so that it no longer can fly. I sorta felt sorry for the roosters and so went only once.

A couple of our GIs also had fighting cocks that they entered into contests. One guy kept his tied near our welder's welding tanks. They were always crapping on his equipment. He told the guy to move them. I guess the guy figured he didn't have to, so he didn't. The welder asked Walke and I if we'd like a couple of roosters for lunch and we said, *"sure!"* He said he'd bring them to us. We built a fire, put a tub of water over it and dipped the dead birds into hot water to pick and skin them. Then we roasted them over the fire. We each had one, only eating the parts we liked. It was a better meal than we were getting over at the mess hall. A couple of days later the GI that owned the roosters came over to us and said, "Heard you cooked a couple of chickens the other night." We said, "Yes, we did." He said, "I'm missing a couple of fighting cocks," and wondered where we got the roosters. We told him that we didn't know anything about it. He knew we'd eaten his fighting cocks. There were two of us and there was nothing he could do about it. Our welding friend, Walke and I all had a good laugh about it when we got together later on. The rest of the guys back at the camp heard about it too. They would smile and ask if we enjoyed our chicken dinner.

The next day Walke and I decided to cook some of those big fat white grub worms the Aussies told us we could eat in an emergency if we were in the jungle without food. We built a fire in the middle of the path that all the GIs followed on their way to the mess hall. It was near suppertime when the first bunch of guys on the way to the mess hall stopped and asked what we were doing. We told them, "cooking grub worms, as you can see." We had a dozen or so that we found inside an old bombed-out coconut tree. We told them how the Aussies had taught us in their jungle survival course that they were edible. They were about three times the size of grub worms back home. They asked, "Are you going to eat them?" We told them, "That's why we're cooking them." They hurried on by, looking at us like we were really crazy. Some guys saw the grubs in our skillet and told the others that hadn't yet left for the mess hall to have a look. They all came out to see, making a wide circle around us. Unfortunately we cooked them until they were black and so they didn't taste very good.

Walke and I had some more fun with these big grub worms later on. They were easy to find in the rotting palm trees. We had several artists in our camp publication department. They lived in the same area of our camp and all had monkeys for pets. Walke and I would collect several of the grubs and bring them over to where the monkeys were kept in their cages. They'd put the grub's head in their mouth, bite it off and spit it out. Then they would squeeze the grubs like a tube of tooth paste and eat the green stuff inside. The artists sure hated to see us coming, which made it even more enjoyable for us. We nearly died laughing. Tonight I was feeding one of the monkeys beetles. It sounded like it was eating popcorn: crunch, crunch, crunch. I just caught a grasshopper that flew into the light and took him to the monkey. Crunch, crunch and he was gone.

This morning Dick and two of the Australians temporarily attached to our squadron walked to town to take some pictures of the natives. They are quite fierce-looking characters too, with their long hair shabbily kept and a gleam in their eyes. These are not the native inhabitants but instead had come from neighboring islands to trade. They came in outrigger canoes, some beautifully carved. They

"Lt. Egan has his head out the pilot's window just above our squadron's insignia on our plane. I always figured him to be a great pilot and a real good guy. In civilian life, before the war, he was a cop in New York City. Our navigator, First lieutenant Carmody, has his head out the top hatch where he took sextant readings for our position we were flying." *Thompson family collection.*

were loaded with fish fresh and dried. The dried ones gave you a wonderful appetite. You can smell them two blocks away. They eat, sleep and live in their boats that smell awful because of the dried fish that the flies have worked over for weeks.

The natives all along the wharf have things to sell: shells of all types, Japanese money and other things. Dick and Bill (the Aussie) took several pictures of the colorful scenery. We also took some pictures of cute Filipino girls bathing near the shore. On the way back to camp we bought some native cigars to smoke. They taste like corn silk. Back at camp I worked on my coconut pipe dish and cut my finger again. After our siesta, Dick, Bill and I walked to a native village and watched a wedding ceremony. The groom was all dolled up and doing a dance to an interesting drumbeat. The village was really filthy. Naked kids with sores all over their bodies ran through the streets. We went back to our town to eat. I had lemonade, fried rice, fried fish and coffee. The others had fried eggs in place of the fish. I guess they were still thinking of the fish along the waterfront.

The next day we went to do some mapping of

#20

#21

Top: "How this family ended up with this horse, I can't imagine. We had heard the Japs killed all the horses, cattle, even dogs and cats for food while they occupied the Philippines for two years. They must have had a good hiding place for their horse. They were sure proud of their horse and buggy, no doubt, the only one in town."
Bottom: "Now I can understand the Ox. The Japs left some of them so the natives could work their rice fields. The Japs didn't leave the natives here with much though, and treated them pretty rough — we were told." *Thompson family collection.*

#12

#13

Top: "Well, when your shoes hurt, take them off and rest your feet. That's what this Filipino lass is doing. She's also using the trunk of the palm tree to help her out. She can still smile though. It must have been her new shoes or the long walk that made her feet sore — probably used to going bare foot. She was nicely dressed and friendly, however we didn't press our luck. Just thanked her for letting us take her picture." *Thompson family collection.*

Bottom: "This Filipino woman is busy cleaning the pulp out of coconuts. She and the girl with her arms folded didn't really want their picture taken. At first, they didn't seem to know if they could trust us. They were still worried, remembering about their treatment by the Japanese, I guess." *Thompson family collection.*

#35a

#36a

"That's 'Fire-fly' with me and Swede." *Thompson family collection.*

Borneo. The Japs had an anti-aircraft gunner there called "Two-Shot Charlie." If Charlie missed you on the first shot he'd get you on the second. We skirted his domain. He usually wouldn't fire at you if the bomb bay doors were kept closed. As we neared the area three Jap Zeros came up after us. We checked our guns. The navigator couldn't get the nose guns to fire. Our radio operator tried to fire guns in the top turret but they wouldn't fire either. The engineer's side guns worked OK. One of the guns in the tail turret worked, the other did not. Templeton got into the ball turret, lowered it and

fired a few rounds before it jammed. I fired the one tail gun that still worked at the Japs but they were still quite a ways away. They never came any closer as we turned around and circled away from them. The Japs only followed us a short way, thank goodness. We then completed our mapping mission. Our gunner caught hell. There was talk of busting him but he never had been given a chance to test the guns since leaving the States. The next trip all the guns worked.

After finishing our missions from Zamboanga, we moved up to Manila on Luzon Island. There was no jungle there or any other place of much interest. We spent most of our time in camp. We hired a young Filipino to clean our tents. The women in Manila seemed to be a happy and cheerful lot. The woman who cleaned the tent always brought her ten-year-old daughter with her. She liked to hang around in our tent. We got a kick out of trying to communicate with her and she tried to teach us her school songs in Spanish. She was always happy and singing most of the time. We called her "Fire-fly." She sure was a morale booster in our nothing-to-do camp.

On one of our flights from Manila, Egan asked us if we'd like to buzz a town on Japan's coast. I was to take pictures of the place with the big K-18 camera. I forgot how close buzzing meant with Egan. We came in real close and at maximum speed. The rear end of our plane was vibrating faster than the rear end of a hula dancer. Jonsey and Swain held the camera close to the window. It was all they could do to keep it there. I was praying for a miracle but the pictures were blurred. We tried anyway.

From Manila we flew to Okinawa in September of 1945. Of course, we found ourselves in another tent city. This time it was on top of a plateau. We had to walk quite a ways to the mess hall and started taking a shortcut through what looked like an onion field. We collected some green onions to jazz up our crummy meals. Someone later told us they were fertilized with human manure. We quit picking onions although we never did get sick.

From Okinawa we mapped the Japanese islands. The war had come to an end but some Japs didn't believe it so you still had to be cautious. We hadn't been on Okinawa too long before a big typhoon hit the island. It leveled everything. The natives there have their ancestors buried in caves dug into the hillsides. The caves are left open so they can bring food and gifts. Some of the GIs hid out inside some of these caves to weather the storm. The sheet metal roofs of buildings were flying around like leaves. Our tent was the last to go down. I had a cold and felt so bad that I just wanted some place to lie down. I propped up part of the tent over a cot, crawled in and slept through most of it. When I woke up, the storm was over, my fever was gone and everything was a mess. We lived two weeks on GI rations and were left to fend for ourselves. I made a shelter using two small trees and parts of tents — a sort of large nest-like affair. Walke and some of the others used lean-tos fashioned from parts of ruined tents.

In a few weeks we were issued new tents and things got back to normal but everyone was eager to get back home. Most of the bombing squadrons had left and some of our guys went with them. There wasn't much left to do. I'd take off in the morning by myself, go down the hill and thru a small village to the ocean. I'd walk along the beach and sometimes fire my revolver at tin cans floating in the water.

General Arnold had orders not to let any photographers go home until we'd finished aerial mapping all the Japanese islands. One of my last flights came close to Mount Fujiyama. We flew in close so I could take a picture with the K-18 camera out the side window. It was really beautiful.

I took a slow boat back to the States. We slept in hammocks hung along the wall. In the daytime we saw flying fish and once I saw a whale. At night the water, and especially in the wake, was alive with different-colored lights from the animals and plants that lived in the ocean. I'd never been on a boat this long before and enjoyed it all.

On the way back to the States our boat passed

"My shot of Mt. Fuji." *Thompson family collection.*

close to the southern Aleutian Islands. They told us we were going this far north just in case some Japanese submarine officer hadn't heard the news.

We entered Puget Sound and it was a long waterway into Seattle. What a mess. GIs were getting rid of clothes they didn't want to keep. Shoes mainly — they were floating in the water all around the ship. We all talked it over. Once we got ashore we were going to order the biggest, thickest milk shake they could make before doing anything else. We came to a bar along the way and figured a drink first wouldn't hurt. We never did get those milk shakes that night. It was November 1945 and it was snowing in Seattle. It was great. They told us it was unusual for it to snow that early. I guess it snowed for us. We sure enjoyed it.

## Futomi Hosoda

# OUSHOU OBOEGAKI

Iwo Jima is approximately 2 miles wide and 4 miles long. Volcanic vents on the island are active, giving rise to its name: Iwo Jima means "Sulfur Island" in Japanese. National Archives photo #80-G-310939.

Iwo Jima is located halfway between Tokyo and the island of Saipan. Its location and two large airfields gave Iwo Jima great tactical importance during the war.

In May 1944 Prime Minister Tojo chose Lieutenant General Kuribayashi to defend Iwo Jima. Tojo told him, "The entire army and the nation will depend on you for the defense of that key island."

When Kuribayashi arrived on Iwo Jima in June he quickly rejected the traditional water's edge defensive strategy. The army suffered from a shortage of warplanes and the navy was in retreat. Without a navy or sufficient aircraft, a beach defense would be vulnerable to American air and naval bombardments. Kuribayashi decided instead to fight the entire battle from underground positions, a concept that was unique in the history of warfare. Under the direction of mining engineers, his men cut sixteen miles of interconnected tunnels and hundreds of rooms into the island's soft volcanic stone with hand tools. The exhausting work was complicated by water shortages, malnutrition and disease.

On 19 February 1945 the Americans began their amphibious assault on Iwo Jima. The ferocious thirty-six-day battle that followed accounted for one-third of all U.S. Marines casualties during the Pacific War.

Sixty-eight years later I discovered a Japanese notebook in a small Midwestern bookstore. At first glance only a few words and dates were decipherable — Saipan, Lockheed and 20 June 1944. Not until several pages were sent to Kazunori Tanoue, my translator in Japan, was the diary's true nature revealed. It is an extraordinary account written by Futomi Hosoda, a *Heichou*[1] serving with the Imperial Japanese Army garrisoned on Iwo Jima in the months leading up the battle.

His diary has two types of entries: descriptions of daily experiences as the men prepare Iwo Jima for battle, and short reflective essays. These essays appear in italics throughout the text.

---

1   *Heichou*: the equivalent of a Lance Corporal.

## *Oushou Oboegaki*[2]

*"I will write down my thoughts and observations until the day I die. When that will happen I do not know."*

### June 20, *Shōwa* 19[3]

I have joined the 63rd Unit located in the eastern area of Japan and belong to the Wakatsuki squad[4] known as the 8th Independent Anti-Tank Battalion ammunition platoon. I said farewell to my friend Ryozaburo after he presented me with my uniform. It was a pathetic farewell due to the rain.

### June 23

Our platoon was reorganized into the 2nd platoon squad. We departed Kofu[5] at 9:16 p.m.

### June 24

All of us got off the truck at the Mizuho pier in Higashi-Kanagawa. I was surprised to see Shinichi Kikushima. He has been assigned to the staff of the 9th Battalion headquarters. I also saw Hachiro Sasaki, Fukai Kihei, Yukio Hasumi, and Ishida and Hitoshi Nagata. We were all comrades training with the 570th 1st Educational Corps in Pyongyang.

### June 27

We finished loading the ship with equipment and supplies. By 3:30 p.m. they began boarding soldiers. At 6:20 p.m. we departed Yokohama and headed towards Iwo Jima on transport ship No. 153. We fight to bring glory for the homeland. I will never step on its soil again.

### June 28

We practiced various escape drills, tried on our life jackets and received instructions on how to abandon ship in the event of a catastrophic submarine attack.

### June 29

The sea is calm today. Our airplanes search the sea for signs of the enemy. Those flying close to the sea seem particularly strong-hearted.

### June 30

We landed safely at Iwo Jima. I worked all night unloading the ship. Military units have already taken up residence on the island. I am relieved to see the airfield in place.

### July 1

Everyone was commanded to dig trenches. I have been assigned to table setting duties.

### July 3

An enemy plane raided the island this afternoon. We should win this battle, we can never lose. I served soldiers tobacco and caramel after roll call.

### July 4

The air-raid alarm rang around 4 a.m. Fifty enemy planes gave us a good pounding. Our airfield was bombed heavily but we were able to shoot down two enemy aircraft. There were a total of four air strikes. We were also attacked from the sea at around 11:00 a.m. A warship, four battleships, several destroyers and battle cruisers bombarded the island with such ferocity that I wondered if Iwo Jima was going to sink into the sea. Our airfield did not have defensive measures in place and many people were injured. The 8th and 9th Independent Anti-Tank Battalions were then informed of an enemy landing which turned out to be untrue. After all the hectic preparations and non-stop encounters with enemy planes, I was convinced I would die. At 7:30 p.m. the squad was put under the battalion

---

2   *Oushou Oboegaki* means "A Draftee's Memorandum" or "A Draftee's Diary." *Oushou* means "respond to the call-up notice for military service," which is similar to the draft. *Oboegaki* means "memorandum" or "memorial" — written words to be remembered. *Oboe* literally means "memory," and *gaki* means "writing."

3   *Shōwa*: The traditional Japanese calendar was based on the reign of the emperor; years were given the name the emperor will assume after death. In this case Hirohito was to be known as *Shōwa* ("Enlightened Harmony"), and that period coincides with his lengthy reign from 1926 (*Shōwa* 1) to 1989 (*Shōwa* 64). Thus the nineteenth year of Hirohito's reign corresponds to 1944 on the Gregorian calendar.

4   Squads are named after the squad leader. Wakatsuki was the name of the soldier who was squad leader.

5   Kofu is a city 63 miles west of Tokyo.

commander's direct control. A gun was placed at the battle command post at battalion headquarters. After the attack we cleared the field of debris and preparations for installing the rapid-fire cannon were made. Everyone worked all night preparing for combat.

### Ship in Distress:

*I can't help but think back to when half of the 2nd troop, the entire 3rd troop, and some of our own comrades boarded the Noto-maru at Chichi Jima[6] and set sail for Iwo Jima. If only these men could have boarded ship No. 153 with us at Chichi Jima for the journey here. The Noto-maru sank because of an enemy air raid and all but twenty soldiers went missing. I look out at the Pacific Ocean and wish everything we have lost in this war could be rebuilt. I feel regret for the soldiers who ended up as honorable sacrifices. My heart is moved as I remember them. So much has been lost — the people, weapons, and soldiers on sunken transport ships. When I think of them, I am at a loss for words.*

## July 5

I've left the artillery position and returned to camp. The enemy attacks that we were so worried about never materialized. Still, I am surprised to be alive. This evening there was unexpected news. Almost all of the enemy ships that had so recently bombarded us were sunk by our own combined fleet. I shouted victoriously and everyone had a joyous drink to celebrate our unexpected triumph.[7]

## July 7

The construction of our defensive installations continued as we prepare for combat. I was nervous when I saw eleven ships on the sea and wondered if they belonged to the enemy. I vomited outside

and was also suffering from a violent bout of diarrhea. I finally managed to rejoin the troop later in the afternoon for some work.

### Iwo Jima Sketch:

*Iwo Jima is a small island measuring 6km from east to west and 4km from north to south. The island does not know four seasons and is usually summer-like all year round. Such a climate is unexpected for a place that is not so far south of Tokyo. There were about 150 houses with residents but they were evacuated from the island by mid-July. The residents were growing coca and sugarcane. They also grew fruits such as pineapple, mango, coconut, etc. as their specialty produce — fair enough for a southern region. It was surprising to find so many flies on the island after we had landed. There are also crabs which strain their eyes while walking sideways and forwards. The ground of the island is soft, like its name — Iwo Jima. There is also a hot spring near the beach. It is 135 meters in depth and from it comes boiling sea water. Fresh water is the biggest problem on the island. No one can drink seawater but there is a way to have drinking water. I drink water by collecting and storing rainwater. The pouring rainwater is collected from the roof into a bucket. I now have a better understanding of how important water is after having lived on this island. When I first arrived I always had diarrhea because I could not get used to the water.*

## July 14

I went to see the doctor because of my high fever and continuing battle with diarrhea. Two B-24s made a surprise attack at 6:40 p.m. One of our troop transports that was just about to land was attacked by the enemy and three soldiers died. It was truly an unfortunate event.

## July 19

Pitiful news this morning: Saipan has fallen and all of our comrades have perished. Prime Minister General Tojo has quit and a navy minister resigned

---

6    Chichi Jima is located 150 miles north of Iwo Jima. Both are part of the Bonin Island archipelago, also known as the Ogasawara Islands.

7    Japanese propaganda turned defeats into victories. On 19-20 June 1944, the Imperial Japanese Navy suffered a devastating defeat in the Battle of the Philippine Sea, where it lost three carriers and hundreds of airplanes. Their defeat left Japanese army forces defending Saipan without resupply. The victory Hosoda refers to never occured.

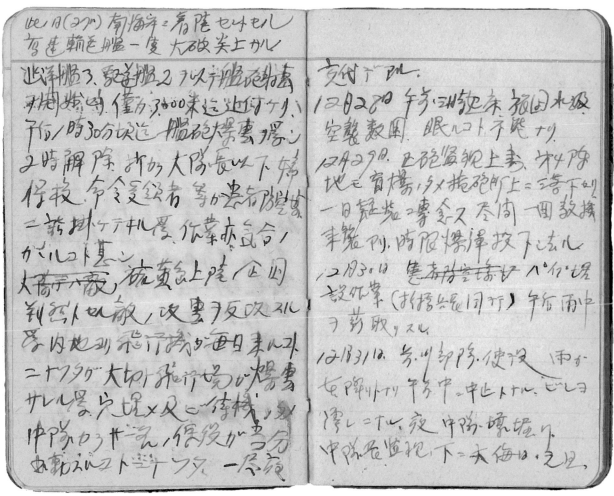

Futomi Hosoda's diary. *Author's collection.*

from the Imperial Headquarters. Our enemies will surely shift to Iwo Jima for an all-out attack, and much more. What then will become of us? I worked the whole day with a platoon of two squads installing long-range rapid-fire cannon. I soaked myself in a hot spring by the south pier after that.

## July 20

It has now been one month since my military conscription. The Tojo Cabinet has resigned because of what happened on Saipan: the death of everyone there and the downfall of our fleet. This news will weigh heavily on the morale of soldiers fighting on the front lines. The Abe squad took over our barracks and are now using it for their camp.

## July 21

I collected water into a drum from the south pier as commanded by Staff Sergeant Tanaka. News spread that there will be a cabinet formation and it is to be commanded by Admiral Mitsumasa Yoneuchi. Also, there will no longer be any need for the Tojo Cabinet to be dismissed as a body since Foreign Minister Shigemitsu himself had resigned. I'm already confused as to what information is correct and what is not.

**July 23**

Last night we were notified that Chichi Jima was under attack from enemy aircraft. Then a terrible storm destroyed our camp which we had made such an effort to build. I had to find a hole to sleep in. We no longer expected an air raid so the alert was called off.

*Women:*

*There are many married men among us and all we talk about in camp is women. That is, how good wives and sweet girlfriends are: it was the women's encomium. I feel a little lonely because I have been living for 26 years and have never had a girlfriend. The talk from comrades about women is enviable as an unmarried man, and it makes me lonely. Now, I have made a decision to get a wife the moment I return from here.*

**July 24**

It was cloudy today. I worked at the camp of the 1st squad of the 20th Independent Artillery Mortar Battalion. I read a letter Shinichi Kikuchi received from Corporal Koyabayshi. I was surprised to discover in his letter the news that Kihei Fukai was killed last July 4th during an enemy naval bombardment. I was at a loss for words and have lost another sworn friend from the 570th. Around ten more comrades arrived here today.

*Kihei Fukai's Death in Battle:*

*Today I received a letter from Shinichi Kikuchi. He told me that Lance Corporal Fukai with the 9th Battalion at headquarters was killed during the attack from a warship on 4 July. I was surprised when I received the news. Back in the days of the 570th we met every day and talked about Manchuria and boasted to one another about which of us was in charge of the barracks. We both attended the same elementary school and had a close relationship. But now he is dead only four days after landing here. Whenever I think about his life I am in agony. We drank sake together which we*

*brought from Yokohama, but I never knew it would be the last cup. AH!*

**July 25**

Today I was laying gravel on the east coast. I asked the driver from the 9th Battalion if he could deliver a letter to Shinichi.

**July 26**

Have been suffering from a headache for days now. Reports of desperate fighting have arrived from our paratroopers who have landed on Omiya Jima.[8]

**July 29**

I have a slight fever and have been suffering from a cold for the last few days. I really feel unwell and lay in bed the whole day.

**July 30**

My fever has gone down a bit. I was put back to work in the 6th position of the 2nd company. There is this unpleasant guy among us. He is First Lieutenant Yamada. Because every soldier is given a nickname, we decided to call him *"Man-gun."*[9]

**August 1**

We were attacked before the break of dawn. Lance Corporal Itabashi and First Class Private Haneda were injured. An enemy ship took a few potshots and sailed off before we had a chance to respond. We were furious afterwards.

**August 4**

The air raid alarm rang out at around 10:30 a.m. We were bombed three times today. An SB ship[10] was sunk. We have been allowed to send one postcard. I sent one to Ryozaburo.

---

8  Omiya Jima: Guam.
9  *Man-gun*: Manchurian army.
10  SB Ships: Shallow-draft vessels and motor-driven barges of seagoing capability, similar in design to American LST ships. Most could run onto beaches for unloading. Since Iwo Jima did not have port facilities, troops and materiel were unloaded at Chichi-Jima and transferred there by SB ships. American submarine torpedoes sank so many SB ships that fewer than half of the tanks destined for Iwo Jima arrived safely.

**August 5**

Again the alarm was sounded because enemy ships were roaming the sea nearby.

**August 7**

I was assigned to an anti-aircraft emplacement. Kondo and I remained on duty at the *kanshi-jo*[11] all night.

**August 8**

The squad returned to the camp of the company. I stayed at the camp of the 1st squad of the 1st platoon.

**August 9**

For the first time in a while I took some time off. I wrote a letter to *Syocho* Danno[12] and another letter to Mitsuo.

***Mitsuo:***

*I was pleased to meet you again.*
*I will die earlier than you, though.*
*Don't ever lose the war.*
*I will give my life in order to win.*
*Take great care of yourself and serve the country well.*

**August 12**

I have been feeling very sick for several days now. A long night on watch preceded by guard service the night before has worn me out. The doctor says I have a gastric catarrh. I rested and later ate a Japanese pumpkin. It was very delicious. What a good green vegetable!

***What I Would Have Told Otake-kun:***

*The call-up papers came and you went up to Tokyo. You and I both know that call-up papers are not sent to a soldier who is sick or wounded. However,*

---

11   *Kanshi-jo (Kansi-go)*: An observation post or surveillance position, scattered throughout Iwo Jima, where soldiers watched for enemy ships or aircraft. Reports would be telephoned to a command center which would sound the alarm.
12   *Syocho* Danno: "Chief of Police Danno." Futomi Hosoda was a policeman in civilian life. Danno was the chief's last name.

An example of a Japanese SB Ship unloading. Photographic source and location unknown.

*your attitude in those days was very hard to watch as a friend. The only reason you were home was because of an army oversight and I was sorry to have discovered your true colors. Otake-kun, there are many sick and wounded soldiers here on Iwo Jima. If I could see you now, I would wonder if you could adequately serve the country in a place like this. You should know the current situation in Japan. I would like to ask you to reflect on your behavior.*

**August 14**

It was time for the early morning drills. Everyone looked sharp and ready for action. I am still in sickbay. Sergeant Major Ishii said he thought I looked jaundiced. I became very anxious after hearing these remarks even though I was diagnosed as having a gastric catarrh by the naval surgeon.

**August 15**

Enemy aircraft raided around 10:30 p.m. They flew in formation and bombed at an elevation of 50 meters. Several people were hurt.

**August 17**

I had the naval surgeon examine me because of my yellow appearance. He said it was nothing to be worried about. Still, I was very uneasy. An enemy plane attacked at around 2 p.m. and was soon engaged by one of our fighters. Recently the enemy

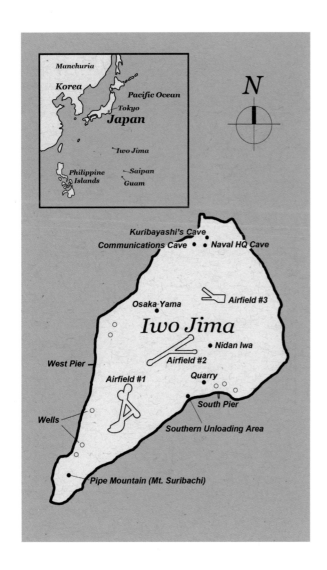

appears to be focused on killing troops rather than destroying our installations.

### The Jaundice Disease:

*The color of my eyes began to turn yellow in early August when I was diagnosed with gastric catarrh. My entire body felt languid for several days and I had a poor appetite. Sergeant Major Ishii noted my jaundice. Everybody else in the company was also complaining about the same thing. We would become anxious after seeing ourselves in the mirror; our eyes were haggard and yellow, and our lower body appeared a pale yellow as well. My urine was tinged with yellow weeks before and slowly became reddish brown as the condition worsened. Eventually it became obvious to me that I had jaundice, but the army surgeon said that I should not worry.*

### August 20

There was an inspection of our weapons. I took a rest in the afternoon.

### Tobacco and a Soldier:

*Tobacco is a friend of the soldier. On Iwo Jima, we in the army are hungry for tobacco and are not satisfied with the meager allotment. Soldiers in the navy are supplied much better. They get fifty cigarettes a month, many sweets and alcoholic drinks. We appeal to soldiers in the navy to barter with us for tobacco. This behavior is unique to the army and would never be seen back home in rural areas.*

### August 21

Shinichi Kikushima visited here. I received a can of beef and one small *ohagi*.[13]

### Eating a Fly:

*An island that is full of flies spells trouble for a soldier. It is said that originally there were not that many flies on the island; but as the number of men increased, so did the number of flies. I end up eating a fly with each meal. Every day there are at least five or six flies that sink into my soup. They also get mixed into our cooked food that the Army serves us. During daytime I can't take a proper nap because flies hover over me and land in my mouth, nose and eyes. Flies even travel along with me when I walk on the road. There are flies wherever we go. Horses, cows, human dung and dead crabs are all blackened with flies. One could say that flies are one of Iwo Jima's specialties.*

---

13  *Ohagi*: rice cake coated with sweetened red beans.

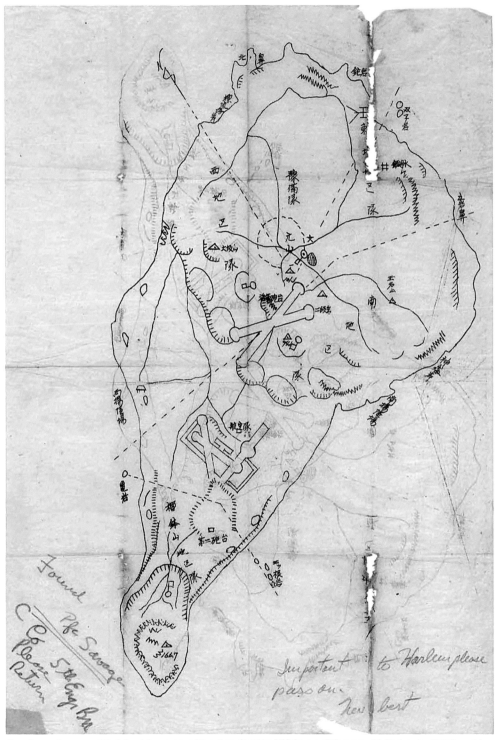

An unknown Japanese soldier's hand-drawn map of Iwo Jima, found by PFC Savage, C Company, 5th Engineering Battalion. *Adam Speak collection*.

## August 23

At 8:20 a.m. the air-raid alarm rang out. It rang again at around 10:30 a.m. One enemy plane attacked four times without warning while we were sleeping. The force of the Grumman fighter attack was tremendous, causing great damage to the airfield and an aircraft. Cheekily it came, throwing its bombs and then heading for the hills. At night, the air-raid alarm rang twice for approximately two hours.

## August 25

Thirteen large-sized enemy airplanes attacked and bombed an airfield around 1:00 p.m.

## August 26

Twenty enemy planes attacked again around 10:40 a.m. One of them dropped a bomb that exploded before it hit the ground and made a sound that was beyond description. I thought it would be the end of me. Someone said that a soldier manning a *funshinho*[14] died instantly. The war situation has become so dire that I no longer think of seeing tomorrow's light.

## August 27

There was another air raid around 10 p.m. and I took shelter for about an hour. The petty officer of the week and Corporal Hongo had an argument today. I suppose there are many problems because of the class differences in the military. Although yielding is a shame, I waited for one to give in. I am now classified as "fit to work."

## August 28

I received orders from the first lieutenant at headquarters to cut reeds and fix the roof. An enemy airplane attacked at 12:40 p.m. I felt the enemy's attack every minute. The alarm was raised again from 7:30 p.m. to 10 p.m. I have heard that General Commander-in-Chief Toyota of the combined fleet felt responsible for recent military failures and killed himself. In Europe, the U.S. and British armies are on the move and there is fighting in the streets. The situation looks very bad.

## *The Deterioration of the War Situation and Soldiers' Morale:*

*The enemy is close to the mainland of Japan, Paris was recaptured from the Germans and the war situation looks very bad. On Iwo Jima, the enemy is close by and executes air raids every day. The enemy is attempting to destroy us and all is not well. In fact, the loss of the combined fleet has become a huge problem and is apparent to every soldier. As the war situation deteriorates, so does in many cases the soldiers' morale.*

## August 31

It's 2:30. The same sixteen enemy planes that have been attacking us day and night are at it once again, this time at a very low altitude.

## September 1

The air raid alarm rang at 6:00 a.m. and a total of fifty enemy fighters made strafing attacks. This afternoon an enemy battle cruiser and a destroyer bombarded our position and Osaka-Yama. Reports indicate that the enemy navy has attacked Chichi Jima. I must reluctantly admit that the enemy has excellent military capabilities.

## September 2

It's 5:00 a.m. and the air raid alarm has sounded. The enemy who has attacked every day since the end of August is at it again. Like yesterday, machine gun bullets rained down upon us as enemy fighter planes attacked the island continuously. Around noon, six enemy warships appeared on the horizon. They approached the island gradually and then bombarded us everywhere. During the attack I took food and weapons to soldiers who had been standing watch. I then departed to the 4th *Jinchi*[15]

---

14 *Funshinho*: The *yonshiki yonjyu-senchi funshinho* was a 400mm rocket mortar first used in combat during the Battle of Iwo Jima.

15 *Jinchi*: A military position or encampment. In his diary Futomi identifies

with Haneda. Enemy warships launched another attack centering on the airfield for about two hours. It was mortifying and the sound of the explosions damaged my ears. Since yesterday's attack destroyed most of our airplanes, there was no way to counterattack. The enemy ships were in plain sight but there was nothing we could do to stop them. Enemy formations showered us with bullets from machine guns and the attacks continued even after the naval bombardment had concluded. Five airplanes were firing down upon us at the same time. I returned to the 4th Jinchi and joined the others for watch duty at the kanshi-jo during the night.

## September 4

Today I was very cautious because days with the number four are considered unlucky. However, only a few enemy planes attacked and so it turned out to be a good day after all. I worked watch duty at night and I was joined by Corporal Okazaki. An enemy plane came around 8:00 p.m. but there was no damage.

## September 5

I went to the 3rd Jinchi for practice drills conducted by First Lieutenant Nakamura. During the drill the air-raid alarm rang and a few enemy planes attacked. Later, at around 9:30 a.m., the alarm rang again and a few enemy planes attacked. I evacuated to safety. They attacked again in the afternoon.

## September 6

During quarry work at Pipe Mountain[16] enemy

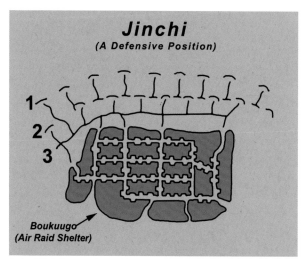

A simplified diagram of a jinchi on Iwo Jima. On Iwo Jima the main component of each jinchi was a man-made underground shelter or naturally occuring cave, called the boukuugou, which acted as company headquarters and air-raid shelter (dark grey). Each jinchi also had a network of tunnels that connected the command shelter with other parts of the jinchi (not shown). In this illustration, tunnels in the command boukuugou have rooms used for sleeping and storage cut into their walls. Also shown are three defensive perimeters outside the jinchi's boukuugou (these are not to scale — they would have extended much further away from the boukuugou). Each of these lines of defense would be further divided into three more defensive lines, and would have included gun pits, spider holes, light artillery, mortar emplacements, and concrete-reinforced pillboxes in staggered positions with interconnected fields of fire. Lines 1, 2 and 3 in the illustration are connected by open trenches. Although it is not the case with the above example, most jinchi on Iwo Jima were connected to one another by a network of tunnels.

planes attacked from two directions at around 12 o'clock. I hid between the rocks. After work, I missed my ride back and returned to the camp on foot, arriving at 6 p.m.

*A Draftee and an Active Soldier:*
*A draftee serves the country as a beginning soldier, a second-year soldier, and a third-year soldier, using his energy to the utmost for those three years of duty. An active soldier is someone who previously worked as a draftee and is now on his second tour of duty. Unlike the draftee, he understands army life backwards and forwards; his attitude and performance is natural and calm. However, I am surprised that so many active soldiers serving their second tour are simpletons and are easily excited despite their experience.*

---

several of them by number as places where he worked and slept. A typical jinchi had several defensive perimeters consisting of firing trenches, artillery installations, concrete-reinforced pill boxes, and bunkers positioned in front of an underground air-raid shelter known as a *boukuugou*. The boukuugou housed the command center, sleeping nooks and storage rooms for each jinchi, and were designed with several passageways for escape. A jinchi might be further identified by its design: for example, at the north end of Iwo Jima was the *fukkaku jinchi* ("honeycomb defensive position") which surrounded Lieutenant General Kuribayashi's underground command center. Jinchi were sometimes identified by their purpose or location; for example, *yobi jinchi* was a "reserve defensive position" and *zenshin jinchi* was an "advanced position."

16  Pipe Mountain: another name for Mount Suribachi. Sulfurous gas and water vapor rising from its crater gives the appearance of a smoking pipe when viewed from the sea.

**September 7**

We came under attack at the start of my watch, which began around 11:30 p.m. Patrol is First Lieutenant Takahashi's special talent.

*Younger Brother:*

*Iwo Jima is one solitary island in the distant sea. Everybody often reminisces about home. However, my feelings for home are exceptionally strong. I always feel very anxious when thinking of home. Most especially, I am anxious about Mother who is old and probably lonely, my brother Mitsuo who is now in the army, and my friend Ryozaburo who has been sick with tuberculosis for a long time. As Mr. Juro Mimura would say, "I love these things strongly." When I was at home I did not easily express my love. But all that has changed in a war where nobody knows what will happen tomorrow.*

**September 8**

My watch is over and so I rested for awhile. Later, I washed myself and my clothes. It was a good feeling. The air-raid alarm rang at 10:30 p.m.

**September 9**

Today, and for the time being, we have a new schedule to accommodate a new work detail: rise at 3 a.m., breakfast at 5:00, lunch at 10:00, afternoon nap from 1 - 2 p.m., and supper at 5. I looked up at the moon in the dark dawn as I worked.

**September 10**

Anti-aircraft surveillance. At 5:30 p.m. the air-raid alarm rang out for one hour. An enemy plane approached and was met by one of our own. During the ensuing air battle the enemy dropped a block-buster that produced a gaping hole in the road leading to the Kuritsu unit.

**September 13**

I was able to stay at the 4th Jinchi last night because the number of those assigned to anti-aircraft surveillance was increased. After I awoke, I helped

with the construction of a pillbox at the 9th Jinchi. I took charge of the water works section until my shift ended at 12:30. I took the rest of the afternoon off.

**September 14**

I carried meals to soldiers on anti-aircraft surveillance. At 11:30 the alarm rang and I evacuated to the 3rd Jinchi with First Class Private Takenoue. A bomb landed nearby and there was very much damage.

**September 15**

I helped with the digging at a boukuugou located on the eastern part of the island. I performed anti-aircraft surveillance in the evening. A few enemy planes snuck in and dropped bombs.

*The Story of Reinforcements:*

*On September 15 our reinforcements arrived at Iwo Jima. They had been in Kofu as reservists but were transferred to help load ships at Mizuho pier in Yokohama a few days later. They worked there for about twenty days before being reassigned to new duties on Chichi Jima. After a while, they were sent here to Iwo Jima and reported for duty at the 3rd company. Hajime Wada and Second Class Private Sima were assigned to the ammunition platoon. Lance Corporal Tanide, who was in the Nakamura squad of the 570th in Korea, has also arrived. Other soldiers from Chichi Jima also came in turn to do their part. Iwo Jima will be a very dangerous place for them.*

**September 19**

I was mobilized last night to draw water for the battalion. I rested in the morning and collected sea water for various tasks at the south coast in the afternoon. Today we all received tobacco as a gift from the Emperor and the Imperial family.

**September 22**

After anti-aircraft surveillance I helped with dig-

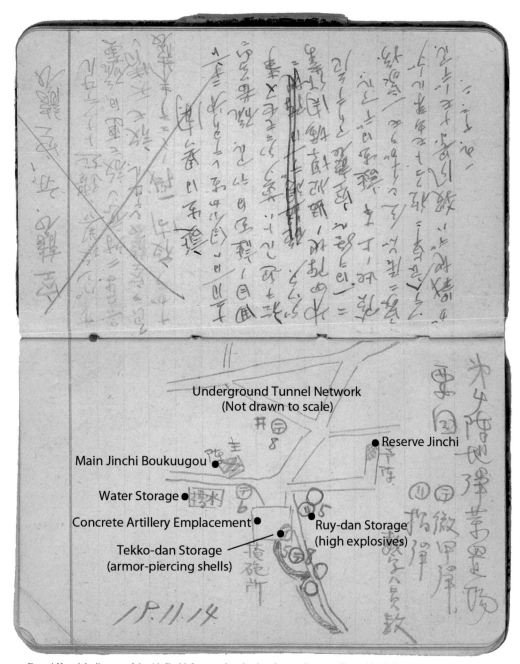

Futomi Hosoda's diagram of the 4th Jinchi. Its exact location is unknown, but according to his 18 October entry it is just over an hour's walk from Mount Suribachi. Hosoda's 24 December entry gives a second clue, suggesting that the 4th Jinchi was located in the vicinity of the west pier. The **Main Jinchi Boukuugou** marks the location of the underground command bunker. Hosoda refers to digging firing pits at the first, second and third line of the 4th Jinchi (not illustrated in his diagram). A system of interconnected tunnels link the 4th Jinchi to its storage areas, underground gun emplacements and a yobi "reserve" jinchi which could be used if the main jinchi was destroyed. The tunnels also permitted movement of men and materiel between other parts of the island during battle. *Author's collection.*

ging at the boukuugou. We had a heavy rain and I was able to save large amounts of rainwater. I read *Shōin Yoshida* by Minetaro Yamanaka.[17]

**September 27**

I have been dealing with a dreadful case of diarrhea for the last few days. Am abstaining from food but still I shit about thirty times a day. I feel so bad.

**September 28**

I am in extreme pain and have been excused from military drills.

### *The Battlefield and Sōseki Natsume:*

*The island has now become a battlefield. In such a hard-pressed and tense every-day atmosphere, it is inevitable that the minds of some become wild. It is neither despair nor ambition that drives me to try to improve my soul in this situation. For this, there is Sōseki's book[18] for me to read, for I know that when I read Sōseki's novel I can forget the present painful moment, and feel the wealth of a higher soul.*

### *The Story of First Lieutenant Shibata's Disaster:*

*Today First Lieutenant Shibata of battalion headquarters was sent by airplane to bring back weapons from Japan. He also brought with him about 10,000 yen in soldiers' remittances intended to help households back home. Ten minutes after his departure from Iwo Jima he encountered an enemy fighter returning from an assault on Chichi Jima. The encounter left Shibata's damaged aircraft smoking badly and so he returned to the airfield. It was regrettable that First Lieutenant Shibata was injured in the face as well and had to postpone his trip. However, I must say that the thought of returning to the air and facing more relentless attacks was a fearful burden for him.*

---

17   Shōin Yoshida was an important intellectual of the Tokugawa Shogunate (1830-1859).
18   Sōseki Natsume: a novelist (1867-1916) often considered to be the greatest writer in modern Japanese history.

**September 29**

One enemy plane attacked at around 7:20 p.m.

**September 30**

I have sent about ten letters to a friend since my arrival on Iwo Jima but have not in return received a single reply. There should have been at least one reply because I expressed myself very clearly in hope of getting the desired response. Perhaps the letters were never delivered — marine transportation is difficult beyond description. Many transport ships are sunk by enemy submarines and airplanes and the letters and their replies have most likely suffered the same tragic fate. Ah.

### *Diarrhea:*

*I started having diarrhea every day from September 20th due to my bad stomach. When I went to dig a field hospital boukuugou at headquarters on the 26th, I dug one shovel full of earth and had a bowel movement. I then went to the toilet about ten times. I was diagnosed by the army surgeon the next day. The surgeon said, "Is there anything you can think of that would have caused this?" I answered "Nothing." That day became a day of fasting for me because anything I ate would run right through me. I went to the toilet many times and could not sleep. My stool sometimes appeared as the white of an egg with blood and mucus. In rural areas this type of an illness is considered contagious and the carrier is isolated. The pain was awful and I thought how good it is to be healthy.*

**October 2**

Today I was given a second vaccination. The condition of my stomach has improved considerably. During the evening the air-raid alarm rang out three times. There was no time to sleep.

### *The Theoretical Possibility of a Transfer:*

*When soldiers have been on Iwo Jima for three months or more, they begin to think about requesting a transfer. The theoretical possibility of a trans-*

*fer to Hachijo Jima, Taiwan, or the Boshu defense*[19] *appeared and then disappeared as the war situation deteriorated. And now we are being paid a bonus of three months' salary for some mysterious reason. I guess I will just have to see how it goes for a while. I now find myself in a difficult and dangerous transport situation. I want to think of moving forward and not look back. The monotonous daily life and hard labor has made Iwo Jima a very unpleasant place.*

## October 4
I worked as *Toban*[20] for the company. Nagata-kun[21] and I were suffering from exhaustion and were given orders to rest.

## October 5
I resumed work again.

## October 7
I switched from Toban and was reassigned to other work. I carried quarry rock from the east coast under the supervision of Second Lieutenant Yamada. I can now see the importance of Yamada's leadership skills. At night I stood watch at the Kanshi-jo.

## October 8
I worked digging the boukuugou at the 4th Jinchi with corporal Okazaki. Today was clean-up day and I went to the hot spring and took a bath. Later in the afternoon I got some rest.

### About Going to Iwo Jima Hot Springs:
*There is a hot spring that can be found near the island's south pier. The waves of the sea come into a spot that is surrounded by stones that are exposed to the heat of the sun. If the soldiers happen to work near there, they take time to soak in it. The only problem is that it is sea water and not fresh wa-*

*ter. When I soak in the hot spring, I place a board under me to sit on or else the sand on my feet and legs becomes too hot. Staying there can prove to be dangerous though. Yes, being swallowed by a large wave is dangerous enough. What is even more dangerous is not knowing if the island is under attack.*

## October 9
I helped dig the boukuugou at the 4th Jinchi. Nineteen enemy airplanes attacked without warning at 9:30 p.m. and dropped a large number of bombs. Even if I had evacuated to a cave I would not have escaped the dangerous vibrations. I went back to my anti-aircraft surveillance duties after dinner.

## October 11
I assisted the *Kohei-tai*[22] with their tunneling under the airfield near Pipe Mountain. I dug about 70cm deep and about fifteen *tsubo*[23] in sandy ground. We worked all day in scorching heat under the blazing sun. More soldiers have been assigned to anti-aircraft watch duty tonight.

## October 12
There was a lot of digging today. We dug again in sandy ground and assisted the Kouhei-tai just like we did yesterday. Two enemy airplanes appeared around 9:30.

## October 13
Anti-aircraft surveillance, and then it rained and I was able to gather a great quantity of rainwater. It tasted delicious. We fired at two enemy planes but accomplished nothing.

## October 14
I finished my watch at the Kanshi-jo and immediately went to work digging the boukuugou for hospital patients. Shinichi Kikuchi gave me five cigarettes.

---

19   Boshu defense: the air defense of eastern Japan.
20   *Toban*: the person on duty, such as a clerk who staffs a desk, or someone with a similar level of responsibility who assists in the running of the company.
21   Nagata-kun: Nagata is a person's name, and *-kun* is an enclitic of endearment used when referring to a friend or a younger person.

22   *Kouhei-tai*: engineering troops. Engineers were stationed on Iwo Jima to supervise the digging of the underground tunnel network and defensive installations.
23   *Tsubo*: a measurement of area equal to 3.3 square meters.

**October 15**
I worked at the 14th Jinchi with the Kouhei-tai who were tunneling at the foot of Pipe Mountain. I finished at 2:00 p.m. A transport ship arrived and I went to help with the unloading and carried food to the accounting room. Fifteen soldiers who remained behind in Kofu arrived on the island today. Also, First Lieutenant Ardo from the 570th and First Lieutenant Seya Ito arrived from Chichi Jima. We celebrated their arrival with sake. Anti-aircraft surveillance was put on alert.

**October 16**
I went directly from the 4th Jinchi to help with the well drilling. Work stopped in the morning due to the arrival of two SB ships.

**October 17**
More soldiers were assigned to anti-aircraft surveillance watch. After my shift, I went to help with the well digging. After that I went directly to the 1st Jinchi to make up for lost work yesterday. I carried hard clay.

**October 18**
I assisted the Kouhei-tai with their tunneling at the foot of Pipe Mountain and finished at around 4:00 p.m. I returned to camp by foot which took more than an hour. Sergeant Major Ishi stopped by while on patrol. There was another increase in the number of soldiers standing watch.

**October 19**
I stood watch at the kanshi-jo and cleaned my rifle which had become covered with a light coat of red rust.

**October 21**
Ten enemy planes attacked without the alarm sounding at around 11:30 a.m. One of our pilots bravely crashed into an enemy aircraft. Another enemy was shot down and a third was blasted from the sky. Three of our planes never returned while other pilots bailed out by parachute.

***Information About a Plane:***
*It is a miserable sight to see the countless Japanese planes that lay in ruins. Parts, bits and pieces of airplanes are scattered everywhere — some are even pulverized. There are unexploded bombs all around and our own spent artillery shells and machine gun casings litter the ground. At the airfield, we line up broken planes and even pieces of planes as decoys. I feel a great sadness when I think of those who must deliberately sacrifice their lives just to fight. I am angry toward our incompetent navy.*

**October 22**
The squad commander and Corporal Okazaki were transferred to company headquarters. Lance Corporal Kotaka took temporary command of our squad. Staff Sergeant Tanaka went to assist the third troop.

***The Story of the Police Staff:***
*It was written in a bulletin on October 22 that any soldiers with a police background should step forward. My own guess, from information gathered, is that command is searching for experienced police staff to carry out prison guard duties on Chichi Jima. It's true that I would like to be done here on Iwo Jima and transfer to Chichi Jima. However, the situation at sea is extremely dangerous and I am not sure I would survive the journey. Iwo Jima has become a very unpleasant place. A change of scenery is desirable.*

**October 24**
It seems that the battle on the east sea of Taiwan has become a hard fight.

**October 25**
Today I assisted the Kouhei-tai.

**October 27**
I went to the lumber mill at Nidan Iwa and worked to get lumber for the squad.

**October 28**

I worked until 5 o'clock for the Kouhei-tai who were busy pouring a concrete bunker.

**October 29**

Stood anti-aircraft surveillance watch duty. I have neglected my diary for a few days so today I brought it up to date. I finished reading the book, *One Plane Never Returned*, by Jun Sakakiyama.

**October 30**

I went to the south coast to draw water for the company's work detail. In the afternoon I lost my footing in a wave and fell, bruising my waist and left shoulder.

**October 31**

The doctor took a look at my bruises but they were not serious. I swapped work assignments with Second Lieutenant Miyazaki because of tomorrow's brigade drill. I waited for the doctor in the Buddha Room[24] because the medical room was overflowing with patients.

**November 1**

I spent the day working Second Lieutenant Miyazaki's shift as messenger. Ten enemy planes attacked.

*The Arrival of Letters:*
*The long-awaited letters have arrived. A letter from Otake-kun came first and three from Ryozaburo followed several days later. After I read the postcard from my uncle in Ako, a postcard from Otake-kun arrived. It took about one or two months for this mail to make its way here to the island. Only one of three letters from Ryozaburo arrived in my hand; the first and second letters sank into the sea. It was a miserable fate, although many letters from other acquaintances did arrive. I read the letters over several times and was relieved to know that everyone was facing the battle at home in good health.*

**November 3**

Watch duty was put on alert last night. The air-raid alarm rang in two separate locations but no enemy planes appeared this time. Today is *Meiji-Setsu*[25] so I took a day of rest.

*Meiji-Setsu on Iwo Jima:*
*I was able to take a day off on Meiji-Setsu as expected. When I was in Manchuria, I went to the military store and was able to purchase some sake, sweets, and food for a big dinner. Here on Iwo Jima our celebratory feast consisted of one can of mackerel that I ate with six others at supper. Then I ate some boiled dry Japanese radish with soy sauce and dried cuttlefish and drank about five shaku[26] of sake. We mellowed out with the five shaku sakes and attended a party in front of the officers' room at battalion headquarters.*

**November 5**

More soldiers were assigned watch duty again last night. I took a day of rest — brigade's orders. Forty-five Boeing B-29s attacked around 4 p.m. and the bombing continued for about an hour. Watch duty was on alert in the evening. The air was very cool.

**November 6**

I worked digging a firing trench at the Jinchi.

**November 7**

I had regular anti-aircraft surveillance watch duty.

**November 8**

I worked at the 1st Jinchi until 11:50 p.m. Then there was an air raid.

**November 9**

I pinched and injured the middle finger of my left hand while firing the anti-aircraft gun during watch.

---

24   Buddha room: where soldiers pray for the dead.

25   *Meiji-Setsu*: the birthday of the Emperor Meiji (Hirohito).
26   *Shaku*: a traditional unit of measure equal to 18ml (.60 oz.).

**November 10**

We were digging at the 4th Jinchi when enemy planes attacked at around 10 p.m. The ground shook violently, even inside the boukuugou.

**November 11**

A flare suddenly shot into the sky at midnight and lit up Iwo Jima as if it was broad daylight. A tremendous naval bombardment commenced and continued without interruption for an hour and fifty minutes. The airfield was the focus of the attack and received twelve barrages. The sounds of gunfire were terrible and the earth shook violently. When the firing stopped, our battalion commander came to the Jinchi for *Ko-haibi*.[27] Although we prepared for combat, there was no invasion so the troops disassembled that afternoon at 3 p.m. Later we learned that the naval attack was from a fleet of ten ships that had sailed from Saipan. Fortunately the aircraft carriers were not among them. For the rest of the day I stayed at the 4th Jinchi and stood watch.

**November 12**

I wondered if warships would attack again tonight, but all was quiet. I transported steel rods for the Maekawa squad during Jinchi work. Later on, I went to the west coast for the first time. Anti-aircraft surveillance watch was put on alert and there was an air raid at 11:30 p.m.

**November 13**

I gathered up my things and moved to the 3rd Jinchi of the 12th Independent Anti-Tank Battalion. We hauled hard clay in the afternoon. There was an air raid at 3 p.m. and another one at 7 p.m.

**November 14**

It was the company's drill day. Later on I stood watch. All of us in the squad were punished after Private Odaka was caught stealing food from the medical room.

*Sashikuri:*

*This is an army term for stealing or manipulating the numbers. If the supplies are insufficient, soldiers will find a way to steal them for themselves. Soldiers have never thought of this as a bad thing and find pleasure in stealing ingredients for cooking meals. It is thrilling to be stealthy and then enjoy the spoils. Sashikuri can never be taken away from the troops.*

**November 15**

After watch duty I worked at the company's 1st Jinchi. I rested in the afternoon but it wasn't very satisfying. I let out a shout because I am so homesick.

**November 16**

I worked digging a firing trench at the 4th Jinchi. After dinner, I stood watch for Private First Class Nagata because he was sick.

**November 17**

Digging continued at the firing trench. Later that morning during the air-raid I heard some troubling news. A telegram arrived that told of a tense situation from the Imperial Headquarters last night. An unusual and rarely seen Lockheed twin-engine, twin-bodied airplane[28] appeared today and attacked our position. I worked all day until I fell from exhaustion.

**November 18**

I finished watch duty and gathered wood for headquarters later in the day.

**November 19**

After lunch there was an air raid. A bomb fell near the 4th Jinchi. Kikushima sent me a postcard.

**November 20**

After dinner, Shinichi Kikuchi dropped by and

---

27   *Ko-haibi*: the call to battle stations.

28   Lockheed P-38 Lightning was a twin-boom, twin-engine airplane with a single, central nacelle containing the cockpit and armament. The Japanese name for the P-38 was *Ni hikōki ippairoto* —"two planes, one pilot".

gave me some tobacco. I went to unload an SB ship headed for the southern coast early this morning. Shortly after departing Chichi Jima, the SB ship was attacked and its stern was blown apart. The damage made it impossible to land and so the unloading work was cancelled. I spent the rest of the day doing odds and ends. Watch duty was on alert during the evening.

**November 21**
Second Lieutenant Miyazaki was found dead last night. Life is so ephemeral. I took part in his cremation ceremony later in the afternoon.

**November 22**
I stood anti-aircraft and artillery watch as usual. In an article published by the weekly *Asahi Shimbun,*[29] Yoshizo Ishikawa wrote that people are quick to assert their rights and tend to forget their responsibilities. I thought, Indeed! Here was something Jun Kawada, Soichi Yoyogi and Hideki Yukawa need to read.

**November 23**
We assisted with the airfield expansion effort this morning. One of our army planes arrived today and I thought it may be here in preparation for an attack on Saipan. I pushed a *torokko*[30] for the first time in my life. Work was finished at 3 p.m.

**November 24**
I stood watch again. Today the battalion conducted live-fire drills. In the afternoon I worked as the artillerist, firing cannon from the 4th Jinchi.

**November 25**
I got up early this morning and went to work at the 3rd Jinchi. It was a rainy day and I got soaked. Work was finished at 4 p.m.

**November 26**
We continued pouring concrete at the 3rd Jinchi until 6 p.m. Watch was on alert after dinner and then the air-raid alarm sounded.

**November 27**
Today I did construction work at the airfield. Twice this afternoon I ran to the 4th Jinchi because of air raids. About ten enemy airplanes dropped delayed-fuse time-bombs. It was very dangerous.

**November 28**
Although I was scheduled for a rest, I exercised for two hours at the 3rd Jinchi because it was the battalion's drill day. I sent a postcard to Ryozaburo, Otake, and Uncle Shinpachi after returning to the camp and then collected firewood in the afternoon. I am having trouble relaxing on my day off. I suppose it is my state of mind. I accompanied the petty officers on patrol after dinner. I stayed overnight at the 2nd Jinchi for the first time. There was only one air raid today.

**November 29**
The 800-meter runway took the brunt of the most recent attack and is now full of holes. There were in fact an amazing number of holes and I was mobilized to repair the damage. The air-raid alarm rang again around 4 p.m. and I evacuated by car to the safety of a nearby firing trench. Nineteen enemy airplanes attacked. They dropped several delayed-fuse time-bombs and made their escape. Later on we were caught by surprise when one of the bombs detonated near the airfield.

**November 30**
There is a shortage of tobacco. I went to the *shuho*[31] to pick up my monthly ration of cigarettes, which is now two packs of Kinshi and one Homare.[32] I was then mobilized to help expand the airfield. Lunch was boiled rice mixed with meat and vegetables.

---

29   *Asahi Shimbun* is the most widely read newspaper in Japan.
30   *Torokko*: a mining cart that travels on rails and was used on Iwo Jima to haul rock and debris.

31   *Shuho*: a Japanese military shop, canteen or post exchange.
32   Kinshi and Homare: brand names for cigarettes.

It was delicious. Twenty-three enemy airplanes attacked around 1 p.m. and I took cover at the 4th Jinchi. A large number of delayed-fuse time-bombs were dropped. I returned to the airfield after the bombing for about forty minutes to help repair the damage. I then resumed my regular work. The air-raid alarm rang again around 4 p.m. More bombs were dropped and the alarm was dismissed at 5 p.m. Thirty minutes later the delayed-fuse time-bombs began to explode and continued doing so here and there for the next fifteen hours. The explosions continued into the night as I stood watch. Two more attacks came before the night was over.

**December 1**
Today is my 26th birthday. I never thought I would have my birthday on Iwo Jima. If I had stayed at home, I could go with my family to have a meal rather than be in the current condition I find myself in. But here I am, now weary on the battlefield. I finished digging out a trench near the cannon position at the 4th Jinchi. Twenty-one enemy airplanes attacked around 2 p.m. They dropped delayed-fuse time-bombs for about an hour and twenty minutes. We received a very disturbing report that Tokyo was bombed four times. It was an extremely dangerous birthday for me.

**December 2**
I got up at 3 a.m. and stood watch. All of us were scheduled to unload cargo from the SB ship that arrived today. The enemy airplanes attacked at 2:30 and dropped a large number of delayed-fuse time-bombs.

*Tobacco:*
*Shinichi Kikuchi resupplied me with tobacco. I find it difficult to cope with my normal army ration of thirty cigarettes every five days. Tobacco is like a meal to me and I cannot endure without it. First of all I must admit it: I have become piggish and am ashamed. So it is a great blessing from heaven whenever Shinichi Kikuchi brings me tobacco. He*

*has connections with the accounting room of the 9th battalion and with the navy as well. He said he could get tobacco even when it is restricted.*

**December 3**
From last night to this morning the enemy attacked by air three times. I am exhausted from so little sleep. During the day I worked at the 3rd Jinchi. There were more attacks in the evening. I take off my hat to the enemy for their effective and persistent attacks.

**December 4**
I got up at 3:00 a.m. and went to the brigade to draw water with First Class Private Kusama. The driving rain made this task all the more difficult. I finished work at 6:30 p.m. and then did the laundry. There were a few air raids after returning to the camp. An enemy reconnaissance plane was seen circling overhead.

**December 5**
Soldiers from the brigade continued with their well drilling. Meanwhile, soldiers from the 4th squad trained at the 4th Jinchi. The company commander was very unpleasant during today's drills.

**December 6**
I have been staying at the 4th Jinchi since last night because watch is on alert. I helped with construction at the kanshi-jo at the 4th Jinchi, and finished at 3:30 p.m.

**December 7**
Today I worked at the 1st Jinchi.

**December 8**
It is the third anniversary of the Greater East Asian War. The battalion held a formal reading ceremony in front of headquarters. Company drills were scheduled to last three hours. After that we were supposed to gather firewood for an hour-and-a-half and rest in the afternoon. These plans were inter-

rupted at 8:30 a.m. when the alarm sounded. Enemy planes attacked and gave us a terrific pounding. Then, at around 12:45, eight enemy warships began their bombardment of the island. I took cover at the 4th battalion Jinchi and ate *kanpan*[33] for lunch during the attack. The bombardment from the sea ended at 1:50. A few minutes later the air-raid alarm was turned off and I watched with regret as the enemy ships escaped unharmed into the distance. There was nothing I could do but praise the enemy's bravery and military might.

## December 9

I went to the south pier to fill holes caused by yesterday's attack. Rain began to fall as soon as I arrived and I got soaked. An air-raid alarm sounded at the 3rd Jinchi and we took cover.

## December 10

With my clothes still soaked from yesterday, I headed off to work in the early hours of the morning. I worked at the Maekawa camp.

## December 11

There was an air raid while we were digging a trench at the 3rd Jinchi. The weather was more agreeable today. Additional troops stood watch duty this evening.

## December 12

I exercised in the 3rd Jinchi till 8 a.m. and went to gather firewood at 9 a.m. I got a three-shot vaccination and then dined on a freshly-caught octopus in the afternoon.

## December 13

The enemy is conducting a war of nerves. They attacked four times during the night and into the morning. The alarm then rang three more times. After a Lockheed finished with its attack, a reconnaissance plane appeared to assess the damage. Then a B-29 came and dropped more bombs.

---

33  *Kanpan*: hardtack.

## December 14

From last night to this morning the alarm rang eight times with one or two airplanes attacking on each occasion. A bomb with a time-delayed fuse was dropped and later exploded. I am a wreck and have the jitters due to a lack of sleep. I stood watch and helped First Class Private Haneda dig the boukuugou.

### The Time-Bomb:

*At the end of November enemy planes dropped delayed-fuse time-bombs. They are a different and very dangerous type of bomb that does not explode within a known time frame. No one except the manufacturer can determine when it will explode. The bomb penetrates a few feet into the ground. When it explodes, the blast does not move horizontally but instead spreads vertically. Therefore, the safest thing to do is to lie down ten meters away because fragments will only fly upwards.*

## December 15

I exercised in the 3rd Jinchi. I cut down trees in the afternoon for making a company's restroom. There was a scene during an air attack where one of our pilots bailed out of his plane and parachuted down to safety. There was a lot of bombing during the night.

## December 16

I dug a firing trench at the 3rd Jinchi.

## December 17

I received two months' salary today. I decided to send 50 yen home. Hachiro Yoyogi and I worked together to dig out a boukuugou for the sick and wounded. We worked under the supervision of First Lieutenant Yamada.

## December 18

Today I caught the largest number of octopus since landing on Iwo Jima. Spent the entire day working in Maekawa's squad but frequent air raids limited our ability to get much done. Watch duty was put on alert this evening. Five or six raids occurred during the night and five bombs exploded in front of the Jinchi. I narrowly escaped death.

### Octopus:

*Although I have seen many an octopus since landing, I only recently discovered that the taste is very similar to peanuts. We are forbidden to cook for ourselves and so soldiers eat whatever they can find to supplement the food shortage. I broke apart the octopus and ate it with a long needle. It was good eating and I hid it from the others during my lunch break. Octopus is somewhat oily and is especially delicious. It seems that the octopus of Iwo Jima have nearly all been eaten up.*

### December 19

Although the plan was to dig a firing trench, it was changed to camouflage work in front of the Jinchi. The alarm rang out at 9 a.m. and company commander First Lieutenant Shibata took cover in the boukuugou. He was scolded by the battalion commander because he failed to notice the alarm was cancelled and continued to remain underground. After that, he fired us up with drills at the 4th Jinchi because today just happened to be the company's day for drills. First Lieutenant Shibata took out his frustrations by screaming immoderately at us the whole time.

### December 20

I worked with Maekawa's squad today.

### December 21

I worked digging the company boukuugou. I was cold from 4 a.m. till 12 p.m. because of the rain. I stayed at the 2nd Jinchi all night and accompanied Sergeant Kobayashi on patrol. There were two air-raids.

### December 22

Brigade commander Major General Sadasue Senda came to patrol for the first time. The company practiced *Nikuhaku Kogeki*.[34] I dug the company's trench in the afternoon. It stopped raining by 8 p.m. and the moon came out.

### December 23

I worked with Maekawa's squad. Watch duty was put on alert again this evening.

### December 24

Today was unforgettable. It was the fifth bombardment from a warship. I returned to the company in darkness before the sleeping dawn awakened. First Class Private Nagata told me during watch duty that there would be a ship to unload. I came to the south pier after breakfast. Bad weather and rough seas made it difficult for the large-sized SB ship to dock and so it set a new course for the west pier. I crossed the airfield and went to meet the ship. I had been unloading the SB ship with a two-wheeled cart for only a short while when a Lockheed suddenly attacked with its machine guns blazing away. All I could do was pray for God's help as my life hung by a thread. When the Lockheed left, ten enemy warships began their naval bombardment. Unloading work was cancelled and all of us in the squad were quickly dismissed. I got into a naval car with Corporal Matsui and Saito, Mochizuki from third company, Lance Corporal Nihei and First Class Private Odaka. We made it halfway to the shelter when one of our own large-sized airplanes took off from the airstrip. It approached our car at such a low angle that we all jumped out onto the ground. The plane barely missed us as it flew over the car. It was extremely terrifying. We all then hopped back in the car and sped to the entrance of the Osaka Yama Jinchi of the 9th Independent Anti-Tank Battalion. I took shelter in a natural cave. At around noon an

---

34  *Nikuhaku Kogeki*: "Human bullet assault" troops assigned to attack tanks with explosive satchels. A soldier would attempt to place his explosives on the tank's tracks to disable it — sometimes by hiding in a prepared underground pit (a *tako-tubo*, or "octopus pot"), and other times running directly at his target. The suicide version of this tactic was known as *tokkou* ("suicide bomb attack") — *Tokkoutai* is the word for "suicide squad."

enemy air attack took us by surprise. During the attack one of our airplanes took off and engaged the enemy in a dogfight. Another naval bombardment followed and lasted for an hour and fifteen minutes. When it was all over, an enemy flying boat flew overhead at a low altitude to assess the damage. I got into the car and returned to the company which was near Nidan Iwa. The island was unrecognizable from the onslaught. We were concerned about those who were caught by surprise unloading the ship when the attack came. It turned out that they had safely evacuated to the 4th Jinchi. It began to rain and I was put in charge of a work detail repairing the road to Nidan Iwa. I worked during the evening digging the company's boukuugou. There were a few more air raids again that night. It seems that the enemy is at last focusing its energy on the capture of Iwo Jima. An SB was bombed, strafed and hung low in the water off the southern coast.

### December 25

I awoke this morning at 3 a.m. and went to the brigade to draw water with First Class Private Wada. The navy was unloading supplies from an SB ship that was damaged by yesterday's attack. I asked them for a biscuit and tobacco. I envy the navy for this large stash of food. I finished work at 4 p.m. There were two air raids. I shared tobacco with First Class Private Namiki. Enemy planes attacked seven times in the night. I only got a few hours' sleep.

### December 26

I got up at 3:40 to help with digging the company boukuugou. My head was heavy from a lack of sleep. Just after breakfast I was ordered by First Lieutenant Yamada to fill holes behind the officers' billet at headquarters. Just then a delayed-fuse time-bomb was dropped. This all happened at around 10:40 a.m. and it wasn't long before more time-bombs were dropped yet again. Big holes were blasted in two places on the road in front of the Muto squad. During the attack, ten soldiers from the Kuritsu squad went into a cave for protection but were buried alive when the cave filled with sand. One of the buried victims still lay half exposed when I went to stand watch later that night. I was digging a hole when two delayed-fuse bombs exploded. I escaped death by a hair's breadth. One of our planes returned from a bombing run on Saipan. A gleaming light safely guided it to the center of the runway. First Class Odaka stood anti-aircraft surveillance watch with me throughout the night.

### December 27

I worked digging the hospital boukuugou at headquarters. Suddenly a Lockheed flew by with machine guns blazing away at around 9:30. A group of thirteen B-24s, eleven Lockheed airplanes and three B-29s soon followed with their own attack. This was in turn followed by another group of ten attacking enemy planes. According to intelligence, enemy troop transports were headed northward. The bombardment from three battle cruisers and two destroyers began at noon. The warships came to within 3,000 meters of the island. Naval bombardment continued till around 1:30 p.m. and the alarm was cancelled at 2 p.m. The battalion commander and instructor Hoshi supervised work at the hospital boukuugou. Everyone concentrated and the work went smoothly. Because of the anticipated American invasion of the island, Japan is sending us an airplane every day in order to build up our defenses. The airfield is of critical importance and eleven soldiers from our company have been assigned to keep it repaired. It was day-and-night shift work. A high-speed transport ship which was going to land on the southern coast was destroyed and burned today.

### December 28

A few air raids occurred during my time spent drawing water for the brigade. Sleep was impossible.

**December 29**

I stood watch today. A bomb was dropped on the cannon position at the 4th Jinchi. I spent the whole day concentrating on camouflage. There was one attack today from a small group of enemy airplanes. They dropped their delayed-fuse time-bombs and flew away.

**December 30**

Lance Corporal Orihashi and I buried pipe [water pipe?] today. I gathered firewood in the rain.

**December 31**

I worked for Maekawa's squad. The rain came down in earnest and so the morning's work had to be suspended. I was thoroughly soaked. In the evening I dug out the company's trench. New Year's Eve came while I stood watch. I passed the old year and welcomed the New Year in a trench.

**January 1, Shōwa 20**

The *Kyujo-Hohai*[35] was held in front of the squad's headquarters at 5:20 a.m. Here on Iwo Jima we had an unexpected treat: two pieces of *mochi*[36] were served for New Year. I received a medicinal glass of alcohol, two pieces of *manju*[37] and three cigarettes as a special ration. In the afternoon I collected firewood for about one hour and thirty minutes. I spent the rest of New Year's Day eating octopus. Tonight's watch was put on alert and just then the air-raid alarm sounded. I shouldered the *tenage-bin*[38] and hurried to the Jinchi with First Class Private Nagata.

**January 2**

There were military drills at the 4th Jinchi. Later on in the afternoon I worked at the 3rd Jinchi. The second day of the New Year has gone. There were eight air raids during the night and I was hardly able to sleep.

**January 3**

I dug out the company's trench from early morning until noon. A Lockheed plane came for reconnaissance at around 1:30 and enemy planes attacked at 3:30 during work at the 3rd Jinchi. The bombing was intense and one of the targets of the attack was very near our camp. I thought my life was going to end at any moment. Company Sergeant Tanaka was injured in the head and chest from an attack later that evening.

**January 4**

I went to stay at the 4th Jinchi last night. During the day I worked with Maekawa's squad. It was a beautiful day and I became so sleepy because of that. Watch duty was at the 4th Jinchi and we were on alert throughout the night. The bombing raids seemed to go on forever. One of the bombs exploded on the road to the cannon position of the Jinchi yesterday.

**January 5**

While working with the Maekawa squad yesterday I was beaten with a stick of lumber until it broke in two.[39] Three Lockheed airplanes suddenly attacked at 7 a.m. One was shot down into the sea to the right side of Pipe Mountain. After that ten B-24s came. Bombardment from a warship began at 2 p.m. and continued for about two hours. There was no great damage. I evacuated to the cave of the Musashino squad. I worked all night, from 8 p.m. to 4 a.m. at the company's boukuugou.

**January 6**

After working through the night I stood watch at the kanshi-jo. I worked with the artillery crew and fired the cannon of the 4th Jinchi today. First Class Privates Hiroyoshi Miyazawa and Shoji Sawada were injured during the night from a bomb explo-

35   *Kyujo-Hohai*: a worship ceremony of the Imperial Palace.
36   *Mochi*: rice cake.
37   *Manju*: steamed cake.
38   *Tenage-bin*: breakable jars filled with gasoline, similar to a Molotov cocktail, used in attacks against tanks. *Tenagedan* = "hand grenade" and *bin* = "bottle."

39   Any minor action by a Japanese soldier that irritated a superior could be cause for corporal punishment.

sion at the 3rd Jinchi. The air raids have become more and more intense.

## January 7

In the morning there was repair work at the 3rd Jinchi. I dug the company's boukuugou from 12 p.m. until 8 p.m. The parcel came from Ryozaburo. The air raids had become intense, and so I stayed in the company's shelter where I had been digging, but I did not sleep at all.

### A Parcel Just Arrived

*The long-awaited parcel from Ryozaburo was delivered to me on January 7th. When I opened the package, it was as if I was brushed by a gentle breeze from home. There was a flowery belt I bought before my military service and a bamboo pipe purchased with one sen[40] while I was still in training. There was a souvenir pipe from Truk Island and a magnifying glass bought instead of matches, both of which I have inherited from the now-deceased Hiroshi Otake. There was a copy of Rembrandt's biography and some cigarettes. As I read Rembrandt, I felt like I was back home, and smoked until I was satisfied.*

## January 8

I dug at the company's boukuugou from the early morning. Our position there is dangerously exposed and so we have been digging every day to complete the work. I gathered firewood, took a break, and ate octopus in the afternoon. I stayed overnight at the 4th Jinchi.

### Impressions of the Beginning of Shouwa 20:

*The endless fighting in Shouwa 19 has finished and Shouwa 20 has finally arrived. Last year was a very busy one. When I look back, I realize I had wandered between life and death many times since my landing on Iwo Jima six months ago. In the meantime, it was regrettable that I finished the year without any spiritual enlightenment. Perhaps this*

*was because I find it difficult to consider without regret that I may die anywhere and at any time. Perhaps I regret being born into this world. In order to fulfill my last assignment as a brilliant soldier, I disregard my own desires and pledge a brave fight.*

## January 9

I went with First Class Private Odaka to draw water for the brigade. Our enemies on Saipan and Tinian have launched air raids on the mainland one after the other following the Tokyo raid in November. As a feint measure, the enemy carries out aerial bombardments over Iwo Jima for a minimum of six to ten times daily. The enemy bombs us day and night with regular and delayed-fuse time-bombs. They intend to kill as many of us as possible. Therefore, everywhere is dangerous and it is especially dangerous near the camp. We dug the main trunk of a large-scale tunnel according to brigade orders. The work went on day and night until the tunnel was large enough to hold every soldier inside. Intense work continues every day.

### Bombardments From Warships:

*The same ships that took part in the Tokyo air raid bombarded us for two days. On December 24th and on the 27th, battle cruisers and destroyers bombarded us for one hour and thirty minutes each day. A Lockheed came in at a low altitude and viciously strafed us, but radar could not detect it. After that, B-24s approached undetected and dropped bombs. After the bombing, a flying boat wandered impertinently above the island to assess the situation. Shortly afterwards, the naval bombardment started up all over again. I became somewhat anxious when several of our airplanes were blown up and destroyed by fire.*

## January 10

I stayed at the 4th Jinchi last night. In the early morning I worked for the first line of the company's boukuugou. An enemy bomb caused damage to the

---

40   Sen: 1/100 yen.

camp of the *siki-han*[41] at 3:30. Watch was put on alert in the evening and I went to the 4th Jinchi. That octopus I ate has given me diarrhea.

## January 11
Today I worked digging a firing trench and managed to find time to dash off a postcard to Ryozaburo and Otake-kun. I helped with the digging at the company's boukuugou from 8 a.m. to 11 p.m. I then slept until 2 a.m., awoke, and resumed work packing and digging sand until 5 a.m. I am completely exhausted.

### About the Excessive Malnutrition:
*I have not eaten many fresh vegetables since landing. All the cooked food is made from dried vegetables and is causing malnutrition. These dried vegetables include Japanese radish, sweet potato, carrot, kanpyou,[42] kombu,[43] and a wakame.[44] Living under such conditions makes me realize how happy I was in Japan. The voice of "rationing" is everywhere, but when I think of how it will be on the battlefield, I must admit that I am better off now and certainly happier. I think I must recognize and appreciate what a gracious country the homeland is.*

## January 12
Because today was drill day I was mobilized to work through last night and into the early morning hours. I trained with the artillery crew of the 4th Jinchi until 8 a.m. and then dug at the company's boukuugou from 12 p.m. till 8 p.m. I stayed overnight at the third boukuugou.

## January 13
I worked at the first defensive line of the boukuugou from 4 a.m. to 10 a.m. Night bombings have decreased over the last few days.

## January 14
Today I was engaged in repair work at the yobi-jinchi of the 4th Jinchi in the afternoon. According to reports, third company's First Class Private Fujisawa was killed in action during an air raid near the SB ship at the southern coast.

## January 15
In the afternoon I made repairs to the first line of the boukuugou at the 4th Jinchi.

## January 16
Today I worked for the first line at the company's boukuugou.

### Darkness:
*My comrades often talk in secret. They talk about someone who bought something and paid several times the official price from a broker, and of someone who sold three bags of rice for 1000 Yen and the police caught the wrong person. They also speak of things done successfully in the dark. If I were to pursue these criminals, as I would have done in my former life as a law enforcement agent in the rural area, all of them should be eating a stinking meal in a police cell by now. However, I couldn't care less about what they are doing while they are in the army.*

## January 17
I did simple work during the day and dug the company's boukuugou throughout the night. I was sick to my stomach and was miserable the entire time. There were four air raids.

## January 19
I had worked all night until morning and was scheduled for rest. Instead, I was mobilized for drills. In the afternoon I skipped work and slept because my head hurt and stomach ached. I went to the 4th Jinchi in the evening and stayed there overnight.

---

41  *Siki-han*: a command group. Each company had one siki-han. The members of this group gave the initial command to fire artillery.
42  *Kanpyou*: dried gourd strips.
43  *Kombu*: sea tangle.
44  *Wakame*: edible brown seaweed.

## January 20

I worked at the 2nd Jinchi this morning, in the afternoon at the second line of the company boukuugou.

## January 21

A bomb exploded in front of the 4th Jinchi around 9:15 last night. The blast broke a concrete wall at the cannon position and injured First Class Private Nagata who was sleeping there. I worked for the Maekawa squad and later met Shinichi Kikuchi for lunch at the 9th Battalion. We enjoyed *kuzuyu*,[45] tea, and a few other treats. I returned home with three cigarettes and three Japanese radishes. I was expecting another all-nighter working the third line of the company's boukuugou, but at 10 p.m. my schedule was suddenly changed. It turns out that tomorrow I will be unloading a ship. I stopped working and slept outside in the trench.

### *Notes From a Visit With Shinichi At the 9th Battalion:*

*I went to work today with the Maekawa squad near the brigade. During my lunch break I visited Shinichi in the 9th battalion. He was at the office and was putting sugar into his kuzuyu. The group leader and other soldiers welcomed me; they took out pickles and served tea. The group indulged me with tea and some idle talk, it being the first time we met since arriving here on the island. They gave me three cigarettes and three Japanese radishes as a souvenir when I left. They asked as a favor that I bring Japanese radish and other vegetable seeds to them in return. Although I did not know if such seeds existed in the 8th Battalion's accounting room, I agreed and left. Several days later, Shinichi said I should stop by and help myself to a pig that recently died in one of the enemy naval bombardments. Unfortunately, I had to refuse his offer because I was running late.*

## January 22

We originally planned to unload two ships this morning at the south pier but work was rescheduled to the afternoon. Two ships arrived. I used a *daihachi*[46] to carry loads of food and ammunition. While there, I took advantage of this rare opportunity to fill up on canned food. I finished unloading at 8:00 p.m. I went to the 4th Jinchi for watch duty which was on alert because of the many air raids today.

## January 24

I went with Private Oba to draw water from the well. We had an air raid at around 10:30. Not long after that, enemy ships (one battleship, three cruisers and four destroyers) arrived. We were pounded without mercy and I took refuge in a firing trench. One of our pilots deliberately crashed his airplane onto the deck of an enemy ship and sank it. We were ready to draw water at around 7 p.m. but no vehicle arrived. An aerial attack burned the petty officers' room of the siki-han later in the evening.

## January 25

I worked for the Kouhei-tai. There were a few air-raids.

## January 26

Takeoffs and landings were impossible because enemy naval guns have once again destroyed the airfield. I went to work filling up the holes under the command of First Lieutenant Takahashi. After work, as I returned to camp, there was an air raid and so I evacuated to the 4th Jinchi. I stayed in the stairway of the third boukuugou.

## January 27

Today, like yesterday, I continued working to repair the airfield. I was quite surprised at around 3 p.m. in the afternoon when a B-29 suddenly flew by and I took cover. The *dentan*[47] was malfunctioning which made me quite angry. I wrote a postcard to

---

45   *Kuzuyu*: a type of starch gruel.

46   *Daihachi*: two-wheeled carts.
47   *Dentan*: radar.

Ryozaburo.

**January 28**

I quite unexpectedly received a parcel from Ryozaburo; it was my birthday gift. In the parcel were two books: *Manon Lescaut* and *The History of Aviation Development*. I worked artillery surveillance. Today was the battalion's day off. After finishing repair work on one of the artillery pieces, I laid down.

**January 29**

For those who were not able to take a holiday yesterday, today became their holiday. I went to the south pier to take a bath. I soaked myself in fresh water inside a metal drum. This was my second bath since landing on Iwo Jima. Goods were unloaded and brought to the supply and accounting room in the afternoon. An air raid took place while I was unloading rice.

**January 30**

I drew water for the brigade early in the morning. First Class Private Soneda and I worked together and we finished by one o'clock. I went to the 4th Jinchi in the evening and stayed overnight. I was given ten Kinshi cigarettes.

***Death from Disease in the Second Company:***

*The other day, Lance Corporal Oyagi died from an illness caused by malnutrition and Sergeant Sugasawa came down with typhus. Both of them would still be alive if they were living a normal life, but that is impossible here on Iwo Jima. Death by sickness is very painful and it is not honorable, and has brought the unfairness of war close to me. This is a lesson that should be taught everywhere.*

**January 31**

The brigade drill was carried out at 4 a.m. I went to repair the huge crater in the road right in front of the Musashino squad that was caused by today's afternoon attack. After patrol with Corporal Saito I

stayed at the 2nd Jinchi and slept well for the first time in a long time.

**February 1**

My work assignment at the 3rd Jinchi was suddenly changed by company command. I was sent to work filling up holes at the first airfield.

**February 2**

I worked at the first line of the boukuugou. In the afternoon I was employed in the supply control and accounting room. Watch duty was on alert status this evening.

**February 3**

Worked at the 4th Jinchi and read the *Manon Lescaut* during my lunch break. Several Lockheed aircraft attacked around 12:00 p.m. and opened up on us with machine-gun fire. One was shot down. B-24s attacked in the evening. I stayed at the boukuugou. I ate five bean seeds in celebration of *Setsubun*,[48] the eve of the beginning of spring.

***Notes About Radar:***

*I was told that the radar on Iwo Jima was excellent and was capable of detecting aircraft as far away as 200 kilometers. I have my doubts. Headquarters often sounds the alarm after a B-29 has flown overhead, throwing everyone into confusion and scattering us in all directions. Today I was part of a work crew repairing holes in the first airfield made on February 2nd. Although the radar indicated that the enemy was still flying seventy to eighty kilometers away at 2 p.m., the alarm had not sounded when I noticed nine B-29s flying overhead. I evacuated by vehicle to the cave of the Nagata squad at Pipe Mountain. It was an unnerving experience.*

---

48  *Setsubun*: the day preceding *Risshun* (3 February), the first day of spring in the Japanese lunar calendar; roughly equivalent to New Year's Eve. There is a custom of throwing roasted soybeans (*mamemaki*) out the door and chanting *Oni wa soto! Fuku wa uchi!* "Out with Evil! In with Fortune!" in order to banish evil ogres from one's house.

### About <u>Manon Lescaut</u>

*Ryozaburo mailed me my paperback copy of <u>Manon Lescaut</u>, published by Iwanami Shoten. It seemed that Otake-kun had it. Although the old paperback was in my hands for a long time, I only recently began reading it. To my surprise, the more I read this old paperback, the better it gets. It has turned into an amazing love story and I get very aroused while reading it. However, it is a famous book with a good reputation, and is full of well-turned phrases. Best of all, I like the way Manon manipulates Chevalier; it is described so well. I am also impressed by how Chevalier desperately struggles to satisfy Manon's taste for luxury and, in doing so, gradually becomes a villian. Reading this book provides me with a pleasant escape during an air raid.*

*3 February 1945 was Futomi Hosoda's last entry. On 19 February the American invasion began. Written on the last few pages are his farewells.*

**To Ryozaburo:** I am hoping you are in good health. The rest is up to you. Extend love to my mother. Take care of her in my place. I am thinking it may be good to send Mother to Koshu, depending on the circumstances. It may also be good for you to send Mother to live with Mr. Abe, or to Mikawashima, so that she might be better able to cope until Mitsuo returns. It will not be good to cause Mr. Abe any more trouble. Be sincere towards them.

**To Mother:** I will die early without being able to be a good son. I would prefer if you could go to the countryside and settle there. Stay healthy always.

**To Mr. Abe:** I wanted to thank you for giving me my uniform. It is improper to say good-bye at this point without saying my thanks. Thank you very much for everything you have done for me. Give my best regards to your wife. Please do take care of yourself.

**To Mr. Yamachi:** Thank you very much for your kindness. I regret to inform you that I will die earlier than I expected. Please take care of yourself always.

**To Otake-kun:** I have always appreciated our friendship that lasted so long. Give my best regards to Nishihara-kun. It looks like I will be the first among the three of us to cross the Sanzu River[49] on my way to the afterlife. I intend to die well.

---

49  Sanzu River: the way to the afterlife in the Buddhist tradition; similar to the River Styx in Greek mythology.

# Thirty-Five Days in Hell

Howard McLaughlin, 1945.

This story began when I acquired a Japanese helmet covered in a tangle of camouflage. The name of the Marine who found the helmet outside a blown-out bunker was PFC Howard N. McLaughlin, Jr. When I located McLaughlin's son, Doug, through his father's obituary, I asked about the helmet and Doug confirmed its authenticity. I then asked if his father had ever written about the war. Doug said that his father co-authored a book with another Marine,[1] but that a second, more significant manuscript existed.

Several months later, a massive five-volume manuscript arrived in the mail. The story that follows is from Volume III, *Iwo Jima*. It features never-before-seen combat photographs taken by one of the men in McLaughlin's unit.

## *Thirty-Five Days in Hell*

The harsh notes of the bugle sounding over the ship's P. A. system and the accompanying shrill notes of the bosun's pipe announced to all hands aboard that today was officially started. None of this ear-piercing noise had really awakened any of the probably four hundred men in our compartment. All night long people had nervously wandered back and forth to the adjacent heads for a smoke or had drifted out on deck. There they silently lined the rail, gazing into the dark, lost in silent contemplation.

In between the nervous wanderings, these people had tried to get comfortable in their cramped little bunks. But this evening, sleep would not come. After you had cleaned and oiled your weapon for the fourth or fifth time, the best anyone could do was just lay in your cramped little space and stare at the bottom of the bunk above.

For all men there was the continually recurring fear that was uppermost in every man's thoughts. After all the months of openly boasting about your fearlessness and ease that you would be able to face the enemy in combat, the time to put up or shut up was at hand. Now there was that terrible dread that after all you might not measure up to being a Marine in the eyes of your buddies. And no matter how indifferent any man had acted, this past night had been a time for private thoughts, reflections and praying. This tension was far too great for anyone to have slept.

Now this blaring noise on the USS *Darke*'s

1   Howard N. McLaughlin and Raymond C. Miller, *From the Volcano to The Gorge, Getting the Job Done on Iwo Jima* (Tower Publishing, 2010).

loudspeaker system was telling us that today was the day that we had all been trained for. In place of the eerie red night-battle lights, the white compartment lights were turned on. This harsh light clearly showed the tension on peoples' faces, and the somber mood of the men was accentuated with the jumbled piles of equipment and field packs stacked in the isles and passageways.

All of us had trained for well over a year-and a-half for this day. Many of these people had practiced particularly hard during our last four months in the staging area of beautiful Hawaii. Today was the day that many of us would take the final test: a test that allowed for no second guesses, and there was a severe penalty for mistakes. This was D-day for the landing of two divisions of the U.S. Marines on the Japanese-held island of Iwo Jima.

I was a member of the repair section (heavy equipment), Headquarters and Service Company of the 5th Engineer Battalion of the 5th Marine Division. Although as Marines all of us mechanics in H&S Co. had completed combat infantry training before being assigned to the combat engineers, our training had never progressed beyond the rudiments that were taught just out of boot camp. We didn't really know any more about what the real infantry would be doing than what we had learned in elementary training.

Once in the combat engineers, we had additional training in the duties of combat engineers before our assignment to line companies. From line companies, selected individuals were picked due to some skill and transferred to H&S Co. In combat the line companies did the fighting, while H&S Companies were considered support troops, i.e. rear echelon troops. H&S Company engineers was where all of the specialized engineering people were assembled. Any man that had an engineering skill or was knowledgeable in construction was put in H&S Company.

In an emergency, theoretically, any Marine could be infantry, and was expected to be. Any time there was a serious depletion in the ranks of combat

Mount Suribachi, which means "grinding bowl" in Japanese, was known to locals as Pipe Mountain. Sulfur gas and water vapor sometimes rolls out from the caldera, giving it the appearance of a smoking pipe when viewed from the sea. National Archives photograph.

outfits during combat situations, any warm body was used to fill the holes in the dike. This ability to use service troops in among regular infantry during emergencies to reinforce depleted units proved its worth on several occasions during previous landings.

In theory this was wonderful. However, for those chosen to serve in an emergency, this wasn't so good. Although we in H&S Co. had been in the Marines as long as people in the infantry, they had been practicing for combat every day. We hadn't practiced at all. It is a documented fact that the longevity of fresh, untrained people placed in active combat units results in a high percentage of losses among the newcomers. However, it is better military strategy to lose a few untrained men than to lose the battle. Since we had been overseas we had only had a few days training of landing practice at the beaches. And we had not done any calisthenics since boot camp. Not even occasionally. Our job called for more brains and less brawn. The brawn was the combat engineers in the line companies. Our job was to repair damaged heavy equipment: dozers, cranes and all kinds of heavy trucks. Our only job was to assure that the rest of the engineers were able to fight. But by Corps mandate, when bodies were needed to fill a hole in the line, physically conditioned or not you had to go.

In keeping with this line of thinking, on the tables of organization for the division, H&S Co. was shown as being made up of twenty .50-caliber heavy machine-gun crews and twenty .30-caliber light machine-gun crews. In the invasion orders this was to be a combat landing. So even though the shooting was supposed to be all done and the fighting all done, if any of us from the repair section went ashore, when we landed we would still carry all of the equipment necessary as machine-gun squads.

In the pre-invasion scheduling, as heavy equipment mechanics we of the repair section had been assured that we didn't have to worry. With our specialized training, we were too valuable to be used as infantry. Unless we were specifically needed to repair damaged engineer equipment, we weren't even to go ashore on this little island. However, if we were needed on the island to repair damaged engineer equipment, it would be well into the third day before we went ashore. We were assured by the Division Command that by then the fighting would be all done. And the Navy's high brass had assured the Marine commands that their fabulous marksmanship would destroy everything that had been constructed by man on the island. The Navy high brass had continually assured us Marines that this entire landing would be a short, easy operation. If the taking of this island went as smoothly as the Navy predicted, then we mechanics would not even go ashore on Iwo Jima.

Although I had joined the Marines wanting to win some medals, now that I was actually this close to combat the idea of landing after the fighting was over sounded just fine with me. With my new-found maturity, I preferred to learn about combat a little at a time, not just be dumped onto the beach in the middle of the battle.

# D-day

D-day breakfast was the famous "last supper": steak and eggs — cooked any way you wanted, and all you wanted. But I don't think there were many people that really chow'd down this morning.

The ship's cooking galleys were closed at 0530 hours. The mess hall eating area was on one of the hatch areas that had to be uncovered and opened. Once the pallets of artillery ammunition were removed from the holds below the mess hall deck, the hatch covers would be set back in place on top of the hatches. On all the ships the troops' mess hall area would be used as a hospital when needed.

Out on the weather decks, other members of the crew had begun to unleash the landing craft that each transport and cargo ship carried. The USS *Darke* carried twenty of these little landing craft. The correct name was Landing Craft Vehicle and Personnel: LCVPs. Each had a crew of three. The front was hinged to drop flat, so troops and supplies could unload onto the beach while the landing craft was still afloat. These small craft usually carried thirty-six combat Marines, or a jeep and a small trailer plus several men.

While we had been eating our breakfast, our bunks had been dismantled and stacked far away from the hatch areas that opened through the deck of each compartment. In the storage holds below were stored jeeps and light trucks. These would be off-loaded on to LCMs[2] and taken ashore for the landing. LCMs were about one-and-one-half times bigger than the LCVPs.

Once the holds were open we mechanics did our thing, checking trucks and equipment to make sure they would start and releasing tie-downs off trucks and artillery pieces. As soon as the checks were completed, the ship's cranes began hoisting the equipment out of the holds. The equipment was then loaded on the LCMs that were beginning to come alongside. The LCMs also had a front ramp

---

2   Landing Craft Mechanized were about 50 ft. long.

that could be lowered at the beach, allowing equipment, at least in theory, to drive off directly onto the dry beach.

The landing team I was assigned to was in reserve. Remember, I was not scheduled to land until possibly the third day, and then only if it became necessary to repair damaged engineer equipment. So when we had finished our work down in the holds, several of us went topside to find seats along the bulkheads to watch the show.

It was still dark, but all the troop transports around us had turned on their deck lights for the sailors loading the landing craft. With all the ships lit up, we could see that there were now four or five as many times the number of ships that had been in our convoy out from Hawaii. There were ships on all sides of us, for as far as the eye could see.

Off the starboard bow, ten miles in the distance, was the dark hulk of the island of Iwo Jima. In the darkness it was all asparkle with the flashes of U.S. naval shells bursting on its surface. The shelling was from ships between us and the island. In all of our briefings, it had been predicted by the Navy that the pre-invasion shelling from their ships would pulverize everything on the island. The Marines would be able to walk across the island without having to fire a shot.

As dawn broke and visibility improved, some of the warships moved in closer to the landing beaches. They were firing almost point-blank at some of the shapes that were overlooking the landing beaches. Looking through field glasses at the area where the shells were exploding, we agreed that they looked like pillboxes and gun emplacements. However, any feature or structure on the island that could be seen was by chance. The beach area of the island looked like a big cloud of smoke.

It was also quite a show to watch the Navy and Marine planes dive bomb and strafe the lower slopes of Mount Suribachi. The real crowd pleaser were the specially converted large LST landing craft that normally carried tanks. These ships moved in really close to shore and disgorged thousands of fiery-tailed 4.5-inch rockets in streams onto the landing beaches. A couple of destroyers then moved close to the landing beach. Their work could be easily followed as they searched for targets. The streams of tracer bullets were like fiery fingers probing the smoky shores of the island.

By 0815 the transports moved in towards the island. I would guess that there were almost a thousand in the water. It looked like you could get from one transport to another by walking on all the little landing craft in the water between them. There were also amtracs, amtanks, control boats and many LCMs, LSMs and the much bigger LSTs.[3] The whole ocean was covered with little circles of landing craft waiting to form lines to become part of the landing waves.

At 0845 the intensity of the shelling increased and included every naval gun that could possibly fire at the landing beaches. Smoke and dust in the air obscured everything from sight. It was impossible to even make out where the landing beaches were anymore. From where we were it was impossible to even see the island anymore.

In the midst of this barrage, a single green star shell fired into the air signaling the start of the mad dash toward the beach for the first three waves.

Our ship's loudspeaker had been set on the command radio frequency of the landing units of the 27th and 28th Marines. At 0902 these units began calling back to command units still onboard ship. They were saying that they were on the beach and that there was no return small arms fire. They also reported that the Japanese shelling of the beach was very light. More units on the beach reported the same and everybody breathed a sigh of relief. It sounded like this was going to be a fairly easy landing. Maybe the Navy was finally right for a change.

---

3  Amtrack: Landing Vehicle Tracked (LVT) was an amphibious landing craft used to carry assault troops. LVTs were approximately 26 feet long. Amtank (LVT-A4) was an armored LVT fitted with a turret. These light tanks provided fire support to the Marines in the early stage of the landing. Landing Ship Medium (LSM) was an amphibious assault ship roughly 200 feet long with two front doors that swung open onto the beach. Landing Ship, Tank (LST) was about 380 feet long and used to carry vehicles, cargo and landing troops directly onto an unimproved shore through two bow doors. LSMs and LSTs can be seen on the beach behind Mount Suribachi in the photograph on page 197.

As soon as the LCVPs had landed the third wave, they raced back to the troop transports for more Marines. The fourth wave was already lined up and ready to start towards the beach as soon as the third wave was clear of the beach. The idea was to get as many people ashore to steamroll over any enemy that might choose to fight.

The amtanks that went ashore were equipped with a 75mm cannon and a .50-cal. machine gun, and as the name implies, they were amphibious and capable of movement on land once they left the water. On landing, the amtanks stayed on the beach till the first three waves were all ashore. Then they were to move inland with the advancing troops to provide fire support, just like a tank, until the island was secured.

Each amtrack was equipped with one .50-cal. and one .30-cal machine gun, and carried about twenty-four Marines inside a steel hull. Once on dry land the amtrack's rear door dropped to allow the Marines inside to exit, with the amtrack giving protection against small arms fire. Once unloaded, the amtracks returned to the ships for more troops and supplies. They were also responsible for returning any wounded to the ships.

With the landing of the fifth wave the euphoria of a possible easy landing evaporated. The radios indicated that there was a lot of mortar and artillery fire now on the landing beaches. Still, there seemed to be nothing to get alarmed about because only the new landing units were complaining. The radios of the earlier waves were silent, and everybody assumed they were silent because there was no time to report back about their progress.

Shortly, however, from the working radios the true word began to get back to the transports. The majority of troops were still on the first hundred yards of the beach. They hadn't been able to move inland as planned because Jap shell-fire was cutting the Marines on the beach to ribbons. The command and control radios were reporting that if they couldn't be reinforced right away, they would soon be pushed back into the water.

Back on the ships we listened intently to the radios. Command was querying them, trying to discover why there was such a terrible difference in radio reports. As we listened to the radios on the beach they would go silent in mid-conversation. Finally it was explained to command that many of the units couldn't complain as the incoming fire was extremely accurate. And while the losses for all units ashore were getting heavier, it was the radios and their operators that were being singled out for pinpoint shelling.

There was now no communication with many of the units on the beach. Most of the officers with radios ashore were wounded or dead. Those officers on the beach with radios still operating were frantically calling for help. They needed tanks and demolition explosives if they were to stay alive! There were too many pillboxes and bunkers that were undamaged! Until these were destroyed it would be impossible to get off the landing beaches.

By the time the next wave began to land on the beach, the beachmaster[4] and shore parties' radios began describing the accuracy of the Jap artillery fire. Most of the LCVPs were being destroyed as they dropped their ramps to unload troops and they stressed that this was true all along the landing beaches. The beachmaster's radio estimated that over half the LCVPs had been destroyed in the fourth wave. That percentage increased to two-thirds destroyed by the time the sixth wave had unloaded its troops. Most of the amtanks and amtracks ashore were now useless junk. Most had bogged down in the first few yards of loose sand on the beaches where they were systematically destroyed by accurate shell-fire. Those that were able to move inland were being destroyed by accurate gunfire from "destroyed" pillboxes that had come back to life.

Now that the naval shelling was over, the smoke and dust was lifting. Even out on the troop ships

---

4   The beachmaster organizes the landing area, establishes a coherent flow of men and equipment onto the beachhead and beyond, and directs the evacuation of the wounded and dead.

there were many times the number of concrete pill-boxes, now visible from their muzzle flashes. The radios from the beach said there were even more pillboxes that could not be seen from the ships. The job of camouflaging them was superb, and very few had been damaged enough that they were not firing on the landing Marines. The assault units were saying that most of these pillboxes were firing 20mm automatic guns or .50-cal. machine guns, with a few firing 47mm anti-tank guns. Each pillbox or bunker would need to be destroyed by infantry and line company engineers. The artillery and mortar shelling raining in on them was coming from some-place else on the island. The radios stressed that the troops could deal with the pillboxes they could see, but there was no place to fight or hide from the artillery and mortar fire. There was no way that the troops could fight what, for them, was causing the most concern.

The Navy moved several of their ships very close to shore and began using the onboard gun batteries to replace the lost firepower of the destroyed amtanks and amtracks. It was quite apparent that this landing was not going well at all.

Meanwhile, a little after 1100 hours, all of landing team 3/26 was called to our debarkation stations on the double. At each boat station there were enough troops for at least two and, in most cases, four LCVP boat loads. Standing at our boat stations we assumed they wanted work details to load cargo from the holds. After all, the landing was only three hours old. True, the landing was going sour fast but there should be plenty of trained infantry to land before they called on us. And besides, according to the original plan, landing team 2/26 would be called to land ahead of us.

Quickly, senior Marine officers began walking down through the assembled ranks, pointing out those selected, of which I was one, to step up to the front rows. When they had selected enough people for eight boatloads, the rear ranks were ordered to stand fast. Those selected for the front rank were told to go and get all their combat gear on the

double and be back in ranks in five minutes.

Our packs and all our combat gear had been packed last night and were piled around the edges of where our bunks had been. All we had to do was find them and put it all on. The machine guns and ammo was quickly lowered into the waiting boats for us. A trip to the head was our only deviation. By the time we got back to our boat stations there were eight landing craft under the debarkation nets along our side of the ship, each already loaded with piles of boxes. Officers took our names and we climbed over the railing, starting the long descent down the cargo nets to the waiting landing craft below.

We were heavily weighted down with all the things we had to carry. Because of the cold weather, most of us had on our long johns. Besides those, I wore a wool shirt and we all wore wool-lined field jackets rather than thinner dungaree jackets. We wore leggings under our dungaree pants, strapped tight to help support our ankles. Our engineers' helmets were without the distinctive Marine cam-ouflage cover. Each man had a rifle, bayonet and a cartridge belt full of rifle clips. Attached to it were two canteens, two first aid pouches and two combat field dressings and a combat knife. Then you wore a combat pack. This had your blankets rolled in a wa-terproof poncho rolled around the top half of your pack, with an entrenching tool attached to the back. The bottom half of the pack was carried in on trucks and was to be picked up later. In addition to all this we each had a gas mask and two extra bandoliers of rifle clips. There were two hand grenades attached to the cartridge belt suspenders. As 2nd gunner, I carried the tripod to the machine gun — 100 to 120 pounds of stuff to run with.

As we climbed down the cargo nets and neared the small boats, it was plain how bad the swells really were. The swells were so bad that the small boat would raise to the top of the swell and then sink suddenly in the next trough by as much as fifteen to twenty feet.

To board the LCVPs in heavy seas you climbed down the cargo net to a point even with the top gunwale at the top of the swell. You hung on to the landing net as the LCVP receded to the bottom of that trough and waited till it started back towards the top of the next swell. As the LCVP neared the top, you and several others jumped and prayed. If you missed your jump, it was all the way to the bottom of the ocean with your equipment before you could get it all unbuckled. For safety, we still had on the mandatory inflatable life belt. In an emergency the belt was inflated to the size of two balloon bicycle tire tubes by two little $CO_2$ cartridges. The inflatable life belt might work if you had to abandon ship without equipment, but they were worthless under the weight of all that gear.

Once loaded, our landing craft left the ship right away and headed out to join one of the circles of landing craft. The coxswain who steered the boat had a helper called a boatswain mate. His job was to get the front ramp down and the troops and gear off as fast as possible when the boat touched the beach. This LCVP had a gunner in a partly armored turret positioned alongside and a little higher than the coxswain. His .50-caliber machine gun fired over the heads of the landing troops.

There were about twenty-five men on board. Eight were engineers. When the call had been for engineers, I am sure what they really wanted were line company engineers for demolition work. We were mechanics, carpenters and bridge builders being sent in as a machine-gun squad. I don't know who the other people in the boat were or their units. The back of the craft was filled with boxes of materials.

The little landing craft really gave you a roller-coaster ride in the heavy swells and there were a lot of green faces. But thank God for small favors, our boat didn't circle very long before another small boat came alongside us. By bullhorn a naval officer told the coxs'n of our landing craft, and I can still remember his exact words: "You will be a certain number boat from the right. Form up on boat number something, the one flying the yellow pendant from its aerial. You are to land on Red Beach, just

to the left of Fatatsu Rocks. This is wave number thirteen. When you see the signal flare go off, start for the beach at full power. Don't lag behind the boats alongside of you, and don't stay at the beach. Unload and get out. The beach is still hot. Good luck."

It was about a three-mile dash to the beach. A cold wind was blowing and the sea was rough. The roar of the engine drowned out most other sounds except for the deafening sounds from the salvos of naval shells passing overhead. So all communication in the LCVP was by hand signal or somebody yelling in your ear. Then the call was passed down: "Lock and load. Check the man's gear ahead of you and remember your training. The beach is very hot." Then the word was passed that it was time to kneel down in a crouch. We were reminded again of our training: "Keep your heads down till the boat hits the beach. When the ramp goes down, run like hell. Once on the beach, remember to keep your ass down."

Water splashed into the landing craft from enemy shellfire. Then there was a nearby explosion that really rocked the boat and everyone got soaking wet. We had been instructed that it was not unusual for water to enter the barrel of your rifle during amphibious landings. A rifle fired with water in the barrel could explode the breach. To protect our weapons from water in the barrel, each man had been issued a cellophane sleeve to slip over the weapon till you landed. None of us had our weapon protected by the sleeve. The old-timers from previous landings told us not to use the sleeve because you couldn't fire the weapon with the sleeve on. You had to be ready to fire when the ramp went down and there would be not time to stop on the beach and remove the sleeve. Instead we unsheathed condoms and rolled one down over each muzzle to keep the water out. As soon as the rifle was fired, the condom was blown away.

Everything I saw for the next few hours is still visible if I close my eyes. There was a lurch as the forward motion of the boat abruptly stopped and

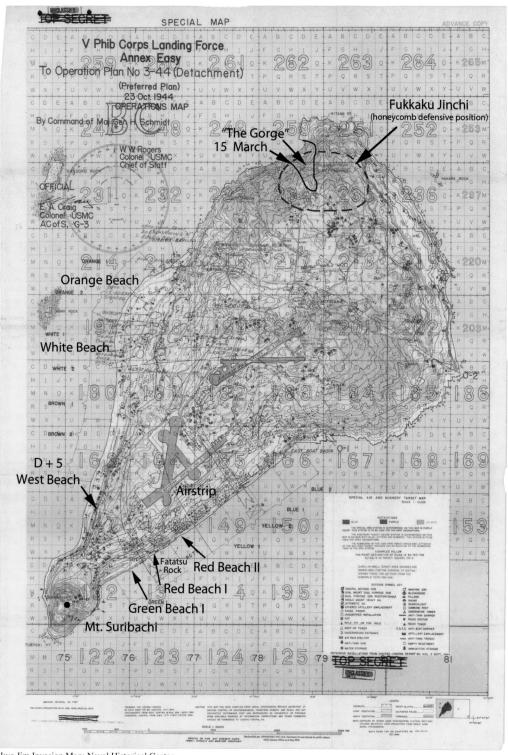

Iwo Jim Invasion Map; Naval Historical Center.

everybody was thrown towards the front of the craft. As the ramp went down, we stood up, adjusted our gear and after what seemed like hours moved out of the landing craft into the unknown.

We were ashore to the left of a partly sunken ship and the bow of the landing craft was on the hard sand of the beach. Later I found out that we had landed on Red Beach II, not Red Beach I which was closer to Mount Suribachi. It was the only open space along the shoreline where the landing craft could reach the beach.

Looking ahead as I came out of the landing craft, the beach had a gentle upward slope that ended in a steep upward slope, 150 to 200 feet from the mouth of the landing craft. To my right, for almost as far as I could see, was a wide flat beach. To my left the beach got narrower in a very short distance, and beyond that was Mount Suribachi looming over us like a giant.

On the flat area of the beach on either side of me were all kinds of amtracks, amtanks, Sherman tanks, artillery pieces and their tractors. They were wrecked, laying at odd angles, torn apart, tracks off and some burning. There were boxes of supplies laying around where they had been dropped or blown. Among this mess I could see the tops of camouflaged helmets in hastily deepened shell holes.

At the high water area ahead of me were Marines — shoulder to shoulder. They were in closely packed lines of newly excavated foxholes and shell holes, and all hunched down as far as they could get. The geysers of sand from the exploding shells let you know, even before getting far off the boat ramp, that the incoming shellfire was very heavy. The screaming noise of the heavy artillery shells was terribly unnerving, but at the same time the thundering noise from the explosions was so deafening that the beach seemed somehow silent.

At that time all the shelling seemed to be aimed at the ramp of our landing craft. We ran off the boat in three lines. I was near the back in the far left line. Just after I had taken my first step off the

boat ramp the man just ahead and to my right was hit. He stumbled and fell but I could not stop to help. Move, move faster! That was the word that had been drilled into all of us. If one stopped, it might cause those behind to bunch up and bunched up people are prime targets for enemy fire.

The first few steps out of the boat were on hard-packed wet sand and the running was easy. A few steps later and you were on dry sand and it became impossible to run under all the weight we were carrying. The blasts from the explosions constantly peppered me with sand. Wherever I looked there seemed to be many shells bursting.

I instinctively looked for shell holes to duck into as I ran up the beach. My rifle was in my right hand, the machine-gun tripod in my left. Most shell holes seemed too shallow to be of much use but at least you could kneel down and catch your breath while you determined where and when to run next. The shelling was so heavy, there was really no safe time to run. But run forward you did. Scared shitless.

As I ran up the beach, sliding in and out of shell holes, one fairly large shell hole that I jumped in had another Marine already crouched in it. He was laying on his stomach, arms flexed, elbows in the sand, holding his rifle out of the sand. One leg was cocked up, poised, ready to make the sprint forward to the next hole. As I slid in beside him I thought "This man was lucky, he didn't have to wear his field pack." I noticed the name Patterson stenciled on the back of his field jacket. The front visor of his helmet was resting on the sand like he was trying to close his eyes and hide from the shelling. I reached over and grabbed him by the shoulder. I started to yell, *"Let's go, Mac."* But as soon as I started to shake him I knew he was dead.

When I reached the high water line at the base of the first sandbank there was a solid mass of Marines. One look at these men huddled together in the shallow foxholes told the story of the landing. They were all wounded and waiting to be taken off the island. All around them were dead Marines wrapped in their ponchos. They were being used as sand bags to protect the wounded from the blizzard of shrapnel. People were being wounded faster than the corpsmen could treat them. Once wounded, they were often hit again by shrapnel with many of the men dying from multiple shrapnel wounds.

After removing my pack and all equipment except for my cartridge belt, I turned and faced the water to find the boat I had landed from. Kneeling on one knee, it took a minute to decide where to start. The beaches at the water line on both sides of where I thought I'd landed were littered with wrecked landing craft and equipment. In many places there were wrecks two-and three-deep out from the waterline. I got ready to run towards the landing craft, looking in either direction as if getting ready to cross a busy street. I got to my feet and began to run but was knocked flat on my ass from the concussion of an exploding shell. Laying there in the sand and on my back, I thought I was already a casualty. After some quick checking I was convinced that none of the shrapnel had hit me. Up again and running I found the right landing craft where a corpsman was working on the kid who fell next to me coming off the boat. He seemed to still be alive.

Back in the landing craft I picked up two thirty-pound pouches of high explosives (Composition C) and took off up the beach again. Without my pack and without the suspenders holding up my cartridge belt, and with both hands full, my cartridge belt began to slip down over my hips. Before I could find a place to stop and hitch it up, the belt slipped down around my ankles and I tripped, falling face-first into the sand.

At the high water line I dumped the explosives, along with the offending cartridge belt, next to our packs. I took a deep breath, turned, and started back for another load. Halfway back down the beach I saw the landing craft disappear in a cloud of smoke and debris. It had taken a direct hit. When the smoke cleared, all that remained was the bottom of the hull floating in the surf while the landing ramp

held it to the beach. After the battle, the wounded kid the corpsman was working on in our landing craft told me that he was being loaded onto another landing craft down the beach when a Jap shell hit the landing craft we had been on, setting off the rest of the explosives still on board.

I returned empty-handed this time to the high water line. The seven of us engineers gathered on the beach near our packs, flat on our faces, yelling to one another, trying to decide where to find a place to start digging holes to crawl into. With my face buried in the sand I realized that it was not regular beach sand. It was a very dark gray, almost black, coarse, volcanic ash. Each grain of ash had been worn smooth and round so that there was not cohesiveness to it. It was like thousands of little ball bearings.

An officer slid down the steep sandbank ahead of us, said he was sure glad to see us, and then commandeered the first thirteen able-bodied Marines he could find — which included all seven of us. He told us to leave our gear and bring our rifles, cartridge belts, gas masks and any extra rifle ammo we could find. Each man was to carry two pouches of high explosives, or as many bandoliers as he could carry, and follow the man he pointed to. We were on our way to the front lines.

Our guide was a wounded and bandaged infantryman from the 28th Marines. He pointed up towards the sandbank in front of us and told us to climb to the top. Trying to climb the steep sand slopes was real work. You sank up to your knees in the black volcanic sand. For each step forward you seemed to slide two steps back. The weight and unwieldiness of the swinging packs of explosives hampered our movement, and trying to carry our rifles in a way that kept them out of the sand left us with no hands to assist during the steep climb.

We climbed as fast as we could in the loose sand. There were three or four twenty-foot-wide terraces, each about twenty feet above the previous one. Each terrace could only be reached by climbing steep slopes of black volcanic sand which were yet unmarred by a single footprint. This was virgin territory.

Even though we paused at each terrace to get our breath, the stops were not long enough and we were completely winded by the time we reached the uppermost terrace. From atop this terrace we looked back down on the landing beaches which looked like a garbage dump from 20 yards out into the water to the height of the high water mark. There was no more space along the beach to land boats. All kinds of wrecked jeeps, small trucks, Sherman tanks and amphibious tractors littered the beach. Dumped among them were piles of materials and hundreds of Marines trying to find places to hide, digging foxholes anywhere to get out of the shellfire.

As I faced the beach and to my right was Mount Suribachi, eight hundred yards away. It towered, impressive and forbidding from where we stood. The Jap artillery spotters up on the mountainside had a perfect view of every move the Marines made. Just off Suribachi were two U.S. Navy battleships. They had moved in, almost up to the beach of the 28th Marines' landing area at the foot of Suribachi, their starboard gun batteries exchanging shellfire with Jap gun emplacements on the mountainside. Whenever a Jap gun fired at the Marines, the battleships would fire at the muzzle flash of the Jap gun. Until the Japs fired their guns, they were mostly invisible to the naked eye.

About one-quarter of the way up Mount Suribachi were large artillery pieces protected by mammoth steel doors. We found out later that these guns were in concrete emplacements dug from tunnels inside the mountain. Each gun was mounted on tracks. After being loaded and aimed the gun moved forward, causing the steel doors to open long enough to let the gun fire before being withdrawn back into their caves with the doors automatically closing behind. The ships firing eight-and ten-inch shells were not able to damage these doors. Battleships with fourteen-and sixteen-inch shells fired salvos and were able to jam the doors with direct hits. This took a long time. Some of the doors were in places that naval gunfire could not reach and the Japanese guns inside continued attacking into the second day.

While resting on the top terrace, our guide told us we were going to the foot of Mount Suribachi. He told us that there wasn't as much artillery fire up there but that there was plenty of rifle and machine-gun fire from pillboxes protecting the base of the mountain, and to keep our eyes open because there were still lots of live Japs behind our lines that were sniping at any target that presented itself.

Starting our trek again, we moved out in a staggered single file. The ground was much flatter, but still all sand and slightly uphill. We were moving up a shallow draw that protected us from the shrapnel and rifle bullets that snapped and cracked as they passed over our heads. We were headed up and away from the beach towards the south end of the first airfield.

At the head of the draw were the remains of a well-concealed concrete pillbox. There were small shrubs and plants growing on the surrounding slopes and in the sand that covered the top of this concrete emplacement. The firing aperture was badly damaged and blackened by fire. The interior had been destroyed by high explosives and by flamethrowers. Around the back of the blown pillbox were six or eight Japs who had tried to escape out the back entrance, all dead. Their bodies were scattered behind the pillbox and along the trail we were on. One of the Jap bodies lay spread-eagle across the trail on his back. His body was almost completely naked except for split-toed shoes, his uniform being either blown off by the explosives or burned off from flamethrowers. His wide-eyed, grinning but visually undamaged dead body saluted each Marine that passed with an erection, swollen in death to several times its normal size.

After we passed this pillbox we turned left out of the little draw. We were now headed towards Mount Suribachi. The ground was much flatter but still all sand and slightly uphill. However, up here most of the sand was covered with low growth. It reminded me of what you would find on the sand dunes along our ocean beaches. Our line of travel was along the top of a slope, out on the flat part of the island where we were protected from the shrapnel coming up off the beach below. But we were not protected from stray rifle and machine-gun bullets snapping by from the front lines, which in the relative silence at the top of the slope was sobering. It was really eerie up there on that hike. Back on the beach there wasn't room for another person, but here, and other than the dead Japs at the pillbox, we had not seen a single living person or any sign of the Marines having been through.

The 28th Marines had landed on the left of the 27th Marines and were closest to Mount Suribachi. It was their job to take the mountain. Our guide told us that although there was a ring of Marines around its base, the 28th was stopped cold as they tried to climb the lower slopes which were protected by pillboxes and a myriad of spider holes. As we neared the foot of the mountain we angled further out into a flat area, putting us under direct enemy observation and within range of aimed rifle fire. The terrain was very uneven and covered with leafless scrub brush that had grown to about six feet in height above the ground cover. In clumps, this leafless scrub was almost impossible to penetrate.

Soon we were on a zig-zag road that a dozer had cut through the area. It was headed toward the base of the mountain in the center of the island. We were warned to keep well spread out. Following the example of our guide, we moved ahead in short dashes, crouching low as we zig-zagged forward. At the end of each dash forward we ducked down behind the scrub brush along the sides of the road.

In a staggered line around the base of the mountain were pillboxes looking down on us, each about two hundred feet apart. In some spots they were staggered in tiers three deep, the upper tiers covering the approaches to the lower pillboxes. The road ended right at the base of the mountain and here I did not see anyplace to hide. We were

waved into some shell holes where there was nothing to protect us from rifle fire from above. Every time I looked up at the nearest pillboxes, the muzzle flash of the machine guns firing from the apertures was clearly visible.

Dirty, and with their clothing ripped, line company engineers and infantrymen showed up almost immediately to take our pouches of high explosives. I recognized one engineer. He dropped in the hole with me for a minute to bum a cigarette. As we talked he told me how easy the landing had seemed in the beginning, but after half an hour or so the shelling, machine-gun and rifle fire, it had become something else. He told me that despite the shelling and bombings, the Japs hadn't been hurt at all. As soon as the Marines landed and the Navy shelling stopped, the Japs began to fire from almost completely destroyed pillboxes and blockhouses, and from behind tiny clusters of shrubs. The Japs would saturate an area with murderous fire, but as soon as Marine and naval artillery opened up to counter the fire, the Japs would disappear until the shelling ceased, then quickly emerge again to begin blasting away at the Marines. I asked him where Sgt. Wolover was. Wolover was a member of C Company of the engineer training school. The man nodded over to an adjacent shell hole where ten or more ponchos covered dead Marines.

On that sobering note we were told our job was complete and that we could return to our units on the beach. Back down on the beach we located our little pile of packs and the machine gun. Everything was covered with sand and a couple of packs were damaged by shelling.

We were then told to move whatever gear we could salvage from the beach and move it up the hill towards the 28th Marines. Back up the steep sand slopes we went, but more fatigued this time under the weight of our heavy packs and machine-gun parts. Once at our destination, near the line between Green Beach I and Red Beach I, we were directed to dig in where a steep slope broke over onto the flat top of the island. We were soon joined by several other H&S Co. engineers that were from another ship. They were as bewildered as we were as to why we were chosen to land early. There were now about twenty of us in all, but we had all the parts for three machine guns. We were told to dig in and get the guns set up to fire across the island this evening. From our new positions we had front-row seats to watch the havoc on the beach where officers frantically tried to get all able-bodied-men off so they would be able to fight tonight.

It was about 1600 hours when we began digging in and setting up the guns. Some of us from H&S Co. were sent back to the beachmaster of the 28th Marines. The beachmaster separated us into small groups and scattered us among nearby shell holes. Then, visiting each group, he told us that the wave we came in on over three hours ago was the last one able to land. The shelling was so accurate and heavy that it was impossible to land boats long enough to unload before they were hit, and that we were running out of supplies. He told us that a banzai charge was expected that night. Our job on the beach was to pick up all the weapons we could find so the Japs that might infiltrate that night couldn't use them against us. We were also told to salvage any rifle and machine-gun ammo, first aid gear and drinking water we could find. We were to remove these items from the tide-washed beach to higher ground.

In comparison with the beach and slopes, it was very quiet down along the waterline. Now that the tide was out there was quite a steep area of newly exposed sand beach. With the majority of the shelling up on the old beach one hundred feet from the present waterline, this was great. The wrecked landing craft and big equipment that we were going through along the beach protected us from spent shrapnel. In one of the wrecked landing craft I found myself a Thompson sub-machine gun. All of the people on the work detail rearmed themselves with the weapon of their choice. Some of the landing craft even had pump shotguns. We worked at this for about two hours until it was too dark to

be safely moving around. When we returned to our group we brought with us a couple of bundles of sacks for sandbags. There was no shortage of sand.

While we were gone, those who stayed behind had stripped the machine guns and gotten the sand out of the firing mechanisms, draping blankets over the guns to keep out the flying sand. After we made a little sandbag parapet in front of each gun to provide some protection to the gunners, we laid on our backs in our foxholes and field-stripped and cleaned our rifles. This would become an urgent necessity many times a day because of the sand and dust from the incessant shelling.

Finally we had a chance to rest and eat our evening meal; hard chocolate, but it sure tasted good! It had been a long and exhausting day. The old-timers told us that the way to make the nights easier was to divide it into shifts. So we divided the night up into two-hour watch shifts. We hoped that we could get some sleep but there was to be no rest for anyone.

We were shelled steadily all night long. The sky was continually filled with parachute flares and their greenish light lent an eerie look to an already chaotic landscape. There were times when the volume of small arms fire directed at the units ahead of us increased till it sounded as if the expected banzai charge had finally started. It had, but it never got back to where we were. The most nerve-racking part of this was that all night long, from dusk till dawn, we were subjected to traversing fire from a Jap 81mm mortar in a forty-nine shell pattern. Yes, forty-nine, I counted them all night long. After several hours of this you no longer had to count the shells dropping. You subconsciously knew when the next mortar shell would be the one to arrive within ten to fifteen feet of you.

Nobody was supposed to be moving at night and we were all supposed to be quiet — you stayed in your foxhole. Marines were told to shoot at noises and anything that moved. This assured us that those moving in the dark would be Japs coming to attack us. Yet it was necessary to keep those around you informed of what was going on in the area, so there was lots of talking between foxholes. Information passed up and down the line by word of mouth. We received many reports of probes and feelers of the line in front of us in Jap territory. From down along the beach we received word that Japs were swimming around and coming in through the wrecked equipment. Before long, the beach was alive with Jap snipers.

Looking back at the landing beaches behind us in the light of the flares, it seemed as if there were almost as many Marines up and moving about as if it was daytime. Pioneers[5] and some of the engineers were trying to get damaged equipment off the beach, ignoring the incoming shellfire and snipers. If the equipment wasn't serviceable then the dozers pushed it into big piles. Other men attached cables to wrecked landing craft so the dozers could pull them up on the beach, out of the way.

The Jap snipers were swimming out from Mount Suribachi, drifting into the beach and hiding in the piles of debris. Any time our armored dozers passed a pile of debris, they would doze the pile around a little to silence any snipers hiding inside.

Several times during the night, from out on the flat area ahead of us, word was passed back that the Japs were on their way. We fired our machine guns just over the heads of the line of infantry ahead of us. We were doing the firing so that the infantry to our front didn't have to fire and give away their positions from the muzzle flashes of their weapons. Until the Japs were within hand grenade distance of the Marine lines, their location was uncertain to the enemy. Once the Marine infantry in front of us started firing, we would stop firing. This way we wouldn't hit any of them if they had to leave their holes for any reason.

We were firing the machine gun so much that every so often we had to stop to give the barrel a chance to cool off. We'd then scoop up all the empty shell casings out of our foxhole to make

room to move around. Before morning we began to run out of belts of machine-gun ammo and so we opened salvaged rifle clips and put the cartridges into the empty canvas gun belts. This was almost impossible to do in the semi-darkness while trying to keep sand out of the belts during shell bursts. With every shell burst came a shower of sand, and the people behind us reloaded under ponchos to keep the falling sand out of the belts. The machine guns in our row fired all night long, but I never saw anything that looked like a Jap even though we were being hit by bullets every so often. Each hit was announced by a sharp crack and a peppering of sand that sprayed over us.

## D + 1

After the darkness of night it was wonderful to see the skies beginning to lighten. We were jubilant to have made it through the night, but the return of visibility brought back to life the Jap artillery spotters up on Suribachi. The intensity and accuracy of the shelling increased rapidly. Jap small arms and machine-gun fire intensified enough so that no one was fool enough to stand up. Our old friend dropping mortar shells now had all kinds of help.

Then we got a new twist. The enemy artillery was sending in two types of shells bursting 200 feet over our positions. The first type burst with a puff of dirty gray smoke, raining shrapnel down on the men below. The second type burst in the air with multi-legged white bursts, like those from exploding skyrockets during a Fourth of July fireworks display, but there was nothing pleasant about them. These were phosphorous shells and they were pure hell. The temperature of burning phosphorus is so high that it will burn through clothing, skin and bone. It cannot be extinguished with water and must be dug out with a knife or allowed to burn itself out. In a foxhole it is your job to use the point of your combat knife to dig out any pieces of phosphorus that falls onto your partner before it can burn too

---

5   A Pioneer Battalion was a specialized unit that conducted shore-party operations during the initial landing. Pioneers performed a variety of military engineering duties such as clearing minefields, demolitions, moving equipment and unloading supplies.

deeply into him. He does the same for you.

In the midst of this phosphorous shelling our friend finally dropped a mortar round into our foxhole. I was lying on my left side, right leg flexed, left leg almost straight, knife in hand and facing Kenny, who I shared a foxhole with. The round hit only inches away from the bottom of my left foot. The force of the explosion jammed my left knee up almost to my waist. The sound of the exploding mortar shell made my ears ring for quite a while. Luckily, by hitting in the sand, the cone of shrapnel went up and over us as we were hit by a wave of air, heat and flying sand from the concussion. In that instant I knew for sure that there was a God and that I had been saved for some reason. I knew instantly that I would get off that island alive. Later I wondered if Kenny felt the same thing. After the intensity of the shelling that morning I never again came close to being that terrified. Sure, I was scared a lot after that, but never again in the same way.

Later in the morning, at around 0800 hours, we were ordered to move the machine guns to new positions ahead and to the west of our previous position by about 500 yards. Our new position was in a relatively flat area near the edge of the 28th Marines, near the narrowest part of the island. The sandy slope where we had been during the night was now going to be used as a parking area for salvageable equipment.

Our new location was out on the flat part of the island. The only cover was some shrubs about eighteen inches to two feet tall among the sand hillocks, marred only by a few bomb craters and shell holes. When you stood up it looked to be less than 1,000 yards from the front lines of the 27th Marines to the north. They were partway up the south end of the first airfield. It was about 500 yards to the lines of the 28th Marines along the foot of Suribachi to the south of us. The west beach, which was mostly held by the Japs, was about 500 yards directly ahead.

Our new foxholes were in big shell holes plainly visible to the observers on Suribachi, but outside the limit for aimed small arms fire. However, there was still enough stray small arms fire coming from the front lines on either side of us to make you keep down when it was not absolutely necessary to be up and moving. While some of us were picking out fields of fire for the guns, others were making the numerous trips to move all our gear.

It was now overcast and quite cold. We weren't half dug-in when dozers started digging out gun pits right next to us for artillery pieces that were salvaged off the beaches. As soon as the dozers appeared with the 105mm howitzers in tow they began drawing enemy artillery fire. As more sleds of shells began arriving from the beach, the whole area came under the scrutiny of the Jap spotters up on Suribachi. Even though anything that moved was getting shelled, our people continued setting up the gun batteries. Soon they started counter-battery fire against the Jap artillery to the north of us.

We set up our machine guns to fire towards the west beach, which as I said still belonged mostly to the Japs. The machine guns were laid out with interlocking fields of fire. This meant that the area in front of our gun could be covered by guns on either side of us. If one of us were put out of commission, there would be no hole in the line. One of my side-limit markers was a dead Marine covered with a poncho. His helmet was on his rifle, stuck into the sand next to him. I was told that this dead Marine was Master Gunnery Sergeant John Basilone, a Congressional Medal of Honor winner on the island of Guadalcanal.[6]

Part of our job protecting the artillery batteries was conducting night patrols. As soon as it was dark, ten of us were sent out into the cold drizzle on night patrol. We slithered down the steep slopes onto the west beach. The patrol was to stop any Japs, particularly messengers moving between the north and south ends of the island. The west beach was nice and level and about thirty yards wide. We went back up the slope, found a good place and scooped out some shallow foxholes.

---

6   Basilone was also awarded the Navy Cross for his actions on Iwo Jima. He was killed near airfield #1 by Japanese mortar shrapnel.

With all the slipping and sliding I had managed to get the breach mechanism of my M-1 full of sand. I laid down on my back on the sandy slope of the beach and took my rifle apart, laying the parts on my chest, then wiping off each piece with my shirt tail and reassembling the rifle while working in pitch blackness. I had brought my M-1 because with it you could hit something farther away than fifty feet, which was the limit with the Thompson.

Once settled in our holes, several of us started sniping at the occasional passersby. These must have been stragglers. During the six hours we were on that cold and wet beach no one saw any large groups of Japs. Maybe they were smart enough to stay out of the rain.

We then returned to our machine-gun positions. There would be no peace between the continual Jap shelling looking for the location of our artillery. The word passed that we had Jap infiltrators in front of, behind, and amongst us and so another night passed without any sleep. During the night a light mist began to settle over us, turning to a drizzle that would not let up. It made the cold even colder.

## D + 2

With the exception of a few men left to guard our machine guns, those that didn't have to go back down to help on the landing beaches were sent on a short patrol towards the west beach. We were looking for stragglers, and did turn up several moving out ahead of us. I don't remember that we ever received any serious answering fire.

In mid-morning when we got back from this patrol we were told to move again. This was because artillery was rapidly expanding with pieces being successfully landed on the island. Our people continued setting up the new gun batteries even though they were constantly being shelled by Jap artillery batteries north of us. The only protection afforded them was that the whole area around the guns was clouded in smoke.

We moved again, closer to the west beaches, but at least it was farther from the artillery. This was the area that we had been patrolling in for the last two days. The infantry had been through this area on the first day during the mad dash to cut the island in half, although it truly wasn't cut in half yet. The area still contained snipers and stragglers. Some had played possum during the sweeps of the last two days.

Our machine guns were again positioned to protect the artillery from a Jap attack off the west beaches. During mid-afternoon the mist and drizzle that had been falling since last night turned into a light rain. Soon we were soaking wet. This was not the place to be wearing a poncho because it restricted your movement. If you were in a shell hole, maybe you could drape it over your shoulders until you had to move. Then somebody came up with the idea of using sticks to hold up the center of the poncho, like a tent, staking down the outer edges. These little shelters worked well for those of us in the rear areas. Here the danger of infiltrators and snipers was reduced by the large number of people moving around. Within a couple of days the whole south end of the island looked like a giant shantytown and people were flying small U.S. and Confederate flags from their tents.

We walked back down to the landing beaches to get supplies. Well, really, we were sent there. The beach was still being shelled, but not quite as bad as two days ago. There were several tank landing ships nosed in and moored to the beach with cables. Each ship had the bow doors open with its ramp extending out to the beach. A couple of the ships were filled with boxes of supplies being unloaded by labor gangs. Lines of men snaked out of each ship and down its ramp as Pioneers moved materiel to a series of storage dumps away from the beaches. There were maybe four lines of men snaking out of each ship, like tentacles of an octopus, with each man handing a box to the man to their right.

This chain of men hardly shied away when a shell exploded near them, ignoring all but the closest shell bursts, each man not wanting to be less of a Marine than the man next to him, and all scared shitless. I nonchalantly shouldered a case of supplies and walked casually back up to our area. I was bound and determined that it would not be me that broke and ran from the incoming shells at the beach. We carried back cases of K-rations, .30-cal rifle ammo and five-gallon jeep cans of water.

Just before dusk, all our help returned from the beach, bringing some more engineers that they had found during the day. We now had almost thirty-eight engineers in our little group, and a total of four light machine guns.

Early that evening, even though I protested that I didn't feel well, I was one of the lucky ones that got to go back down on the west beach again. Some of the people found some shadows to shoot at but again I didn't see anything. Due to lack of activity we returned to our foxholes at about one-thirty. Now I was really miserable with a high temperature, headache and all my joints aching. Although my clothes were cold and wet I was burning up with fever. I pulled my poncho over myself and laid down in the wet sand. That's all I remember till I woke up the next morning.

### D + 3

We moved again mid-morning. This time up to the southwest end of the first airfield. Now we were back in the center of the island. The airfield was built on the extension of a shallow plateau. The runway at the portion of the airstrip where we were was built up about twenty-five feet above the surrounding plateau. We were about two thousand yards from the foot of Mount Suribachi. The front lines of the 27th Marines were a thousand yards ahead to the north. The 4th Marine Division was on the other side of the runway at this point.

It was still drizzling in the morning and shellfire seemed to be lessening. However, the shelling did not stop — there were just lulls when somebody else was getting yours.

We still didn't have any officers from H&S Co. on the island and so we were under control of Division Headquarters. While we waited for our officers to arrive they found make-work for us. Four of us mechanics were sent out to the equipment park and told to look over the damaged equipment and repair something — anything. But we didn't have our tools or equipment to make repairs with, yet. So we spent most of the day working down in the Engineering Battalion salvaged equipment area, not really repairing anything, just tagging things we thought were salvageable and repairable. It drizzled on and off all day. There were no night patrols. This was the first night the Japs fired their rockets at us — the "Orange Blossom Specials."

### D + 4

It was still drizzling in the morning when we were told to stand fast until the rest of H&S Co. arrived later that morning. Now that many of the Japanese batteries had been destroyed, their accuracy of their shelling seemed to be getting poorer. However, the random shelling did not cease; there just were longer lulls in between the shells in your sector. These lulls were dangerous because they gave you a false sense of security, catching you out in the open when the next shell arrived.

In mid-morning, word was passed that there were Marines up on the sides of Mount Suribachi. They were plainly visible to us from where we were. Everybody was passing field glasses back and forth, watching as the patrol neared the top of the mountain. We lost sight of some of them for a few minutes. Then, with a yell heard all over the island, the patrol was seen putting up an American flag. It was small, but it was visible to everybody around us, even without field glasses. We reasoned that if we had people up on the heights, this would explain why the accuracy of the Jap shelling seemed to be so much poorer. The showing of the flag was

met with increased shelling where we were. The Japs were letting us know that they were still on the island and could still put up a good fight.

Early in the afternoon the rest of H&S Co. started arriving on the island. We were told to move again, back to the west beach. It was our responsibility to protect the left flank of the 27th Marines from possible enemy landings on the west beaches. With the arrival of the main part of the company, we now had a couple of 6 x 6 trucks to help with the move. The only trouble being that the trucks drew artillery and mortar fire any time the Japs could see them. I rode on the right running board as one of the

trucks moved our gear over to the west beach. Out on the running board I could exit fast if need be. The driver drove with his door open, one foot on the accelerator and the other out on the running board in case he had to jump. True enough, that piece of moving equipment drew incoming fire. I jumped off while the truck was still moving, landing on my feet in the sand as my left ankle turned under me.

After a few rounds, the shelling moved on. The

Above: The camouflaged Japanese helmet captured by McLaughlin: "The helmet came from a pillbox down in the southeast corner of the Island from one of the outer rings of the defense of Mt. Suribachi . . . and was picked up on the afternoon of February 23rd." From a 2007 email retrieved from Howard McLaughlin's computer on 8 August 2014. Courtesy Doug McLaughlin. *Author's collection.*

truck must have rolled to a stop in a place that was out of the Japs' vision. My ankle hurt real bad. I couldn't walk on it and it quickly started swelling. A corpsman looked at my ankle and assured me that it was only twisted.

Two of the guys helped me limp over to where we were setting up the machine gun. I started digging a foxhole while Kenny carried over the rest of our gear. This time we dug our line of machine guns in along the top edge of a bluff. Our field of fire was down and across the wide beach below. Now, however, there were ten amphibious armored tanks on the beach. We were their only protection and we were to shoot anyone that approached the tanks. The Japs usually tried to disable the tanks by blowing a track off with an explosive charge carried by a suicide runner who would dash out towards the tank, activate the delay fuse on the satchel, and throw it under or into the caterpillar type tank tread.[7]

Kenny and I dug our hole at the break in the slope. Several rows of riflemen dug in behind us to protect our backs. H&S Co. now had a total of ten .30-cal. machine guns set up along the edge of the terrace. The guns were set about twenty-five feet apart. The row of ten .50-cal. H&S Co. machine guns were set up back about a hundred feet behind us. In between these rows of machine guns were several rows of infantry.

The riflemen behind us were all new to the island as of that afternoon. Tonight would be their first night in combat. We had dug in during daylight and they were supposed to memorize our locations so they wouldn't fire at us by mistake. These riflemen were specifically instructed not to fire until they were sure that the Japs had gotten around or through the machine guns in front of them. The riflemen could not see down the slopes behind us or any of the beach from their positions. Only the

people manning the machine guns could see the amtanks below and might fire to protect them.

Just after dark there was an air-raid alert for six twin-engine Bettys. The ships all around the island fired at these possible Kamikaze planes. During the raid one of the planes flew down the beach right in front of us. He was almost at the same height as we were and was traveling from north to south. Our machine guns fired as he went by and the Betty crashed on the beach near Mount Suribachi. The whole raid was over in just a few minutes. It was time to settle in.

Kenny had the first watch. He was crouched at the front of the foxhole, keeping an eye on the beach. I was leaning against the back of the foxhole, sort of dozing. Kenny poked me, whispering, "The shit is about to hit the fan. There is someone coming up the slope." Kenny raised up a little to look down the slope, there was a shot, and Kenny fell back on top of me. I yelled to the hole on our left, "Kenny is hit!" just as another shot was fired. I knew Kenny was hit because I could feel the slimy wetness (blood) all over me. But in the darkness I was unable to find where the wound was, and I couldn't expect any help from a corpsman at night.

Kenny was unconscious and sprawled on top of me. There wasn't any way to get out from under him without standing up. In the darkness I followed the trail of wetness to its source: a wound with a small piece of bone protruding from Kenny's forehead. The wound was about two inches long and was where the headband of his helmet would sit. Now that I had the site of the wound I started to put a field dressing on it. As I wrapped the tails of the dressing around Kenny's head, I slipped my hand under the back of his head to raise it up. The little wet hole my finger slipped into told me not to bother — Kenny was dead.

I assumed from all the yelling going on behind me that there were more infiltrators so I didn't dare call to anyone anymore. I didn't want to give away the fact that Kenny was dead and that I was alone. I reached for one of my grenades and pulled the

7  Called "Satchel Charlie" by the Marines, the *Nikuhaku Kogeki* ("human bullet assault") troops were assigned to attack tanks with explosive satchels. A soldier would attempt to place his explosives on the tank's tracks to disable it — sometimes by hiding in a prepared underground pit (a *tako-tubo*, or "octopus pot"), and other times running directly at his target. The suicide version of this tactic was known as *tokkou* ("suicide bomb attack").

arming pin. I was poised to throw the grenade at any outside sound before some Jap could jump me. Working with one hand while holding the grenade's safety lever in place with the other, I extracted myself from under Kenny's body. I got out a pistol, crouched in one corner of the foxhole and waited under the faint light of the sky, watching around the rim of the hole for any sign of movement, ready to shoot.

In the morning, as soon as there was enough light to move about, Frank from the machine-gun hole to my left came over to see what had happened. The first thing he tried to do was get the live grenade out of my hand. He had a hell of a time doing so because my hand muscles bound up like a claw from holding the safety spoon in place all night.

We found out that a new man in the hole right behind me had also been shot. The realization that he was wounded caused him to panic and seek help. Disobeying orders, he left his foxhole and somehow managed to run and crawl back through our company lines without getting shot again. He was helped out of the night lines when it was discovered that he had a head wound.

A few hours later we learned that the wounded Marine was back at the engineer command post. This command post was at the very back of our unit. On his head was a bloody bandage indicating a serious wound. He told the people at the command post he was supposed to be evacuated to a hospital ship but had refused to go. He also said that he had shot a Jap inside our perimeter just before he himself was shot and wounded in the head.

These people he was talking to in the command post were also new to the island yesterday, so to them he was a real hero. So some clown officer immediately wrote him up for a Silver Star, and another countersigned it. The colonel sent the recommendation up to division within the hour, never bothering to check out his story. They never asked any of us what really happened.

Meanwhile, back at the beach line, in talking it over amongst the old-timers on the island, the whole shooting incident didn't seem right. Kenny's body had been removed from the foxhole, put on a nearby stretcher and covered with his poncho. Finally, to settle the argument, one of the men went over to look at Kenny's wound in daylight. He removed the field dressing and saw that the wound went from the back to the front of his head. There had been only two shots fired. Frank fired the second shot at the muzzle flash of the first shot.

The new hero arrived back amongst us, eager to see the Jap he had shot. When we ignored him and all his boasting he became infuriated. He truly believed that we were trying to deny him his glory because we were so jealous. When queried by the old-timers as to where he shot the Jap, he assured us that he had seen him right there in front of his hole. He had looked up and saw this head silhouetted in the light ahead of him. He knew that the head he saw had to be a Jap infiltrating our lines. He took good aim and shot the dirty Jap, and almost as soon as he fired, another dirty Jap fired at him, and now he wanted us to hand over the sword that the Jap undoubtedly must have been carrying. When someone tried to explain what had happened, he wouldn't believe him — this man would never admit that he might have erred and shot Kenny by mistake.

The doctor of our unit came by later to see how the rest of us were taking Kenny's death. When we told him what had really happened he was flabbergasted. He told us that when our hero was brought in last night, he was scared shitless and pleaded with the doctors at the aid station to send him out to the hospital ship. The aid station doctor had sent him back here; his wound was only skin deep.

Yet as much as the old-timers protested, those stupid officers in the engineer command post never asked division to cancel the Silver Star to the hero for his bravery. I guess that would be losing face to admit that they were wrong — even this once.

*Repair Section D+6*

## The Next Few Days

I vaguely remember that for a couple of days after Kenny was killed I spent my days helping move H&S Co. engineer equipment. We were moving equipment up from the east beaches to our designated area on the west part of the island. Revetments were dug in the sand with dozers for our machine shop trailers and places to park trucks and jeeps. Once the big trailers were in place, camouflage nets were slung over the tops, to hide as much as possible from the expected aerial attacks.

By the seventh day I was sent up on the big landing beaches on the west side of the island. These were called Orange and White beaches. The plan was to try to open this beach area for easier supply of the 26th and 27th Marines, and quicker removal of their wounded. On these beaches was where the Japs thought we would make our original assault landing. So the area was very heavily mined.

Above: "The sandbagged foxholes in the foreground are part of H&S Company." — Howard McLaughlin.
One of the engineers in McLaughlin's demolition squad carried a camera to document their combat operations on Iwo Jima. This and all subsequent photographs are reproduced with permission from Howard McLaughlin's son, Doug McLaughlin. Each photograph was provided with a caption line that was written by Howard McLaughlin.

There were forty-eight of us being sent to clear these beaches. We were six newly-formed eight-man teams, of H&S Co. engineers. There were three teams of demolition men and three mine disposal teams. I was the assistant squad leader of the 1st Demolitions Squad, known by our code name "Nutcracker 1." Both Frank, the squad leader, and I were PFCs; everybody in the squad outranked us. There were at least two sergeants and one master technical sergeant. They were to be riflemen, not having any demolition experience. We were the "experts."

This big, relatively flat beach we went to covered about fifteen to twenty acres. It was still under sniper fire from pillboxes all along the north and east face of the slopes surrounding the beach. What hindered our work was that to protect this big flat beach from erosion by the wind, the Japs had planted grass. This grass grew in clumps about six inches in diameter, that were now about eight to ten inches tall. These clumps of grass were about eighteen inches apart, in rows about eighteen inches apart.

Because of the continual sniping, in trying to find and remove these mines that were hidden in the sand, you had to crawl along the rows on your belly. Checking the clumps of grass on each side of you with your bayonet as you crawled forward. You stuck the bayonet in under each clump of grass at about a forty-five degree angle. You probed very carefully. If the point of the bayonet was stopped in any way, you stopped pushing it in immediately. It only took five to ten pounds of pressure to set one of these mines off. You carried two colors of little flags. White meant you had cleared a row to the point of the farthest little flag. A red flag meant that there was a land mine there or at least something suspicious was in that location. The types of mines varied, but there were plenty of them. They were usually hidden in the clumps of grass. But if you believed this was the only place they were, they would never be able to find enough of you to bury.

As far as a man was concerned, the small

*N & S Area D + 7*

anti-personnel mines were the worst. There were at least two varieties. One was about fourteen inches in diameter and six inches thick. From the top there were three piano wires about eight inches long sticking out, which when moved only a short distance in any direction would electrically short out the mine and set it off. So it was necessary to look carefully at each clump of grass, as that was a favorite spot to put them.

The other common mine was a pressure mine. It was about eight to ten inches in diameter and two inches thick. It had a little knob on the top that took about ten pounds of pressure to set off. There were non-magnetic versions of both of these mines, so the use of a mine detector wasn't feasible.

When it was time to remove these mines after they were found, you had to be very careful. Some of these mines had another booby trap mine under the top one, and in removing the top one you set the bottom one off.

There were also 250 lb. and 500 lb. aerial bomb

Above: H & S Co on the west beach, D + 7. "The repair section is now pretty well dug in." — Howard McLaughlin.

mines. These were stood on end and had a yardstick mine on the top of them that was three feet long, about two inches in diameter, and had three separate sets of feelers on the top.

Before long, because of the large number of mines, when we had some mines to remove, instead of digging them out, we detonated them in groups. We wired a line of small charges together, with Primacord, placing a charge on top of each mine to be removed. Then from a safe distance the whole string was destroyed at one time.

After the six squads of H&S Co. engineers were sent up to remove mines, we were never returned to the H&S Company area. We were no longer under the control of our battalion, belonging to division, for assignment to whatever unit was in the most need of engineers on that day. The H&S Co. area for us became a true rear area. These rear echelon people became strangers to us. Never again were these people whom we had known for almost a year ever again the close friends we left out on the ships. There was no longer a common bond. Later, back together in Hawaii we hardly knew each other anymore. In our conversations it seemed like we were not even talking about the same things.[8] Our outlooks and understanding of life was no longer the same. Their conversation and interests seemed mundane, even juvenile. Conversely, we were not able to articulate to them what we had witnessed because of the horrors they recalled for us. Their nightly bull sessions, celebrating the glories of heroes, were unnerving to us in their innocence. Back in Hawaii, because these scenes were still so vivid yet, we had become quiet, we had pulled into our protective shells. Because of that, we were more and more excluded from their gatherings. They wanted John Wayne-movie-type stories, with lots of heroics to tantalize and whet the mind. These Hollywood-type stories, we knew, were not the way combat was. When these entertaining stories were

not forthcoming from us, they felt we were aloof and uncaring in our attitude towards them. They reciprocated by shunning us like we had the plague. We were no longer asked to drink or play cards with them.

These stories they wanted to hear, I understand now, were the only tie they had with the war. Having been two or three miles behind the lines was almost like they were still back in Hawaii. They wanted to hear dazzling stories of heroics and people that were winning medals. Now I can see that they needed these stories to bring home, to tell their folks and in later years to tell their children what they did in the war. They had lived [on Iwo Jima] in a relatively safe area with very few inconveniences. They worked regular hours every day, had clean clothes, hot meals, showers, and were able to get regular sleep. It was almost a lark for them. They would be heroes at home, so they needed first-hand war stories to pass on as they drank beers and told sea stories at the VFW meetings. They wanted us to entertain them with exciting tales of life on the lines. We wanted a chance to forget war and think of pleasant things, like home and girls. But even if you did try to explain to them about one of our own engineers doing something out of the ordinary, they had no gauge or guide to apply to it. Without knowing how impossible it was to even move at the front, it was impossible to impress upon them what actual feats some of these stories actually were. They had no understanding of the fact that in combat doing ordinary or normal things was in itself heroic.

For them, medals are the only criteria as to who the real men are. Yet, to the man on the line who received this medal for this thing now called a heroic act, he is bewildered. Chances are that this act of heroism was a common occurrence. He doesn't feel he did anything that any other man hadn't done a hundred times. Up on the line, life and dignity survive because of caring. The best analogy I can think of is the Golden Rule; do unto others . . . you have to help each other if anyone is to survive. It's

---

8    On 27 March, the 5th Marine Division was sent to Camp Tarawa, Hawaii for an extensive liberty program. Once new equipment and replacements arrived, training for the invasion of the Japanese mainland began.

as simple as that. No one took blind chances. Everything that was done was a calculated risk. Sometimes the cards didn't turn up right, and you paid with your life, but you always tried. A man pinned down or in trouble could always count on help. A wounded man knew that he would be gotten back to medical aid by somebody, as quickly as possible . . . and the Marines never left their dead.

## *Life on the Lines*

In a way it seems hard to believe that for the first twenty days I never saw more than a fleeting glimpse of a live Jap. So much of the time when you tried to move forward, it was through a hail of mortar and artillery shells. True, we were fired at, and we shot back, but we were only shooting at muzzle flashes. It was always an unseen enemy that we fought. You could never really see anybody behind the muzzle flashes in the darkness of the pillboxes and caves.

Later it wasn't much better, but on occasions I did see running Japs. They were generally flushed out of pillboxes and bunkers by high explosives. With the appearance of a live Jap, the frustration of the people on the lines would boil over. People would stand up, holler and shout like kids at a football game . . . everybody firing at the running Jap. For an instant, he was merely a duck in the shooting gallery at the county fair. The hollering and cheering as he was hit and went down made the whole episode an exhilarating relief from the otherwise seriousness of our existence . . . a chance to pay the Japs back in some small way for our misery and the death of our friends. But mostly the whole time we fought against an unseen enemy. You knew he was there, because somebody was shooting at you. It was just that you couldn't see them back in the darkness of the caves or through the small slits of the pillboxes or bunkers.

Probably the most disheartening sight to us during all the time that we were on the island was

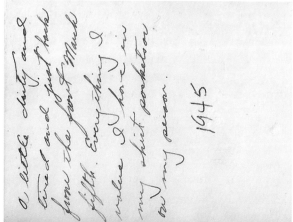

"A little dirty and tired and just back from the front March 5th. Everything I value I have in my shirt pockets or on my person. 1945."

the visible number of dead Marines and the absence of any dead Japs. After I saw those six dead Japs by the pillbox on the first afternoon, I would say that, if you were lucky, you might see one or two dead Japs on most days till much later in the fighting. If and when they were killed, they were inside of caves, pillboxes, spider holes, etc. You fired at muzzle flashes, but you very seldom saw a dead Jap.

As you will be able to tell from now on, there are many things that I still vividly remember. Some of these scenes are burned so vividly into my mind, that I still see every graphic detail . . . whether I want to remember them or not. So now I'll enter a period of time in which a structured account of events is impossible; all continuity disappears . . . .

In the beginning our work consisted mainly of sealing off the mouths of all types of caves. This we did by using explosive charges to cause the roofs to cave in, thereby hopefully sealing the ingress and egress from these caves. This denied their use as places for snipers and machine guns to set up and harass the backs of the advancing Marines. This also included following the heels of the infantry, closing and sealing off those caves, and destroying those bunkers that had been purposely bypassed in the mad rush forward. These caves still had Jap defenders in them to contend with . . . and nobody wants to be buried alive, so there were lots of arguments. Arguments from the occupants over our right to seal them up in their cave.

The caves, once they were found, were fairly easy to seal. Usually the caves were scattered, being limited to areas with ridges or gullies. In the center of the island most of the caves we tackled were no longer covered by supporting fire from other caves or machine-gun emplacements. The infantry had taken care of that for us. However, some were still protected by snipers, hidden in well-concealed spider holes.

As the attrition rate among line company engineers trained in demolitions stripped some rifle companies of their ability to advance when faced with these Japs dug in hardened positions, we began to get more requests for help. Thank goodness we had a chance to practice for a few days before the requests got us up with the riflemen.

The farther north we got on the island, the more elaborate the protection was for the caves and the occasional pillboxes we encountered. Up here, every cave and pillbox was covered by fire from two or three adjacent positions or machine-gun emplacements. These caves and bunkers that were covered by supporting fire from other positions required help from the infantry. The infantry provided supporting fire for us. They fired into the mouths of the caves or the firing aperture of the pillboxes as we worked our way up to eliminate them on by one.

Caves were destroyed one at a time. Once a cave was found, and it was targeted for destruction, a blueprint was followed. The extra riflemen in our squad, along with borrowed BAR[9] men from the infantry, would fire into the mouth of the cave. This kept any people inside from firing out of the cave. With them pinned down inside the cave, two of us could work up towards the cave. One of us working towards the mouth on each side of the entrance.

When we were in place, the two of us, one on each side, would each sling one of those thirty-pound packs of explosives in to the mouth of the cave the first chance we got. The two almost simultaneous explosions usually caused the collapse of the roof in on those inside.

These charges had thirty-second delay fuses on them, so we had to ignite the fuse and count a while before we threw them, so that there was not enough time for anybody in the cave to throw the charge back out before it went off. It is easy for the recipients to throw back one charge, but two charges thrown almost simultaneously caused enough confusion that both never got thrown back at us.

Before long we had graduated to destroying the reinforced pillboxes or bunkers that were a permanent part of the Jap defenses. These naturally were harder to eliminate. They were usually just recently surrounded by the infantry and still had snipers or other light guns covering them. The rest of the squad was then placed in front of the pillbox and they were to fire into the firing aperture. Hopefully keeping any live Japs inside from shooting at Frank or I as we crawled forward on each side in a pincer action. The infantry, and sometimes tanks, fired at any other sources of Jap fire that might cover the pillbox.

For pillboxes, the two of us crawled forward, one on each side, dragging the special "shaped

9   Browning Automatic Rifle; a portable, light machine gun (machine rifle) with a 20-round magazine.

"1st and 2nd Demo squads moving out first thing in the morning. As a rule, we accompanied tanks. This must have been pretty well back for us to be bunched up like this." — Howard McLaughlin.

charges." We generally started wide and then worked in from the sides or back. Once you were up to the back of the pillbox, you placed the "shaped charge" on the top, pulled the igniter strip, and ducked down beside the back wall and waited. It takes thirty seconds before the charge goes off. You must stay down behind the back of the pillbox as the people out in front are firing into the aperture at the front of it. Sometimes they only stopped firing long enough for you to make the last sprint to the back of the pillbox.

The "shaped charges" were a conical-shaped hollow charge encased in a steel shell. They weighed about thirty pounds, were shaped to a cone-like point at the top, about twelve inches in diameter, eighteen inches long, and had two handles — one on either side to carry them with. If you looked at the underside of the charge it was a hollow cone. Once the charge was set in place and the igniter was pulled, my work was done. When the charge goes off it will cut a hole in the top of a reinforced concrete pillbox, just the same size as the charge. There is no danger to me although I may be only ten feet away. In fact, it was not unusual

"This is our first Jap car. We took this back to Hawaii with us . . . fixed it up and ran it around the island until we left [to occupy] Japan." — Howard McLaughlin.

that the explosive charge only stunned any Japs still alive inside. So that as soon as the charge goes off, the people in the front must run up and kill any Japs still alive inside. This was done by sticking the nozzle of the flamethrower in or tossing hand grenades in the firing aperture. Usually, as soon as one charge went off, the second charge would be set on top of the pillbox and exploded. This was done to keep the people inside stunned long enough for the infantry to get up to the firing aperture.

The farther north we went, the fewer reinforced concrete pillboxes and bunkers we ran into. But there were many more caves and machine-gun emplacements cut into the steep sides of every canyon and gully that we entered.

The demolition squads did not have to stay on the front lines at night. Although we never returned to the safety of the H&S Co. area, we were allowed to drop back from the front lines in the evening and form a part of the secondary line. This allowed us to escape some of the infiltrators that seemed to continually harass the front lines. But the snipers and the mortar-shelling were almost as bad — if not worse — back where we were. It may sound

"This would be about a third of the way through the fighting and there appears to be active snipers about." — Howard McLaughlin.

as if the secondary lines were way back. To us it was a long way, sometimes being almost a hundred yards back. Being "back" we were sometimes able to sleep in shifts, to be "fresh" for the next day's work. The only trouble with this was . . . you had to steel yourself every morning to get up and advance up to where the lines were mentally.

As I sit here decades later writing some of these things down, one thing makes me think of another and it goes on from there. I can't tell the whole story — many things I experienced were too terrible to put into words. I have no way of even

beginning to convey what you feel as you see another human being torn apart, mangled, or maimed; no way to put down on paper what uncontrollable fear feels like, the screaming terror that lasts till you can't scream any more. That kind of terror numbs the conscious part of your brain and makes you just a living body . . . responding to events in ways you were conditioned to by your training.

After all of these years I have not found what type of trigger causes these scenes to surface in my mind. When I first came home, it was especially bad on Helen when we were first married. She would be the innocent victim of my nightmares. In these to me very real happenings, my actions were brought on by a learned reflex. In real time if you were laying down, it was always sort of a crouch. You always keep one foot pulled up for leverage. Then when the emergency arose you were able to instantly jump or throw yourself up and over into another nearby hole for cover. Now, in the middle of the night, I would react to this dreamed threat in the same manner. If Helen was lucky, I went out of bed on my side, onto the floor. But sometimes I tried to jump towards her side of the bed. When this happened, I usually became entangled in the covers and fell on her. Sometimes Helen was hit in the face or chest as I wildly threw an arm back as I tried to move. After all of these years sometimes I still have these nightmares. To me, they are just as vivid as ever, but in some ways these present dreams are worse. Now they seem to run in a pattern of inability to do something to either help someone, or to do something to save myself from some impending catastrophe. There is still terror in these dreams, but now much frustration also.

Which now brings up the subject of the time that I was most seriously hurt: the day the island was declared officially secured. At the front there would be eleven more days of deadly fighting to get to the north beaches, but because of the public outcry over the high number of casualties on Iwo, for public consumption back home the island had been declared secured. The area I was in this day was on a flat area facing a long low ridge, honeycombed with caves.[10] It was the entrance to "The Gorge."

The caves and spider holes supporting them had this infantry unit stopped. Two infantrymen and myself were standing at the rear corner of a tank. I was talking to the tank crew on their extension phone, on the outside right back corner of the tank. We were discussing what we were going to do, how and when, so they would tell the other three tanks by radio not to shoot at us. By this time there was no Jap artillery fire, and very little of the heavy mortar fire, especially when Marines were in the area to spot any firing and call in our own shelling on them. Anyway, we were standing at the back corner of the tank, I was in the back and the others were on the side. That is all I remember.

When I came to, I was on my back, tightly bound to a stretcher, and was unable to move. My eyes were completely bandaged. From the hissing sounds just before the explosions around me I knew that we were being shelled by Jap knee mortars.[11] I couldn't dodge the bursts, and worst of all, I couldn't see the falling mortar shells to get out of the way. My only contact with the world was a radioman in the next shell hole over trying to get help: "BAS,[12] this is Blue Cannon George . . . ." He was calling frantically for help, and was not being received by anyone. It seemed like hours that he was calling and never got an answer.

Finally, a corpsman came back and, in answer to my questioning, he told me I was strapped down so I could be moved. Under further questioning, he finally told me that the other two men who had been with me were dead. The firefight had heated up and there were now two of us wounded that had to be moved back to the battalion aid station. I was at a collecting point, back several hundred yards

10   McLaughlin had entered the *fukkaku jinchi* at the north end of the island (see map on page 203). On Iwo Jima a new policy of "endurance engagements" had replaced the old policy of "decisive engagements" which was based upon the belief that the Japanese fighting spirit (including banzai charges) would overcome the American reliance on technology for victory. By 1944, however, many Japanese commanders believed that defeat was inevitable. A change in strategy to endurance engagements would buy time and make American victories so costly that Japan might be offered better negotiating terms. The phrase "fukkaku jinchi" was integrated into the terminology of the Imperial General Headquarters around mid-1944. While the origin of this phrase is unclear, it means the "utilization of underground honeycombed defensive positions." The large fukkaku jinchi at the north end of the island protected Lieutenant General Kuribayashi's underground command center, the communications cave, Rear Admiral Ichimaru's Naval Headquarters cave, and the surrounding area. *Fukkaku* literally means "castle on the plains" or "the multiplex of castle walls." The

word *jinchi* means "defensive position" or "encampment." A typical jinchi on Iwo Jima had underground shelters, pill boxes, machine-gun pits, firing trenches and bunkers with interconnecting tunnels.
11   The Type 89 Grenade Discharger *(hachikyu-shikiju-tekidanto)* was a portable, short-ranged mortar. It was operated by one soldier or a crew of three to increase the rate of fire. It fired a variety of small explosive projectiles fitted with a propellant base. The tube assembly had a curved support plate that was placed on the ground or against a fixed object for support. The term "knee mortar" is a misnomer. Allied troops mistakenly believed that the curved support plate was positioned on the thigh, just above the knee when kneeling, before firing.
12   Battalion Aid Station.

from the fighting now. When questioned further, he told me that it appeared that I might have a head wound, as I had been unconscious for some time. He didn't know about my eyes, he had not put the bandages on. There were mortars falling and a call for a corpsman, so he left me.

Laying there thinking about being blind for the rest of my life, I felt sorry enough for myself that I started to cry. I must have cried a lot as the tears diluted the blood sealing my eyes shut and allowed light in under the bandages. When the corpsman came back I told him I could see light, so he agreed to at least change the eye bandage. When it was removed, I could see. I had been unconscious and my face, I later found out, was covered with blood from the other two men, so as a precaution my eyes had been bandaged. I was unstrapped and checked over. Other than a bad headache, ringing in my ears, and being covered with the remains of the other two men I was OK and could return to my unit.

Upon returning to the line and finding my squad of engineers, as I was the assistant squad leader, Frank told me that the Navy had sent their apologies for the short round. The other two men that I was talking to were killed instantly, the explosion being almost on top of them. The corner of the tank had saved me from the shrapnel.

Once the island was declared secured on the 15th of March, all of the fighting was concentrated in trying to enter and take the last pocket of resistance. This area was called "The Gorge" and fighting went on there until the end, which for us was on the 25th of March.

The Gorge was saved on purpose until after the island was "secured." Although trying to take it from the Japs was going to be deadly, it was saved until after the island was secured because of the hue and cry from home about the high number of Marines that had been killed and wounded on Iwo. This way all of the killed and wounded fighting here could be conveniently added to the total at some later date and most people wouldn't realize it. The Gorge was saved until the end because of our intelligence from

the captured laborers and discovered documents. By all indications this area contained the Japs' island command post and the hospital. Most of the Imperial Marines that had been brought to the island were believed to be guarding the command post. The presence of the command post, and the Jap Marines guarding it, assured us that we were down to fighting real diehards.

In anticipation of the savageness of the impending fight, it was decided to mass all the American troops possible for the final push. So the front lines moved up to the edge of The Gorge and stopped until everybody else caught up and closed in around the edges. But they didn't bring in any fresh troops, they just massed the tired, worn-out people to make the final push.

I don't know where to begin in a description of The Gorge. The Gorge was less than one mile square. This area was long, wide, and fairly deep at the sea end [of the] ravine. It was approximately 700 yards long and was about 500 yards wide at the entrance, narrowing down to less than 200 yards at the sea, and the sides were cut with smaller lateral canyons — and the entire length was jumbled with rock and lined with machine-gun and rifle positions. I guess the only good thing was that up here . . . there were fewer reinforced concrete pillboxes and bunkers. There were probably more caves in The Gorge area, per given area, than anywhere else on the island. It appeared, although by this time there was no one left that was adventurous enough to enter these cave openings to find out for sure, that most of them were connected in groups by connecting tunnels.

The Gorge was deceptive to the superficial observer. It was entirely possible to stand at the edge of the mouth of The Gorge and study at leisure the steep slopes and cliffs. There was no sign of the Japs, no movement, and lots of times no shots — generally, only silence. It was even possible for small patrols to move around on parts of the gully floor, yet anytime they approached too close to a cave, or the Japs decided that they were a profitable target, then there would be a flurry of small arms fire from several well-hidden locations.

The Gorge itself was heavily fortified with a few pillboxes, lots of caves, machine-gun emplacements, spider holes, trenches, and lots of boulders and big rocks. The backs of the pillboxes and machine-gun emplacements were dug into the sides of the walls of the ravine. This way the opposing sides of The Gorge covered the fronts of caves and pillboxes facing them, and there was no way back to defend. When we did find reinforced concrete pillboxes, there was always an elaborate defense system dug in around them to protect them from attack.

There was really only one way into the area, and armored dozers struggled in the hard rock to cut a road down the middle of the floor of The Gorge. Every so often they would back out and the tanks would enter to neutralize the caves in as far as they could reach. Then the tanks would back out and the dozer would return to work on another fifty feet of road. We started at the wide end and worked our way towards the narrow sea end. Someplace in this area the Jap Admiral[13] and most of his staff were

holed up in some of these caves. And the Jap troops protecting this command were sure acting like true Imperial Marines.

It was possible sometimes for troops standing on the rim of The Gorge to fire anti-tank rockets at cave openings once they were discovered. But the camouflage was so good on these openings that they were never discovered until they opened fire on a patrol or group. Most of the machine-gun emplacements had very narrow fields of fire, but all

---

13    McLaughlin is referring to Rear Admiral Rinosuke Ichimaru, commander of 27 Air Flotilla at Iwo Jima. With all his aircraft destroyed by American carrier raids, he put his 2300 men under the command of the army commander Kuribayashi. Ichimaru disagreed with Kuribayashi's strategy of moving the Japanese defense underground, feeling his troops should either defend the beaches or concentrate around the central airfield complex. He led a final attack of 60 men on 18 March 1945, but survived, and was later killed while leaving his cave on 27 March 1945. Discovered in Ichimaru's cave was a letter addressed to President Roosevelt that sought to justify Japan's decision to go to war. Ichimaru's letter is archived at the United States Naval Academy, Annapolis.

*Rear Admiral R. Ichimaru of the Japanese Navy sends this note to Roosevelt. I have one word to give you upon the termination of this battle.*

*Approximately a century has elapsed since Nippon, after Commodore Perry's entry to Shimoda, became widely affiliated with the countries of the world. During this period of intercourse Nippon has met with many national crises as well as the undesired Sino-Japanese War, Russo-Japanese War, the World War, the Manchurian Incident, and the China Incident. Nippon is now, unfortunately, in a state of open conflict with your country. Judging Nippon from just this side of the screen you may slander our nation as a yellow peril, or a bloodthirsty nation or maybe a protoplasm of military clique.*

*Though you may use the surprise attack on Pearl Harbor as your primary material for propaganda, I believe you, of all persons, know best that you left Nippon no other method in order to save herself from self-destruction.*

*His Imperial Highness, as clearly shown in the Rescript of the Founder of the Empire "Yosei" [Justice], "Choki" [Sagacity] and "Sekkei" [Benevolence], contained in the above three-fold doctrine, rules in the realization of "Hakko-ichiu" [the universe under His Sacred Rule] in His Gracious mind.*

*The realization of which means the habitation of their respective fatherlands*

*under their own customs and traditions, thus ensuring the everlasting peace of the world.*

*Emperor Meiji's "The four seas of the world that are united in brotherhood will know no high waves nor wind" (composed during the Russo-Japanese War) won the appraisal of your uncle [sic], Theodore Roosevelt, as you yourself know.*

*We, the Nippon-jin, though may follow all lines of trade, it is through our each walk of life that we support the Imperial doctrine. We, the soldiers of the Imperial Fighting Force, take up arms to further the above-stated "doctrine."*

*Though we, at the time, are externally taken by your air raids and shelling backed by your material superiority, spiritually we are burning with delight and enjoying the peace of mind.*

*This peacefulness of mind, the common universal stigma of the Nippon-jin, burning with fervor in the upholding of the Imperial Doctrine may be impossible for you and Churchill to understand. I hereupon, pitying your spiritual feebleness, pen a word or two.*

*Judging from your actions, white races — especially you Anglo-Saxons — at the sacrifice of the colored races are monopolizing the fruits of the world.*

*In order to attain this end, countless machinations were used to cajole the yellow races, and to finally deprive them of any strength. Nippon in retaliation to your imperialism tried to free the oriental nations from your punitive bonds, only to be faced by your dogged opposition. You now consider your once friendly Nippon a harmful existence to your luscious plan, a bunch of barbarians that must be exterminated. The completion of this Greater East Asia War will bring about the birth of the East Asia Co-Prosperity Area, this in turn will in the near future result in the everlasting peace of the world, if, of course, it is not hampered upon by your unending imperialism.*

*Why is it that you, an already flourishing nation, nip in the bud the movement for the freedom of the suppressed nations of the east? It is no other than to return to the East that which belongs to the East.*

*It is beyond our contemplation when we try to understand your stinted narrowness. The existence of the East Asia Co-Prosperity sphere does not in any way encroach upon your safety as a nation; on the contrary, it will sit as a pillar of world peace ensuring the happiness of the world. His Imperial Majesty's true aim is no other than the attainment of this everlasting peace.*

*Studying the condition of the never-ending racial struggle resulting from mutual misunderstanding of the European countries, it is not difficult to feel the need of the everlasting universal peace.*

*President Hitler's crusade of "His Fatherland" is brought about by no other than the stupidity of holding only Germany, the loser of the World War, solely responsible for the 1914-1918 calamity and the deprivation of Germany's re-establishment.*

*It is beyond my imagination of how you can slander Hitler's program and at the same time cooperate with Stalin's "Soviet Russia" which has as its principle aim the "socialization" of the World at large.*

*If only the brute force decides the ruler of the world, fighting will everlastingly be repeated, and never will the world know peace nor happiness.*

*Upon the attainment of your barbaric world monopoly never forget to retain in your mind the failure of your predecessor President Wilson at his heights.*

*— Rear Admiral Ichimaru*

"This picture of a cave being sealed off is typical of the whole north end of the island. All volcanic rock and lots of places for snipers to hide. But the bad terrain had really started down around the beginning of the first air field and gotten steadily worse as we moved north. As we moved north, the ground got harder and harder, so there were more and more holes, caves or what have you that had been dug back into the near vertical faces of the canyon and gully walls. To us up there still fighting, there didn't seem to be any end to the number of caves that still faced us. It looked more hopeless every day. There were no replacements, just a few tired worn out people left up there. It seemed that the only way out was to get killed or wounded." — Howard McLaughlin

were cleverly concealed, and with smokeless powder the only way to spot where the fire was coming from was to see the muzzle flashes of the weapons.

Up in this area death from the Japs was swift and sure. All our injuries from the Japs were by a single sniper bullet and generally in the head. The only way to get to the Japs up in this area was with explosives and flamethrowers. If artillery was needed, a tank was brought in that could fire directly into the firing aperture from the roads being cut in with an armored dozer. Because of the terrain there usually wasn't enough maneuvering room to allow us to bypass any of the fortified positions. The field of fire that they covered meant that everybody was stopped until it was eliminated.

There may have been no Jap artillery or mortars, but some misguided souls on our side made up for the Japs' lack of harassment by "helping" us. One day there were eleven batteries of artillery firing into The Gorge.

"The far northwest end of the island. The road was put in by engineer dozers and at this time completely circled the top part of the island, although the area to the left of the picture is still in Jap hands . . . it being The Gorge, and as you can see there was nothing but volcanic rock up at this end of the island and the trees are like leafless Manzanita." — Howard McLaughlin.

Artillery fire up in this area was useless. These pillboxes and machine-gun emplacements were cut into the face of the cliffs, so only a direct hit could do any good. And the artillery fire didn't seem to do any damage to the spider holes and snipers. The Japs in them just moved back in the tunnels until the artillery firing was over, and then they would crawl back up through the connecting tunnels and were ready to shoot at us again.

The artillery that our noble officers fired could only impact the north side of The Gorge, and although it kept the Japs away from the entrances until the firing stopped, it also kept us away. It was only possible by a direct hit from a tank cannon or an anti-tank rocket to close them off long enough to blow the mouths shut with explosives. Even then it was not unusual to have Japs sniping at you from there later in the day.

Although I have said that towards the north end of the island most of the deaths were by a single bullet, I should add that there were still lots of wounds by shrapnel . . . caused by our own people, as all of the targets were generally so close to us. And to keep things lively, there were always short

rounds that burst in amongst the Marines. These were all wounds by friendly fire, and there was no need for their happening.

By now there were lots of artillery pieces on the island, and there was an over-abundance of unused artillery ammunition because there just weren't any targets left to shoot at, so there were no calls made from the lines for support fire. These "helpers" (that I referred to earlier) were officers that needed to have some combat time, and there were still plenty of officers that needed some medals. So they would come up to the front, direct some artillery fire, win their medal and then go back to the south end of the island and crawl into their safe dugout. There was no way that any of these artillery shells that they asked to have fired could have gotten into the caves up on the sides of The Gorge, but so what. All they did was impede our work and cause us casualties. Artillery barrages hindered us in our work, but we had no officers to complain to, to stop this foolishness.

Very few Marines wore steel helmets up here as they did not stop rifle bullets. I wore a fatigue cap, like a baseball cap. It was less trouble when you had to run. However there was not much running up here. There had been no replacements in this time and there weren't many of us left. Most of us had been on the lines for at least the last fifteen to twenty days without any relief, and we were extremely tired. Those of us that were left were so tired that, if we moved, it was like zombies; you had no strength left, you were even so tired that you couldn't run anymore. By this time you just accepted the odds as being against you, and were merely waiting for the shock of the bullet.

This was bad because it dulled your senses. You were no longer observing as you had been, and I'm sure this added to the number of casualties — needless casualties — that we suffered. Nerves were frayed from artillery and demolition explosions, and there was not a man there that wasn't wounded or bandaged in some manner — we were all walking wounded. I read later that, by the time

"The far northwest corner of the island, showing the ruggedness of the area. — Howard McLaughlin

we entered The Gorge, the combat efficiency of the Fifth Marine Division was rated at 34%; it looked more like 2% when I was up there.

One morning (March 25th) at about ten o'clock, my squad was relieved, taken out of the lines, and sent back to the rear area. We were to report someplace, but I remember none of this.

Anyway, we were relieved and taken down to the west landing beaches. We were to board ship that afternoon. I don't remember going to the beach or really much about it. This part of my story was told later to me back in Hawaii. I'm sure we

were the cruddiest-looking bunch of people you have ever seen . . . and we all stank so bad that people shied away from us, but none of us cared from being so tired. I can remember these people sorting us out were in clean uniforms. These nice clean rear-echelon types were careful that none of this trash brushed against their clean uniforms. They were taking your name, serial number and unit, trying to find out who was still left alive. I was told by the others later . . . that I was standing in one of the lines of men waiting in single file to board small landing craft (LCVPs) to be taken out to the transports. I was taken by the arm and led away from the people I had come to the beach with. A couple of corpsmen pulled me aside and took me to another landing craft, a bigger one. I can remember being on what I think was an LCM, going out to the ship. It was great; there was no line to stand in as they helped me onboard. There was even room enough in the boat that I could sit down against the side and go to sleep. I did.

It turned out that this LCM had only wounded on board and we were taken to the USS *Zeilin*, a hospital ship. Once out to the hospital ship the badly wounded, still on their stretchers, were placed on pallets and lifted to the deck of the hospital ship by cranes. Several of us were walking wounded, so when the LCM tied up alongside a landing net hanging from the deck of the *Zeilin*, we just assumed that we had to climb the nets. A corpsman told us that if we wanted to we could climb the rope nets, but that we could ride up on the pallets after the more seriously wounded were all removed.

I guess I thought I was OK, so with several others I started to climb up the rope net. Partway up I panicked. I locked my arms through the rope nets and hung on for dear life. I couldn't climb up any farther, I was too weak to continue climbing. My hands and arms were so weak that it felt like I was going to lose my grip on the ropes and fall back into the ocean. I froze. I was afraid. I thought for sure that I would fall into the LCM or into the water and drown. Two sailors quickly came down the net and helped me up to the deck. I just didn't have any strength to get more than halfway up. This was the only time I ever boarded a US Navy ship and didn't salute the officer on deck and request permission to come aboard.

Once safely on deck, I and the others were told to strip down bare-assed naked. Everything off: clothes, cartridge belts, canteens, first aid pouches, helmets, shoes all went into a pile on deck to be buried at sea. You could keep your weapon, after a sailor checked the magazine for live rounds, and your combat knife. We were told to put any person-

al items we wanted to save in a  little pile.[14] I used my fatigue hat to save my KA-BAR knife, my Boy Scout pocket knife, my Zippo lighter, my crimping pliers for explosives, and my waterproofed picture of my wife, Helen.

Once stripped, we were pointed at a hatchway entrance to the cabin area and told to take a shower. Naked, carrying my M-1 and my hat with all my belongings, I entered the passageway and was directed to pile my stuff in a pile against the bulkhead and pointed into a locker-type room. There, one at a time, we were given a quick boot-camp style haircut. That done, we were pointed to a fresh hot water shower and told, "You may stay as long as you like, there is shaving gear on the wash basins, there will be clean clothes and hot chow when you are ready."

There were only maybe twenty of us that were able to walk. After a long shower, time out to shave and more soaking under the hot shower, we were given all new clothes, all standard navy issue: shoes, blue dungarees and white skivvies. We were also given an oversize army dungaree jacket for the cold weather.

After we were dressed we were taken to the crew's galley. I don't remember what we had to eat, but it was hot, it was good and there were several main dishes and it was served sit-down style. During the meal the cooks looked on appreciatively

---

14    McLaughlin left behind some of his gear and several Japanese items in the H&S Co. Engineer Battalion rear area. These included the helmet on page 213, a case of defused grenades (to trade with), and his bullet pierced blanket roll. McLaughlin wrote, "The first proof positive that I was nearly hit with a bullet, which maybe even that day was far more often than I ever want to know about, was on the first afternoon of the landing beach. This was after we had returned from carrying explosives up to the 28th Marines. I was climbing the slope with my pack on my back. I was 'slapped' sharply on the blanket roll above my left shoulder and to the left of my head when it was hit by a bullet. The pack had my blankets rolled as prescribed, in a horseshoe shape, on the top and sides of the upper pack. The bullet must have traveled from Mt. Suribachi, a distance at which (although it was out of accurate aiming distance) it was still well within the lethal distance for killing. I still have those blankets today with several neat little holes punched in them." McLaughlin's extra gear and Japanese artifacts made their way back to Hawaii with the salvageable equipment. McLaughlin wrote, "Any of the Engineer's trucks and heavy equipment that were salvageable had been brought back [to Hawaii] from Iwo and lined up in our equipment park. It was about a third to a quarter of the equipment that we had left with. However, added to this were some of the strange things that various engineers had acquired along the way." These "strange things" included Japanese motorcycles, trucks, and the car pictured on page 222.

as we devoured the food — all we wanted to eat, and I do remember that at the end we all had all the ice cream we wanted. Then we were told, "Eat all you want to eat, any time, for the next several days in this galley."

We were shown bunks in the sick bays. "You may sleep as long as you want till we are back in the Hawaiian Islands. You will be checked over by a doctor in the next couple of days."

The troop ship I came out on had 2,000-plus Marines on it, and we had about 400 men in a troop compartment. Each man had an area six feet long, and about two feet wide and eighteen inches high for you and all of your gear, packs and rifle, etc. Now I was on a ship that could carry 6,000 troops easily, but there were only about 300 wounded on board. In the sick bay compartment that I was in there were less than thirty wounded. The aisles were wide and the bunks were only two high. One bunk was about chest height to the corpsmen that were tending the more seriously wounded. The other bunk was below that, about four inches off the floor, and when not in use was chained up out of the corpsman's way.

In my compartment there were four of us that were considered as walking wounded; the rest were semi-ambulatory patients. We got up and went to chow and helped the corpsman keep the compartment policed. The others were waited on and fed by corpsmen. If it was necessary for them to be up, and for some it was possible with help, they were helped around by corpsmen. Never in all my time overseas did I ever see a navy nurse, except those I saw on the streets of Honolulu.

After a couple of days of eating and sleeping I was examined by a team of doctors. When they finally got through with their examination, and then several surprise nighttime checks, it was decided that all I had was combat fatigue. Amongst the troops it was called "The Thousand-Yard Stare," otherwise known as "Shell Shock." I would live.

I told them about my poor eyesight and hearing on the left side, but they seemed to think that it would go away with rest. Well, it didn't. Fifty years later I still have headaches all the time, just sometimes worse than others, and I have trouble with vertigo. I get sick very easily if I turn or move fast in certain ways, but that's a small price for still being alive.

Now that the ship was underway, all of the walking wounded who had been released by the doctors were asked to help run the ship. I was assigned to the crew's mess. The old chief took one look at me and assigned me to run the bread slicer in the galley. Just before every meal I had to put the fresh-baked loaves of bread thru the slicer for any of the seven galleys on the ship that wanted some. Sometimes this work took ten or fifteen minutes. Other mess men came and got the sliced bread, I didn't even have to deliver it. The rest of the time was mine, and I was to eat with the cooks as I now worked for the bakery. I was the only Marine in the galley and they all treated me like a little kid. All I did was eat and sleep — just what the doctor ordered.

# IWO JIMA REDISCOVERED

Coast Guard combat photographer Merrill Allen was sent ashore on 21 February 1945, the third day of the Battle of Iwo Jima. His mission was to film the Marines on the beach. Allen remembered the nightmarish attack: "It seems like a dream now. Iwo Jima was the first combat I had seen. I had orders to take some film footage of the landing and to report right back to the ship, but the first day I didn't shoot any film, it was a matter of survival." The young Coast Guardsman, who had virtually no combat training, stuck close to the highly-trained Marines: "We'd be in a shell hole and then run to where another explosion hit and dig in there. I relied strictly on my speed to make it through the day."

Above: The battle-damaged Japanese helmet Merrill Allen brought back from Iwo Jima. *Author's collection.*
Opposite page: Clips from Allen's film showing the flag from the second flag raising on top of Mount Suribachi (left), and a mortar strike at the base of Suribachi (right).

On 23 February, Allen began his ascent of Mt. Suribachi. "I was going up and met Joe Rosenthal coming down." Rosenthal was the photographer who snapped the famous photograph of the second flag raising on top of Mount Suribachi. "We stopped and had a cigarette together. I asked Joe what was going on up there and he said, 'Nothing much of interest, just the boys putting up the flag.' I continued up to the top and filmed the flag and some of the men."

Allen used up the last of his film on top of Mount Suribachi. As he made his way down the slope of the volcano and toward the beach, Allen picked up a battle-damaged Japanese helmet as a reminder of that day.

When he returned to the USS *Bayfield* and climbed over the netting to come aboard, the crew greeted him with stunned looks on their faces. He was overdue and presumed dead. "That ship never looked so pretty to me in all my life," said Allen.

His exposed 16mm film was sent to a darkroom on Guam for processing. "Extra copies were sent back to the ship and the skipper called me into his stateroom that night and gave me a copy of the film. I didn't need any more souvenirs than that."

Life calmed down for Allen after Iwo Jima: "I became the ship's photographer, taking pictures of the boys for their hometown newspapers."

After the war, Allen's Iwo Jima film stayed in

Before digital remastering.

After digital remastering.

his closet. Years later he spliced together segments of his color footage with black-and-white footage taken by a combat photographer friend who also filmed the battle. Allen, a native of Stanton, Nebraska, would show his 40-minute reel to local groups: "I showed it a couple of times, but by the late 1970's it became brittle with age — it was put together rough."

The film begins in Hawaii with scenes of Marines practicing amphibious landings. Next were scenes of equipment being loaded onto the USS *Bayfield*, followed by footage of the voyage to Iwo Jima where *Bayfield* was unloaded in preparation for the amphibious assault. The film then documents the landing and scenes on the beach, and concludes as the *Bayfield* departs for Saipan with several Japanese prisoners-of-war aboard.

Japanese prisoners-of-war taken on Iwo Jima were brought aboard USS *Bayfield* for interrogation. Allen filmed these same prisoners as they were off-loaded in Saipan. National Archives photo # 127-GW-327-143141.

Before his death on 6 March 2010, Allen donated the 40-minute reel to the Nebraska State Historical Society. His footage of the American flag atop Mount Suribachi cannot be found in the film collection at the National Archives, making it historically significant.

The story of the remastering of Merrill Allen's film began in 2014. I tracked down his son David, and explained that I had just acquired the battle-damaged helmet that his father picked up on Iwo Jima; David confirmed the authenticity of the helmet and then told me about his father's film and its fragile condition.

A year later I called David and said that I would like to have his father's film digitally remastered as one of the projects for my book. I explained how color film stock has a lifespan of no more than seventy years; after that, it becomes so brittle and deformed from shrinkage that restoration is no longer possible. David was enthusiastic about the prospect of having his father's film preserved and helped me obtain the 40-minute reel from the Nebraska State Historical Society.

To remaster Allen's movie digitally, the film was first cleaned and then fed by hand through a sprocketless viewing device where a high resolution scan was made of each frame, resulting in several terabytes of data before editing. Special software used during the scanning process removed scratches and made adjustments in color and contrast. Allen's audio track was also remastered to remove background noise and improve fidelity. The two files were then merged and digitally compressed. The whole process was very time-consuming, but the result made it possible to see details that were not previously available to the viewer.

Opposite page: Armed only with his 16mm camera and a .45 sidearm, Merrill Allen boards the USS *Bayfield* after filming the landing at Iwo Jima. National Archives photograph #26-G-89A-27.

# William Glavic

# YORKTOWN DIARY

USS *Yorktown CV-10*. National Archives Photograph # 80-G-471017.

While under construction as *Bon Homme Richard*, this Essex-class carrier was renamed USS *Yorktown CV-10* in honor of USS *Yorktown CV-5*, sunk at the Battle of Midway in June 1942. She was commissioned on 15 April 1943, beccoming the fourth U.S. Navy ship named Yorktown since the American Revolutionary War.

USS *Yorktown CV-10* participated in Allied offensive operations in the Pacific, beginning in 1943 and ending with the defeat of Japan in 1945. She received the Presidential Unit Citation and earned eleven battle stars during World War II.

William Glavic, V-3-R, worked as a radar operator in *Yorktown's* Combat Information Center, the nerve center of the ship charged with keeping the *Yorktown's* commanding officer and higher commands informed of the location, identity and movement of friendly and foe aircraft and surface ships within their area of operation.

Glavic's diary records the actions of his ship, their battle group and all the sister ships throughout the Pacific Theater. Many of the entries are highly detailed and reflect his unique access to information within the CIC. Glavic had a natural talent for comprehensively detailing the action with a lean narrative, yet in the most intimate way he takes the reader to the decks of the *Yorktown*. His self-effacing manner makes a compelling personal history, and one cannot help but admire the reserve and strength of character that belies his fears.

## *The Diary of William Glavic*

**October 9, 1944**
Left Bremerton, Washington, bound for San Francisco, California.

**October 11**
Arrived in San Francisco and stayed two days at Alameda Airfield, California.

**October 13**

Left San Francisco, bound for Pearl Harbor, loaded with jeeps, trucks, planes, pretty rough crossing.

**October 19**

Arrived at Pearl Harbor, same old place, Fox 13, then went to the Navy Yard.

**October 24**

Left Pearl headed for Eniwetok at 1500. Will take us six days.

**October 30**

Arrived Eniwetok at 0900. It's in the Marshals, northern part, will leave tomorrow morning.

**November 3**

Arrived at Ulithi and found a lot of shipping, first time in this place. The *Franklin* was here, which was hit by a suicide bomber. First carrier ever hit by this new method of attack. Was aboard her and the damage was all on the hangar deck. Fire damaged most of the hangar deck. Will stay here two days and then join the fleet.

**November 5**

Left Ulithi with 27 ships, here we go again.

**November 11**

Met the fleet and are now ready for action. We answered MacArthur's call for help by sinking a convoy west of Leyte. He got all the credit for it, he always does.

**November 13**

Sent strikes over Luzon airfields, doing all the damage we could around the field. We saw two planes that day.

**November 15**

Steaming westward, destination unknown.

**November 16**

Refueled today. 38.2[1] joined us today which was the *Intrepid*, *Hancock*, *Independence*, further operations are unknown, we are 38.1 in the third fleet.

**November 17**

Cruising in circles west of the Philippines, nothing doing now.

**November 18**

Still around the Philippines, shot down a twin engine plane today (a Nellie),[2] will strike Luzon tomorrow.

**November 19**

Sent in strikes to Luzon, shot a twin-engine plane down trying to get at us. Can expect more, shot some more down today; by sunset the total is 10 planes shot down trying to get at us. (By us I mean the carriers.)

**November 20**

Still around Luzon, waiting for the Japs to make a move. No luck!

**November 21**

Everything is peaceful around here, got a little mail today.

**November 23**

Thanksgiving today, had a pretty good chow. Still cruising around looking for trouble (still no luck).

**November 24**

Pulled in Ulithi today, got mail and plenty of rest (1500 when we pulled in). Saw Joe Diemert.

---

1   38.2 refers to Task Group 38.2. A Task unit has 3-5 ships, task groups have 4-10 ships, a task force has 2-5 task groups, and fleets are made up of several task forces.

2   Glavic refers to a Nellie, which was more commonly referred to as a Nell, a twin-engine G3M 96 Attack Bomber.

**November 26**
Went over the Island of Mog Mog and had some beer and looked around.

**November 27**
Still in Ulithi and the *Intrepid* got hit by Jap suicide bombers (she will be going back now). They keep this up and we won't have any carriers left.

**November 28**
Had G.Q. last night, but it turned out to be friendly. We are only 60 miles from a Jap held base. I don't think they know we're here yet. (I hope.)[3]

**November 31**
Still in Ulithi, had a meeting of all radar operators. They were telling us that the Japs have our IFF (that's how we tell our planes from the Japs).[4] Looks like we're going to have trouble, oh well, you can't live forever.

**December 1**
Pulled out of Ulithi today at 0600. MacArthur is having trouble so here we go again. Destination unknown.

**December 2**
Everything was canceled so we pulled back in Ulithi to wait for further orders.

**December 10**
In Ulithi all this time, pulled out this morning at 0600, at a meeting we were told that we would cover the landings on Mindoro Island, then go up to Luzon and try to knock their airforce out up there, we're doing pretty good so far.

**December 14**
Had G.Q. last night and we shot a Jap flying boat

down, 22 miles away at 0417, planes came back from the target and they said they did pretty good.

**December 15**
Second day of our strike, no Japs. Looks like they're afraid to come out and fight. Guess we'll get away with it this time. A fellow walked into a propeller while it was still going and he was killed instantly, I saw it where I was standing, boy it was a mess (Lt. Comd. Heiss).

**December 16**
Still striking Luzon, had G.Q. last night, but we missed the old bastard, so that's another Jap that lives to see another day. Our air group commander was shot down but he bailed out over the target, found out later that he's now with fighting Doug.[5] Had a plane crash today and the plane turned over, the pilot died of head injuries (Funeral No.10 so far).

**December 17**
Went out to refuel but it was too rough, called off.

**December 18**
Last night we ran into a typhoon (0200) and it lasted 13 hours. It sure was a bad one, all ships were having trouble, some only had 15% of their fuel left. The *Monterey* caught on fire, the planes broke loose and started banging against each other, that's what started the fire, she was dead in the water, we left her behind and kept on going. The *Cowpens* also had a little fire but they put it out right away. The CVEs with our replacement aircraft were dead in the water, visibility was only two miles, so we're having a hell of a time dodging all those ships.[6] In an hour's time we had sixteen men washed overboard (I stayed down below). The waves were coming over our bow and right down the flight deck and took everything loose with it. We had to eat chow on the deck that day because the tables wouldn't

---

3   G.Q. stands for General Quarters or Battle Stations.
4   IFF: Identification Friend or Foe was an radio operated identification system. It enabled ground control to determine the bearing and range of an aircraft fitted with a transmitting IFF radio device. Its name is a misnomer; IFF can only identify aircraft that carry the IFF device.

5   Douglas MacArthur.
6   CVE is the hull classification symbol for an escort aircraft carrier.

stay still, we listed 30 degrees, sometimes more, we had a foot of water in where we slept. I sure as hell don't want to go through that again, the waves were 60 feet high, that's nothing to sneeze at out there.

## December 19

It's all calm and peaceful today so we refueled, we got the word today that we lost three destroyers out there. Fred Grubham, who was on the *Monaghan*, also lost the *Spence and Hull*, they only picked up about 30 men out of a thousand. Still searching for more.

## December 20

Still looking for the men, all we find is the life jackets and rafts, but no men, picked up a couple of bodies but they were dead.

## December 24

Pulled in Ulithi — received all our Christmas packages.

## December 29

West and Small got transferred, lost two swell guys.

## December 30

Pulled out and our operations will be around Formosa this time.

## January 1, 1945

Our position at the time of midnite was 18°- 08.5, Lat 130°- 00 getting colder as we go north.

## January 2

Refueled today, but no mail, tomorrow we strike Formosa.

## January 3

We hit today, weather was pretty bad, we now are wearing jackets.

## January 4

Shot down four planes today: 1 Zeke, Betty, Irving;

we lost two pilots of our own, a destroyer was under attack by a Jap fighter, they got strafed, but they also got him.[7]

## January 5

Pulled out to refuel.

## January 6

Sent planes over Luzon today. No excitement. Shot a Betty down later.

## January 7

Still sending planes over Luzon, we shot down a Jap torpedo bomber (Jill)[8] and the Jap didn't have his helmet on and no rear seat gunner, they think that he was one of those things they call a suicide bomber. He was after us but never got here. Just heard that the 7th Fleet got hit by suicide boys, 12 ships got hit (7th fleet are CVEs and the older battle ships). They go in on the invasions and stay there till they secure the beach.

## January 8

Pulled out and refueled.

## January 9

Sent strikes into Luzon and Formosa again. Shot down a twin engine plane today that passed right over our heads. The invasion of Luzon started today. Everything is going good. Another fellow walked into a spinning prop, I went to his funeral

---

7   During the first year of the Pacific War, Allied personnel struggled to quickly and accurately identify Japanese aircraft. Several code systems were tried but added to the confusion. In mid-1942, Captain Frank McCoy, assigned to a U.S. Army Air Intelligence Unit in Australia, devised a simpler method. Together with Technical Sergeant Francis Williams and Corporal Joseph Grattan, McCoy divided the Japanese aircraft into categories. Fighters and single-engine-float planes were given men's names. Women's names were given to bombers, transports and reconnaissance aircraft. Bird names were given to gliders and tree names to trainer aircraft. McCoy gave many of the aircraft hillbilly names, such as Zeke, for the Mitsubishi A6M Zero, a long-range fighter plane, and Rufe, the Nakajima A6M2-N single-engine float plane — all names he encountered while growing up in Tennessee. Others were given names of friends or people he knew personally. The Mitsubishi G4M twin-engine bomber, with its large gun blisters, was named Betty in homage to a busty female friend of Williams. Irving was the Nakajima J1N Gekko (Moonlight), a twin-engine aircraft used for reconnaissance, kamikaze missions and as a night fighter.
8    Jill was the Allied reporting name for the Nakajima B6N *Tenzan* (Heavenly Mountain) and was Japan's standard carrier-borne torpedo bomber.

(No.11). Tonight we will go to the China Sea, we will go thru the Bashi Channel, it's between Luzon and Formosa. Started thru at 2100 and sure was a tight fit.

**January 10**
We shot three twin engine bombers down while going between Luzon and Formosa, sent out searches to find the Jap fleet but no luck as of yet. Saw a convoy but didn't bother it.

**January 11**
Refueled today (we brought our own tankers right with us). Also shot down three Jap fighters 45 miles away.

**January 12**
Today we sent in strikes to French Indochina, Saigon Area, all together sank 30 ships in the harbor and shot 15 planes out of the air, still no Jap fleet. We lost one plane. Tomorrow we will go up to Honk-Kong in China. Also tried to refuel but weather is too bad.

**January 13**
Refueled today. Weather much better.

**January 14**
Sent in strikes to hit the western side of Formosa, weather got bad so we called it off.

**January 15**
Refueled today, taking no chances of running out of oil.

**January 16**
Sent strikes to hit Tokyo also the Honk-Kong area, weather is pretty bad and cold.

**January 17**
Today we tried to refuel, but water is still rough. No luck.

**January 19**
Finally got some good weather and will try to refuel, heading north and having a little trouble trying to get out, weather is rough and cold.

**January 20**
Japs finally found out where we are and it cost them 11 planes, we are still trying to get out, well we are finally going thru, started thru at 8 p.m., we were so close to land that we could go out on the flight deck and see it at night, when you do that, then you know you're close. It was midnite before we were all clear of all land.

**January 21**
We are striking Formosa today, this time from the Pacific side, 15 suicide planes started out for us, the results, 1 DD[9] hit (*Maddox*), several killed, many injured, the *Ticonderoga* also got hit, Capt. and the Exec. were injured, the hangar deck was all burned out and she cannot operate her planes, 15 planes out of 90 were in operational order, the *Langley* was also attacked and hit, results, 1 killed, two injured. All carriers hit will go back to Ulithi. Shot down 19 planes in all, we're having a little clean up session out here, also shot down two of our own planes by mistake (OS2U),[10] pilots and crew were picked up and they weren't hurt.

**January 22**
We were under attack last night, shot down a twin engine plane (a Betty) that now makes it seven to our credit.

**January 23**
Refueling today, also some mail, first mail since Dec. 30.

**January 24**
On our way back to Ulithi.

---

9   DD is the hull classification symbol for a destroyer.
10   Vought OS2U Kingfisher was a catapult-launched shipboard observation floatplane..

**January 26**

Anchored in Ulithi, changed our radio call from Cobra to Ruler, we also changed from the Third Fleet to the Fifth Fleet, *Saratoga*, *Bennington*, *Randolph*, *Bunker Hill*, all came out from the States, went over on the beach and helped sort mail, also took some pictures.

**February 10**

Left Ulithi and are going up to hit Tokyo also the Bonin Is., we will invade Iwo Jima on Feb. 19, 1945 at 0830.

**February 14**

Heading for Tokyo with 5 groups, there will be eleven big carriers with 58 Task Force and 5 small (CVL),[11] we will be with the *Randolph*, *Cabot* and *Langley*.

**February 16**

D-3-Day. Hit Tokyo today, sent in planes a hundred miles off the shore, we caught them by surprise, we ran into a lot of little fishing boats, sank all we met, got a prisoner off of one of them, there were 11 to start but the others got killed. We bombed an aircraft plant and destroyed it, destroyed all planes that we saw. One pilot was shot down, but a sub (ours) picked him up 5 miles off the shore. The weather sure is cold 41° out . . . a jump from 104 to 41, boy if that isn't something, the pilots saw snow on the ground over the target, but didn't bring any back. Didn't see a Jap plane all day, we will be here tomorrow again.

**February 17**

Hit Tokyo again. Still no Japs came out, guess we shot down all we could see. The total was 385 planes shot out of the air that day (yesterday).

**February 18**

Pulled out to refuel, we ran into 7 P.C. boats (patrol craft), sank them all and only took one prisoner.

**February 19**

Invaded Iwo Jima today, we were right there with our fighters to help out. Strafed and bombed the island.

**February 20**

Refueled today, also took on some mail.

**February 21**

Went back to Iwo Jima, they're having a little trouble, the *Saratoga* went into the beach to help and she was hit by 4 suicide planes, one in the island structure, one on the water line and two on the fight deck, she was really a mess. Casualties were very heavy.

**February 22**

Still at Iwo Jima, the CVE *Bismarck Sea* was hit with a bomb and sunk. The suicide boys were there again.

**February 23**

Pulled out to refuel today, also saw the island, looks like a big rock in the middle of the ocean.

**February 24**

Heading towards Tokyo again, we had another carrier's plane land on us today and when he hit, his belly tank came off and hit the prop and exploded, causing a big fire, we put it out after a while, his guns went off and sprayed our island structure hitting a couple of men, Elliott from our division was hit in the mouth and in both legs, he will be alright, 13 men were hurt from the fire. It always seems to be a plane from another carrier that causes all the trouble, a *Liscome Bay* plane killed 5 of our men once, the same thing happened there only it happened at night that time.

**February 25**

We are still hitting Iwo Jima, bombing and strafing.

---

11   CVL is the hull classification number for a light aircraft carrier.

MARCH 26
Today we are hitting Okinawa, Saw 52 mine sweepers getting ready to clean the place of mines, the were eleven miles from us. Battle wagons pulled out to get ready to go in a shell the beach, Just got word that the British are out here 4 CV's, 2 BB's, 4 CA's, and a destroyer screen. They are hitting the islands farther south of Okinawa, shot down two planes last night, two Bettys.

MARCH 27
Everything went ok today 58.1 was under attack (Jocko's outfit) they shot down 7 with the AA Fire. One ship got hit with a torpedoe, it went right thru it without going off
Okinawa has a population of 500,000, has three big airfields. Neveda, Biloxi were hit by suicide bombers, 40 killed 17 injured, 44 on Biloxi (AA cruiser) injured.

MARCH 28
Refueled today, also took on Amunition from a AE, took it over by pulleys, this is the first time we ever tried that, worked out pretty good, had several sub contacts inside the screen, had to make several emergencies turns, boy we'll be a darn lucky bunch if we live thru this operation.

MARCH 29
Got word that another typhoon is coming our way, still around Okinawa, sending our planes in over every little Island around us to see that the Japs don't try anything (Anami Shima, Tokuna, Kikia, and some others) A Judy (Jap dive bomber) followed our planes back and he tryed a suicide dive on us and he missed by about two feet, I seen that and I sure was scared, we shot two of our own planes down, they were trying to get him also, the Jap really exploded when he hit.

William Glavic's diary was acquired by the author from a Canadian bookseller. *Author's collection.*

**February 26**
Refueled again.

**February 28**
Heading towards our home base. Good old Ulithi.

**March 1**
Arrived in the afternoon.

**March 9**
Went out for one day, we had gunnery exercises.

**March 11**
While at anchor of the eve of the tenth, a Jap suicide plane got in and hit the *Randolph* in the fantail, the Jap flew right over our bow at about a hundred feet and right into the *Randolph*, setting two thousand yards on our port beam, I was at the movies at the time. The movies started at 7:30 and we saw two shorts and a newsreel, then all of a sudden a big explosion on our port side, fire broke out and we went to general quarters, pulled up our gangways and all ready to get out of there, the fire lasted three hours.

**March 12**

Fire was all out and the damage wasn't too bad, a repair ship fixed her up. She asked for 19 graves over on the beach so I guess 19 got killed. She didn't look so bad.

**March 14**

Isn't safe around here so we are pulling out and this will be the longest operation we will ever be on. We will be gone three months, get supplies, ammunition, mail etc. at sea operating with the *Intrepid, Enterprise, Langley*, will strike the Neisi Shoto Is. today or tomorrow.

**March 18**

My birthday.[12] Feel like an old man, we are hitting Kyushu today.

**March 19**

Still striking the island, it is in the southern part of Japan. We had bogeys all night long and very little sleep, we were attacked today, we got two near misses and a hit, it hit the signal bridge, came thru a row of gunners and exploded on the starboard side, right next to the ship fitter shop. Two men were hit on the guns. One fellow got both legs cut off, the other only got one leg off. They both died, three men in the ship fitter shop got killed, one officer (Lt.) and two enlisted men. It put a 15 foot hole in our side and destroyed three compartments, ship fitter shop was destroyed, second deck (Q.M.)[13] compt. blown out, third deck full of holes, fourth deck full of water (store room). I was on the second deck in the next compt. and I was sleeping, it threw me out of my sack on the deck, lucky I wasn't hit but it sure scared the hell out of me, smoke filled our compt. so we had to get out, there was a fire but it was put right out. The *Enterprise* also got a bomb hit, hers was a small bomb (250#). Ours was a 600#. The *Franklin* got the worst of all of us, she was ready to launch planes for a strike, planes had bombs on and full of gas, the Jap dropped the bomb right in the middle of all the planes. So there was 21 explosions counted from our ship, they had to tow her back to Guam, she had 500 men left on her out of 3,000, many lives lost. All C.I.C. personnel were killed, they have their C.I.C the same place we have ours. 1600 men were picked out of the water. *Halsey Powell* also got hit (DD) can only make ten knots. Our group will stay behind them and protect them from the Japs. They got the best of us there but they'll pay for it.

**March 20**

Buried our five men today, was pretty quiet today.

**March 21**

Still bombing the Japs. The Japs sent out everything they had but we had more than they did.

**March 22**

Pulled out to refuel. Chaplain told us what we did over Tokyo, shot 500 planes out of the air, one CVE was sunk and smaller ships in the harbor were sunk, hit installations (every bomb is a direct hit there because they are so close together). Told us we will cover another invasion on April 1st but we will hit them with everything we got before that. We are resting up today.

**March 23**

Our invasion will be Okinawa in the Nansei Shotos, we will hit it for ten days straight without a let up. Saw no Japs today, weather was bad. One bogey got within 40 miles today, he was shot down before he knew what hit him, he didn't have a chance. Refuel tomorrow.

**March 25**

Refueled today from tankers, received mail today, Glavic got one letter (just about the limit for me).

---

12    William Glavic was born on 18 March 1924.
13    Quartermaster is an enlisted man in charge of the watch-to-watch navigation and the maintenance, correction and preparation of nautical charts and navigation publications.

**March 26**

Today we are hitting Okinawa. Saw 52 mine sweepers getting ready to clean the place of mines. They were eleven miles from us. Battle wagons pulled out to get ready to go in and shell the beach. Just got word that the British are out here 4 CVs, 2BBs,[14] 4CAs and a destroyer screen. They are hitting the islands farther south of Okinawa. Shot down two planes last night, two Bettys.

**March 27**

Everything went OK today. 58.1 was under attack (Jocko's outfit).[15] They shot down 7 with the AA[16] fire. One ship got hit with a torpedo, it went right thru it without going off. Okinawa has a population of 500,000, has three big air fields. *Nevada*, *Biloxi* were hit by suicide bombers; 40 killed, 17 injured, 94 on *Biloxi* injured.

**March 28**

Refueled today. Also took on ammunition from a AE, took it over by pulleys.[17] This is the first time we ever tried that, worked out pretty good. Had several sub contacts inside the screen, had to make several emergency turns. Boy we'll be a darn lucky bunch if we live thru this operation.

**March 29**

Got word that another typhoon is coming our way, still around Okinawa, sending our planes in over every little island around us to see that the Japs don't try anything (Anami Shima, Tokuna, Kikia, and some others). A Judy (Jap dive bomber)[18] fol-lowed our planes back and he tried a suicide dive on us and he missed by about two feet. I seen that and I sure was scared. We shot two of our own planes down, they we're trying to get him also. The Jap really exploded when he hit, we only found one pilot the other was killed. Typhoon still heading this way and were still waiting for it, the invasion will be Easter Sunday (April 1, 1945) at 0830. One of our pilots was picked up off the beach, he spent 3 days in a cave, said he walked all over the island, he stole a horse and did some riding, gave us a lot of information on the Jap gun construction. Bogey closed our group at 2330, *Alaska* opened up on it but missed, night fighters from the *Intrepid* went out to get it, shot it down at 40 miles from us, (1 Betty).

**March 30**

Was 40 miles from Okinawa and still sending in our planes to knock out the place, no Jap planes were sighted today. (Thank God.)

**April 1**

(Easter Sunday) The invasion started this morning, 60,000 troops went ashore and we went in on the N.W. side of the island, we fooled the Japs because we pulled a fake invasion on the southern tip of the island, so when we went ashore on the west side, they met no opposition. Today at 0830 and at 1000 they reported that they were in 5 miles inland without seeing a Jap, so far everything is going along swell, but we don't know how long it will last. At 1600 they were in to 6.5 miles, still no Japs, 3 miles across the island. The *Indianapolis* was hit by a suicide bomber. The bomb went right thru the ship and exploded in the water, 1 killed, 14 injured, 5 missing. We shot down a Betty 15 miles from our formation, we are still helping out with the invasion, sending in all our planes, strafing and bombing, Tokyo reports half our fleet sunk, she sure hit the fleet but she hasn't sunk it yet and I hope she doesn't, another report from the beach, they are 8.5 miles inland, the *West Virginia* got hit by a suicide

---

14    BB is the hull classification symbol for a battleship.

15    As the war progressed and as ships became available, U.S. naval forces were organized into formations called "task groups." These were groups of ships assembled to perform specific tasks. An "assault group" of attack transports, minesweepers and destroyers would be formed to invade an island after it had been bombed by a "bombardment group." Task Group 58.1 consisted of two heavy carriers, two light carriers, five battleships, three heavy cruisers, five light cruisers, and twenty-four destroyers. Task Group 58.1 was commanded by Admiral J. J. "Jocko" Clark, who called it "the largest assemblage of naval power ever in a single formation."

16    AA stands for anti-aircraft fire.

17    AE is the hull classification symbol for an ammunition ship.

18    Judy was the designation name for the Yokosuka D4Y *Suisei* (Comet) Navy carrier dive bomber. It was one of the fastest dive bombers of the war.

April 11, 1945; "Today the Japs sent out an all-out attack on us, in which it lasted all day and half the night, two suicide planes tried to hit the *Missouri*, only one hit it without much damage." National Archives photo # NH 62690.

bomber, boy the Japs are sure using up a lot of their suicide pilots, I hope they run out pretty soon. You can kill the bastards by gun fire, but they still keep coming, sometimes they're on fire when they hit, they are getting to be a pain in the _ _ _.

## April 3

Last night the *New Jersey* hit the *Franks* (DD). The Captain of the destroyer was hurt and later died, the DD went back to the States. One of our officers was on there for the ride but he is alright ( Lt.

Brand, one swell guy). The typhoon is breaking up, so I guess we won't get hit by it, we're getting a little of it, the water is pretty rough but everything is under control. Too rough to refuel so we'll do that tomorrow.

## April 4

Refueling today, rough outside but we have to go thru with it, we took on oil, gasoline, bombs, mail (none for Glavic) and some chow. We will go back to Okinawa after we refuel, it seems like we stay out three days (going 400 miles a day) and on the fourth day we refuel. We've been out since March 14th and still no signs of going back. The patch where the bomb hit started to come apart but they fixed it again, the water was pretty rough.

## April 5

We are taking the British's place while they go out to refuel, they are operating south of Okinawa and we're up north, we shot down two Bettys when they tried to land on the island, also ran one into the ground and one got away. Besides that nothing else happened.

## April 6

Refueling today, about 1500 we got word that 58.1 + 58.3 are under heavy attack, they shot down a total of 150 planes that day. *Calhoun* & *Bush* (DD) were sunk by suiciders.

## April 7

Still striking Okinawa, also we sighted the remains of the Jap fleet 1 BB (*Iowa* class) 2 CAs[19] and 10 DDs. All task groups sent in planes and there was a total of 386 planes in the attack, results, the battle ship took 13 torpedo hits and six 1,000 lb. armor piercing bombs, it then blew up and sank,[20] the cruisers also took the same and sank, three DDs were sunk, and 3 more damaged, they really took a beating. Good to hear that. We all got a "well done." The *Hancock* (CV)[21] took a suicider in the number elevator, she went back also, there are only five carriers out here now: *Hornet*, *Bennington*, *Essex*, *Yorktown*, and *Randolph*. Shot down 30 planes today, I saw a couple of them go down, they were only a thousand yards away, one made a run on the *Wisconsin*, dropped two bombs and missed, and tried to suicide in a DD also missed.

## April 8

*Randolph* and *Enterprise* joined the group, shot down two planes today: a Frances[22] and a Nick[23] at 15,000 ft. Our CAP[24] got one, still sending our planes into Okinawa, we are only 60 miles away.

## April 9

Place: Okinawa, sank a sub today. Got the contact at 1000 and stayed with it all day believed to be two of them. No air attacks today. The island was attacked by 6 Vals (dive bombers)[25] and two suicided the *Sterett* (DD 407) on the water line and the other in the super structure. The rest were shot down with no damage. Going to refuel tomorrow and I hope to Christ I get some mail, sure miss it and Marge. P51s are hitting Tokyo from Iwo Jima.

## April 10

Refueling 300 mi. off of Okinawa. We got mail.

## April 11

Today the Japs sent out an all-out attack on us, in which it lasted all day and half the night, two suicide planes tried to hit the *Missouri*, only one hit it without much damage, the other plane made a run on us (torpedo) and we shot it down about 1,000 yds. off our starboard beam. I saw him coming and saw him shot down. Boy he really came in fast but we were faster. Another DD was hit with 16 killed, but later heard that 20 were killed, total planes shot down today by (AA fire) are 4 Judys, 3 Zekes, 7 Tojos[26] and two Bettys. CAP got 1 Nick, 1 Kate,[27] 5 Bettys, 5 Zekes and 1 Mavis.[28]

---

19    CA was the hull classification symbol for a heavy cruiser.
20    Glavic is referring to the sinking of Japanese battleship Yamato. She and her sister ship, Musashi, were the heaviest and most powerfully armored battleships ever constructed.
21    CV is the hull classification for an aircraft carrier.

22    Frances was the reporting name for the Yokosuka P1Y *Ginga* (Galaxy), a twin-engine land-based bomber.
23    Nick was the reporting name for the Kawasaki Ki-45 *Toryu* (Dragon Slayer), a two-seat, twin-engine fighter used by the Imperial Japanese Army.
24    CAP stands for Combat Air Patrol.
25    Val was the Allied reporting name for the Aichi D3A carrier-based dive bomber and participated in nearly all Japanese naval actions.
26    Tojo was the designation name for the Nakajima Ki-44 *Shoki*, a single-engine fighter. Shoki is the Japanese pronunciation for Zhong Kui, a figure of Chinese mythology regarded as a vanquisher of ghosts and evil beings.
27    Kate was the designation name for the Nakajima B5N, the standard carrier torpedo bomber of the Japanese Navy.
28    Mavis was the designation name for the Kawanishi H6K, an Imperial Japanese Navy flying boat used for maritime patrol duties.

## April 12

We were under attack again last night and shot down 3 planes by the night fighters, then in the morning the Japs sent another all-out attack, these attacks came between 0800 to 1000 and 1400 till 1800. We shot down 1 Myrt,[29] 31 Zekes, 23 Vals, 3 Bettys, they did not hit any of our ships but they got two near misses and a suicide miss on the old *Enterprise*. The time now is 2210 and we are just securing, we heard a Jap broadcast that they are going to send an attack on us at 2320, about an hour from now, I hope they don't because I'm sleepy and would like to get some sleep.

## April 13

No attack last night, thank God. Was pretty peaceful today and didn't see any Japs.

## April 14

We are still around Okinawa, it is a month today and they still don't have all of the island which is only sixty miles long. Shot down a Zeke last night. We are now under attack and the results will come later. They sure were coming. The total is 23 planes shot down 18 Bettys, 3 Zekes, and 2 Judys. The *Hunt* and *Sigsbee* (DDs) were hit by bombs, no damage report yet.

## April 15

Splashed two Bettys last night by night fighters. Today the ship is two years old. 58.1 + 2 were under attack and shot down several planes, heading back to give them hell, vise versa.

## April 16

Was under attack again in the morning and again in the afternoon. 61 planes shot down by our fighters and 5 AA, *Intrepid* got a suicide, port side (No. 3 elevator), will leave formation to estimate the damage, she put her fire out in about an hour's time. One B25 was shot down during a small dog fight,

six ships were hit by suicide planes at Okinawa (1 DD sunk) picked up 5 men of the B25, one was killed. VF(N)[30] got 4 twin engine jobs after dark, was a very good coordinated attack by the Japs. They reported a torpedo heading for us after a Betty or Frances made her run, we made an eng. turn and missed it. One of our night fighters got 3 out of the 4 shot down during the night.

## April 17

Another large raid coming our way. We tally-hoed[31] them and there were 35 planes at 40 miles, our fighters (YKTN) got 21 of them, one pilot getting six before he ran out of ammo. Some of them got thru to our picket line (5 DDs ahead of us 50 miles).[32] One DD shot 6 of them down, received two near misses + 4 suiciders which glanced off, she still was making twenty knots. Pilots say the planes looked to be new, must be running them right out from the factory. Picked up an observer from a Frances we shot down 7 miles from us, he had a back injury when they brought him aboard, he looked to be about 17, when they bring the Jap aboard he doesn't have any clothes on, what a girl wouldn't give to be out here. Made the 23,000th landing.

## April 18

Still sending in strikes to Okinawa. The army still has ¼ of the island to go yet, no Bogey contacts all day, can't figure it out, must have shot all the planes down they had. Summary of what the TASK FORCE 58 has downed so far. From March 16 to April 18th: total 1660 Jap planes.

## April 19

Still no bogey contacts, they must be getting all their planes ready for a grand slam at us. 4 DDs

---

29    Myrt was the Allied reporting name for the Nakajima C6N *Saiun* (Iridescent Cloud). It was a carrier-based reconnaissance aircraft.

30    VF(N) was the U.S. Navy's designation for night fighter aircraft. The V indicates "fixed wing" and comes from *voloplane*, French for an aircraft sustained in the air by lifting surfaces as opposed to a hot air balloon or Zeppelin. The F indicates fighter aircraft and N stands for night fighter.

31    Tally-ho is what pilots said to their controller when visual contact was made with an enemy aircraft. It is a British phrase that originated from the activity of hunting with hounds, shouted when the rider following the hounds sees the fox.

32    Pickets were radar-equipped ships positioned around a force to protect it from surprise attack.

found a sub and stayed with it for 16 hours before they destroyed it.

## April 20

Refueling again, took aboard ammo from a AE and chow from a AK.[33] After that we will head back to the hot spot (northern tip of Okinawa). No bogeys today.

## April 21

At 0105 a Betty search plane was shot down by night fighters, not far from our formation, another one at 0220, sent CAP over the island, 94 fighters in all. Only 3 bogey contacts all day. All day only one passed over us at 31,000 ft. Too late to send fighters up that high, somebody shot him down, others were shot down by CAP. Betty came in at 2345, our fighter had bad radar so the other task group got it.

## April 22

Had another Betty shot down by VF(N) at 0140, then another at 0250 11 miles from the ship. Our front line pickets got one by (AA) YKTN. CAP shot down a Myrt at 30,000 ft. 20 miles from the formation, he was right over our heads once, Jill was shot down at 35,000, 80 miles from our formation, those high planes were painted all white, 25 planes were shot down over Okinawa.

## April 23

No Japs whatsoever, for once we get some rest and a good night's sleep.

## April 24

Refueled and took on ammo, *CV-38* U.S.S. *Shangri-La* joined our task group. She makes things look a little better out here, it's about time they're bringing some of the carriers back out here. Switched captains, Capt. Comb left on a tanker, Capt. Boone took over. No action on Okinawa.

## April 25

Still in the fueling area, took on chow today, our chow has been getting pretty bad lately. Headed back to Indian country (Jap territory).

## April 26

Still no bogeys all day, pretty good duty now, were up to Okinawa and saw the island — B29s have been hitting Kyushu for the past couple of days, guess that's what's holding them back. Few bogeys over Okinawa, but nothing serious.

## April 27

Still around Okinawa, no bogeys, B-29s still over Kyushu, we had a barrage balloon at 48,000 ft. last night, then another at 15,000. Night fighters hit it because we followed it right down to the water, you can tell a balloon because it goes the speed of the wind following the same course. Okinawa was under attack at night, the hospital ship U.S.S. *Comfort* got a suicide hit, 40 killed, the plane landed right in the surgery, she had spot lights on the red cross but it didn't stop this Jap. It was a 50 plane raid — 27 shot down. Pretty bad night.

## April 28

Refueling today, Ward was transferred to a tanker for duty in Uncle Sugar.[34] No bogeys.

## April 29

0300 *Shangri-La* night fighters shot down a Betty 40 miles east of our formation, the first plane she has to her credit. Pretty quiet in the morning, in the afternoon we picked up a big raid at 70 miles + intercepted, VF[35] shot down 3 Zekes + the others got in to us. *Wisconsin* (BB) shot down one with our help (I saw that), he was diving on the (BB) and fell in the water about 500 feet from it, they were pretty lucky. Two DDs got hit by suiciders (the *Hazelwood* + *Haggard*). *Hag.* got 2 hits and *Hazel*

---

33   AK is the hull classification symbol for a cargo ship.

34   Uncle Sugar: the U.S. government's waste of taxpayer's money, or stinginess of not providing the expected equipment. In this case, Glavic means that Ward was transferred to a less than desirable ship.

35   VF was the designation for a fighter squadron.

1, but they did a lot of damage. Hag. is under tow by a CL[36] *San Diego* + *St. Louis*, what a life, where in hell is my transfer. Another attack was sent at us at 0130, 2 planes were shot down, they kept us up till 0345 and we had to get up at 0450, so you see how much sleep we got. Was only 65 miles from Okinawa.

**April 30**

3 Tonys[37] were shot down near our group about 0800 by the CAP at 24,000 ft. Guess they were looking for us and found us. No other bogies all day (thank God).

**May 1**

45 miles away from Okinawa. No Japs around yet, we landed three F4Us from the beach who were lost, they were low on gas and it's the first time they ever made a carrier landing (2 Marine Capt. and a Major). All three came in perfect. Still sending our planes to the beach to bomb what land we don't have. Just got word that Mussolini was executed, one down and two to go. Made Second Class. Nine months to go before I make 1st Class.

**May 2**

Refueling today, no bogeys, all was peaceful, the hospital ship *Bountiful* was here to pick up the fellows that got hurt. Saw a couple of nurses, first women I saw since I left Frisco on October 13th. Sure were a sight for sore eyes.

**May 3**

No bogeys today, weather was pretty bad, B-29s are hitting southern Tokyo and they're doing a good job of keeping the Japs away.

**May 4**

Night fighters started things off by shooting at an Emily (flying boat, 4 motors).[38] He was just about to land when the night fighter helped him down. 0130 then the other VF(N)-3 got himself three Bettys within a 1½ hr. So I guess the Japs are looking for us again. 0930 we sighted (on our radar) a big raid coming down from the north. All carriers sent all their planes after them, *Yorktown* getting 35, *Essex* 35, *Shangri-La* 10, *Independence* 4. Then the beach had three night fighters there too, estimated 300 planes came down, none got into the formation, but some did get into the beach, hitting and bombing the ships. Since we've been out on this operation, we covered 23,000 miles, 400 miles a day, boy, that's moving around when you don't go anywhere. We have been out 52 days so far and still going strong. We're eating no fresh vegetables or fruits, all canned stuff or powdered, very little meat or sugar, no milk, sometimes no bread, boy they're really making us tighten up our belts, but the longer we stay out here, the sooner the war will be over. Our speed is 18.5 kts. (average). Japs tried to land behind our troops, 13 full barges of them, about 600, the barges were caught and sunk and all troops killed, none got in. A (CVE) U.S.S. *Sangamon* was hit by a suicide boy and was burning fiercely but they later put the fire out and everything was under control, last report only 300 survivors but they think they have more on other ships. Marines have moved south to help the Army, they are already making gains and making the army look sick. U.S.S. *Biloxi* was hit by a suicide boy. No report on damage. 7 destroyers were sunk off Okinawa, one DD took 3 suicide hits, boy, they sure are using a lot of "Special Corp" men.

**May 5**

Very peaceful today, no bogeys.

**May 6**

Same as yesterday, no bogeys.

---

36   CL was the hull classification symbol for a light cruiser.
37   Tony was the designation name for the Kawasaki Ki-61 *Hien* (flying swallow). It was used by the Imperial Japanese Army Air Force. It was the only mass-produced Japanese fighter of the war to use a liquid-cooled inline "V" engine.

---

38   Emily was the reporting name for the Kawanishi H8K flying boat, used for maritime patrol duty.

**May 7**

Refueled today, took on ammo + chow (22 tons). Had AA practice. Was repairing the fight deck because it sure is tore up from the landing planes.

**May 8**

Weather was bad, ceiling zero, rained all day. Only had search planes (ours) from Okinawa and they were flying by their instruments. We had no flights and no bogeys.

**May 9**

Weather is better, sent in planes to the beach. One of our planes came in (TBM)[39] and folded his wings and at the same time fired his guns, killing one man and injuring 19. Three men are pretty bad. One man who died was an Ensign, one Chief lost his left arm. The rest I don't know how they are. Besides that it's quiet out.

**May 10**

We had a bogey come in the morning and got 30 miles to the south of us and the *Shangri-La* planes shot it down (A-26 1 Judy). When going down he threw out a parachute with a silver box on it. Planes shot it down. Then in the afternoon another came in at 30,000. He came in to 7 miles, but turned away, he also threw out a big parachute with a box on it, I wonder what they're up to now with these parachutes and boxes, they might use them to give our position away or RCM gear to jam our radar.[40] Buried the Ensign today, otherwise quiet out today. Made our 25,000 landing by Fox 17.

**May 11**

The *Langley* just came back to our Task Group. Went out to fix its boilers. Had a bogey at 0145 last night, sharp shooter (*Shangri-La*) nighters tried to shoot it down but missed, chased it for 100 miles or more, then it got away. Secured at 0300 (no

sleep again). Well here we go again, picked up our first bogey at 0800 and shot it down, a Judy, then at 1000 we had a couple more, 58.3 was under attack and the *Bunker Hill* took two suicide bombers, one in No. 3 elevator, the other frame 70 (C.I.C. frame 86). Nothing went below the hanger deck, fire rooms were smoked out but were later back in. *Sullivan* picked 151 men out of the water, *Waldron* picked 97, other DDs picked up 10. All together there were 269 picked out of the water. We passed a couple of bodies but they were dead already, the only bogey came in to 18 miles from us. She will go back to the states again. Got a report that DD *Hadley (DD774)* shot down 23 and CAP, 12, the island was under attack all morning and it was quiet in the afternoon, we pulled out and are now heading for Ulithi (900 miles). It will be two months that we spent up here at Okinawa shooting down over 2,000 planes, traveled over 24,000 miles. Ate beans, rice, and hamburger. Pulled out at 1830.

**May 12**

Well we're on our way back now and will have gunnery exercises, fired, and had simulation air attacks, beside that it was the same, had muster and chaplain gave a victory pray. Had movies on the hangar deck; have the mid watch tonight.

**May 13**

Mother's Day. Hope mom got the flowers. Still on our way to Ulithi, boy it will feel good to get away for awhile. Holding AA practice.

**May 14**

Anchored in Ulithi 1215 and started to load the ship, boy they don't waste time.

**May 15**

Alongside repair ship *Jason*.

**May 16**

The *Bunker Hill* just pulled in and she was hit by suicide plane, boy she really was beat up.

---

39   The Grumman TBM Avenger torpedo bomber. TBM was the designation for aircraft manufactured by General Motors.
40   RCM stands for radio countermeasure.

**May 17**
Still in Ulithi and it really is hot in here.

**May 20**
Painted the ship a different color — took the camouflage off and painted it all blue. The *Enterprise* pulled in today and she was also beat up by suicides, the *Bunker Hill* and *Enterprise* will be going back to the states. Another big carrier came out from the states, called *Ticonderoga*, she had the "Fighting Lady" painted on her stack, boy that's robbery.

**May 22**
Bishop was transferred today —

**May 23**
Had AA practice all day —

**May 24**
Pulled out of Ulithi at 0600 for another operation, where it will be I don't know as yet, more than likely back to Okinawa, the ground forces have seven miles to go yet and the Japs are sending all their zoot suiters (suicide planes).[41] So I guess that's where we're going. It never fails, we're always looking for trouble, we should reach there in a couple of days, we are now under a new exec., Comdr. Evans, he doesn't seem so good, but time will tell.

**May 25**
Still on our way to Okinawa, had AA practice, heard that the weather was pretty hot there; about 80 degrees, oh well it wouldn't be the first time. Still having trouble there with zoot suiters, 500 B-29s hit Japan today.

**May 26**
Nothing doing today, routine —

"The *Bunker Hill* took two suicide bombers, one in No. 3 elevator, the other frame 70 . . . . " National Archives photo # 80-G-274266.

**May 27**
Refueled today, joined 58.1 and 58.3 (we're 58.4). We are changing from the 5th Fleet to the 3rd Fleet, Halsey's the boss now and he's on the *Missouri*.

**May 28**
At Okinawa now and sending in our planes. Our group shot down 4 Japs so far, 38.3 got 11 Japs, total shot down 77 for the day, weather bad, raining.

**May 29**
Still at Okinawa, no Japs yet, weather still bad, we have Cedric Foster aboard (commentator) and he made a broadcast to the States by way of Guam, to date 59,000 Japs have been killed but more will follow, we had 25,000 casualties and 5,000 which are dead, a Jap plane landed on Okinawa and a bunch of Japs came a running out throwing hand grenades at our parked planes, they got a couple of them but none of the Japs are alive to tell it.[42] 500 B-29s are

---

41  "Zoot suiter" may be a slang derivative from the 1943 Zoot Suit riots in Los Angeles. Marines and Sailors fought with migrant Mexican youth who were perceived as being anti-American because of the extravagant zoot suits they wore during a time of rationing and wartime clothing restrictions.

---

42  The attacks on the parked planes is a reference to the *Giretsu Kuteitai* (Heroic Paratroopers) an airlifted special forces unit of the Japanese Army. The unit was formed from Army paratroopers in November 1944 as a last-ditch attempt to reduce and delay Allied bombing raids on the Japanese Home Islands.

hitting Yokohama today. Also 105 P-51s, B-29s by day and P51s at night and that keeps them on the run. The zoot suiters got a couple more DDs (destroyers). It seems that the Japs are picking on our DD's instead of the carriers, weather is still bad and they're only gaining by the yards on the beach. The DDs hit yesterday were *Lloyd*, *Lenore* and *San Luel*, the DD *Drexel* was hit and sunk, 38.3 left us to go to Ulithi or Leyte.

## May 30

Strikes against Okinawa, Army and Marines gained a little more today. 3 more DDs hit: *Anthony*, 5 killed, *Schubert*, many killed, and the *Brane*, so far 60,000 Japs have been killed and still going strong. The last B-29 raid on Tokyo reported that 51% of the city was destroyed, 115 Jap planes were shot down on a big raid on Okinawa (Monday). Steak for chow.

## May 31

Foggy weather, couldn't do much today, sent planes over Okinawa. They only have 3 more miles to go yet and then we'll have their island, mud has stopped the trucks on the road. DD *Schubert* announced 11 killed and 28 missing (blown overboard or else jumped). It was hit by a suicide plane carrying a phosphorus bomb, 435 hit Tokyo again, destroyed 16 square miles and lost 7 planes, six were seen getting into rafts which a PBM[43] dropped to them, the PBMs have destroyed 92,000 tons of Jap shipping and splashed 32 Jap planes since they have been on search sectors. 437 Jap planes were shot down in the last 11 days, the war correspondents are leaving and their names are Cedric Foster — Mutual Broadcasting, Mr. Luce — Time Magazine, Lt. Brity — Navy Dept. We had fried chicken for chow.  8 Japs were shot down today,

APD[44] — *Tantrun*[45] splashed 4 and then was hit by a zoot suiter.

## June 1

Refueled today — no mail — will start north to hit Kyushu, that's where we got hit on March 19, my birthday.

## June 2

Surprise no Japs came out after us, T.G.[46] 38.1 sent planes in for Okinawa, 38.4 (that's us) sent 130 fighters into Kyushu to look for Jap planes, they have to go over 300 miles one way, bad weather made it hard to find their target, they did destroy 14 planes on the ground, damaged 11, the only opposition were two float planes which were shot down with no trouble at all, one of our pilots was forced down in the bay at the southern tip of the island, a PBY-4 was sent in to pick him up.[47] Well, the PBY-4 crashed in doing so, then we sent in a PBM to pick up the 12 men, they were in sight of the Jap airfield, the field had barrage balloons around it, but the men were picked up OK. At Okinawa a DD *Griswold* fired one shot and knocked a Betty out of the sky (good work on that). Also one of our subs captured an island 150 miles south of Honk Kong, they shelled the Is., then sent a landing party ashore and captured it. They destroyed a weather station and buildings. Iwo Jima was under attack and 3 were killed, 25 wounded. Our planes took pictures of Kyushu and the B-29s sure did a good job of bombing.

## June 3

Sent strikes into Kyushu, no Japs were out, weather was bad. Five of our pilots were shot down over the target, photos show that every hangar on six airfields were destroyed by B-29s. We catapulted 80

---

Giretsu operations were to be undertaken at night. Commando units would be inserted onto a target airfield by crash landing their transports. On the night of 24 May the Giretsu attacked Yontan airfield on Okinawa. Five transports managed to crash land. Ten raiders, armed with submachine guns and explosives killed two U.S. servicemen, destroyed 70,000 gallons of fuel, nine aircraft and damaged 29 more before being killed.

43   PBM: The Martin PBM Mariner was a patrol bomber flying boat.

44   APD: Destroyers and destroyer escorts that were converted into high-speed transports. AP stood for transport, D for destroyer.

45   USS *Tatum APD-81*.

46   Task Group.

47   PBY: The Consolidated PBY Catalina was an amphibious aircraft used in anti-submarine warfare, patrol bombing, convoy escorts and search and rescue missions.

planes for a new record, we are nearly up to our 4,000 mark without an accident. Still fighting on Okinawa, things are slow because of the rain and mud, all units are bogged down. T.G. 31 (ships in Okinawa) reported the following loss and damage to the ships up to May 31, sunk 10 destroyers, 1 mine sweeper, 1 APD, 10 landing craft, 3 AKs, 2 AM, 174 damaged [?], 44 DDs, 8 BBs, 2 CA, 2 CL, 19 DEs[48] and 13 transports. Several DDs were hit twice and repaired, but the DD *Cowell* was hit three times and repaired, 13 Japs were shot down off Okinawa today, looks like they'll never give up. Most of these are suicide planes, that's what is doing all the damage to the ships in the harbor out there.

## June 4

Typhoon heading our way, so all flights canceled and we're heading east to avoid it doing 25 knots. Trying to miss it but the typhoon is moving at 75 knots with an 80 knot wind. Still moving slow on Okinawa, we are dropping supplies by parachute to the troops because of the mud, 36 Japs were shot down over Okinawa, so far 1,442 Jap planes have been shot down over Okinawa. Ships in the harbor got 435 since May 11, 64,000 Jap troops killed so far, they think it will be over 100,000 because they still have a little to go yet.

## June 5

We got the tail end of the typhoon and it was pretty rough out, no damage was done to our group, but 38.3 thought they would go another way and they got right in the middle of it and here's what happened. The CVs *Hornet* and *Bennington* had their flight decks cave in because of a big wave. The CA *Pittsburgh* lost its bow (100 ft.) at 1845, the bow stayed afloat, so they towed it in to Guam where they will reassemble it. We didn't refuel today because it's too rough, the tankers have mail for us. We are suppose to hit Okinawa tomorrow, but I guess they will change their minds.

## June 6

Sent planes over Okinawa and also refueled. Haven't seen any Jap planes around lately, made the 26,000 landing today, we also catapulted our 4,000 without an accident. Boy that's good. A fellow was hit by a prop, got him right behind the right leg. He's ok, heard that Russia entered the war, that's good to hear. Maybe it will all be over soon. The *Hornet* + *Bennington* destroyed 25 ft. of their flight deck. The cruiser *Louisville* was hit by a zoot suiter yesterday, 8 killed, 17 wounded. Little gains on Okinawa. Operations in their final stage (I hope).

## June 7

Our planes found 4 Japs and shot them down, still sending planes in to parachute supplies to the troops. Our planes found 7 more Japs later in the day, looks like good hunting for our boys. One of our planes (SB2C)[49] crashed into the water. Pilot was killed but the crewman got out. 65,000 Japs killed, 573 P.O.W. The fighters from the beach got 20 Japs today, not bad (Marine pilots). The BB *Mississippi* was hit by a zoot suiter, one killed, 4 wounded, one of our subs sank 19 small ships with its deck guns south of Honk Kong.

## June 8

Decided to send our planes up to Kyushu, also sent more planes to Okinawa to drop more supplies. The island is just about secured now and TG 31, report 5,964 casualties around Okinawa (Navy casualties). Two patrols (PBMs) shot down 3 Japs while on their patrol, funeral was held for Ensign Watson who was killed in the SB2C crash, funeral at 1300. We are going to Leyte.

## June 9

Refueled today. A P-38 showing off crashed on the *Randolph* killing 4 and destroying 10 planes when it was going into Leyte Gulf.[50]

---

48   Destroyer escort.

49   Curtiss Helldiver, a carrier-based single-engine bomber.
50   The Lockheed P-38 Lightning was a twin-engine, twin-boom fighter aircraft with a central nacelle containing the cockpit and armament. On 7 June, two P-38s

**June 10**

No excitement, had AA practice, found two King Fishers that were on the water for 3 days, they belong to the BB *New York* in Leyte, what they were doing out here we don't know. Pilots were OK. Today we started for the Philippines (Leyte). Beer situation there is bad (darn it all). DD *Porter* was hit by a zoot suiter, boy I'm glad we're getting out of there.

**June 11**

B-29s (300) are hitting Tokyo today with 100 P51s as escort, it will be the second time in 24 hrs. 1 B-29 was lost. 26 Japs were shot down. Army Air Force hit Kyushu + Formosa. 27 Japs were shot down + 7 surface craft were sunk. 392,116 dead Japs have been counted in the Philippines. The Japs have been forced into the southern end of Okinawa, there are 20,000 Japs + 50,000 civilians in that corner. Weather is hot.

**June 12**

DD *Porter* who was hit by zoot suiter is now reported sunk. Will get to Leyte tomorrow. It's hotter today.

**June 13**

Anchored in Leyte at 1545, nice looking place with high mountains + green grass. It's really hot here. Eight months ago today we sailed from Frisco.

**June 14**

Raining — 71,000 Japs reported killed on Okinawa this date.

**June 15, 16, 17**

Raining — Air Group 9 left us and Air Group 88 coming aboard. Had G.Q. at 2130 turned out to be a C-54.[51]

**June 18, 19, 20, 21, 22**

Still loafing in Leyte, we went ashore a couple of times to drink beer and look around. Not much there.

**June 23**

Okinawa is ours now, the invasion was on Easter Sunday and ended this date. It lasted 82 days. We were there 60 days. 89,000 Japs killed so far and 4,096 Jap planes destroyed, we lost 91 ships (sunk), 54 damaged, 9,600 killed and 25,000 wounded. So you can see we both took a beating but the best man won.

**June 26**

Left San Pedro Bay at 0610 to qualify Air Group 88, AA practice and plane drills, suppose to return about 0900 in the morning. A bomb was thrown over board and the damn thing went off and shook the hell out of the ship, nobody was hurt.

**June 28**

Returned to San Pedro Bay this morning and anchored at 0835.

**June 29**

Loafing as always. Got word that Luzon was secured, it was invaded Jan. 2 and 113,000 Japs were killed there alone. Admiral Nimitz announced that from March 18 to June 10, our navy had 4,907 men killed and 4,825 wounded, that was while we were up at Okinawa. The complete total is 12,000 killed and 34,000 wounded, so far they have 9,500 Japs who have surrendered on Okinawa.

**July[52]**

Pulled up anchor at 0655 and started out of San Pedro Bay, don't know where we're going, but they are giving us winter clothing, so it must be up north (Tokyo).

---

buzzed the *Randolph* at anchor off Leyte. One of the pilots cut it too close and crashed on deck, killing himself and eleven sailors.

51  Douglas C-54 Skymaster was a four-engined transport aircraft.

52  The first two entries for July 1945 appear without dates.

**July**

A 17 gun salute for Asst. Sect. of Navy for Air who is on the *Shangri-La*. He and Admiral Fitch landed aboard the "Y" at 1330 for a visit with Admiral Radford. It's getting a little cooler —

**July 4**

Turkey for chow, ice cream, pie, cigars, AA practice.

**July 5**

Going north.

**July 6**

Just got a report that the DD *Porter* and *Twiggs* were lost at Okinawa cost them 244 men killed. (Boy that ain't good.)

**July 7**

Had our first accident on the catapult, the plane, an F4U,[53] was thrown in the water and caught fire, the pilot got out alright, we have 37 F4Us aboard.

**July 8**

Refueled today, mail, the British are just north of us and they have a flag ship, BB *King George V*, 6 cruisers, 3 carriers + 17 destroyers.

**July 9**

Closing in on Tokyo, about 300 mi. out. At 2000 will launch our planes from a distance of 140 miles. YKTN will launch 140 planes, all Task Groups (38.1 — 38.3 — 38.4) altogether there will be 1,440 planes launched at Tokyo, then tonight B-29s will hit Tokyo, so it will go on day and night.

**July 10**

Reveille 0200, launched strikes against Tokyo, pickings were slim, all air fields in good condition, good flying weather, lost two planes, one pilot rescued. 1 small ship sunk, 2 planes destroyed and 100 destroyed on the ground, no planes air borne

at 1345 we had a little action. Three Japs tried to get at us. 38.1 shot down a Frances. *Cowpens* shot down a Dinah,[54] the other got away, at 0745 a fellow took a chock[55] from a wheel of a plane as it was warming. The chock hit the prop and it flew back and hit him (R.B. Miller). Well he died of internal injuries, they couldn't do a thing for him, I say that because I saw him right after he got hit.

**July 11**

Reveille 0130 AM, going north. Results of yesterday's strike on Tokyo, our group (*Yorktown*) dropped 46.3 tons of bombs and 14 rockets were used. They destroyed 22 planes on the ground, 21 damaged, no Japs seen in the air, TG 38 damaged 249 planes on the ground they reported 439 single engine and 94 twin engine Jap planes damaged on the ground. Also seen 279 dummies on the ground.

**July 12**

Refueling today, no mail. Raining and cold outside, sleeping under blankets + wearing jackets. We will strike tomorrow, northern Honshu and southern Kuriles.

**July 13**

Nine months ago today left Frisco. All strikes cancelled due to bad weather. Reveille 0130. Taps 2000 (8 p.m.).

**July 14**

Rev. 0130, the BBs *Mass.* + *Indiana*, *South Dakota*, cruisers *Quincy* and *Chicago*, nine DDs went into 3 miles of Honshu and shelled the beach, Kamashi, Honshu, sent planes in also, no planes airborne. Several destroyed on the ground but 60 small ships sunk, 2 Des, 3 railroad ferries sunk, 2 damaged, one left burning at the dock. 27 rail road locomotives destroyed, one large merchant ship sunk, several

---

53  F4U: Vought F4U Corsair single-engine fighter aircraft.

54  Dinah was the reporting name for the Mitsubishi Ki-46, a twin-engine reconnaissance aircraft.

55  Wheel chocks are blocks made of wood or some other sturdy material that are placed in front and behind the wheels of an aircraft, holding it motionless, and are removed before take off.

factories destroyed, dropped 36.9 tons of bombs on them. Shot a Jap Betty down at 1225, 75 miles from the ship.

**July 15**
Strikes on Honshu and Hokaido going on today. Also the BBs *Iowa*, *Wisconsin*, *Missouri*, *N. Carolina* and *Alabama*, cruisers *Atlanta*, *Dayton* and Destroyers for screen. Went into the beach to shell it. They picked on the iron works at Hokaido. Admiral Halsey is on the *Missouri*. A Navy PBY (Dumbo) picked up six crewman from a B-25, the load was so great that she couldn't take off so she taxied to base (Iwo) 125 miles. The work of the day, 15 ships sunk, 24 damaged, 429 planes destroyed or damaged, the BBs poured 1,000 tons of "sixteen" shells into the iron works at Hokaido. The result is that the iron works are no longer there.

**July 16**
Refueled, no mail, British fleet refueled with us.

**July 17**
Very bad weather, all operations cancelled, all our battleships, cruisers, and destroyers left the group to shell the coast of Honshu north of Tokyo.

**July 18**
The BBs did alright last night. Several tons of shells were fired into Honshu. Weather bad this morning, but strikes sent in this afternoon, the target was a Jap battleship in dry dock, the planes got four direct hits and two near misses, 1 flak barge armed with 20 AA guns was sunk, 1 DD left burning, one of our planes failed to return. The *Bon Homme Richard* lost two night fighters due to bad weather.

**July 20**
Refueled and mail (Glavic none).

**July 21**
Taking on bombs and food.

**July 22**
Still fueling because BBs take a long time to load 16 inch shells.

**July 23**
Finished refueling, rearming and taking aboard supplies. Heading for Jap land. Shot down a balloon today, was carrying a bomb, one of those they launched toward the States; I saw it, it was a white balloon porcupine bomb with 20 foot cable lines dangling below. It didn't explode, but we didn't fool around with it when it landed, it was at 10,000 feet and we had it on our radar.

**July 24**
Striking today — results — strafed ships, a small carrier hit (CVE). Several planes destroyed on the ground, no airborne, a cruiser was found and 11 bombers went after it, *Yota* class. Also hit the BB again, smaller ships were hit, 3 locomotives destroyed, 3 damaged, 3 of our planes were shot down, they were jumped by 12 Jacks. Four of our planes low on gas landed in the water. All pilots saved. Shot down a Frances near our group.

**July 25**
Bad weather over target. Most strikes cancelled. Several Japs were shot down trying to get at us. A Myrt + Betty were shot down near us. The others were shot down by "Limeys." I saw them shot down. It's a lot of fun to see them hit the water. Otherwise it is no fun. A PBM made an emergency landing inside our group, he was in the air 13 hrs. and low on gas, made a 600 mile trip to pick up a downed pilot, he got back to us and landed, then all hands got in a boat and went to a DD standing by, then the DD sank the plane.

**July 26**
Refueled + rearm. No mail.

**July 27**
Rearmed — AA practice.

**July 28**

Striking Honshu, damaged 33 planes, destroyed 2 hangars, AA fire was heavy, 5 of our planes were hit but made it back, a sub picked up seven downed pilots from other ships, one Frances was shot down by 38.3.

**July 29**

Pulled out for a day of rest, had a movie on hangar deck. Only 120 miles from Japan, our BBs, CLs and some DDs left this afternoon to shell the coast. They use about 1,000 tons on every shelling. We sent in night fighters to cover the bombardment group.

**July 30**

Striking again and this time we were in to 45 miles of the island (that's too damn close). Japs sent a suicide group to Okinawa and they sank two of our DDs. The planes they sent were made out of plywood and only could do 90 kts. Boy the Japs are really hard up for planes now. 5 Jap subs were sunk in Kure naval base. Another PBM landed in our group and we sank it, he landed at night. Two destroyers turned their search lights on to help him: he made it alright.

**July 31**

Refueled, no mail.

**August 1**

Took on provisions for the group. Will stay here for a while till we get further orders.

**August 2**

Just got word that the cruiser *Indianapolis* was sunk by torpedoes.[56]

**August 3**

Still roaming around out here waiting to see what will happen, so far everything is going along alright.

**August 4, 5 + 6**

Still in the same place + no dope yet.

**August 7**

Pres. Truman gave the Japs six days to surrender, we strike tomorrow for the first time since July 30. A Jap hospital ship was sighted and so we sent a destroyer (*Taylor*) to investigate her, a force went aboard and found contraband, she was coming from Wake Island and so she had to pull in one of our ports, they will take all men off of her and sink it, that was a sight for sore eyes.

**August 8**

Pretty foggy out today. All strikes cancelled. Shot down a Dinah, 35 miles away. The Chaplain gave us some dope on the atomic bomb. Boy, some weapon.

**August 9**

Strikes launched against Honshu. Raid after raid came after us, 13 in all. One Jap Myrt made a suicide dive on the *Wasp* (CV). We opened fire on it and it was hit, so he missed the *Wasp* by 10 yds. 3 men were burned from the explosion when he hit the water (I saw that). It was only 4,500 yards away from us. Too close for comfort. 20 planes destroyed on the ground. BBs and CLs shelled the coast again, heard B-29s dropped second atomic bomb. DD *Borie* was hit by a Jap suicide plane, 45 miles from us.

**August 10**

Still in the same place, no Japs as yet, sending strikes in, 1 plane was shot down but the pilot was picked up by one of our subs. The sub shelled the

---

56  After delivering the world's first operational atomic bomb to Tinian Island on 26 July, the *Indianapolis* reported to CINPAC (Commander-in-Chief, Pacific) Headquarters at Guam for further orders. She was directed to join the battleship USS *Idaho* at Leyte Gulf in the Philippines to prepare for the invasion of Japan. The USS *Indianapolis,* unescorted, departed Guam and at 14 minutes past midnight on 30 July, midway between Guam and Leyte Gulf, she was hit by two torpedoes. The first blew away her bow, the second struck midship on the starboard side adjacent to a fuel tank and powder magazine. The resulting explosion split the ship to the keel. Within minutes she rolled to starboard and sank. Of the ships

1,197 crewmen, only 317 survived. It was the greatest single loss of life at sea in the history of the U.S. Navy.

coast with 5 inch shells, just for the hell of it. Made 29,000th landing today, at 2100 the Captain announced over the loud speaker that the Japs were ready to surrender, we were at lat. 37° - 50'. Long. 144° - 59'.

## August 11
Japs surrender not confirmed but we're all waiting anxiously. We are refueling today.

## August 12
Still no word from Japs about final surrender, if nothing comes in before morning then we will strike, they picked 10% of the fleet to go ashore on Japan when surrender terms are final, no one from our group can go.

## August 13
Striking today, shot down 21 Japs who were trying to get their last crack at us (they all had bombs on them). They kept coming out from early morning till 6 at night. Still awaiting word from Japan. Will refuel tomorrow.

## August 14
Got word that there will be a ship coming out with 3,339 bags of mail for our group. The Japs finally took our terms but nothing official yet. We will strike till the word comes to "cease firing."

## August 15
THE WAR IS OVER. 3 years, 8 months, 7 days. We launched a strike and the planes were ten miles from Tokyo and were told to return (0634). 16 Jap fighters jumped our formation and we lost 4 planes. But 14 Japs were shot down. We were told if we saw any more Japs that we should shoot them down in a friendly manner. At 0812, the President said that all hostilities had stopped, we are 100 miles from Tokyo. Long 142° - 12' Lat 33° - 57'. Raised peace flags and Admiral's flag (two stars for Radford). At 1115 then at 1125 a Jap Judy was shot down. So we still have to keep our eyes and ears open. Admiral

Halsey made a speech to the group and while he was talking, six zeros were shot down. In all, 22 Japs have been shot down today. We are moving out to 210 miles from Japan, just for safety measures. MacArthur made Supreme Commander of all allied groups.

## August 16
Nothing much doing. From May 12th to August 15th T.F. 38 is credited with the following: 290 planes shot out of the air, 1,301 destroyed on the ground, 1,374 damaged. Refuel tomorrow.

## August 17
Adm. Nimitz said that when the war ended, the 3rd Fleet had 105 warships and 28 British.

## August 18
Refueled. Mail boat was here and we unloaded mail for our group on to the *Yorktown* and it took all day.

## August 19
Jap envoys headed for IE Shima (island where Pyle was killed) for a conference with Doug.[57] After they get to IE Shima then one of our planes will take them to Manilla. The Japs were supposed to fly an all white plane with a green x on its side and wings, they got there too in that color plane.

## August 20
Essex and eight British ships joined our Group (38.4) including *King George V*. All our Marines were transferred to a transport *Ozark*. They will go in to occupy Japan. Lt. Gen. Wainwright was rescued from the Japs. BB *Penna* was hit by a suicide plane August 14th. Extensive damage done to the BB. Doug says he will go ashore in ten days.

## August 22
Still nothing doing. We're standing by for the landing, just in case something goes wrong. Landing

---

57   Ernie Pyle was a Pulitzer Prize-winning American journalist.

will be made next Sunday. All planes of TF 38 were launched at 1130 for a group picture. What a sight. 981 planes were launched, 543 fighters, 124 fighter bombers, 182 torpedo planes, 12 bombers, 16 British Sea Fires, 4 Fire Flys. *Essex* didn't launch, no reason. Getting hot.

## August 23
Still cruising around. Got word on the atomic bombs. The 1st killed 60,000, wounded 100,000 and left 200,000 homeless. The second did worse. 120,000 killed, 200,000 wounded, left 250,000 homeless. Boy, I wouldn't want to be there at the time.

## August 24
Still cruising around doing nothing —

## August 25
Bad weather. Occupation of Japan delayed two days. Three typhoons in our vicinity (oh my God). Getting cool.

## August 26
Still loafing — weather very bad. Two P-38s landed in Kyushu and the Japs greeted them. Boy, those people changed in a hurry. Then a B-17 landed and picked up the pilots.

## August 27
A Task Force led by the *Missouri* entered Tokyo Bay. The landings will be made Thursday. The group in the Harbor will consist of 12 BBs, 18 CVs, 4 CVLs-6, 20 CA and CLs and 101 DDs. They're going in with their guns loaded.

## August 28
15 planes landed at Atsugi Airfield. They were technicians and the Japs greeted them and they were well treated.

## August 29
Refueled — no mail.

## August 30
MacArthur landed at Tokyo. First American General to set foot in Japan. Most of the fleet moved into Tokyo Bay but the *Yorktown*, *Shangri-la* and the *Bon Homme Richard*, stayed out and did patrol duty. Admiral Nimitz moved into Tokyo Bay aboard the Battleship *South Dakota*.

## August 31
Occupation of Japan. Everything going along swell — no trouble. 2 years today we first attacked Marcus Island. Boy that was the day. War Dept. announced the casualties for this war: 1,070,000. Of this number, 200,000 killed, 120,000 prisoners, the rest were wounded.

## September 1
*Essex* left us and went to the U.S.A. (God's country). Still doing nothing.

## September 2, 1945
Surrender terms were signed aboard the *Missouri* in Tokyo Bay at 1044. President Truman proclaimed September 2nd as V.J. Day. I saw land today for the first time in 64 days. We moved in to 20 miles off the coast. The mountain of Fujiyama was visible at 1700, although it was 77 miles away. All planes from the 3 Task Groups plus 500 B-29s flew over the *Missouri* while the surrender terms were being signed, 117 days after V-E day.

— V.J. Day—

# References

### Atsushi Takizawa
## LONG SHADOW AT NOMONHAN
Translated for the author by Kazunori Tanoue

### Cleon Stewart
## KING RAT

Telephone interview with C. Leslie Carpenter, 22 July 2015.

Telephone interview with Belinda Carpenter Koenig, 23 July 2015.

Email correspondence with Mary Gage, 7, 12 and 13 February 2016.

Email correspondence with Rebecca Carpenter Heindel, 7 May 2016.

Tape recorded interview with Belinda Carpenter Koenig, 16 January 2016.

Excerpts from Air Vice-Marshall Sir Thomas Howell's diary printed with permission from his daughter, Mary Gage.

Travis Monday, *W. F. Matthews: Lost Battalion Survivor* (Lulu Enterprises 2007), 22-28.

Left: Nina and "Les" Carpenter, 1946. Photo credit: Rebecca Carpenter Heindel. Below: Carpenter's Changi Prison shoes. *Belinda Carpenter Koenig collection.*

### John Alderman & Crew
## USS McFARLAND AVD-14

Office of Naval Records and History, Ship's Histories Section, Navy Department, *History of USS McFarland (DD-237)*, 1952, 260.

Action Report, USS *McFarland AVD-14*, Serial 052, 15 December 1942.

Kent B. Brown, *Lt. Col. Harold William "Indian Joe" Bauer* posted at http://acepilots.com/bauer/usmc_bauer1.html.

A. B. Feuer, "Day of Battle Sealark Channel," *Sea Classics* (August 1994): 17-22.

Norman Edward Chalmers Archive, courtesy his daughter, Sande McLaughlin.

Telephone interview and email correspondence with Sande McLaughlin, 23, 26, 27, 29 and 30 October 2014.

Helmke  Nielson  Touchtone
Delong         Waughtel

Paul Helmke, who is featured in USS *McFarland AVD-14*, sent me this photograph. When asked where it was taken, he replied, "It was at Sherman's Dine and Dance in San Diego on my first liberty back in the USA after leaving the *McFarland* in Pearl Harbor. It was around Easter in 1943. I was waiting for my orders to new construction as the nucleus crew for USS *Bradford DD-545* at Bethlehem Shipyard, Terminal Island, Long Beach, California." A nucleus crew consists of selected experienced or specialized personnel who were assigned to inactive ships, or to a new ship 12 months prior to delivery, and typically consisted of two-fifths of the vessel's normal wartime complement of officers and men. This included specialists in fire control, gunnery and engineering who lived aboard and became familiar with the lay of the ship, its turrets and boiler rooms. The ship could be brought to operational readiness after delivery through the addition of relatively untrained crew members. I also asked Paul, "What was in the bottle that you were holding. Was it rum?" "Could be," said Paul, "but with my 92 years of memories, I'm afraid that detail is lost forever. Now, I did like rum and Coke, and the next morning I woke up under a car in a parking lot. I still had money in my pocket so I hadn't been rolled." *Author's collection.*

Telephone interview with Paul Helmke, 10 October 2015.

Email correspondence wth Paul Helmke, 9 June 2016.

Additional quotes taken from Paul Helmke's letter written to E. Andrew Wilde, 14 May 1995.

## Frank Schwable
# NIGHT FIGHTER

### General Reference Material

Aircraft Action Report VMF(N)-531, 13 November 1943, 20-23.
Aircraft Action Report VMF(N)-531, 14 - 15 November 1943, 23-26.
Aircraft Action Report VMF(N)-531, 3 December 1943, 1-18.
Aircraft Action Report VMF(N)-531, 12 January 1944, 16-20.
Aircraft Action Report VMF(N)-531, 5 February 1944, 21-26.
Aircraft Action Report VMF(N)-531, 9 February 1944, 27-32.
Aircraft Action Report Narrative, VMF(N)-531, 14 February 1944, 33-37.
Aircraft Action Report Narrative, VMF(N)-531, 16 February 1944, 38-43.
Aircraft Action Report Narrative, VMF(N)-531, 2-3 March 1944, 52-55.
Aircraft Action Report VMF(N)-531, 13 March 1944, 56-62.
Aircraft Action Report Narrative, VMF(N)-531, 10 April 1944, 47-48.
Aircraft Action Report VMF(N)-531, 10 May 1944, 60-62.

Oral history transcript of Brig. Gen. Frank H. Schwable, (USMC). Interviewer: Benis M. Frank. Marine Corps Combat Development Command, Marine Corps University, Research Archives, Gray Research Center, Quantico, Virginia, 1983.

Lt. Col. Robert O. Bisson (USMC), Calibration of GCI equipment over water in the South Pacific Area, 22 November 1943 Report to the Commandant, Headquarters, U.S. Marine Corps, 1-8.

Combat Experiences of VMF(N)-531, The Pioneer Twin Engine Night Fighter Squadron in the South Pacific, Serial #00347, 13 November 1943 – 13 March 1944, 1-13.

Combat Experiences of VMF(N)-531, The Pioneer Twin Engine Night Fighter Squadron in the South Pacific, 28 April 1944, 1-13.

Maj. William Moore (USMC), *Under the Cover of Darkness: A History of the First Night Fighter Squadron of World War Two* (Quantico, VA: Marine Corps Command and Staff College Education Center, May 1981).

Col. Charles Quilter II (USMC) and Capt. John C. Chapin (USMC), *A History of Marine Fighter Attack Squadron 531* (History and Museums Division Headquarters, U.S. Marine Corps, Washington D.C. 2001).

Col. Charles Quilter II (USMC), *A History of Marine Fighter Attack Squadron 531 (Part 1),* working draft (unpublished), History and Museums Division Headquarters, U.S. Marine Corps, Washington D.C. (June 1987). Charles Quilter II, the author of this unpublished manuscript, was also a pilot and joined Marine Attack Squadron 531 (VMFA-531) in 1965; he flew 252 combat missions in Vietnam with VMFA-323. His wife, Ann Hutchinson Quilter, is the daughter of Homer Hutchinson, who flew night missions with the RAF in England and was the executive officer of VMF(N)-533, which deployed to the Pacific in 1944 in Grumman Hellcats. It was the most successful American night fighter squadron in history. Quilter's unpublished 82-page working draft *A History of Marine Fighter Attack Squadron 531* was edited down to form the first 20 pages of a book by the same name published in 2001.

Col. Frank M. Schwable (USMC), Report of Marine Night Fighter Squadron 531 Operations in the South Pacific, 25 August 1943 – 25 November 1943. Report to the Commandant, Headquarters, U.S. Marine Corps, 1-9.

Col. Frank M. Schwable (USMC), Report of Marine Night Fighter Squadron 531 Operations in the South Pacific, 25 November 1943 – 25 February 1944. Report to the Commandant, Headquarters, U.S. Marine Corps, 1-11.

Col. Frank M. Schwable (USMC), Report of Marine Night Fighter Squadron 531 Operations in the South Pacific, 4 February 1944. Report to the Commandant, Headquarters, U.S. Marine Corps, 1-20.

Frank Schwable, *Warfare Operations Report A16-3.* This typescript 38–page document is part of the Schwable group of artifacts. *Author's collection.*

Robert Sherrod, *History of Marine Corps Aviation in World War II* (Presidio Press, 1980). 164-169.

War Diary Summary VMF(N)-531, May 1943, 1-3.
War Diary Summary VMF(N)-531, September 1943, 1-7.
War Diary Summary VMF(N)-531, November 1943, 1-18.
War Diary Summary VMF(N)-531, December 1943, 1-13.
War Diary Summary VMF(N)-531, October 1943, 1-15.
War Diary Summary VMF(N)-531, January 1944, 1-15.
War Diary Summary VMF(N)-531, February 1944, 1-20.
War Diary Summary VMF(N)-531, 20-21 March 1944, 17.
War Diary Summary VMF(N)-531, April 1944, 1-24.
War Diary Summary VMF(N)-531, May 1944, 36 -38.
War Diary Summary VMF(N)-531, June 1944, 2-14.
War Diary Summary VMF(N)-531, October 1944, 10-12.

### The Squadron's First Victory

Deck Log and War Diary for the USS *Denver*, 1-30 November 1943.

Action Report, USS *Columbia*, Report of Night Fighter Interception at 0420, 13 November 1943.

Videotaped interview with John O'Brien conducted by Paddy O'Brien, 2000.

Above: Leonard "Red" Martin's Arisaka rifle that he picked up while the USS *Denver* was in port. It was this rifle that led me to Martin's story about the torpedoing of *Denver* and the ship's connection to VMF(N)-531. *Author's collection.*

### The Squadron's First Combat Death

Col. Frank M. Schwable (USMC), Report of Marine Night Fighter Squadron 531 Operations in the South Pacific, 25 August 1943 – 25 November 1943, 4.

### Vindication

Combat Experiences of VMF(N)-531, The Pioneer Twin Engine Night Fighter Squadron in the South Pacific, Serial #00347, 13 November 1943 – 13 March 1944, 5 -7.

### Dupuy and Hicks Liason

Col. Frank M. Schwable, (USMC), Report of Marine Night Fighter Squadron 531 Operations in the South Pacific, 25 November 1943 – 25 February 1944. Report to the Commandant, Headquarters, U.S. Marine Corps, 1.

### The Art of Airborne Interception

AI Mark IV radar information provided by Norman Groom, Pitstone Green Museum, Pitstone, Buckinghamshire, England.

### Citizen Sailor Dupuy

Aircraft Action Report Narrative, VMF(N)-531, 14 February 1944, 35-36.

Email correspondence with Kyle Lemons (Dupuy's stepson), 25 April 2014, 25 August 2014.

Email correspondence with Sheilah Dupuy (Dupuy's daughter), 7 February 2014, 4 August 2015.

Samuel Eliot Morison *History of United States Naval Operations in World War II,* Vol. 6, *Breaking the Bismark's Barrier, 22 July 1942-1 May 1944* (Boston: Little, Brown and Company, 1950), 303.

Lt. Comdr. James S. Hunter (USN) and Lt. Max Hodge (USN), "Radar Cues the Navy Fighters, Part 1," *Popular Mechanics* (February 1946): 1- 6, 169-174.

Lt. Comdr. James S. Hunter (USN) and Lt. Max Hodge (USN), "Radar Cues the Navy Fighters, Part 3," *Popular Mechanics* (April 1946): 164-168, 238-240, 242.

James L. H. Peck, "Radar, Magic Eye That Sees the Invisible," *Popular Science* (September 1945): 65-71, 210, 214, 218, 222, 226,

IFF System Information:  VK2DYM's Radio and Radar Information posted at www.qsl.net/vk2dym/radio/iff.htm.

"Outline of Policy and Study Course," 10 April 1943, appendix V to Gray, "History of CIC School," NDL/HR.

Timothy S. Wolters, *Information at Sea: Shipboard Command and Control in the U.S. Navy, from Mobile Bay to Okinawa* (Baltimore: Johns Hopkins University Press, 2013), 214.

CIC [Combat Information Center] Manual (RADSIX), Radar Bulletin No. 6, posted at http://www.history.navy.mil/research/library/online-reading-room/title-list-alphabetically/c/cic--combat-information-center-manual-radsix.html.

### Relieved of Command

Merrill I. Skolnik, *Introduction to Radar Systems* (New York: McGraw Hill, 1969), 9-11.

### The Squadron's Last Days

Barrett Tillman, *U.S. Marine Corps Fighter Squadrons of World War II* (Osprey Publishing, 2014), 17.

Special thanks to Bob Gill for making the Schwable story possible.

Special thanks to fellow collector and militaria dealer Jeremy Severn for making the William Duffey story possible (page 94-95).

## Jones, Benoit, Wade, Karcher & Pollard
# 2nd MARINE DIVISION

### Bud Benoit

Interviews with Bud Benoit conducted by the author, 16 December 2014 and 24, 25 and 28 August 2015.

Videotaped interview with Bud Benoit by Steve Adams, 2006.

### John Wade Photo Montage (page 131)

Telephone interview with John Wade III, 4 June 2015.

Email correspondence with Juli Wade, 7 June 2015.

George Pollard's sketch of Red "Swede" Norvik, drawn on deck of the USS *Zeilin* as it steamed toward Tarawa. Norvik is mentioned in several passages of Robert Sherrod's book, *Tarawa. Norvik family collection.*

### Anthony Karcher and Kinoshita's letter (page 132)

Email correspondence with Dennis Karcher (Anthony Karcher's nephew), 23-27 January 2015.

### George Pollard

Interview with George Pollard conducted by the author, 1986, 1992 and 1998.

Interview with George Pollard, Don Jones, and Sakae Oba conducted by the author, 14 September, 1986.

Paul Galloway, "If We'd Found Him, We Would Have Killed Him," *Chicago Tribune*, (15 September 1986), posted at http://articles.chicagotribune.com/1986-09-15/features/8603080984_1_saipan-japanese-mythic-porportions.

## Robert Thompson
# SHANGRI-LA

Robert Thompson photo archive, courtesy of the Thompson family.

Telephone interview with Pamela Thompson (Robert Thompson's daughter-in-law), 20 November 2014.

## Futomi Hosoda
## OUSHOU OBOEGAKI
Translated for the author by Kazunori Tanoue

The Japanese Ministry of Health and Welfare confirmed Futomi Hosoda was a soldier stationed on Iwo Jima from June 1944 until the Japanese government declared him dead on 16 March 1945. The Ministry identified Hosoda's rank as *Heicho* (lance corporal) and also contacted his family about the diary. Hosoda's nephew is his only living relative; he did not respond to the author's inquiries.

## Howard McLaughlin
## THIRTY-FIVE DAYS IN HELL

McLaughlin's manuscript, *Iwo Jima, Thirty-Five Days in Hell,* edited and reproduced here with permission from the McLaughlin family.

Telephone interview with Doug McLaughlin (Howard McLaughlin's son), 30 March 2014.

Email correspondence with Doug McLaughlin, 6 April 2014 – 10 August 2014.

It was from fellow collector Jeremy Severn that I acquired McLaughlin's helmet. Severn is also a dealer in rare militaria: www.ww2germansteel.com.

## Merrill Allen
## IWO JIMA REDISCOVERED

Special thanks to David Allen, Jeremy Severn (from whom I also acquired Allen's helmet), and the Nebraska State Historical Society for making this story possible.

## William Glavic
## USS YORKTOWN

Diary reproduced here with permission of the Glavic family.

Telephone interview with Deneen M. Porter (Glavic's daughter), 14 September 2014.

# Additional Sources

www.goldenarrowresearch.com

www.ginamcneely.com

www.fold3.com

NARA (National Archives Records Administration), St. Louis, Mo.
http://www.archives.gov/st-louis/

www.battlemaps.us

www.ancestry.com

www.upwork.com

William Glavic, right, and Dr. Jack Griffeth, left, who served as a "medical" guardian on the 4 May 2009, "honor flight" for veterans from Atlanta. Honor Flighs were conducted by non-profit organizations dedicated to transporting United States military veterans to see the war memorials in Washington, D.C. at no cost to the veterans. Glavic died four months after this photo was taken on 3 September 2009. Photo courtesy of The Honor Flight Network.